Renaissance Feminism

Renaissance Feminism

LITERARY TEXTS AND POLITICAL MODELS

Constance Jordan

CORNELL UNIVERSITY PRESS

ITHACA AND LONDON

First published 1990 by Cornell University Press.
First printing, Cornell Paperbacks, 1990.
Second printing 1992.

International Standard Book Number (cloth) 0-8014-2163-2
International Standard Book Number (paper) 0-8014-9732-9
Library of Congress Catalog Card Number 89-46172

Printed in the United States of America

Librarians: Library of Congress cataloging information
appears on the last page of the book.

♾ The paper in this book meets the minimum requirements of the
American National Standard for Information Sciences—Permanence of
Paper for Printed Library Materials, ANSI Z39.48-1984.

For Wilson,
Andrew, and Geoffrey

Contents

Acknowledgments

THIS book has been a collaborative enterprise and I am happy to thank those who contributed to it. My first debt is to Thomas M. Greene, whose learned yet elegant scholarship has been a model to me from my first days as a graduate student; for his support I am very grateful. The institutions that have helped to fund my research on this project are numerous: the National Endowment for the Humanities, the Folger Institute, the Newberry Library, and Columbia University, which awarded me a Chamberlain Fellowship and a Junior Faculty Research Grant. K. J. Wilson, who initially suggested that I write on defenses of women, is in some sense this book's father; it has also had many heroic midwives: I thank Albert Ascoli, Rebecca Bushnell, David Damrosch, Heather Dubrow, Margaret Ferguson, Joan Ferrante, Paul Gehl, Gail Geiger, Hope Glidden, Robert Hanning, Carolyn Heilbrun, Ann Rosalind Jones, Donald Kelley, Marshall Leicester, Joseph Loewenstein, Richard Mallette, Richard McCoy, Michael Murrin, David Quint, Mary Beth Rose, Gordon Schochet, James Shapiro, Richard Strier, and Nancy Vickers for having read and commented on the whole or portions of it at various stages. To my students who have assisted me with their time and ideas, especially Clare Fowler, Bishnupriya Ghosh, Peter Herman, Eve Keller, Karen Kingsbury, Susan Nerheim, and Pauline Vinson, many thanks. The staffs of the Folger Library and the Newberry Library have been unfailingly helpful and encouraging; I look forward to working again with Lena Cowen Orlin, Richard Brown, and Mary Beth Rose. The hospitality of Louisa and Bill Newlin in Paris and of Coline Covington, Anthony Sheil, and Elizabeth Simpson in London made my research in those cities a pleasure. To Edward Golub, who never turned down my invitations to discuss the subject of Renaissance women and their relations with men, is owed much credit for whatever clarity my arguments here have achieved. This book is dedicated with love and respect to my grown-up sons.

CONSTANCE JORDAN

Claremont, California

A Note on Texts and Editorial Practices

For texts in circulation before the sixteenth century or representative of Latin humanism I have used the best modern English translations available. When no English translations exist, I have made my own, consulting the most reliable translations in French or Italian. Whenever possible, I have checked all translations of these texts with the original Latin texts.

For sixteenth- and seventeenth-century texts, I have tried to examine the first or the most comprehensive edition; the editions I have used are indicated by dates in my text, unless my notes indicate otherwise. Interested readers should check further to make certain that earlier or different editions do not exist; in some cases, the number of and differences between editions of a given work may be considerable.

I have retained the original spellings of all texts, but have modernized letters, changing *u* to *v*, *i* to *j*, and *vv* to *w*. I have eliminated capital letters except at the beginning of sentences and proper names; I have added modern accents to quotations in French and Italian as they were needed, and I have altered original punctuation to preserve the sense of a passage when necessary. All translations of French and Italian sixteenth- and seventeenth-century texts are my own. I have included in my translations the words of the original text when they are crucial to its meaning or in some way ambiguous. All translations from works of history or literary criticism are my own, unless I have indicated otherwise.

Quotations from all texts are identified initially in a footnote and thereafter in my text. Titles of sixteenth-century and seventeenth-century texts are cited in their short form, except when they indicate the nature of the subject of the work. They follow standard modern practice with respect to capitalization; exceptions here are the run-on portions of the titles of English texts, which are not capitalized.

Renaissance Feminism

Introduction

Feminist scholarship is predicated on the assumption that women have experienced life differently from men and that this difference is worth studying. How such scholarship is to be pursued, what the parameters of its discourse(s) are or should be, and whether its intentions may or must be to reform those who take note of its productions are questions currently much debated. And as far as I can see, with little apparent consensus. If anything, our discussions have tended to broaden rather than narrow the range of opinion. But I do not believe this outcome has yet to discourage anyone. Like Montaigne, for whom the search for truth was vivifying because it was without term—"C'est signe de racourciment d'esprit quand il se contente, ou de lasseté"—feminist scholars have thrived on their differences as much as on the fact of difference.

History has certainly been on our side. Investigators of the past lives of women as individuals and in communities have been astonished by the wealth and diversity of relevant evidence. It is now realistic to expect that we can accomplish the task so many early feminists urged on their readers: the creation of a history of women, the excavation of its records, the decipherment of the palimpsest of the history of men (for so long history *tout court*) in which texts by and about women have been submerged, apparent and readable only from time to time. It is already clear, however, that this history of women will not be consistent in point of view or methodology, nor will it be ideologically monolithic. As Sally Alexander has remarked, "every moment of dissonance and disagreement within feminism, as well as between women and men, demands recovering and disentangling—demands a historical reading."[1] Con-

---

[1] Sally Alexander, "Women, Class, and Sexual Differences in the 1830s and 1840s: Some Reflections on the Writing of a Feminist History," *History Workshop* 17 (Spring 1984): 129.

versely, one could say that every historical reading of the material proper to women's history, which demands a recovery and a disentangling of evidence and interpretation, generates (at least some) dissonance and disgreement among feminist scholars.

To such readings I have made this study of Renaissance feminism a contribution. The term "feminism" is of course open to question, and especially when it is applied to Renaissance thought. Safer and less controversial, though more cumbersome in practice, is the term "pro-woman argument"; and in many if not all cases this term proves entirely apt. For early modern texts on women are highly argumentative; as Linda Woodbridge has documented, they generally exemplify the strategies and techniques recommended in contemporary handbooks of rhetoric.[2] Their most important intellectual connections are with the literature of politics and of law. They are often recognizably partisan; what is presented as the reality of the past—of women as daughters, wives, widows, queens and commoners, laborers, burghers, and gentry—is recognizably bound up with the interests of the writers who describe it. Their descriptions are invariably interpretations. How far they can be understood to constitute what most twentieth-century readers would consider a feminist position is debatable. I shall offer some basic kinds of comparison, and it is my hope that this study as a whole will allow the reader a reasonable basis for making further judgments.

In some respects, feminist texts of the Renaissance represent an extension and an amplification of the late medieval *querelle des femmes*. Many are straightforward "defenses of women"; some are didactic works, devoted to celebrating and at the same time circumscribing the nature of "woman"; and, more problematic, a few are overtly misogynist diatribes that by portraying the sturdy resilience of their objects of scorn often transform blame into a kind of grudging or implied praise. In toto, they cover (that is, I have chosen to see feminist argument in) a range of genres: histories, conduct books, treatises on government, letters, popular and courtly dialogues, and prose romances. The positions they take are various and invariably contentious. In the interest of clarity, I have tried to identify and describe the principal arguments praising and blaming woman as a creature, and women as constitutive of a class of person. This task has been made easier than the vastness of the material would suggest because the Renaissance debate on women is to a degree conventional: it is characterized by the repetition of themes, figures, tropes, motifs, and allusions to various authorities. Very similar arguments

[2]Linda Woodbridge, *Women and the English Renaissance: Literature and the Nature of Womankind, 1540–1620* (Urbana: University of Illinois Press, 1984), 13–136.

appear in text after text, often with minor changes. At the same time, it is important to do justice to innovation. This literature is dynamic; it is punctuated by the introduction of ideas that are, I think, novel to the debate and in some cases revolutionary; they mark a progression of thought, a development in ethical and political sensibility. Throughout all these works—and it has been perhaps the only feature they consistently share—is a pervasive concern with questions of authority and subordination, that is, with the origins of the control of man over woman and its expression in postlapsarian history, and with the rights of the woman who is subject to a male superior.

Certain of the terms and concepts I have used require definition, in part because they generally mean a variety of things, in part because the contexts in which I use them may open me to the charge of anachronism. *Patriarchalism* finds its origins in Scripture, where, as Margaret J. Ezell notes, the power of the Old Testament father over the members of his family is practically absolute: he can chastise, sell, and even kill his wife and children.[3] In Renaissance thought, where the term is understood both literally and figuratively, patriarchalism sustains and rationalizes several of the principal relations in which woman typically and women collectively find themselves. As the head of a family, a father (or, in the event of his death or exile, his surrogate, who is usually though not invariably male) controls the social, economic, and political lives of those in his charge—his kin and dependents. His specific prerogatives are enhanced by the categorical superiority he enjoys *as a man*. Men-in-themselves have a generic authority over women-in-themselves; this authority is most often realized in situations that involve the administration of law and the possession of property. And finally, "patriarchalism" describes a concept of government in which magistracy, or the office of magistrate, is said to have evolved in accordance with an originary disposition of power in the hands of fathers, whose paternal functions supposedly embraced legislative and administrative ones as well. Political patriarchalism proves rather unpredictably paradoxical for a certain category of Renaissance woman. Literature defending woman's rule routinely draws on concepts of authority as mystical and absolute to justify the monarchy of a queen regnant—concepts that have a greater affinity with a patriarchal political order than with other kinds of government organized along constitutional lines.

The effects of *power* and the expression of various kinds of *authority* are constant features of descriptions of domestic life and the relations be-

---

[3]Margaret J. Ezell, *The Patriarch's Wife: Literary Evidence and the History of the Family* (Chapel Hill: University of North Carolina Press, 1987), 3.

tween men and women. The terms are closely associated and need not necessarily be distinguished. Leonard Krieger observes that "authority is simply constituted power—that is, any capacity to secure obedience or conformity that carries with it some title to do so."[4] Yet the structure of domestic relations in early modern Europe makes it useful to see power and authority as separate entities. The conception of familial duties entails a consideration of the power available to ensure their performance as well as the authority needed to legitimate them. Subordinates may have considerable power, owing to intelligence, strength of will, and so forth, but because they lack political status, they may not be able to exercise it.

Duties between man and wife, as between parent and child and between master and servant are mutual but never reciprocal, that is, they are predicated on a relationship between political unequals and are contractual rather than consensual. (According to canon law, no marriage is valid without the consent of both spouses, but their subsequent behavior as husband and wife is supposed to be determined by the marriage contract that they have to enter into.) Assumed is that the head of the family will be a man, and generally a father. His will is made manifest by his power to influence or to coerce; it is authoritative in its capacity to determine family policy, which may (but usually does not) require the use of force to carry out. And because most positive law in this period gives the head of a family, first, control of the property belonging to that family, including the property of wives, and second, restricts all legal activities to men, a man in the position of patriarch has a most efficient means of exercising his prerogative. Within domestic social order or household government, the authority of men-in-themselves over women-in-themselves also obtains, legitimated by what is taken for the divine and natural law that institutes man as the head of woman. Wives, daughters, and female servants are therefore under a double set of obligations, those required by positive law and others derived from divine and natural law. A good deal of feminist argument focuses precisely on the difference between authority and power in relation to these points of law and government. Defenders of women point to the fact that women have power within the family and indeed in larger social settings; what they lack is the authority—the title, the office—to give that power a public and institutional character. They can persuade but they cannot rule. The chronic misogynist complaint of women as gossips registers a fear that they may become authoritative in a political sense.

In the societies of early modern Europe, the idea of an *equality* of

[4]Leonard Krieger, "The Idea of Authority in the West," *American History Review* 82, 2 (1977): 253.

authority and power between different kinds of persons, and notably between men and women, had for the most part no endorsement. Though it was a matter of Christian doctrine in both Catholic and Protestant churches that man and woman were spiritual equals, their common standing in the faith did not affect the political order. All the more remarkable, therefore, were the many claims to equality proposed by feminist writers. The kinds of equality at issue vary, but the crucial point to notice in instances in which such claims are made is the extent to which woman's spiritual equality is seen to entail a correlative political status. As a comparable argument develops on the question of the rights of the subject in relation to political authority in proto-constitutionalist thought, the feminist discourse on equality often seems derivative. (In fact, it may be that the language of the rights of the subject derives from discussions concerning the limits of wifely obedience.) To categorize women-in-themselves as wholly subordinate to men-in-themselves was not, however, to rule out the possibility that a woman could secure a political status that permitted her a degree of autonomy in some situations.

A concession of this kind is granted in accordance with the concept of *equity*, which functions to mitigate the rigidity that would otherwise mark household government. With respect to the statuses of man and woman, especially husband and wife, equity provides the grounds upon which the prerogative of the patriarch is judged fair and just. Equity is sometimes represented as manifest in the complementarity of man and wife, especially in the tasks of generation (of children and other forms of wealth) and in their mutual or shared interests. In the legal thought of England the meaning of equity has a particular relevance to women, for it was in chancery and the other courts of equity that women could press for rights to own and manage their own property.

A study of feminism needs to be clear about what is meant by *ideology*—the nature of the thing it both criticizes in its protests against patriarchal practices and, by contrast, privileges in its own self-defense. I have not found such clarification easy, despite (or perhaps because of) the fact that feminist scholarship has been self-consciously ideological from its inception. *Feminism*, as an intellectual position that is grounded, in Catherine MacKinnon's words, in "the theory of woman's point of view" and committed to the "consciousness raising" of her society, implies that our understanding of ideology be relativistic.[5] A theory of a

---

[5]Catherine A. MacKinnon, "Feminism, Marxism, Method, and the State: An Agenda for Theory," in *The Signs Reader: Women, Gender, and Scholarship*, ed. Elizabeth Abel and Emily K. Abel (Chicago: University of Chicago Press, 1983), 247.

point of view assumes that a theory is or may be based on a point of view. As one examines conflicting ideologies and these points multiply, a critique of what they assume takes on the burden of addressing the nature of ideology itself.

The legal historian Albert Venn Dicey describes some of the primary features of ideology (without actually using the word) by referring to "public opinion," and more particularly to "the reigning or predominant current of opinion . . . [that] may generally be traced to certain fundamental assumptions, which at the time, whether they be actually true or false, are believed by the mass of the world to be true with such confidence that they hardly appear to bear the character of assumptions."[6] In short, these are opinions that no longer betray their supposititious character but appear to be true reflections of the world as it is actually constituted. To the extent that an ideological position is characterized by conscious reflection on its hypothetical nature, it becomes intellectually respectable and it can become politically partisan. I stress these points because some Renaissance feminist argument actually exhibits this kind of sophistication, although it never, to my knowledge, becomes politically partisan; it never urges or provides a basis for political action in behalf of all women.[7] It has been up to critics more recent than Dicey to ask, as has Steven Lukes, what are the cultural agents or agencies that create and sustain ideology.[8] In this view, ideology may be considered not only as an aggregate of consciously held beliefs or opinions but as the effect of institutions that determine the very terms in which conflicts of interest are framed. Ideology can therefore be expressed in the actions such institutions take as well as in those they do not take, that is, their behavior in response to overt conflicts of interest and also in keeping certain conflicts of interest from becoming overt.

The feminism that I have so loosely described to this point has a fourfold relation to ideology. The feminism of Renaissance texts represents a (roughly) uniform and consistent theory of knowledge, recognized and recognizable as a theory of a point of view, by which to justify feminist assumptions of the virtue of women and, conversely, to call into question patriarchal assumptions of their inferiority. Less obviously, my

---

[6]Albert Venn Dicey, *Law and Opinion*, quoted in Sir William Holdsworth, *A History of English Law*, 3d ed. (London: Methuen, 1922; rpt. Sweet and Maxwell, 1977), 4:11.

[7]On feminism as a political movement, Sally Alexander notes: "There had to be not only feminine discontent but also a widespread yearning for another way of life. Before a language of rebellion can pass into general speech it must appeal to the imagination of a wide social group. Thus feminism appears at moments of industrial and political dislocation when disparate social groups are struggling to 'find a voice' in the new emerging order": "Women, Class, and Sexual Differences," 130–31.

[8]See Steven Lukes, *Power: A Radical View* (London: Macmillan, 1984).

scholarly and authorial assumptions and questions shadow—and perhaps I should also say discover—theirs. I too assume that a representation of the world from a woman's point of view has validity, and that such a representation entails an understanding of the assumptions held by the various participants in the debate on the woman question. What kinds of issues did Renaissance feminists consider? A few further distinctions may be helpful.

Looking at the history of feminist social thought, Karen Offen makes a fundamental discrimination between a feminism that finds its rationale in a conception of the individual, on the one hand, and a second kind of feminism that posits as its point of critical departure the essentially different experience of women in contrast to men, on the other. The first she associates with a concern for the autonomy of the female subject, particularly in relation to law and politics; the second she links to an appreciation of what women are and do in contrast to what men are and do. The first feminism is therefore individualist, the second relational and, she believes, older: in this tradition, arguments "proposed a gender-based but egalitarian vision of social organization. They featured the primacy of a companionate, non-hierarchical, male-female couple as the basic unit of society, whereas individualist arguments posited the individual, irrespective of sex or gender, as the basic unit."[9] The first feminism, according to Offen typically twentieth-century and Anglo-American in origin, offers women what has appeared to some critics as a kind of "*masculinisme féminine*," and risks endorsing a model of womankind that distorts much of woman's past and experience. The second feminism, typically continental, found a powerful voice in nineteenth-century social thought; it is grounded

> in the seemingly paradoxical doctrine of "equality in difference," or equity as distinct from equality. The fundamental tenets included the notion that there were *both* biological *and* cultural distinctions between the sexes, a concept of womanly or manly nature, of a sharply defined sexual division of labor, or roles, in the family and throughout society following from that 'difference' and that 'nature,' and of the centrality of the complementary couple and/or the mother/child dyad.   [139]

These two historically recent and strongly distinguished approaches to relations between men and women continue to provide alternatives to modern feminists. Prudent historical scholarship would lead one to expect that practically none of the principal issues raised by nineteenth- and

---

[9]Karen Offen, "Defining Feminism: A Comparative Historical Approach," *Signs: Journal of Women in Culture and Society* 14, 1 (1988): 135.

twentieth-century feminists would find representation in the early modern period. In fact, the reverse is the case. *Mutatis mutandis*, in various ways and degrees, Renaissance feminism can fairly be analyzed in individualist and relational terms.

As a rule, Renaissance feminism is individualist. The concept of equity was used too often to support the patriarchal hierarchy of sex and gender for defenders of women to leave it unchallenged. They contradicted writers who, while not hostile to the proposition that woman was as virtuous as man, indeed while arguing that a woman's place and her contribution to society were of great and in some cases supreme value, always concluded by defining that place and that contribution in terms that were actually denigratory. Feminists tended to regard this kind of "praise" as a practically meaningless concession, more particularly because it scarcely ever addressed the most debilitating effect of woman's supposed inferiority to man, that is, her poverty before the law. In theory, Renaissance feminists sought to establish the truth that men and women were first and most importantly human beings; for the most part, they saw little meaning in sexual—that is, physiological—difference. Not surprisingly, their model was frequently the virile woman.

In practice their individualism often led to the celebration of a set of virtues that they identified as feminine as opposed to masculine, and this celebration served to advance arguments for conceiving of human nature as *androgynous*. A person was biologically male or female; but behavioristically both masculine and feminine if virtuous; brutal and effeminate or cruel and vain if vicious. Diagnoses of character based on these distinctions of positive and negative gender attributes found important expression in statements of "policy" or political practice. Attributes of the governor which allowed him or her to be temperate, merciful, and especially secure in the arts of making peace were deliberately and emphatically gendered as feminine. In some instances this argument was made to support demands that the work typically assigned to women be revalued.

Sexual difference and its effects on the human person—the male in contrast to the female—was, as I have mentioned, not on the whole a topic that Renaissance feminists addressed directly. (Discussions of wife-beating and rape are exceptions.) Conspicuously absent are arguments that represent such difference as highly determinative of all aspects of the lives of women, that would posit, to use a sixteenth-century frame of reference, anatomical distinctions as the basis for the discrimination of male from female spheres of activity. Contrast Catherine MacKinnon's brilliant definition of the politics of modern feminism as based on sexuality:

The substantive principle governing the authentic politics of women's personal lives is pervasive powerlessness to men, expressed and reconstituted daily *as* sexuality. To say that the personal is political means that gender as a division of power is discoverable and verifiable through women's intimate experience of sexual objectification, which is definitive of and synonymous with women's lives as gender female. Thus to feminism, the personal is epistemologically the political, and its epistemology is its politics. Feminism, on this level, is the theory of women's point of view. [247]

Renaissance feminists spoke of powerlessness and objectification, but they tended to see the wretched condition of women as the consequence of the moral perversion of men, who failed to live up to the challenge of being fully human. They sought recognition for women as females and exponents of the feminine but also as a reason to reform the distorted humanity of men, to bring the other half of the human race into line. They understood that sexuality was a fact of life but they thought it related only to procreation. Gender was a far more comprehensive and significant category than was sex. For a man to be fully human meant that he had accepted his own obligation to cultivate the feminine virtues and recognized the masculine virtues in women. Women were correspondingly to exert themselves in ways traditionally required of men, to exercise their minds and bodies, in part for the sake of a humanist virtue, in part because such vitality was judged to be the best defense against male abuse.

A final point. The texts I have chosen to represent the case for women in the Renaissance I have divided according to period and country. My concern has chiefly been to establish in each case both the normative patriarchal positions on the nature and status of women and the feminist reponses to them. I have been guided more by the place and date of publication of a text than by the identity of its author—my purpose has been to portray the general character of the Renaissance debate on women as it would have been conveyed to the largest number of persons. This strategy has led to some critical anomalies that need acknowledgment. I have considered no works in manuscript or in Latin, although I have considered them in their printed versions and translation to the vernacular. Hence, although Christine de Pisan's *Livre de la cité des dames* (1405) clearly represents a major event in the late medieval *querelle des femmes* in France, I consider it among English works because it was printed only in England, as *The Boke of the Cyte of Ladyes* (1521), in the (slightly shorter) version of Brian Ansley. Hence, too, I include among English texts Juan Luis Vives's *De institutione foeminae christianae* (1520), written for Mary Tudor, and translated into English as *The Instruction of a Christen Woman* (1540). An exception to this rule of language and place over author is David Chambers's *Discours de la légitime succession des femmes* (1579); this text I consider with the other work on woman's rule written in English for the Scottish queen: John Leslie's *Defence of the Honour of Marie, Quene of Scots* (1569).

To clarify the direction of my own argument, I have analyzed many of these texts in a highly discriminating manner. In some cases I have isolated for comment relatively short passages of novel or suggestive content from a much longer text devoted for the most part to conventional opinion. Here my purpose has been not to assess the literary character of a text in its entirety or to discover what the author's final and developed opinion of women actually was but rather to reconstruct the main features of the Renaissance treatment of the woman question. Because the arguments of defenders which draw on or take issue with interpretations of scripture are likely to rely upon well-established tropes of abuse or compliment, I have particularly refrained from commenting extensively on them except when they illuminate through contradiction and irony an attitude or position that I regard as strongly feminist. In one way or another I have had to rely on my own judgment to decide when an author is using contradiction for the purpose of establishing irony and when he or she is merely representing uncritically a position characterized by contradiction which becomes ironic retrospectively, by virtue of that contradiction. The most persuasive arguments in this literature often use irony deliberately in order to explode coded discourse, whether of courtliness or patriarchy. There is frequently a rhetorical playfulness to this attack, almost a *sprezzatura* effect. Here one needs to ask: Why is this play? What are the rules of these games? And for what stakes are they being played?

I   *The Terms of the Debate*

Renaissance literature in defense of women is roughly divisible into two general categories. The first is motivated by the claims of society and the state against those of the church, and insists on the value of familial as against celibate life. The second—overtly feminist—is devoted to securing for women a status equal to that of men.[1] Most works in both categories refute (or try to) authorities asserting the moral weakness of woman or her ontological inferiority to man, rehearse proofs of her virtue, and attack misogyny. Works in which the status of women is the chief subject also criticize the attitudes and practices of patriarchy, particularly paternal greed and marital brutality.

Some of this literature, such as Mario Equicola's *Libro di natura d'amore*, may be properly categorized as humanistic; but in general it is directed to a popular audience that could read fluently and with some appreciation for the main elements of a classical moral culture that by the sixteenth

---

[1]Throughout this book I refer to "woman" generically, as the common or ideal type. The practice is general throughout both the literature of defense and misogynist satire: *la donna, la femme,* and "woman" or "womankind" are terms used to refer to the class of persons who are female and deserve special treatment by men. As denoting a type, these terms are both sustained and challenged by feminists; they survive particularly in feminist discourse, where "the woman" acquires heroic (sometimes called "virile") proportions and is endowed with feminine virtues that make her the equal of man in every respect. Ian Maclean supposes that insofar as writing on women established a common type, it is largely conservative; as a feature of intellectual history, it is less controversial than other kinds of inquiry; and as an index to social practice, it is inconsistent: *The Renaissance Notion of Woman: A Study in the Fortunes of Scholasticism and Medical Science in European Intellectual Life* (Cambridge: Cambridge University Press, 1980), 1. By contrast, I think, works specifically of protest, committed both to promoting and exploding the idea of "woman," are usually vigorous and heterodox (if not always learned), and exhibit a diversity of concerns that vary with the circumstances of their writers and audiences.

century already had a wide representation in contemporary works on social and political topics. Many works are dedicated to persons of note, as is François Billon's *Le Fort inexpugnable de l'honneur du sexe féminin* to Catherine de Médicis, but apart from treatises defending the right of a particular queen to rule, such as John Aylmer's *Harborowe for Faithfull and Trewe Subjects*, they do not press cases for individual women. The various audiences for this literature are difficult to analyze precisely. Because certain features of a specifically urban life often seem to provide a focus for a given argument, I have generally assumed that the readership for these works was urban and of the bourgeoisie or "middling sort" rather than landed and aristocratic. A few works were clearly intended in the first instance for royal women—Jean Marot's *Doctrinal des princesses*, for example, and Vives's *De institutio foeminae christianae*—but the fact that they were printed (and in the case of Vives also translated from an original in Latin) means that they were also perceived as appropriate for a larger and more socially heterogeneous audience. Works that are primarily facetious, such as the anonymous *XV Joies de mariage* and Edward Gosynhill's *Scholehouse of Women*, may have had a readership that extended to wage laborers, artisans, and tradespeople. Among obviously serious works, few appear to be concerned with women who are not of the gentry or nobility. Exceptions are catechisms such as that of Claude Baduel, the English homilies on obedience and disobedience, and such demonstrably sectarian treatises on marriage as William Gouge's *Domesticall Duties*. This is not to say that persons of lower social status did not read and feel themselves in sympathy with the opinions expressed in these works, but rather to indicate that the popularity I earlier claimed for them did not, I think, extend absolutely throughout all social strata.[2]

In any case, what seems to be most frequently at stake is the autonomy of the woman of the urban bourgeoisie within her family, especially with respect to her husband's more or less absolute authority and power over her. Her autonomy—the independence with which she can make and act upon moral and political judgments—or lack of it is always considered as inextricably bound up with economic and especially reproductive functions that are fulfilled by domestic activities designed to be performed exclusively at home, and by the bearing and nurturing of children.[3] The

[2]I assume that some of the works I shall discuss were known by having been read aloud. For a discussion of this kind of literacy, see Natalie Zemon Davis, "Printing and the People," in *Society and Culture in Early Modern France* (Stanford: Stanford University Press, 1975), 189–226.

[3]The degree to which any person living in early modern Europe could claim to be "autonomous," or self-governing, was determined by social circumstances substantially different from those that obtain in Western Europe and the United States today. The sixteenth-century societies whose ideas on sex and gender are the subject of this book were

ways in which a woman's exercise of her own will is most frequently analyzed suggest that these writers confronted a common social problem: the woman who had lost the opportunity to make decisions for herself or her family, especially decisions that concerned the management of property. As she emerges from the pages of these treatises, the typical woman almost always appears to be a person who is menaced by a kind of redundancy. She is shown as having to respond in one of two ways. Either she is to *reaffirm* the value of her duties as her husband's subordinate or she must *reject* the grounds upon which she has been assigned her role and discover others that provide her with greater scope.

In the first instance, she is to agree to keep busy, to take seriously her household tasks, however menial and in certain cases symbolic (as when daughters of rich gentry are required to spin to take up time), and never to refuse to perform her husband's orders except in the most extraordinary of moral circumstances. Whatever opportunities for autonomy she may have are represented as occasions in which to honor the obligations that arise from the *complementarity* of duties assigned to men and women in marriage. Here the virtue of woman is real, deserves respect, and so forth, but it is always ancillary to that of man.

In the second instance, she is to reject the principal features of patriarchy, often by way of a historicist critique. In light of contemporary circumstances, it is argued, women ought to be allowed to do more than they did in the past, especially if that past is biblical. Writers propose greater degrees of autonomy for the wife vis-à-vis her husband; they valorize qualities thought to be characteristically feminine, particularly those that come into play in the public arena. At its most theoretical, their protest recognizes the systematic nature of patriarchy and envisages a society structured along fairer lines in which an acknowledgment of sexual difference does not serve as the foundation for political distinctions. Once educated, women are to be considered capable of exercising both domestically and publicly the kinds of virtue conventionally assigned to males: justice, fortitude, prudence. Men, for their part, are to

---

organized to provide their citizenry with a highly determined sense of "place" or "office," to whose requirements specific kinds of behavior, designated as social duties, were to be modeled. Despite prescribed limits to most activities, however, there was for Christians a continuous if also ambiguous challenge to honor divine law, which might mean to act in ways contrary to social duties or, to put the matter positively, in response to moral or spiritual duties. The tension between these two forms of obligation is registered throughout the political literature of the period. Often acute when the duties of wives and daughters are at issue, it is examined extensively throughout this book. For a brief survey of the idea of "place" or "office" as it applied to women in this period, see Shulamith Shahar, *The Fourth Estate: A History of Women in the Middle Ages* (London and New York: Methuen, 1983), 1–10.

profit from a society that is in some degree feminized, in which virtues represented as feminine—temperance, patience, charity—are perceived in men as much as in women.

How and indeed whether this literature reflects the actual conditions of life in the Renaissance is difficult to determine. The fact that many works address the situation of the city woman suggests that feminist attitudes may in part respond to the effects of urban in contrast to rural settings on Renaissance family life. For women a move to the city appears to have been generally deleterious, in large part because it coincided with certain economic changes. With the consolidation of mercantile power in the late Middle Ages, families that had previously derived their wealth and livelihood from the land turned to trade and moved to the burgeoning commercial centers in northern Italy, Lyon, Paris, and London. Men of the rural gentry who had routinely delegated portions of their economic and public responsibilities to their wives—either because they were actually shorthanded or because they were forced to seek preferment or settle legal matters at court—now remained at or close to home, conducting their business in their houses or nearby business quarters. A woman who had enjoyed an effective autonomy, in part through unwritten and customary agreements that permitted others to honor her word as if it were her husband's or next male kin's, was now required to live in accordance with what had always been recognized as the natural law of her inferiority but had until this time remained a moot affair, at least for many practical purposes. Law and custom had been at odds, custom empowering women to do things the law forbade; now law superseded custom, writing it out of mind.[4] Men, by contrast, probably gained a degree of autonomy by moving to a city. Sons tended to leave their parents' urban households earlier than they did the more ample accommodations available to families living on the land. A male city dweller might be relatively free of his father's authority at the time of his marriage; a wife's subordination to her husband, inherent in her situation, might well have been intensified in a small household.[5] But were these relatively new restric-

[4]On English practice, Theodore F. T. Plucknett notes: "Local customs frequently keep the woman's property free from her husband's control, accord her liberty of contract (which was denied at common law), and even allow her to trade separately upon her own account": *A Concise History of Common Law* (Boston: Little, Brown, 1956), 313.

[5]Nino Tamassia, *La famiglia italiana nei secoli decimo quinto e decimo sesto* (Milan: Remo Sandron, 1910), 112. How urbanization and the accumulation of liquid capital affected the lives of women in this period more generally is obviously a vast and complex subject. For a general survey of this and related developments, see, i.a., Marilyn J. Boxer and Jean H. Quataert, "Overview, 1500–1700," in *Connecting Spheres: Women in the Western World, 1500 to the Present*, ed. Boxer and Quataert (New York: Oxford University Press, 1987), 19–52; Shulamith Shahar, "Townswomen," in *Fourth Estate*, 174–219; Richard T. Vann, "Toward a New Lifestyle: Women in Preindustrial Capitalism," in *Becoming Visible: Women in*

tions on women not also balanced by a countervailing increase in their freedoms?

Kathleen Casey has pointed out that the social, political, and economic power of medieval women of feudal rank depended upon the assumption, unstated and certainly unwritten, that they would not abuse it: "If feudal society often derogated from its own rules where family interest was at stake, so that some women of feudal rank exercised in fact powers that were denied them in law, it was because most of them, like their male relatives, could be trusted not to alter conventional political objectives."[6] In other words, it was expected that dynastic interests—expressive, as they were, of the interests of the nobility and gentry at large—would transcend in importance all other interests, including those that had to do with women as a group. Some of the motivation for denying *Renaissance* women authority and power may therefore have been a function of a newly acquired ability to articulate interests that were not dynastic and in line with their duties as wives and mothers. If women could imagine a vital difference between their interests and those of men, if they could see that opportunities to achieve political (in contrast to domestic) virtue ought not to be granted to them in exceptional circumstances but rather as a matter of course, they clearly threatened the status quo. Were women to be identified as an underprivileged group irrespective of rank, the justice of patriarchy might be called in question; a basis for a thorough reorganization of society might be imagined, if not immediately, at least at some future time. These were perceptions both creating and created by contemporary feminist protest. Literature defending women may therefore need to be subjected to a double interpretation: feminist protest

---

European History, ed. Renate Bridenthal and Claudia Koonz (Boston: Houghton Mifflin, 1977), 192–216; Kathleen Casey, "The Cheshire Cat: Reconstructing the Experience of Medieval Women," in *Liberating Woman's History: Theoretical and Critical Essays*, ed. Berenice A. Carroll (Urbana: University of Illinois Press, 1976), 224–249; Michael Mitterauer and Reinhard Seider, *The European Family: Patriarchy and Partnership from the Middle Ages to the Present* (Chicago: University of Chicago Press, 1984); Lillian S. Robinson, "Women under Capitalism: The Renaissance Lady," in *Sex, Class, and Culture* (Bloomington: Indiana University Press, 1987), 150–77. For a theoretical overview including an analysis of women in modern capitalism, see Heidi Hartmann, "Capitalism, Patriarchy, and Job Segregation by Sex," in *The Signs Reader*, ed. Abel and Abel, 193–225. On the cities of northern Europe, see Martha C. Howell, *Women, Production, and Patriarchy in Late Medieval Cities* (Chicago: University of Chicago Press, 1987); for an English case, see Mary Prior, "Women and the Urban Economy: Oxford, 1500–1800," in *Women in English Society, 1500–1800*, ed. Mary Prior (London and New York: Methuen, 1985), 93–117; for a study of urban women in Tuscany, see Judith C. Brown, "A Woman's Place Was in the Home: Women's Work in Renaissance Tuscany," in *Rewriting the Renaissance: The Discourses of Sexual Difference in Early Modern Europe*, ed. Margaret W. Ferguson, Maureen Quilligan, and Nancy Vickers (Chicago: University of Chicago Press, 1986), 206–44.
    [6]Casey, "Cheshire Cat," 234.

records poverty, abuse, humiliation; it also testifies to some degree of literacy, education, leisure time—in short, the means by which to respond to the challenge of reform.

The possibility returns us to Joan Kelly's seminal essay, "Did Women Have a Renaissance?" itself a reply to the prevailing opinion that their experience was like that of men, an opinion traceable to Jakob Burckhardt's thesis that the Renaissance was a period of universal betterment.[7] Kelly's case is supported by evidence from economic and legal history. Although practices varied considerably according to time and place, in most cases it appears that with the development of more complicated economic relations, women were given progressively less legal control over property they owned outright or jointly with a spouse. In her essay on the loss of status for women in this period, Susan Mosher Stuard writes that the creation of a commercial economy altered the function of legal documents effecting the transfer of property. Wills, and similar instruments "whose original purposes were to provide inter- or intra-familial systems of exchange, became the formalized instruments of commerce, banking and trade, in other words, devices for the transmission of business capital." This change was part of a larger economic transformation: with the development of "an increasingly elaborate bureaucratic structure whose rationalized relationships might be defined with precision," women were "defined out of positions of prominence and authority."[8] They were at a greater disadvantage in cases of inter-regional commerce, where their businesses went beyond the limits of the communities in which they worked.[9]

These developments presumably had the greatest effects on women in the higher ranks of society, who had substantial amounts of property in their families, either owned in common with a spouse or in the form of a dowry. In various ways, the conditions of women of lower ranks were also altered. The thesis of Alice Clark's classic study of working women in seventeenth-century England—that their economic position deteriorated with the advent of wage labor and industrialization—is still held to be largely valid.[10] The contributions of more recent historians have

[7]Joan Kelly, "Did Women Have a Renaissance?" in *Becoming Visible*, ed. Bridenthal and Koonz, 137–64. For Burckhardt see *The Civilization of the Renaissance in Italy*, trans. S. G. C. Middlemore (New York: Random House, 1954), 292–96.

[8]Susan Mosher Stuard, "Did Women Lose Status in Late Medieval and Early Modern Times?" in *Restoring Women to History: Materials for Western Civilization*, ed. Elizabeth Fox-Genovese and Susan Mosher Stuard (Fund for the Improvement of Post-Secondary Education and the Lilly Endowment, n.p., n.d.), 1:180, 188.

[9]See esp. Howell, *Women, Production, and Patriarchy*, 174–83.

[10]Alice Clark, *Working Life of Women in the Seventeenth Century* (London: Frank Cass, 1919; New York: Reprints of Economic Classics, 1968).

modified it in some details; further adjustments need to be made if sixteenth-century women are under consideration. Roberta Hamilton argues that capitalism, not industrialization, was the factor that precipitated change in the status of women, whether of the peasantry, the middling sort, or the gentry.[11] Chris Middleton describes the relevant form of capitalism as *preindustrial* (i.e., characteristic of the sixteenth and seventeenth centuries), with work going on "in the producer's own home through various forms of the putting-out system."[12] Women then effectively worked two jobs: one for which they were paid plus a second incumbent upon them as women. They were continually employed, according to David Levine: "In addition to her normal chores [i.e., housekeeping, gardening, keeping livestock], the wife of a protoindustrialist or farm laborer was also expected to earn her wages."[13] She might be more or less highly trained. By studying records of apprentices, K. D. M. Snell presents startling evidence of very widespread employment by women in all kinds of skilled trades—a fact that must have enhanced rather than restricted their economic status.[14] But as Natalie Zemon Davis notes, "female wage-earners," who formed a large part of the preindustrial economy, made up, "together with *unskilled* males, a kind of preproletariat."[15] In any case, much of the working activities of *skilled* women did not apparently show up in records other than those of apprenticeships. Michael Roberts writes that while even unemployed men were identified by a trade in contemporary documents, women who practiced a trade were listed simply as a member of the household of their next male kin.[16] And in fact Clark's *principal* point—that with capitalization came a division between work done by men and women for an employer (whether inside or outside the home, whether paid by piece or by a wage) and domestic work done by women, a division roughly translated as one between production and consumption—finds consistent corroboration in sixteenth-century manuals of household govern-

---

[11]Roberta Hamilton, *The Liberation of Women: A Study of Patriarchy and Capitalism* (London: George Allen & Unwin, 1978), 18.

[12]Chris Middleton, "Women's Labour and the Transition to Pre-Industrial Capitalism," in *Women and Work in Pre-Industrial Britain*, ed. Lindsey Charles and Lorna Duffin (London: Croom Helm, 1985), 184.

[13]David Levine, *Family Formation in an Age of Nascent Capitalism* (New York: Academic Press, 1977), 12, 13.

[14]K. D. M. Snell, *Annals of the Labouring Poor: Social Change and Agrarian England, 1660–1900* (Cambridge: Cambridge University Press, 1985), 270–314.

[15]Natalie Zemon Davis, "'Women's History' in Transition: The European Case," *Feminist Studies* 3, 3/4 (1976): 86.

[16]Michael Roberts, "'Words They Are Women, and Deeds They Are Men': Images of Work and Gender in Early Modern England," in *Women and Work in Pre-Industrial England*, ed. Charles and Duffin, 138–40.

ment. There wives are regularly scolded for leaving the house and con-
suming too much of what their husbands bring in. Their own domestic
labor is routinely discounted, a fact that feminists note and deplore.
While their literary protests probably found few readers among wage-
earning persons, treatises do in fact mention women working on farms
or in workshops. On the whole, they claim that although women do the
same work that men do or comparable work, it is invariably judged to be
worth less.

For Burckhardt's thesis there is no comparable evidence. To substantiate it, one has to assume that in some ways, at least, men and women
were equally affected by the intellectual vigor and the artistic achievement that characterized Renaissance culture.[17] In two important respects,
however—education and literacy—the record suggests that women did
not even come near to matching the achievements of the men of the same
rank much before the end of the seventeenth century.[18] Feminists regularly complain about the lack of education for women. We are almost
forced to conclude that the Burckhardtian view of Renaissance women
was wrong. In any case, feminist argument is written and published
largely in response to a perception that women were treated unjustly,
though one may also note that the perception of injustice in itself indicates a kind of freedom.

Interpreting feminist texts presents other challenges. Despite the polemical nature of the debate on women, many texts cannot be characterized as simply for or against women. Treatises ostensibly *defending*
women are sometimes ambiguous because their intention is in fact two-

[17]As Joan Kelly remarks: "On the one hand, aristocratic women lost considerable
economic, political, and cultural power in relation not only to their feudal forebears but to
men of their own class. On the other hand, a new class of women was created according to
a new gender construction of the domestic lady. The contents of early feminist theory
reflect the declining power of women of rank and the enforced domestication of middle-
class women. Yet it owes its very being to new powers of education that some of the
women had at their command": "Early Feminist Theory and the *Querelle des femmes*," in
Women, History, and Theory: The Essays of Joan Kelly (Chicago: University of Chicago
Press, 1986), 67. See also Jean Portemer: "That the tradition enforcing the dependence of
women was made more exigent everything goes to prove: the schedules of notaries and
the records of arrests, memoires, drama, and fiction. That the movement for the liberation
of woman had a direct and unique influence on events is also beyond any doubt, at least in a
highly discreet but very important area (because it concerned not only the present but the
future and guaranteed further development): the area of education": "Le Statut de la
femme en France depuis la réformation des coutumes jusqu'à la rédaction du code civil," in
La Femme, Recueils de la société Jean Bodin, vol. 12 (Paris, n.d.), 470–71.
[18]David Cressy, *Literacy and the Social Order: Reading and Writing in Tudor and Stuart
England* (Cambridge: Cambridge University Press, 1980), 112, 128–29. The number of
women who are represented in literature as reading and writing and the number of works
signed by women in Italy during this period suggest that literate women were much
commoner there than north of the Alps.

fold and to a degree contradictory. They are designed both to praise and to blame women, to allow them a dignified and honored place in society while at the same time demonstrating that this place is beneath that of men, and to make attractive to women their (new) role as social subordinates by stressing its basis in divine and natural law. In a more general way, this literature is intended to guarantee that the authority of men is unquestioned by anticipating and coming to terms with certain kinds of disaffection among both men and women. It attempts to make acceptable the traditional (and probably reemphasized) subordination of women, both by extolling the virtues required by household government (likening them to the civic virtues needed by men) and by severely circumscribing the actual activities in which these virtues are to be brought into play. On the other hand, dramatically misogynist literature can have a feminist dimension; by depicting women as forceful rebels, it can convey their capacity to think and to act. Here I do not mean to underestimate literary misogyny as a means of perpetuating patriarchal privilege, but rather to point to a way in which it can become self-contradictory.

A more critical sense in which this literature defies categorization is with respect to the sex of its authors. Were it to submit to an analysis of its arguments by reference to authorial sex, a reader could safely insist on an interpretation that takes this into account. But in fact the sex (stated or implied) of an author appears to have no clear or consistent relation to the opinions of men and women expressed. (It is not even possible always to be certain of the author's sex. Treatises signed by men may have been written by women and vice versa. Even when the author of a work is well known, some form of collaboration cannot be ruled out.) While it is usually possible to determine whether or not a text presents a woman's point view, although the determination may be ambiguous in ways I have suggested, there are no clear indications that men and women took uniquely distinct perspectives on feminist questions. Their discourse is typically conducted along philosophical and political lines, concerned with rights, obligations, and duties, with relations conceived almost as abstractions. The *personal* experience of women becomes a feature of their arguments on two topics chiefly: first, rape; and second, woman's work, because it is either underpaid or unpaid. On such subjects, treatises signed by men often represent the feminist case the more strongly, because they directly engage its legal and economic aspects. Treatises signed by women differ only (although not consistently) in showing no enthusiasm for marriage; their criticisms of the married state are frequently expressed in utopian visions of a purely female society.

The subject of men in feminism, or male feminists, not new to twentieth-century criticism, may well have been a novelty in the Renaissance.

Stephen Heath, focusing on the position of the male feminist today, has argued that men cannot be feminists in the fullest sense: "no matter how 'sincere,' 'sympathetic' or whatever, we are always also in a male position which brings with it all the implications of domination and appropriation, everything precisely that is being challenged, that has to be altered."[19] This does not mean, Heath later says, that men cannot actively support a feminist position, or that—and this point is germane to our understanding of Renaissance feminism—such a discrimination between the male and female feminist is free from historical determinants. Heath points out that John Stuart Mill's *Subjection of Women* exemplifies the work of a man who interpreted his culture from a woman's point of view in a period when such interpretations could rest largely on impersonal factors. So much the more, I would then agree, does the feminism of an Agrippa of Nettesheim or a William Heale demonstrate a validity quite independent of the personal experience of women—a validity acquired through the relative cogency of abstract arguments.

But it is also the case that some Renaissance treatises signed by men express feminist opinions based on a sympathetic identification with the "female position," a fact that may distinguish Renaissance from later feminisms. The comments of such writers suggest that in the position of woman as the quintessential subject—that is, as politically subordinate, economically dependent, and legally incapacitated—many Renaissance men saw reflected aspects of their own social situations. For whatever his rank, a man of this period would have been obliged to contend with the effects of a social hierarchy. The more rigorous his experience of subordination and its consequent disempowerment, the more his "male position" would have resembled that of the "female." His maleness and masculinity were therefore susceptible to a degree of qualification quite alien to the experience of men in less stratified societies.[20]

This double positioning of the man may account for the emphasis that many Renaissance feminists placed on androgyny. Beyond sex and sexual difference, and more important than anything they determine, Re-

---

[19]Stephen Heath, "Male Feminism," in *Men in Feminism*, ed. Alice Jardine and Paul Smith (New York and London: Methuen, 1987), 1.

[20]It is entirely appropriate that feminists insist on the primacy of sex over class; for the criticism of Marxist views of the oppression of women, see, i.a., Rosalind Coward, *Patriarchal Precedents: Sexuality and Social Relations* (London: Routledge & Kegan Paul, 1983), and Shulamith Firestone's seminal study, *The Dialectic of Sex: The Case for Feminist Revolution* (New York: Morrow, 1970). Yet the question Renaissance feminism asks— "What is sex—specifically in contrast to gender?"—finds an answer that challenges critics who, like Heath, circumscribe the feminism of contemporary men by pointing to their inability to experience life as a woman. While men obviously cannot be female, they can experience many of the effects of behaving in a feminine manner.

naissance feminists represent men and women as sharing gendered attributes, particularly with respect to the work they do: both labor and often at the same tasks. Admittedly, feminists acknowledge experiences in which physiology is determinative: mothers who nurse children behave in accordance with their nature as females, although not necessarily in response to a feminine disposition; men engage in hard labor for long periods because they are naturally strong, although physical work is not an inherently masculine activity. What is stressed overall, however, is the decisive part played by a common and essentially human experience—always seen in this period in a dialectical tension with authority no matter what the subject—in testing and overcoming rigid categorizations of gender that are based on sexual difference.

Doctrine

Scripture

The rhetorical and philosophical terms of the Renaissance debate on women are drawn initially from religious and philosophical discourse concerning the virtue appropriate to particular categories of persons. They become contentious when feminists reinterpret authoritative texts in order to challenge the concept of virtue as sex- and gender-specific. Contemporary social mores were based on the assumption that a person's virtue was to be assessed by reference not to a presumed individualism but rather to the idea of society as a "corporation."[21] A person was known largely by the office in life to which he had been called by God; his value or worth was a reflection of the importance of that office and also of how well he filled it. Questions of virtue thus inevitably allude to a social hierarchy that was generally accepted as a reflection of the hierarchy of creation, an order in nature or *of* nature, instituted not fortuitously but providentially, and therefore not subject to alteration by human beings. And because the hierarchy of creation was instituted providentially, it had a historical dimension; it was to be perceived as unfolding in time, as the scene upon which was played the histories of individual and collective

[21]Harold J. Berman points out that jurisdictional limitations on authority and power in the Middle Ages were conceived in terms applicable to the state as a "corporation," a term (*universitas*; also *corpus* or *collegium*) derived from Justinian: *Law and Revolution: The Formation of the Western Legal Tradition* (Cambridge: Harvard University Press, 1983), 215. See also Ernst H. Kantorowicz, *The King's Two Bodies: A Study in Medieval Political Theology* (Princeton: Princeton University Press, 1981), 193–232, on the "mystical bodies" of church and state.

salvation. The order of nature was thus also an order in and of history and historical time.

In this order the office of woman was what God had made it at the time of Creation according to Genesis 2 and 3. God makes woman because "it is not good that man should be alone," he needs a "helper"; and God instructs woman that her "husband shall rule" over her. Because woman was initially made from the side of man to be his *helper*, and afterward, in her postlapsarian state, ordered to be his *subject*, she was doubly under-privileged. The manner of her creation revealed her *ontological* inferiority, her punishment after the loss of paradise her *political* subordination in historical time. Both limitations are features of patriarchalism and the gross distinction between the worth of men-in-themselves and women-in-themselves.

Woman had, however, an earlier creation, which in effect gave her another nature and status that in the course of sixteenth-century debate came to affect the conditions of her office as they were conceived of in theory. In Genesis 1, she, like man, was created in the image of God, and in this respect she was not different from him. This creation story is frequently adduced as evidence of woman's spiritual equality with man, or, as Erasmus puts it, her "equality as a member [with man] of Christ." The spiritual sameness of man and woman stands both in opposition to and as a complement of their political difference, just as the order of grace, the scene of spiritual struggle, is both opposed to and complemen-tary of the order of nature and historical time in which the social and political effects of spiritual struggle are manifest.

The French historian Jean Dauvillier finds the effects of what might be called a woman's double nature registered in the church's early teaching on marriage and on the position of women in the church. "Christianity established the rule of marriage, a rule that covered a collection of rights and reciprocal duties. The rule is complex, because, with respect to conjugal life, it insists on relations of equality between spouses; but with respect to the society of the family that the spouses constitute, it estab-lishes relations of inequality, founded on the husband's right to govern the family." By the same line of reasoning, women are prevented from holding positions of authority over men within the church: "Therefore, while honoring the spiritual equality [of men and women], the hier-archies of nature impose a certain inferiority upon the woman vis-à-vis the man and, in the structure of the family, of the wife vis-à-vis her husband. . . . She is removed from every function that would give her authority over a man."[22] A woman therefore acquires a twofold sense of

[22]Jean Dauvillier, *Les Temps apostoliques* (Paris: Sirey, 1970), 408, 418.

her own identity and worth as a human being. As one who possesses an immortal soul, she is the equal of man and susceptible to the same salvation and damnation; as one who lives in this world, she is always his inferior and his subordinate. In the language of Renaissance political thought, she is a *persona mixta*: her natural and political self balanced by her spiritual self.[23]

As such, she posed a considerable problem to moralists. How is she to be judged by the same moral standard as her male superiors? And if she is a political subordinate, can she be blamed for what goes wrong? Traditionalists tended to answer the first question by insisting that woman needed more help in the process of salvation than man did; she stood in greater need of grace. They answered the second by arguing that the world's evil arose and continues to derive from the disobedience of woman to her superior, man; she is blameworthy only in that she fails to fulfill her superior's orders. (He of course may be blamed for choosing the wrong course for her to follow.) Both answers fueled feminist responses and throughout the sixteenth century the significance of woman's double nature remained crucial to defenses of her virtue and of her right to autonomy, especially in activities in the public arena.

The complexity of woman's nature recalls features of the typical subject in contemporary political thought. Throughout the Renaissance the political status of the woman vis-à-vis the male head of the family and of the subject vis-à-vis the magistrate are comparable; though the ways in which the domestic and civic forms of government are imagined obviously differ, they are frequently discussed in similar terms. Gordon Schochet has described Renaissance patriarchal theory (particularly in Sir

[23]The concept of woman as a creature with two personae and therefore two ways of responding to experience is central to all discussions of her status in this period. The extent to which she could claim an equality with man on the basis of her first creation was first a matter of theological debate. Ian Maclean notes that for both Augustine and Aquinas she mirrored divinity only by virtue of grace, which had endowed her with intelligence; in other respects she mirrors, and hence is secondary to, man. See *Renaissance Notion of Women*, 13–14, and also, on the question of equality, 20. For an apologetic view of patristic commentary on the equality of man and woman, see Jo Ann McNamara, "Sexual Equality and the Cult of Virginity in Early Christian Thought," *Feminist Studies* 3 (1976): 145–58. For a good analysis of all relevant doctrine see Eleanor Commo McLoughlin, "Equality of Souls, Inequality of Sexes: Woman in Medieval Theology," in *Religion and Sexism: Images of Women in the Jewish and Christian Traditions*, ed. Rosemary K. Ruether (New York: Touchstone, 1974), esp. 215–21. For an acute reading of Gen. 1–3 and their patristic, medieval, and Renaissance glosses, see James Grantham Turner, *One Flesh: Paradisal Marriage and Sexual Relations in the Age of Milton* (Oxford: Clarendon, 1987), esp. 1–95. Turner points out how various were the ways in which Genesis and related passages in the Pauline epistles might be interpreted. For persons not trained in theology, however, these texts were understood directly to support the domestic and political subordination of women.

Robert Filmer's *Patriarchia*) as deriving all legal authority from the "divinely ordained fatherly power of Adam"; the political obligations thus created have a "*genetic* justification, for [they are defended by] the duty to obey in terms of the very origins of political society." The authority of the father is therefore at one with the authority of the magistrate; paternal authority is also political authority. For proponents of constitutional forms of government, the crucial question to ask of patriarchalism was whether persons "who were naturally subjected to the authority of their fathers could nevertheless be *politically* free enough to establish their own governments."[24] In other words, whether a familial and domestic obedience absolutely ruled out the possibility of autonomy in the public arena; whether, in effect, citizens were always children with respect to the authority of the magistrate. Constitutionalist thought had denied the justice of this political infantilism by deriving from the subject's primary obligation to obey God his right and duty to resist what his conscience determined was an unlawful order. In this perspective all persons are equal by virtue of their conscience and their potential for salvation. Their spiritual condition—like that of woman—is guaranteed by their creation in God's image before the institution of household or civil government.[25]

Common to both the purely political and the specifically antifeminist forms of patriarchalism is an acceptance of what Schochet calls the "teleological doctrine," an "acceptance of the genetic proposition that origins determine development" (11). Teleological doctrine is far easier to justify in the case of woman than in that of the political subject, as it has ample scriptural authority in Genesis 2 and 3, and virtually no precedents to the contrary are to be found in what passes for historical record in this period. In this respect, feminists had a harder case to press than did constitutionalists. As Schochet points out, the political issue did not include a dispute as to whether the father had the power of governance within the family [and therefore specifically the husband of the wife], but rather "whether the rights of monarchs could be inferred from this power" (14). On the other hand, the acknowledged differences between domestic and civic patriarchalism were perceived to be favorable to feminist protest. The authority and power of fathers and particularly of

[24]Gordon Schochet, *Patriarchalism in Political Thought* (New York: Basic Books, 1975), 1, 7.

[25]The significance of conscience to the political behavior of a Christian has a long development. It becomes a political issue with the Reformation. For an analytic survey of the concept of a Christian conscience in Reformation politics, see Quentin Skinner, "The Principles of Lutheranism," in *The Foundations of Modern Political Thought*, vol. 2 (Cambridge: Cambridge University Press, 1978), esp. 12–19.

husbands was always bound by divine example. Their duty, inscribed in Scripture and invoked frequently in both learned and popular doctrine, was to love their dependents. A comparable circumscription of monarchic power had much less substantiation. Scriptural references to such power were subject to wide interpretation: a monarch was to be to his people as a shepherd to his sheep; but should his care become lax or abusive, it was possible to argue, as absolutists such as James I actually did, that such a government nevertheless continued to be legitimated by divine law.

Beyond teleological doctrine and ethical imperatives, the use of scriptural authority to justify man's authority and power over woman, particularly in marriage, is vast, and needs to be noted (if only cursorily) because it reveals the scope of what feminist writers had to challenge. To Christians who read Scripture, the Pauline epistles establish for all practical purposes the nature of Christian marriage, and with it the nature of woman. Paul bases his views on marriage on Christ's claims for those who are eunuchs for the kingdom of heaven (Matt. 19:10–12), and in effect creates a moral hierarchy in which celibacy is preferred although married fidelity is permissible (1 Cor. 7, especially 7–9.) A wife provides a licit quenching for the man who burns, but the price he pays for this solace is that he thinks about his wife rather than about the kingdom of heaven (1 Cor. 7:32–33). The opposition here between flesh and spirit is uncompromising and it is not surprising that woman, who instances man's fleshliness, is ordered to remain in subjection. Man is both the head to her body and also, as Christ is to his church, a figure of the eternal in relation to her as an image of the faithful on earth. Paul directs no more emphatic message specifically to woman than that she is to be subordinate to and silent before man (1 Cor. 11:3, 8; 14:34–35; Eph. 5:22; Col. 3:18; 1 Tim. 2:11; 1 Pet. 3:1)—a political condition that, like that of the subject as child, is genetic in origin: "I suffer not a woman to teach, nor to usurp authority over the man, but to be in silence. For Adam was first formed, then Eve. And Adam was not deceived but the woman being deceived was in the transgression" (1 Tim. 2:12–14). This associative logic links the prohibition against speech with an originary misuse of language; as a whole the passage implies that the spiritual persona of woman is inherently defective, that the image of God is seen less clearly in her than in man (a point Augustine and Aquinas later made explicit). Elsewhere in the Pauline epistles the spiritual equality of the sexes is asserted: "there is neither male nor female: for ye are all one in Christ Jesus" (Gal. 3:28). This idea seems to have an echo in the doctrine establishing a mutual sharing of bodies: "The wife hath not power of her own body but the husband: and likewise also the husband hath not power of his own body, but the wife" (1 Cor. 7:4). Yet the "honor" owed to woman is "as unto the weaker vessel" (1 Pet. 3:7), and the love the man owes the woman is as Christ's for his church, from superior to inferior.

The principal Latin Fathers of the early church were virtually unanimous in their agreement with Paul. The notion that celibacy is better than married fidelity is regarded as absolutely unexceptionable and, moreover, is further justified by the certainty that the times are apocalyptic. Observing that the civilized world is everywhere overrun by barbarians, Jerome perceives that the end of the age is at hand and the injunction "Be fruitful and multiply" no longer obtains.[26] Augustine, apologizing for marriage, declares that continence is better; it may even hasten the highly desirable end of the world, which, if "all abstained," would come within a generation.[27] Even if this were not so, the case for associating with woman is usually described as a weak one. As Jerome claims, the history of the gentiles shows that woman is responsible for the world's evil: "In all the bombast of tragedy and the overthrow of houses, cities, and kingdoms, it is the wives and concubines who stir up strife."[28] And Tertullian, making the existence of woman a perpetual sign of human error, sees in the original sin of Eve the cause not only of her political subordination and obligatory silence but also of a continuing guilt. Woman must attempt to "expiate that which she derives from Eve—the ignominy . . . of the first sin. . . . Do you not know [he asks] that you are [each] an Eve? The sentence of God on this sex of yours lives in this age: the guilt must of necessity live too. You are the devil's gateway."[29] Such theological opinions demonstrate how teleological doctrine—that by Eve's creation and sin the pattern for all subsequent relations between men and women is established—could be interpreted to express a fear of woman and of sexuality in general.

Nor did the idea that woman was the spiritual equal of man, similar to him in the order of grace, go unchallenged. Augustine states that the image of God is less perfectly realized in woman than it is in man. While woman, like man, is a human being (*homo*) and therefore created in God's image, as a woman (*femina*) she lacks the essential feature of that divine

[26]St. Jerome, Letter 123, in *Letters and Select Works*, vol. 6 of *Select Library of Nicene and Post-Nicene Fathers of the Christian Church*, ed. Henry Wace and Philip Schaff, 2d ser. (New York, 1893), 234.

[27]St. Augustine, "On the Good of Marriage," in *The Works of St. Augustine*, vol. 3 of *Select Library of Nicene and Post-Nicene Fathers of the Christian Church*, ed. Philip Schaff (Grand Rapids, Mich.: Eerdmans, 1956), 404.

[28]St. Jerome, "Against Jovinianus," in *Letters and Select Works*, ed. Wace and Schaff, 385.

[29]Tertullian, "On Female Dress," in *The Writings of Tertullian*, vol. 11 of *Ante-Nicene Christian Library: Translations of the Fathers down to 325 A.D.*, ed. Alexander Roberts and James Donaldson (Edinburgh, 1869), 1:304.

image, rationality, which is reflected only in man (*vir*).[30] So much is of course also implicit in what Christians were taught to understand about virginity. Eleanor Commo McLaughlin has pointed out that virginity as a condition of spiritual excellence functions differently for a woman than for a man. It was a woman's *nature* to bear children and she must deny it in the interest of her soul. "For the female, virginity is not an affirmation of her being as a woman but an assumption of the nature of the male, which is identified with the truly human: rationality, strength, courage, steadfastness, loyalty."[31] Admittedly, Paul had declared that a woman's salvation would be in the bearing of children (1 Tim. 2:15), but this dictum was effectively superseded by far more widely accepted opinions on the absolute value of virginity.

Nevertheless, the fact that there are two stories of creation, each instituting a different relation among man, woman, and God, did serve at least to suggest the possibility of a defense of woman which took account of her potential for autonomy and for public life. Their contradictions (are the two stories compatible or not?) are eventually represented as elements of a feminist discourse that draws upon the increasingly sophisticated political (and primarily Protestant) discourse on concepts of magisterial authority and representative government. This indebtedness refines contemporary feminist argument. Even in the most rigidly conceived theocracies, the autonomy of the subject is not considered negligible. In the sixteenth century it was the key to the development of theories of the state. In the political sphere it provided a basis initially for determining the religious freedom of conscience, and secondarily for securing what came to be called political rights. In feminist discourse, it was linked to a woman's spiritual equality and to her full participation in the drama of salvation. Because she could not be exempt from judgment, she could not be denied free will; and because she had free will, she had herself to confront, inevitably and notwithstanding any generic deficiency, as her own *moral* authority, the entirely *political* authority of her husband or of the next male kin to which she was subject. The religious freedom of conscience both of the Christian subject and of the woman as

---

[30]Kari Elisabeth Børresen writes that Augustine developed his notion of woman from a need to reconcile Gen. 1:27 with 1 Cor. 11:7, which declares that only men are made in God's image: "The image of the divinity properly understood is not inherent in the soul as a unity in which two elements participate; it inheres only in the masculine element that is dedicated to the contemplation of eternal truths. By virtue of this exalted activity, the masculine element takes charge of the feminine element, which is charged with taking care of the necessities of daily life": *Subordination et équivalence: Nature et rôle de la femme d'après Augustin et Thomas d'Aquin* (Oslo and Paris: Universitetsforlaget and Maison Mame, 1968), 137.

[31]McLaughlin, "Equality of Souls," 234.

subject guaranteed that the authority of the magistrate and of the man could not in all cases be absolute.

This is a well-established principle in virtually all treatises on the obedience of a wife. Clement of Alexandria's is an early formulation of it: "The wise woman, then, will first choose to persuade her husband to be her associate in what is conducive to happiness. And should that be found impracticable, let her by herself earnestly aim at virtue, gaining her husband's consent in everything, so as never to do anything against his will, with exception of what is reckoned as contributing to virtue and salvation." The idea that a woman must follow virtue before uxorial duty also finds corroboration in medieval law. Bracton, for example, insists that a woman must obey her husband in everything—she is *sub virga sua*—as long as he does not order her to do something in violation of divine law.[32]

At the same time, such a guarantee of a woman's autonomy raised the question of the appropriate forms of resistance. In political discourse, this question produced a body of literature on resistance theory, from Luther's early treatises on the notion of passive resistance to the bold reinterpretations of the significance of Romans 13 by such constitutionalists as John Ponet.[33] In feminist discourse, it produced a literature that subverts not only the theoretical basis of patriarchalism but also the concept of a hierarchy of creation which underlies it. One can of course correctly argue that while political discourse affected the conduct of actual governments in later centuries, feminist discourse changed nothing. Before this century, the social and economic hegemony of men in the societies of the West was in practice not challenged, nor was the validity of the assumptions supporting it much examined. Whatever Renaissance feminists claimed as rights for women were not termed *rights*, nor, until the beginning of the seventeenth century, were they demanded except by way of arguing for a modification of existing domestic order. The fact remains that the concepts crucial to the idea of a society organized according to principles inimical to patriarchy—heterogeneity in nature and its creatures, androgyny as the bigendering of each sex, and the

[32]St. Clement of Alexandria, *The Miscellanies*, vol. 2 of *The Writings of Clement of Alexandria*, vol. 12 of *Ante-Nicene Christian Library*, ed. Roberts and Donaldson, 196. For Bracton, see Shahar, *Fourth Estate*, 88; Shahar cites F. Pollock and F. Maitland, *A History of English Law* (Cambridge, 1898), 2:406. On a woman's subordination to her husband in general and without specific reference to conscience, see Maclean, *Renaissance Notion of Women*, 18. A useful guide to the history of women's legal rights is still Eugene A. Hecker, *A Short History of Women's Rights* (New York: Putnam, 1910).

[33]For an analytic survey of concepts of legitimate resistance, see, i.a., Quentin Skinner, "The Duty to Resist" and "The Right to Resist," both in *Foundations of Modern Political Thought*, 2:189–238 and 302–48.

equality of men and women in human society—were enunciated in feminist discourse of the sixteenth century.

Aristotle's Biology

The single most imposing challenge for a defender of women—a challenge that tends to elicit from him or her a guarded acceptance of the necessity of a society controlled by men and, at the same time, the most paradoxical of arguments rejecting this necessity— is the nature of woman's sexuality. Her procreativeness is routinely given a kind of credit. Paul justifies a woman's existence by her ability to have children: "notwithstanding [her original sin] she shall be saved in child-bearing" (1 Tim. 2:15). And defenses remind men that women are related to them in flesh and blood, that women carry in their bodies the next generation and thus the very future. But a woman's sexual difference is more often a sign of weakness—a point feminists discuss with greater intensity and frequency than do their opponents. Woman, it is generally agreed, is not as strong physically as man and, more important, is vulnerable sexually as he is not. Not only because pregnancy and lacta-tion make her dependent on other persons, although this physical depen-dence is clearly important, but because her sexual activity, in contrast to his, can result in scandal and disgrace. Her body can and commonly does signify that she is sexually active whether or not she wishes the fact to be known. Maternity, unlike paternity, is not a discretionary matter, to be acknowledged or not, at will. These biological facts underlie arguments for restricting all woman's activities, particularly those that take her into the public arena. Misogynists tend to perceive her inability to control the effects of her sexuality—pregnancy—as an indication of an inherent moral debility. Feminists had to insist on making a distinction between a nonprejudicial biological condition—pregnancy—and behavior that is and can evidently be proved to be morally culpable—licentiousness.[34] The importance of the virtue of chastity was asserted by both sides. For writers who identified themselves with the interests of men, a woman's chastity signified dynastic integrity; it was the foundation upon which patriarchal society rested. The exchange between men of women and property, and, to a degree, of women as property, was predicated on the value of the woman as a vessel that would generate legitimate children

[34]The twentieth-century interpretation of the effects of this biological difference stresses economics over morals. Once again the prejudice is against women, who in this case are poor if not also sinful. "Our national code of accepted behavior includes the right of men to propagate children, and then desert them": Stanley Lebergott, quoted in Andrew Hacker, "Getting Rough on the Poor," *New York Review of Books*, Oct. 13, 1988, p. 13.

and so perpetuate the family of the man who was legally and morally responsible for her and her maintenance, and not that of some other man. For feminists, chastity was important chiefly insofar as it could lead to a woman's escape from patriarchal proprietorship. A daughter who wished to remain a virgin—and thus to lead a celibate life—was legally under her father's control unless she entered a nunnery, but feminists generally portrayed her as possessing a kind of liberty that was, typically, devoted to intellectual and devotional pursuits.[35]

Much of the rationale for interpretations of female physical weakness as an index of moral weakness comes from popular readings of Aristotle on the biology of animals. Feminists and antifeminists knew that Aristotle had postulated that a female was by nature a defective male; they also knew that he had declared that the male contributed motion and form to the embryo, and the female only matter; and that the male "stands for" the effective and active, and the female for the passive.[36]

[35]This is especially the case for persons who supported the idea that women should undertake humanistic studies. Margaret L. King notes that for women who were not cloistered, a commitment to chastity could serve various ends: "I would suggest that when learned women (or men, for that matter) themselves chose a celibate life, they did so at least in part because they sought psychic freedom; when, on the other hand, men urged chastity upon learned women, they did so at least in part to constrain them. These fearful creatures of a third sex threatened male dominance in both the intellectual and the social realm": "Book-Lined Cells: Women and Humanism in the Early Italian Renaissance," in *Beyond Their Sex: Learned Women of the European Past*, ed. Patricia H. Labalme (New York: New York University Press, 1980), 78. For more on Italian women humanists, see also Margaret L. King and Albert Rabil, Jr., eds., *Her Immaculate Hand: Selected Works by and about the Women Humanists of Quattrocento Italy*, Medieval Texts and Studies no. 20 (Binghamton, N.Y.: State University of New York, 1983).

[36]On the defectiveness of woman: "Now a boy is like a woman in form, and the woman is as it were an impotent male, for it is through a certain incapacity that the female is female, being incapable of concocting the nutriment in its last stage into semen . . . owing to the coldness of her nature." And on her passivity: "It follows [from her passivity] that what the female would contribute to the semen of the male would not be semen but material for the semen to work upon": *Generation of Animals* (hereafter *GA*), 1, 20, 728a1, 729a1, in *The Complete Works of Aristotle: The Revised Oxford Translation*, ed. Jonathan Barnes, Bollingen Series LXXI (Princeton: Princeton University Press, 1984), 1:1130, 1132. For a study of Aristotle's writing relevant to the nature and status of women, see Maryanne Cline Horowitz, "Aristotle and Woman," *Journal of the History of Biology* 9, 2 (1979): 183–213, and esp. in politics, Susan Moller Okin, *Women in Western Political Thought* (Princeton: Princeton University Press, 1979), 73–96. Maclean offers an extended analysis of the effect of Aristotelian ideas of male and female on Renaissance medicine; for physicians of the period, Galen was the preferred authority on the meaning of sexual difference, although in "both Aristotelian and Galenic terms, woman is less fully developed than man. Because of lack of heat in generation, her sexual organs have remained internal, she is incomplete, colder and moister in dominant humours, and unable to 'concoct' perfect semen from blood": *Renaissance Notion of Woman*, 31. Galen did, however, argue that woman had semen, a point that linked his thought with that of sixteenth-century doctors, who, especially after the publication of Gabriele Fallopio's *Observationes anatomicae*, 1561), maintain that each sex, although anatomically different, is functional in

They were aware that according to Aristotelian nature, there is in sexual difference a relation of superior to inferior, and thus that his biology had an obvious correspondence with the view of the beginning of human life in Scripture. To Aristotle, the male is "the first efficient or moving cause to which belong the definition and the form [of the embryo]" (it is not, he later insists, a "material principle" creating mere resemblance [GA 4.1; 765b1, p. 1184]), and as such the male is "better and more divine in [his] nature than the material on which he works [that is, than the female]." (As the male can in some sense be said to "fashion" the embryo from mere matter, he approaches a kind of divine creativity—a point surely not lost on readers who were accustomed to seeing God as the father of mankind and Christ as the husband of the church.) The male is therefore to be kept separate from the female "wherever it is possible and so far as it is possible" and to come together with her only for the "work of genera-tion" (GA 2.1; 327a1, p. 1136). Female passivity and materiality are by definition capable only of being elements of receptivity for the male formative and vitalizing seed. The matter she contributes to generation, the menses, lacks "the principle of soul"; this is contributed only by the male, and in this sense she is a "mutilated male" (GA 2.3; 737b1, p. 1144). She is herself the product of a gestational process that failed to reach full potential. Aristotle writes that a female is created when "the first princi-ple does not bear sway and cannot concoct the nourishment through lack of heat nor bring it into its proper form, but is defeated in this respect" (GA 4.1; 766a1, p. 1185). A struggle therefore takes place within the womb as form attempts to assert itself over matter; a "defeated" form is a female form. Debility characterizes the female for her entire life. As formally less evolved than a male, she is "perfected more quickly," and her entire life cycle is accomplished in a shorter time: "females are weaker

---

generation: ibid., 32–33. In nonscientific circles, Galen's view of human anatomy as divinely ordered may have been important to a reassessment of woman as perfect in her own way: "In the De usu partium (IV, 360 passim) he [Galen] came to the conclusion that in the structure of any animal we have the mark of a wise workman or demiurge, and of a celestial mind: and that 'the investigation of the use of the parts of the body lays the foundation of a truly scientific theology which is much greater and more precious than all medicine'": Lynn Thorndike, The History of Magic and Experimental Science (New York: Columbia University Press, 1923), 1:149. A similar view of woman as well designed is expressed by Aquinas: "With reference to nature in the species as a whole, the female is not something manqué, but is according to the plan of nature [intentio naturae], and is directed to the work of procreation": Maclean, Renaissance Notion of Woman, 8–9, quoting Summa theologica, 1a92, 1. How precise and accurate a reading of Aristotle most Renaissance feminists had is unclear from their defenses. More often than not, they refer to ideas that are attributed to him in contemporary literature on women. But however they cite him, they invariably see him as an exponent of misogyny.

and colder in nature, and we must look upon the female character as being a sort of natural deficiency" (*GA* 4.6; 775a1, p. 1199).

More important to feminists than Aristotle's biology was its impact on his politics. For the female's relative coldness and formlessness implied a whole set of characteristics that made a woman radically unfit for any activity that was not, in essence, a response to a signal or command from a man. Aristotle's politics is in a sense an extrapolation of his understanding of biology and reflects the same preferential distinction for the soul over the body, the intellect over the passions. Because the male, exemplifying the rational element, is superior to the female, exemplifying the passionate element, it is natural, Aristotle writes in the *Politics*, that he rule and she be ruled: "this principle, of necessity, extends to all mankind."[37] Their relations are as between a superior and his inferior or subordinate, and correspond to the natural character of their respective virtues or "excellences." A woman, like a slave or a child, has only a part of the soul that inheres totally in man.

> For the slave has no deliberative faculty at all; the woman has, but it is without authority, and the child has, but it is immature. So it must necessarily be supposed to be with the excellences of character also; all should partake of them, but only in such manner and degree as is required by each for the fulfilment of his function. . . . The temperance of a man and of a woman, or the courage and justice of a man and of a woman, are not, as Socrates maintained, the same; the courage of a man is shown in commanding, of a woman in obeying.   [*Politics* 1.13; 1260a1, p. 1999]

Natural differences eventually dictate social functions that follow rules of decorum determined by character. "A man would be thought a coward if he had no more courage than a courageous woman, and a woman would be thought loquacious if she imposed no more restraint on her conversation than the good man; and indeed their part in the management of the household is different, for the duty of the one is to acquire, and of the other to preserve" (*Politics* 3.4; 1277b1, p. 2027). If these norms are not observed, and a woman rules a man, even within a household, she abuses political propriety and, ultimately, biological nature. The perfect relation between man and wife is "aristocratic": "for the man rules in accordance with merit, and in those matters in which a man should rule, but the matters that befit a woman he hands over to her."[38] If he insists on taking charge of things appropriately hers, he ignores decorum and creates an

---

[37]*Politics* 1.5, 1254b1, in *Complete Works of Aristotle*, 2:1990.
[38]*Nicomachean Ethics* (hereafter *NE*) 8.10, 1160b1, in *Complete Works of Aristotle*, 2:1834.

oligarchy. A woman's rule is always oligarchic. Women can command only because they are "heiresses," and their rule is "not in virtue of excellence but due to wealth and power, as in oligarchies" (*NE* 8.10; 1161a1, p. 1834). At the same time, Aristotle maintains, domestic government is not to be regarded as essentially political, that is, of a kind with civic government, because it does not admit the possibility of a truly, or unqualified, just or unjust action: "there can be no injustice in the unqualified sense towards things that are one's own [as are those of a household]. . . . Hence justice can no more truly be manifested towards a wife than towards children and chattels, for the former is household justice; but even this is different from political justice" (*NE* 5.6; 1134b1, p. 1790). The idea of the wife as a *kind* as well as bearer of property over which her husband has control persists throughout the Renaissance; it is in conformity with the doctrine of woman's inferiority and subordination derived from Genesis 2 and 3.

The influence of Aristotle's view of woman on clerical and scholastic thought is mediated chiefly through Aquinas, who relies on Aristotle's biology to interpret relations between men and women as they appear in Scripture. Early Italian humanists who were interested in developing theories of government for the household as well as for the state—such as Francesco Barbaro and Leon Battista Alberti—went straight to the political writings of Aristotle. For the next two hundred years, scarcely a serious defense of woman fails to contend, in one way or another, with an Aristotelian text. Feminists had, of course, authorities that they could invoke in refutation of some of the claims in the *Generation of Animals* and the *Politics*, notably Plato, who asserts in the *Meno* that virtue is sexless and genderless, and in the *Republic* that "men and women alike possess the qualities which make a guardian [i.e., a person capable of command]; they differ only in their comparative strength or weakness."[39] But Aristotle had criticized his precursor's idealistic vision of a state without distinctions of sex or gender in its notions of government because it ignored the crucial role of property, and of women *as* property, in stabilizing relations between men (*Politics* 2.1–6; 1260b1–1266a1, pp. 2000–2009). No defense that I know of argues for the virtue of woman in a polygamous society in which wives are property common to all men—

[39]*Republic* 5, 456, in *The Dialogues of Plato*, trans. Benjamin Jowett (New York: Random House, 1937), 1:717. Socrates also argues that because, as Meno has claimed, a man rules a state, a woman a household, and both governments proceed by virtue of temperance and justice, then both men and women have the same virtues of temperance and justice: *Meno* 73, in ibid., 351. For Plato's ideas on women in politics, see also Okin, *Women in Western Political Thought*, 15–70.

such an argument is clearly paradoxical in the context of Christian notions of virtue.[40] (Private property also had religious sanction: Adam, it was believed, was endowed with the world's goods and therefore the first property owner.) Humanist exemplum history provided feminists with another kind of strategy. Against claims made in the name of natural or divine law, they could represent historical "facts" concerning virtuous women gathered from Plutarch's *Mulierum virtutes* as well as Livy, Tacitus, and Valerius Maximus. Sixteenth-century writers regarded Boccaccio's *De mulieribus claris* as such a source. But finally feminists, adopting the critical methods of humanist historians, replied to all their opponents by confronting the very concept of authority and what it implies about understanding the order of nature and historical time. As long as an authority was held to speak the absolute truth, to invoke him was sufficient to establish the truth or rightness of a given position or practice, and no feminist could conceive of forms of society that might be alternatives to patriarchy. Their efforts were therefore directed at discovering reasons for ameliorating the condition of woman within existing structures of family and community life. But when such authorities came to be regarded as historically contingent and relevant only to the particular situations they addressed (as they increasingly did during the late fifteenth and early sixteenth centuries), then feminists could propose to legitimate nontraditional views of woman which vitiated patriarchal norms.

REPRESENTATIVE HUMANISTS

Famous Women

Humanist writers touched on feminist issues as a consequence of their concern for the welfare of the *res publica*. Reacting to the clerical preference for the *vita contemplativa* over the *vita activa*, they addressed the moral problems confronting the Christian who had to reconcile civic duty, including the obligation to marry and have children, with his soul's salvation. Boccaccio, for one, saw that politics could be regarded as providential rather than a dangerous distraction; moreover, because the good ruler prevailed while his evil counterpart became the

---

[40]But see Clement of Alexandria, who comments that Plato intended that all property be commonly owned, since division and faction among human beings were the outcome of the ownership of property. This ruling extended, "without doubt, even to wives": Fifth Letter, in *Patrologiae cursus completus, Series latina*, ed. Jacques-Paul Migne (Paris, 1844), 130.57.

victim of fortune, fame was an index of moral status.[41] For other writers, the fate of the individual man was linked to his place in society—both in the family, the seat of domestic order, and in the state, exhibiting a civic order. Marriage, leading to the generation and education of children, became a prerequisite of good citizenship. The family became politicized, its members described in terms of their duties as governing and governed.

The endorsement of marriage for reasons of state entailed both a defense of and, more subtly, an attack on woman which was qualitatively different from anything written earlier. The great medieval source of supposedly misogynist diatribe, Jean de Meung's *Roman de la rose*, charged woman with a fundamental corruption; it was answered by literature extolling her private and moral qualities. Renaissance humanists were less direct in their opinions. Considering how a woman might benefit the state, they praised her for patience and loyalty, qualities that made the political duties incumbent upon her appear to be consistent with her supposed nature. She was chiefly admirable as the faithful lieutenant to her male superiors; her conduct reflected the fact that she had the virtues in the mode not of command but of subordination, as Aristotle had asserted. Were she to prove an exception to this rule and be a Joan of Arc, she was no longer purely a woman. Her virility testified to the rightness of the general scheme privileging man and legitimating patriarchy. In fact, her virility was generally exhibited in action undertaken at a moment of crisis that had as its purpose the preservation of the status quo—the domestic or political order in which she was always inferior and subordinate. Because women did not (and were not supposed to) do anything to earn them public notice, a famous woman was almost a contradiction in terms, either actually infamous or simply fantastic.

In the Proem to his *De mulieribus claris* (c. 1380), Boccaccio reveals the criteria by which he has chosen the women whose histories he writes. The "fame" (*claritas*) they possess is not, he declares, in every case to be

[41]Boccaccio, writing exemplum history in order to benefit the state, illustrates the misfortunes that justly befall evil rulers: "What almighty God (or Fortune, to use their [i.e., the rulers'] language) did to those who were in high office . . . [so that] they, seeing feeble and defeated princes, kings thrown to earth by God's judgment, might know the power of the Most High . . . ; might learn to refrain from mere pleasure": "Proem," in *De casibus virorum illustrium*, ed. Pier Giorgio Ricci and Vittorio Zaccaria, vol. 9 of *Tutte le opere di Giovanni Boccaccio*, ed. Vittore Branca (Milan: Mondadori, 1983), 10. Petrarch simply warns against a desire for fame, which is "a stimulus that excites a generous and modest spirit, raises him up and spurs him on to satisfy the aspirations of citizens, but it casts down wicked and presumptuous characters": "De remediis utriusque fortune," I, 92, in Francesco Petrarca, *Prose*, ed. G. Martellotti (Milan: Riccardo Ricciardi, 1955), 636.

understood in the narrow sense of that term, that is, in relation to "virtue" (*virtus*); but rather more broadly: "I think famous those women who are well known for some deed recognized throughout the world."[42] Initially, he puts the case for the famous woman who is worthy rather than reprehensible in what appear to be positive terms. Distinguishing between a characteristically Christian virtue that derives from an inner and contemplative activity and a characteristically pagan virtue that promotes the public good, the *res publica*, he states that he celebrates the latter because its female exponents, unlike Christian saints, have as yet had no chronicler. His choice restricts the standards by which he will judge the virtue of woman to those supporting the *vita activa*—that is, standards by which women were usually considered to be worthless, whether because naturally incapable of virtuous public activity or because they were legally barred from participating in it. He thus raises the question of the relevance of his own histories to an audience of women. Are they to be understood to provide models for emulation, as his praise of pagan heroines suggests? Or are they to be taken as a warning that to contemporary Christian women the public arena is closed?

> The ladies of sacred history, following the way and the directions of their holy Teacher, often discipline themselves to tolerate adversity almost beyond human consideration. Pagan women, by contrast, attain [glory]— and with what a strength of spirit—either by a certain gift or instinct of nature; or better, because they are spurred on by a desire for the fleeting splendor [*cupiditas fulgoris momentanei*] of the world; and sometimes, battered by fortune, they confront the heaviest of trials. The first kind of women . . . is described . . . in the works of pious men. . . . The merits of the second kind, unpublished in any book, I have undertaken to describe, as if to give them a just reward.   [26]

---

[42]Boccaccio, *De mulieribus claris*, ed. Vittorio Zaccaria, vol. 10 of *Tutte le opere di Giovanni Boccaccio* (Milan: Mondadori, 1967), 24. Boccaccio writes that he intended to dedicate this work to Queen Giovanna of Naples, but realizing that "the little light" of his work would be put out by her "greater" splendor, he has substituted Andrea Acciaiuoli, Countess of Altavilla. For an analysis of this work as a whole, see my "Boccaccio's Infamous Women: Gender and Civic Virtue in the *De mulieribus claris*," in *Ambiguous Realities: Women in the Middle Ages and Renaissance*, ed. Carole Levin and Jeanie Watson (Detroit: Wayne State University Press, 1987), 25–47. My initial reading of this text, concentrating on the apparent humanistic feminism of its proem, failed to grasp the profound irony of its actual histories; see my "Feminism and the Humanists: The Case of Sir Thomas Elyot's *Defence of Good Women*," in *Rewriting the Renaissance*, ed. Ferguson et al., 242–58. The fullest account of Boccaccio's Latin works is still Attilio Hortis, *Studii sul opere latine del Boccaccio* (Trieste, 1879). Hortis considers the question of Boccaccio's misogyny in the *De mulieribus claris* (esp. 81–85). See also Vittore Branca, *Boccaccio: The Man and His Works*, trans. Richard Monges (New York: New York University Press, 1976), and Henri Hauvette, *Boccace: Etude biographique et littéraire* (Paris: Armand Colin, 1914).

Few of Boccaccio's contemporaries, whether men or women, would have undertaken to ignore "the directions of their holy Teacher," here in explicit opposition to the "desire" that prompts action in the fleetingly splendid world, and striven only to secure fame. His women readers would have had cause to reflect even more deeply, for Scripture taught them to obey, not to command. And had they overcome their fear of violating custom and positive law on the one hand and divine law on the other, and taken Boccaccio's text as their guide, they would have discovered an ambiguity that goes deeper than mere contradiction. Not only are his famous women poor examples of virtue, they are also condemned, however covertly, for venturing into a world reserved for men.[43]

Boccaccio's portrait of Dido demonstrates his double and contradictory intention. Deriving his account from Petrarch rather than Vergil or Dante, Boccaccio relates that his heroine, whose name is Elissa, is forced to flee her native land after her brother, the avaricious king Pygmalion, kills her husband, Sychaeus. Now a widow, she vows to remain faithful to her dead husband, and takes the name Dido. She assumes command of her followers, soon to found Carthage under her leadership, through acts of deceit, not conquest. The single exception to this rule—her command to her followers (all men) to get wives by raping the virgins of Cyprus—assumes thematic importance in relation to the second and tragic phase of

---

[43]This strategy of subversion is already evident in the principal text that served as Boccaccio's model, Plutarch's *Mulierum virtutes*, the first extended defense of women to have had wide currency in the Renaissance. The classic statement of misogyny in Greek and Roman antiquity is Hesiod's myth of Pandora (*Theogony* 590–812); Plato and others who engaged in sophistic debate later undertook to defend women from such attacks. See Philip Stadter, *Plutarch's Historical Methods: An Analysis of "Mulierum Virtutes"* (Cambridge: Cambridge University Press, 1965), 3. Echoing Plato's *Meno*, Plutarch declares that the virtues of man and woman are the same; they only appear to be different because "they take on the likeness of the customs on which they are founded, and of the temperament of persons and their nurture and mode of living" (trans. Frank Cole Babbitt, in *Plutarch's Moralia*, Loeb Classical Library (Cambridge: Harvard University Press, 1949), 3:475, 479. Illustrating his thesis by examples, however, Plutarch qualifies the virtue of woman so that its nature and scope correspond to Aristotle's restrictive notion of sex and gender differences. His typically virtuous woman assists and inspires men; if necessary, she sacrifices herself for their welfare or that of the state. See esp. the history of Aretaphila (Love of honor), who, after she has freed her own city, Cyrene, from the tyranny of her husband, "withdrew at once to her own quarters among the women, and, rejecting any sort of meddling in affairs, spent the rest of her life quietly at the loom in the company of her friends and family" (551). The image of a country's deliverer in modest retirement was known to Plutarch through accounts of such heroes as Cincinnatus, who, having rescued the republic, retires to live a private life on his farm—not once but twice. But one needs to note the difference between the particular conditions of freedom due the men of Cyrene and those that their female deliverer accepts as appropriate for her as a woman. By freeing his city, a Cincinnatus secures his *own* liberty; Plutarch's Aretaphila may not be able even to envisage such a condition for herself.

her career, when she is a queen regnant. This phase establishes that whatever her virtues, they are finally irrelevant to her participation in public life. What is decisive is the fact that she is a woman. As such she cannot govern a people, not because there are laws that prevent gynecocracy—in fact, she herself has made the original laws on which her state is founded—but because she can never overcome the effects of her creation as the inferior and subordinate of man.

Boccaccio concludes this phase of Dido's history by extolling her virtuous chastity—the virtue that caused her to commit suicide rather than marry her barbarous suitor, the neighboring king, Massitanus, who pressed his courtship by beseiging Carthage. The poet's tribute to the widowed queen obscures what his history of her implies: woman's rule is a political impossibility. Given the customary relation of husband (head) to his wife (the body, or subordinate), Dido, a queen, cannot take a husband (however civilized) as a king can take a wife. Her subjects fear destruction from her marauding suitor if she does not agree to his proposal; but they could reasonably fear the usurper and tyrant if she did. She cannot be both a queen and a wife. Whatever its moral significance, the chastity of Boccaccio's Dido has chiefly a political reference: she kills herself in response to her fear that her citizenry, left unprotected by the relative impotence of their married queen regnant, would succumb to the demands of the alien authority of her male consort. Her tragic end depends on the fact that she will become politically impotent at the moment of marriage. What we intuitively understand as the meaning of her action—that it actually protects her subjects from a dangerous rule by removing the possibility of a married queen regnant—is made clearer in Boccaccio's account of Dido in an earlier history of the queen, in *De casibus virorum illustrium*. There, having agreed to marry Massitanus, Dido asks for a delay, during which she fortifies her city against the barbarian's army: "She summoned whatever was necessary for the defense of the city, so that she would not leave it undefended after having built it."[44] Satisfied that it is safe, she commits suicide. The impregnable walls of her city are the correlative of her inviolate physical self, and what they protect—the independence of her people—is guaranteed by her refusal to allow herself to be possessed.

The problem of gynecocracy that Boccaccio confronts in his fiction was to require an actual solution later, when the English succession

---

[44]*De casibus vivorum illustrium*, 140–41. Boccaccio, citing chronology, defends his chaste Dido as historically correct by contrast to the amorous Dido of Vergil and Dante. According to Eusebius, Boccaccio declares, Troy was destroyed long before Carthage was built: "I don't think Aeneas ever saw her [Dido]": Canto 5, 1, in *Esposizioni sopra la Commedia di Dante*, ed. Giorgio Padoan, vol. 6 of *Tutte le opere* (Milan: Mondadori, 1965), 300.

required that Mary Tudor become the anomaly Dido had avoided: a married queen regnant. Boccaccio's Dido illustrates, in any case, the *essential* weakness of the woman ruler—her status as naturally and legally vulnerable to men. Dido's most important success (in that without it she would have had no people to lead), her authorization of her male subjects' rape of foreign women, emphasizes the inevitably masculine character of political rule, the rule to which she, as a woman although a monarch, is also at last subject.[45]

Boccaccio's Dido represents his conception of the woman expert in government or "arms"; his Pope Joan exhibits the second of the two attributes of the virtuous citizen, mastery of the "arts." Feminists often commended women for accomplishments in oratory, rhetoric, poetry, philosophy, and even theology. Because a woman need not actually leave the privacy of her family to excel in these arts, however much such a sequestration might seem to be at cross-purposes with her education, praise of her intellectual achievements did not appear to transgress patriarchal norms. Yet the very act of self-expression was often regarded as a violation of the spirit of domesticity. Spoken words might be overheard; written speech might be published; words not known to be a woman's might actually succeed in persuading men to action and so provide her with a basis for achieving authority and power in the public arena. Boccaccio's account of the legendary Pope Joan—whose fame (unlike that of Dido) is a kind of notoriety—illustrates that intellectual activity cannot be undertaken by the female brain, situated as it is in the female body.

Joan is incontestably brilliant. Prevailing over her male competitors, her sex masked by masculine clothing, she is elected to the papacy. Inevitably her intellect propels her into the public arena; inevitably too her political power finds expression in lust.[46] Whereas Dido was the object of desire or, perhaps, its provocation, Joan is an overtly desiring subject. Dido, rejecting desire, was praised for her virtuous self-sacrifice; Joan was punished by God, who, "pitying his people from on high, did not permit a woman to occupy such a high place [as the papacy]. . . . Advised by the devil . . . , elected to the supreme office of the papacy, [Joan] was overcome with a burning lust [*ardor libidinis*]. . . . She found

---

[45]Boccaccio's subtly critical representations of virile women elsewhere in this text stand in problematic contrast to his fulsome praise of Queen Giovanna of Naples, in fact a woman of considerable authority and power, and the last of his subjects in this history.

[46]On the link between female sexuality and eloquence, see the charges against Isotta Nogarola, whose "fluent speech" indicated to the Venetian Niccolò Barbo that she was promiscuous. They are quoted in Lisa Jardine, "Isotta Nogarola: Women Humanists—Education for What?" *History of Education* 12, 4 (1983): 240.

one who mounted [*defricere*] her in secret (she, the successor of Peter!) and thus allayed her flaming prurience" (101, 416). She became pregnant and gave birth ignominiously, in public. Denounced and dishonored, she left the country with her child. Her fate resembles Dido's in that she could not realize her virtue publicly because she was female. Yet her case is also more complicated. By drawing the reader's attention to her violation of the sanctity of *Peter's* office, Boccaccio reminds us, whether or not intentionally, that a pope could in fact beget children and retain the papacy. In this sense, men's bodies can lie; they do not reveal their sexual experience; they cannot signify the virtue of chastity or its opposite, the vice of promiscuity. Women's bodies can and do.

Boccaccio's history of the scandalous Joan conveys his sense that political authority and power are maintained through the creation of a persona that compels the allegiance of the public, and jeopardized when there is clear evidence that a ruler has failed to follow the rules. He also shows that only the ruler who is *publicly* acknowledged as sinful is penalized—a condition that affects women disproportionately. God may be said to have punished Joan because she assumed the papacy (although this was an office for which she was more suited than any of her male peers), and because she committed fornication (a sin male popes committed, too). But her punishment was occasioned by and was a response to her maternity, which was no more than an *expression* of the sexuality that she, a woman—unlike a man who becomes a father—had no way of controlling, hiding, or denying. In effect, although I suspect without full awareness, Boccaccio has distinguished between the moral aspects of sexuality (lust as opposed to continence) and its amoral physical manifestation (maternity as opposed to paternity). Feminists would later attempt to clarify these distinctions by analyzing attitudes toward prostitution and rape.

Household Government

As the populations of cities increased and their government became more complex, it was logical that humanists discussed the feasibility of observing Christian ethics in various kinds of forums: the marketplace, the law courts, the legislature. To lay the foundations for constructive public activity, they studied the conduct of persons within a family, itself a diminutive image of the state. Their treatises describing the rights and duties of husband and wife, parents and children, master or mistress and servants or slaves circulated throughout the fifteenth century; they were printed and reprinted in considerable numbers through the beginning of the seventeenth century. Virtually all urge their readers to marry, although why such encouragement was needed is unclear. Religious scruples—reflecting a belief in the innate evil of woman and in the necessity of solitude for prayer and contemplation—seem less an issue than do fears concerning loss of personal independence due to increased responsibilities, especially financial ones. Most argument is directed at reluctant bridegrooms, perhaps because they were less bound by parental wishes than their prospective brides. Feminists' reactions to these treatises were subtle rather than explicit, in part because many conceded a good deal to the domestic authority and power of the woman as wife or mother. But more often than not, they punctuated their descriptions of marital complementarity with statements of womanly duties that frankly inhibited the actual exercise of a woman's autonomy, and feminists protested these restrictions.

Francesco Barbaro's *De re uxoria* (1416) conveys what were to become the normative terms of the Renaissance discourse on the household— terms that subsequent discussion on the subject had necessarily to consider. Barbaro describes the best means of ensuring dynastic integrity (understandably, since his is a noble Venetian family), and insists on the importance of women as property and property holders.[47] He believes that well-ordered families maintain the stability of the state; and he sees that this order depends chiefly on controlling the activities of women in relation to the production and distribution of wealth.

His thesis exemplifies the kind of reasoning that exponents of patriarchy, particularly as it is manifest in the male control of wealth, could bring to bear on contemporary social and economic developments. Restrictions on women, their behavior in private and in public, appear to have been more stringent in Italy than elsewhere in Europe in the early Renaissance. Kathleen Casey notes that the economic power of Italian women was "earliest and most successfully blocked" from becoming politically decisive. These restrictions followed a "crisis" in which a number of factors, particularly economic, were instrumental. Unlike men, women who lost the occupations they had followed under feudalism and systems of production dependent on the household and the guild

---

[47]The particularly Venetian character of Barbaro's humanism is analyzed by Margaret L. King, "Caldiera and the Barbaros on Marriage and the Family: Humanist Reflections of Venetian Realities," *Journal of Medieval and Renaissance Studies* 6, 1 (1976): 19–50. See also Attilio Gnesotto's introductory remarks detailing the sources, publication history, and social background to Francesco Barbaro, *De re uxoria*, ed. Gnesotto, Atti e memorie della Accademia di scienze lettere ed arti in Padova (1915–16), n.s. 32 (Padova: Battista Randi, n.d.).

were made economically redundant. The "newer paradigms of social structure . . . did not . . . include among them an active independent wife or female worker." She became what Casey terms "an inactive partner" and hence a type on whom could be projected all the anxieties attendant on social change.[48] In Venice, more specific evidence concerning the distribution of dowries suggests how women as property and property holders could affect the stability of families and the patriarchal authority and power directing them. Writing on the distribution of wealth through dowries and bequests, Stanley Chojnacki points out that women who had property to bequeath commonly did so on the basis of affection rather than strict kinship, and more often in favor of female than male relatives. The pattern of inheritance from women therefore tended to undermine the wealth of patrilinear families. To the extent that women could independently hold and pass on property, they represented a potential perturbation to patrilineage and finally to patriarchy.[49] Barbaro's fear of allowing women any degree of independence, especially financial, finds real provocation in the testamentary behavior of contemporary Venetian women.

Like many apologists for what I have called the politicized marriage, Barbaro believes that household government, like civil government, is supported by systems of law. He invokes as authoritative both natural law and its expression in the *ius gentium*, or the so-called law of nations

[48]Casey, "Cheshire Cat," 226–27.

[49]On the power of Venetian women to control wealth, Stanley Chojnacki observes: "The compensation that fathers and brothers traditionally had received for dowry expenditures was the acquisition of economic, social, and even political allies in the persons of their new sons- and brothers-in-law." But, he goes on to note, women, as mothers, aunts, and cousins, also contributed to dowries, and the patterns of their bequests often ran counter to those of men. They contributed to the dowries of women who were outside the patrilineage, to their daughters' daughters as well as to their sons' daughters. Other than dowries, bequests by women were further characterized by a preference for women, apparently determined by affection rather than close kinship. While males and females benefit "almost equally" in bequests by women to primary kin, "among secondary kin beneficiaries (aunts, uncles, nieces, nephews, cousins, etc.), females outnumber males by a considerable margin": "Dowries and Kinsmen in Early Renaissance Venice," in *Women in Medieval Society*, ed. Susan Mosher Stuard (Philadelphia: University of Pennsylvania Press, 1976), 173–98. It was virtually universal practice to maintain a woman's dowry, *dos*, as her own wealth, independent of her husband's property. The husband was entitled to its "use"—that is, the income resulting from its management—but he could not dispose of it, nor could his creditors claim it. At a woman's death, it reverted to her next of kin. Of comparable status was the husband's gift to his wife at the time of marriage, the *donatio propter nuptias*. At the death of her husband, she had the use of this property if she had children; otherwise it reverted to his family. See Charles Phineas Sherman, *Roman Law in the Modern World* (Boston: Boston Book Co., 1917), 2:65–76. For a general assessment of attitudes toward wealth in families, see Hans Baron, "A New Attitude toward Wealth," in *Social and Economic Foundations of the Italian Renaissance*, ed. Anthony Molho (New York: Wiley, 1969), 173–82.

(held to be that law honored by all peoples and the basis of all positive law). These two concepts were epitomized in the biological events of the natural world, and in the history of classical Rome. Together "nature" and "Rome" provide Barbaro with the elements of his ideal marriage and perfect household. In nature, "by which a desire of congress for procreation sake is communicated to every kind of animal," he discovers the reason for marriage; in Rome he sees its political function. By taxing bachelors, Rome caused them to pay the debt they owed in children, a debt justified by the state's natural right to endure. The unmarried violated a civil code; the legitimately married remained within the law and benefited the state: "It hath been experienced that by legitimate marriages children are more disposed by birth to honesty, more gravely educated, and become better citizens, of whom the city consisting, will be more acceptable to its friends in justice, more terrible to its enemies in valour." The importance of marriage in turn guarantees the status of wives. As Barbaro observes, "Cato the Censor said that there was so much respect and veneration due to this state [marriage], that whosoever should offer violence to his wife . . . was equally to be prosecuted and detested with the violators of the images of the goddesses [*simulacra deorum*]."[50] Both abuses are crimes against the state which have symbolic meaning. Wives are "images"; that is, they are not to be protected as the thing itself, whatever that may be, but only as its figuration. What wives stand for in this context is, as Barbaro has said, the ability of the state to reproduce itself. This ability in turn depends, he goes on to say, on the transformation of the competitive and potentially hostile energies of men acting among themselves into the cooperative and amicable forces of attraction bringing men and women together. His opinion recalls Aristotle's notion that the transgenerational stability of a family and hence a society depends on treating each woman as the property of an individual man: "In a state having women and children in common, love [between men] will be diluted, and the father will certainly not say 'my son,' or the son, 'my

[50]Francesco Barbaro, *Directions for Love and Marriage. In two books. Written originally by Franciscus Barbarus a Venetian senator. And now translated into English by a person of quality* (London, 1677), sig. B1–3. I have noted the words of the original text in instances where the translation is dubious. The treatise, composed in 1415, is divided into a preface, "Quid sit conjugium," and a first and second part, "De delectu uxoris" and "De uxoris officio," respectively; it was dedicated to Lorenzo de' Medici, on the occasion of his marriage to Ginevra Cavalcanti. For an edition with Italian on facing pages, see *Prosatori latini del quattrocento*, ed. Eugenio Garin (Milan: Ricciardi, 1952), 105–37. Benjamin G. Kohl translates the preface and the second part of the text into English in *The Earthly Republic: Italian Humanists on Government and Society*, ed. Benjamin G. Kohl and Ronald G. Witt with Elizabeth Welles (Philadelphia: University of Pennsylvania Press, 1978), 179–88.

father.' "[51] For Barbaro, men with generative women as their private possessions can negotiate *peaceful* conquests:

> By this tye [*vinculo*, i.e., marriage] Cadusius reconciled the most seditious Carians amongst themselves; by this alliance Cyrus appeased the Chaldeans that were at enmity with their borderers; and at Rome in the same day the Sabins were both enemies and citizens. . . . And what is more incredible to be spoken, Alexander by this affinity (but not by that stately bridge) allied Asia to Europe.   [B3]

The contribution of marriage diplomacy to the future of states and empires, as it is alluded to here, appears to have suggested to Barbaro the operation of divine will. Woman are "images" of divinity inasmuch as they represent the means of peaceful growth and a way to enlarge the empire without any corresponding diminution of resources.

Yet the imagery of exchange masks the real violence of the actions described. The enmity that threatens constantly to disrupt relations among men is not, as Barbaro develops his argument, simply dissipated in the amorous exchanges of marriage. It is actually redirected to effect the exchanges of women in and through which the growth of the state is sustained. And in order for these exchanges to happen at all, the women exchanged must agree (or be forced to agree) to compliance with the terms of exchange, in short, to become human commodities, objects. Barbaro's description of a wife's virtue suggests why he can imagine that she might offer no objections to this role.

A wife's virtue is first of all to be moral: she cannot run a house unless she can run herself. Beyond that, she is to be exemplary:

> As a prince cannot well govern a city unless he be expert in the common law, the customs of his ancestors, and the publick affairs . . . so neither can domestick affairs be rightly managed unless the excellence of the mistress of the family be a singular example to the rest. And even as souldiers which have an excellent commander are ashamed to desert that place which is appointed them; so men and maid-servants will not forsake that part of the family concern, the custody of which is committed to them by a chaste and prudent mistress.   [B8]

---

[51]*Politics* 2.4, 1262b1, in *Complete Works of Aristotle*, 2:2004. In Aristotle's view, women were, of course, always property; the question was whether they were owned by one man or by many. Women can be exchanged among men in a variety of ways and for diverse reasons: to establish relations among families, to consolidate a political position or party, to acquire land or a public office. For an analysis of these systems of exchange, see Gayle Rubin, "The Traffic in Women: Notes on the 'Political Economy' of Sex," in *Toward an Anthropology of Women*, ed. Rayna R. Reiter (New York: Monthly Review Press, 1975), 157–210.

Her subaltern role is defined by an overriding obligation to obey her husband. She follows two rules: the rule of self-effacement and the rule of transparency. Her actions must be as though they were her husband's: "Let her be so conversant with him, that it may be most certain that nothing will be good to her, nothing pleasant, without her husband." And her thoughts must be entirely clear to him: "Let them [wives] feign nothing, let them dissemble nothing, let them conceal nothing. . . . I would that wives should so live with their husbands, that in a manner they might be of one mind and if it could be done . . . that two should become one" (F2v–3v). Her activities are conditioned accordingly. Barbaro insists that his wife, unlike a Greek wife, is not to be restricted to her "bed-chamber, as in a prison." Yet she must venture into the city only in the company of her husband. She is to be unlike the moon, which shines only in the absence of the sun; she is to be seen only when by her husband, whose light will very nearly (but not quite) obscure hers (Gv). In other words, in public a wife is seen as a "pale reflection" of her husband.[52] Hence, too, she cannot express herself authoritatively; in fact, Barbaro denies that she can "know" anything:

> Socrates [*Isocrates*] exhorteth men to speak either those things which they certainly know, or which, with their honour, they cannot conceal. We enjoin women to concede the former as proper to men, but they may believe the latter also common to themselves; in whom loquacity cannot be enough reproved, by the most prudent and learned persons, nor taciturnity sufficiently applauded.   [G2]

A woman's eloquence is therefore, like her public appearance, also paradoxical: "They should think that they shall obtain the glory of eloquence, if they adorn themselves with the famous ornament of silence" (G3v). In short, none of a woman's duties suggests that she is supposed to have a sense of herself as other than a useful extension of her husband. Barbaro is able to conceive of his ideal wife in these terms because he can make use of Aristotelian notions of a female nature; woman is "naturally weak" in relation to man, who is naturally strong. Woman is "fearful," and her fear brings "care" to preserve household order and direction (H4). In other words, the duties that define a wife are not imposed on her by a superior power, but derive from her innate disposition. Afflicted with a funda-

---

[52]The image, proverbial in the marriage literature of the fifteenth and sixteenth centuries, is Plutarch's: "Whenever the moon is at a distance from the sun we see her conspicuous and brilliant, but she disappears and hides herself when she comes near him. Contrariwise a virtuous woman ought to be most visible in her husband's company, and to stay in the house and hide herself when he is away": *Advice to Bride and Groom* (Conjugalia praecepta), in *Plutarch's Moralia*, 1:304–5.

mental weakness, his typical woman cannot be expected to demonstrate a virile virtue that would permit her to take part in public affairs, or to acquire the kinds of power needed for such activities.

This picture is refuted, to a degree, when Barbaro addresses two situations in which women could, and obviously sometimes did, have real power: the situation of the widow and that of the woman of property. In both cases, he sees dangers that betray his awareness of a female nature different from the one he has described. Widows may prove recalcitrant because experience has given them a sense of themselves that is different from the sense that their husbands expect them to have and, indeed, that they should have, if they are creatures who are comparatively weak: "We can scarce with great ingeny [sic], elaborate industry, and singular care reduce widows, formed both to their own and other humors, to our own customes" (Cv). And a rich wife may prove disobedient: "I think the riches of the wife unprofitable, unless the pattern of her husband's discipline shall appear easie to her, even in penury itself" (D5). The statement can be understood by inference: with riches, a woman may have reason to resist her husband's authority. Not surprisingly, Barbaro is concerned about the effect of a married woman's property on the relationship between spouses. Lycurgus, he asserts, "ordained that wives should be espoused without portions" in order that "Spartan women might not remain unmarried for their poverty, nor be married for their riches, for he foresaw that the Spartanes would seek virtue not riches in wives, and that the women would be far more diligent in the acquisition of virtues" (D6r–v). Barbaro has earlier stated that the virtue proper to woman would constitute her as self-effacing and transparent; here he sees riches as reconstituting her as a true subject, a person who is in some way independent of her husband.

Finally, all Barbaro's stipulations regarding the conduct of woman reflect his concern that her role as a vessel of generation not be compromised. He values a woman's sexuality as essential to the welfare of the family and ultimately to the state, but he emphasizes that it ought not to be the basis for any kind of self-representation:

> Husbands shall accustom [their wives] to seem to be helpers, not of lust, but of necessity: . . . [wives] should so evidence their nuptial honour and modesty, that in their congress decency may accompany their embraces, lest by their avidity and immodesty, they be both defective in their honour, and also less acceptable to their tacite husbands [*mariti tacenti*; i.e., uncomplaining]. [Hv]

Barbaro identifies the expression of sexual desire with speech and makes silence a sign of sexual modesty. A husband's "taciteness" indicates both his reluctance to chastize his wife for her passion and his own indifference or passivity; the implication is that she has had greater pleasure than he. A woman's "modesty" is linked to her silence, and a man's control of her to the forfeit of her sexual and her speaking self. Lacking expression for her self as subject, she becomes merely an object to be used. At the same time she is an "image" of some higher power and has symbolic value. What must be noticed is that her transformation into an object and symbol has depended on a kind of violence. Men agree to cease hostilities among themselves because they can agree to exchange women among themselves. In the process women lose their capacity to speak and be heard; they have value or are virtuous only as the means by which the continuity of society is guaranteed.

Humanists writing on household government did not generally allude to personal experience, despite the intimate nature of their subject. Barbaro's objectivity, like his conservatism, is the rule in this genre. Leon Battista Alberti's *Libri della famiglia* (1441) is unusual in focusing on the mores of his own family in Florence, which, as he laments, is "separated and scattered" by "the conditions of our time, the circumstances of our evil fate."[53] The Alberti wife's part in restoring her family to prosperity is clear and crucial: she is to maintain domestic order by conserving what her husband has acquired. If she fails to do so, she not only hurts her family but also affects the financial stability of the state. For goods that are kept within a family do not enter the marketplace; conversely, those that are lost or sold are put back into competitive play. In excessive quantities, goods in the process of being exchanged can cause men to feel greed, ambition, and an indifference to law. Rather than define her value as that of an object exchanged between men, as Barbaro does, Alberti sees a woman as one who by conserving property *limits* the number of (real) objects to be exchanged among men, and thereby prevents rapid shifts in the fortunes of her family and, by extension, of those of others.

[53]Leon Battista Alberti, *The Family in Renaissance Florence: A Translation by Renée Neu Watkins of "I Libri della famiglia"* (Columbia: University of South Carolina Press, 1969), 94. For a modern edition, see Leon Battista Alberti, *Opere volgari*, ed. Cecil Grayson, Scrittori d'Italia 218 (Bari: Laterza, 1960). Presented to the Florentine Republic in 1441 as a contribution to a literary contest on friendship, Alberti's book was circulated widely in manuscript but not printed before 1734. The text is divided into a prologue and four books; the second, *De re uxoria*, and the third, *Economicus*, contain Alberti's discussion of woman and marriage. For studies of *Della famiglia*, see, i.a., Enrico Aubel, *Leon Battista Alberti e i libri della famiglia* (Città di Castello: S. Lapi, 1913). For an excellent study of Alberti's works as a whole, esp. his development of the idea of perspective, see Joan Gadol, *Leon Battista Alberti: Universal Man of the Early Renaissance* (Chicago: University of Chicago Press, 1969). Watkins provides her translation with a useful introduction and bibliography of works in English.

His disorderly wife stands for a systematic confusion that threatens the well-being of the state itself.

Alberti's emphasis on economics, necessitated in part by the actual financial straits of his family, also reflects contemporary Florentine attitudes toward property and prosperity. He (like Barbaro) draws on Aristotle, particularly the *Economics*, a text translated by his compatriot Lionardo Bruni in 1420 with this apology: "If it is a philosopher's task to study the state, the family, and even the administration and increase of property, then this alone proves that possessions and riches should not be regarded by the wise man with sovereign contempt."[54] Restrictions on the transfer of women's property suggest to what extent the preservation of a family's "possessions and riches" depended on its control. In legal affairs, a Florentine woman was not allowed to be *sine mundio*, without the guardianship (*mundium*) of her father or husband. Her father could claustrate her, reduce her inheritance, determine her dowry, decide whom she would marry. Specifically designed to preserve the wealth of the city was the law that required the widow of a non-Florentine to return to her paternal home in Florence if she wished to keep her dowry, which otherwise reverted to her family.[55]

Della famiglia is written as a series of dialogues in which the principal speakers, all male members of the Alberti family, argue for various positions on the conduct of family life. The family's situation is precarious, in that its head, the middle-aged Lorenzo (Battista's father), is dying. His place is filled alternately in the course of the dialogues by two cousins, the youthful Lionardo and the aged Giannozzo, but the temporary nature of these substitutions underscores the fragility of the unit whose continuity the speakers are trying to ensure. In Book II, titled *De re uxoria*, a dialogue between Battista and Lionardo, the former argues for the dignity of romantic love, the latter for a marriage based on friendship.

Battista's youthful assertion of the value of romantic love is clearly undercut by the evidence he brings to support it. To Battista, "love is a force and a law not altogether deserving contempt and blame . . . something imposed by divine nature on any living creature both to reproduce itself and to increase its kind" (95). It is, moreover, most perfectly realized in marriage: "We may consider the love of husband and wife greatest of all." And it is the basis for a society's wealth: "It rules . . . the whole economy." So much, however, for theory—these statements are immediately refuted when Battista observes: "Yet somehow, I do not

---

[54]Quoted in Baron, "New Attitude toward Wealth," 176.
[55]E. Rodocanachi, *La Femme italienne à l'époque de la Renaissance* (Paris: Hachette, 1907), 292.

know why, it happens not infrequently that a woman prefers a lover to her own husband." And later he notes that romantic love can drive a man to kill his own child, as "Catiline, who for love of Aurelia Orestilla, killed his own son that he might take her to wife." Finally, love is opposed to the interests of the state. Women are generally faithless, Battista admits, and men in love are prone to acts of injustice that have socially and politically devastating results. His description suggests a Senecan tragedy: love, he claims, can restrain "the royal will and royal appetite," raise "an insignificant and meretricious creature to glorious dignity and high estate," make us "despise fame, forget all honor and noble deeds, and lightly tear even the closest bonds of kinship." His interlocutor, Lionardo, can hardly expect an objection when he redefines love as "a limitless folly," "vile appetite," "brutish desire" (98–101).

To clarify what Battista has found perplexing, Lionardo insists on the central importance of the family, and claims that a love "free from all lasciviousness" and characterized as friendship is the only basis for marriage (101). He describes the origins of marriage as a kind of social contract entered into for practical reasons, chiefly for the production of children. Terming a family "fortunate" if it has a "good supply of rich men" (110; see also 127), he discusses marriage in a perspective almost anthropological—men wish progeny, women with progeny require protection, therefore men appropriate and protect women. His principal point, that women are the conduits through which male members of a family must pass generationally, is made clear in his conclusion: the friendship he has extolled is an emotion felt by men primarily for men, and it is expressed by agreements about how women are to be shared and exchanged. In practice, it has nothing to do with feelings that a husband and wife have for each other. "That Pompey of yours," he exclaims to Battista, "amorous as he was, did he not always put friendship first?"

> Though Pompey was aflame with love of [Flora] yet he allowed Geminius to enjoy her. Thus he preferred to satisfy his friend's desire rather than his own strong passion. . . . That was a noble deed of such friendship as always in wholesome minds outweighs the madness of sexual love. Such is the way of true and simple friendship, generous, as you see, and not willing to share and give only property [la roba] to a friend, but to deprive oneself and yield to him in good will and faith even the object of one's personal and, as you say, divine affections and desires.   [103]

The implications of this image of male friendship are clear. The silent Flora who is at the exemplary Pompey's disposal is property; that she is also the object of Pompey's affection means only that he is able to regard property with affection. The fact that he feels affection for a woman does not necessarily mean that he does not regard her as an object that he may acquire or dispose of at will.

In his first two books, Alberti makes a point of distinguishing among kinds of families, those at the crest of good fortune and those, like his own, which are in distress. In Book III, *Economicus*, he sets forth the means by which a family can retain or regain its prosperity. The task depends on a discrimination of public and private duties, and on pursuing them without personal ambition.[56] On the smaller scale of civic order, Alberti imagines a version of the political equilibrium Barbaro dreamed of when he described the diplomatic exchange of women of different nations. Ambition, his character Lionardo claims (introducing the subject of Book III), destroys a person and his family because it leads them to overextend their resources, but it also wrecks the stability that ought to obtain *among families* and within their society at large. He goes on to insist that "fame is born not in the midst of private peace but in public action"; that a citizen ought to desire "the unity, calm, peace, and tranquillity of his own house, but much more those of the country and of the republic." Republics cannot be preserved "if all good men are solely content with their private leisure." But, he cautions, these public actions will not benefit "the country" and "the republic" "if men of wealth or wisdom or nobility among the citizens seek more power than the other citizens, who are also free but less fortunate" (178). That is, the ideal citizen uses power only for the general good, and not to enhance his position by undermining that of another. Giannozzo's answer to the implications of this statement, their substantiation in the actual practice of family affairs, describes the control of familial resources largely as it is effected by the husband's discipline of his wife.

For Giannozzo all public government of the kind Lionardo has extolled must begin with self-government: "One must never . . . for the sake of ruling others . . . cease to bear rule over oneself." And if "private affairs" are not to "get in the way of public ones," there must be a proper division of labor within the house, that is, a man's wife must be his utterly obedient and trustworthy agent. It is she who must preserve the family's "possessions," without which it will lack friends and allies, while her

[56]In her essay on the origins of the notion of female purity as a feature of human society everywhere, Sherry B. Ortner suggests that limitations on the social and economic competitiveness of male heads of families within a given society can be associated with the development of the apparatus of state control. In her view, such men become "domesticated"—that is, they compensate for a loss of power and prestige in society by its exercise within the family, and specifically over wives and children. If correct, her theory explains at least in part why Alberti might link the control of wives with the containment of ambition on the part of husbands. See "The Virgin and the State," *Feminist Studies* 4, 3 (1978): 19–35.

husband exercises an "honorable authority" (179–80). "Nature," Lionardo then observes (elaborating features of his earlier argument from
nature), concurs in this assignment of roles:

> Men are by nature of a more elevated mind than women. They are more
> suited to struggle with arms and with cunning against the misfortunes
> which afflict country, religion, and one's own children. . . . Women, on the
> other hand, are almost all timid by nature, soft, slow, and therefore more
> useful when they sit still and watch over our things. It is as though nature
> thus provided for our well-being, arranging for men to bring things home
> and for women to guard them.   [207]

In fact, as Giannozzo's description of his relationship with his wife
shows, the conduct he expects from her is not in the least natural but
rather the result of his own treatment of her.

Giannozzo begins his description of his wife's education by noting that
she knows nothing of his affairs: although he has shown her his "treasures," he keeps his books and records locked in his study. She "not only
could not read, she could not even lay hands on them. . . . I often used to
express my disapproval of bold and forward females who try too hard to
know about things outside the house, and about the concerns of their
husband and of men in general." He warns husbands not to confide in
their wives: "They are madmen if they think true prudence or good
counsel lies in the female brain" (210). A wife's ignorance is compounded
by her isolation from persons in general. She is not to participate in the
society of women, which is described as frivolous: "I shall be truly glad if
I see that you [his wife] disdain . . . the chattering that some little girls do
all day, in the house, at the door, and wherever they go. They talk now
with this friend, now with that one; they ask a lot of questions and say a
lot of things that they don't know as well as a lot that they do." Nor is she
to converse with members of her own household. She is to talk as little as
possible to her servants or to listen to their opinions or their complaints:
"Too much familiarity kills respect" (217–18).

More crucial than her ignorance and isolation is her humiliation, a state
of mind induced by a process that begins at the time of her marriage with
her renunciation of her mother and her mother's nurturance: she is told
she must behave as an Alberti girl (215). She has to acknowledge that her
mother's instruction has been insufficient and that she seeks one more
perfect—"her mother had taught her only how to spin and sew, and how
to be virtuous and obedient. Now she would gladly learn from me
[Giannozzo] how to rule the family" (218). She herself is made to feel
wholly incapable of correct judgment. When Giannozzo asks his bride
how she would begin her housekeeping, she answers naively that she

would arrange to lock everything up. When Giannozzo points out that it would be impractical to lock *everything* up, she is silent and lowers her eyes. He takes pleasure in her reaction: "I was no little pleased inwardly, seeing that becoming air of repentance on her face." And he congratulates himself on her humiliation: "I could see that she was indeed aware of having been too quick to answer me and that she would, in time, become more and more careful of her words." When she finally responds, it is silently: "After a little while, with humble and modest slowness, she lifted up her eyes to me and, without speaking, smiled" (221). This moment of instruction clearly aims at dehumanizing the pupil. Giannozzo's wife (who never receives a name throughout the dialogue) is forgiven when she behaves like a dog: scolded, she lowers her eyes; after an appropriate interval, she raises them again in a chastened attitude. Giannozzo can proceed with his lesson.

How does Alberti imagine that such brutal methods will be successful? The answer lies in a later passage in which Giannozzo instructs his wife on the need always to be cheerful. He draws a comparison between his own life, which is full of strife and therefore naturally conducive to occasional bad temper, and her own, which is utterly peaceful. His "sour mood" is excusable because he has "spent the day talking and contending with malevolent, scheming persons and with enemies." She, on the other hand, can experience "drooping spirits" only through "the unfortunate results of [her] own mistakes." "You," he declares, "need do nothing but live happily, make sure the household obeys you, and keep the family well. I am doubly grieved when I see you sad, for I know that by your very unhappiness you are confessing some fault" (228). In effect, he makes her responsible for the misfortunes of those around her, and for the accidental mishaps that occur at random in every kind of domestic situation. She cannot escape blame. If she remains cheerful in the face of a domestic disaster, she will be blamed both for it and for being impercep-tive; if she becomes worried or gloomy, the cause will again be her fault, and she will have incurred her husband's displeasure. The success with which Giannozzo can hope to transform his bride into his loyal surrogate in the house turns upon the inculcation of pervasive feelings of guilt.

Given the function of women as guardians of property, the need for such guilt and the kind of control it permits is, I think, clear. For it is by releasing into the public arena goods that can be competed for that hostilities among men are provoked. The woman who threatens social order is therefore the one who fails to keep what she has been given, a fact that explains why the otherwise secretive Giannozzo reveals all his trea-sure to his wife. A careless wife initiates a confusion of categories of belonging, a flouting of proprieties, that is, of decency and ownership.

Such a woman is in fact described by Giannozzo as an example of how not to behave. Asking his wife for "order and system", he declares

> It does not befit a woman like you to carry a sword, nor to do other manly things that men do. Nor is it always and in all places fitting for a woman to do everything that is proper to a woman, for instance holding a distaff, wearing gold brocade, having one's head tied up in a kerchief [all at once]. . . . You shall see that things are done in their proper time. What is needed in autumn is not be consumed in May. What should be enough for a month is not to be used up in a day.   [226]

This image of feminine disorder exemplifies a conflation of categories. Indoors and outside; male and female; past, present, and future are confused, and what is proper to one or the other now becomes universally available. The disorderly woman signifies the putting back into competitive play of objects that have already been assigned a use, a time and place of operation, and an interest or purpose. If, as Barbaro noted, women keep the peace by being property that men can exchange, property that generates property, and if, as Alberti has said, free but unfortunate families are threatened by the ambition of families in power, then the role of women as preservers acquires a double function. By being exchangeable property they alleviate competitive tension among men; by preserving property they relieve men of the need to be competitive. Both functions are important to the stability of society.[57]

For the next two centuries feminists protested the images of women in such treatises as those of Barbaro and Alberti. They saw that according to convention a woman's role was bound up with systems for the allocation of property among men. Her virtue was expressed principally in the absence or negation of activity. Her chastity was valuable because it guaranteed the father's ownership of his children and it pointed to the one

---

[57]Christiane Klapisch-Zuber reports that women who were married at an early age were often a full generation younger than their husbands—a fact that might account for Giannozzo's attitude toward his wife: *Women, Family, and Ritual in Renaissance Italy*, trans. Lydia G. Cochrane (Chicago: University of Chicago Press, 1985), 20; see also 109. According to Richard Trexler, Florentine women had "no legally incorporated identity"; like adolescents and adult salaried workers, they were "objects of trade, being *locati*, 'placed' or rented in countless agreements." As such, women were an element in the "*limina*," made up of "the socially peripheral and disempowered" whose "unorganized potential for disorder" was frightening to men: *Public Life in Renaissance Florence* (New York: Academic Press, 1980), 15–16. Tamassia notes that in those parts of Italy formerly under Germanic law (as Florence had been), the *tutela* or legal guardianship of women by men was the rule. Women were freer in territories under Roman law. "In these regions women, citing their ancient Roman privileges, were able to perform all the legal activities they wished, without the onerous burden of parental and judicial wardship": *Famiglia italiana*, 272–73.

means by which she might be able to gain an easy and surreptitious control of society, that is, by selecting which men would become fathers and which not. Her silence was essential because her status as property, as an object, was in jeopardy if she spoke. Feminists responded by objecting to restrictions on speech, public activity, and the administration of property, especially property that a wife had brought to the family, either by dowry or by her own work. On the other hand, they were most persistently and subtly challenged, not to say confounded, by what one might call Alberti's "Flora syndrome"—that is, the condition of the abused woman who is also loved. Affection itself proved to be an ambiguous concept. A man's devotion to a woman did not appear in any way to preclude her objectification in his eyes; a woman's devotion to a man might be assumed to entail an acceptance of this treatment. The idea of the companionate marriage, so frequently proposed and extolled by all parties, was seen eventually to beg the question. To what extent, if at all, can being a companion mean being an equal?

Christian Marriage

Misogyny was the inevitable by-product of the concept of Christian marriage as the union of rational man with passionate woman; however forceful his control, his association with her made for a moral condition less perfect than that guaranteed by celibacy. The effects of misogynistic attitudes on marriage doctrine were mitigated chiefly by the concept of charity. Beyond emphasizing the importance of a husband's love for his inferior and subordinate wife, marriage doctrine emphasizing charity taught that she (although the weaker vessel) was capable of salvation and therefore ought to be helped to achieve it. By the fifteenth century, however, the humanists' concern with the welfare of the state had put Christian marriage in a new perspective. For them, marriage and the household were political as well as sacramental entities, and relations between spouses and their relatives were determined more by legalistic than religious justifications. The power of the patriarch—in theory limited by his obligation as a father to "love Christ more than a son or daughter" (Matt. 10:37) as well as by his Christlike love as a husband— was enhanced by descriptions of the household as a state or even (as in Barbaro) a military establishment.

Christians could and did find reasons to object to the rigor implicit in the humanists' idea of marriage. To regard the household as a political unit was to diminish the importance of the moral requirement of love; it could also threaten the sacramental character of marriage by giving a father the presumptive right to deny his daughter her choice of husband (as Rabelais was later to see), and, in cases in which she acted independently of him, the binding nature of her consent. The latter issue is expressed in the controversy over so-called clandestine marriages, performed without the consent of the parents of bride and groom. The clergy saw such unions as true marriages because they were based on the consent of the couple; consent had to be mutual, but once it was given, a couple was considered married. Those who objected saw such marriages as invalid because they denied the couple's parents the right to intervene on financial, social, or moral grounds. They argued that no decision as important as marriage should be left to the very young, and they pointed to the practical hardships that could ensue in cases in which such decisions were forced or ill conceived. A marriage without due regard for social status and the distribution of property might place in jeopardy one if not both of the parental families.[58] A woman had reason to fear both a clandestine and an arranged marriage: the first justified if not actually encouraged her seduction or abduction, particularly if she had money or social status; the second made her the pawn of her parents' dynastic ambitions. Both therefore denied her the right to exercise her own discretion and conscience as to whom she would be required to serve and obey as husband. And as important, it denied her the right to determine when she might marry. Rich girls were sometimes married before puberty; after menarche, they were required to live with their husbands. The frequent allegations of feminists that marriage was no more than a kind of enslavement of women reflect the extraordinary punitiveness of many marriages.

Beyond questions regarding what kinds of marriage were valid, Christians who embraced humanistic discipline sought to discover the role of charity in relationships that were also more or less rigidly political.

[58]The most comprehensive treatment of all aspects of marriage and sexual relations in this period is James A. Brundage, *Law, Sex, and Christian Society in Medieval Europe* (Chicago: University of Chicago Press, 1987), esp. 487–575, on the late Middle Ages and Renaissance to the convening of the Council of Trent (1545). For procedures governing marriage as an institution and a sacrament before Trent, see also, i.a., Shahar, *Fourth Estate*, 81–86; Jack Goody, *The Development of the Family and Marriage in Europe* (Cambridge: Cambridge University Press, 1983), 151–53; and Sherman, *Roman Law*, 56–62. See also, for Italy, Rodocanachi, *Femme italienne*, 57–60; Tamassia, *Famiglia italiana*, 150–88. For France, see Beatrice Gottlieb, "The Meaning of Clandestine Marriage," in *Family and Sexuality in French History*, ed. Robert Wheaton and Tamara K. Hareven (Philadelphia: University of Pennsylvania Press, 1980), 49–83; and for a different view of clandestine marriage, see Brundage, *Law, Sex, and Christian Society*, 499–503. On family mores in general, see Donald Kelley, "The Primal Dialectic," in *The Beginning of Ideology: Consciousness and Society in the French Reformation* (Cambridge: Cambridge University Press, 1983), 70–80. For two views of Erasmus's idea of marriage, see E. V. Telle, *Erasme de Rotterdam et le septième sacrement* (Geneva: Droz, 1954), and John B. Payne, *Erasmus: His Theology of the Sacraments* (Richmond, Va.: John Knox Press, 1970), 109–25.

Erasmus, for example, speaks of the husband's authority and power, the wife's subordination and weakness, as elements not only in a domestic order but rather, and primarily, in an interdependence of souls. As he represents it, the function of marriage is not so much to strengthen society as to provide the grounds upon which a personal salvation may be worked out.[59]

Erasmus is not, however, consistent in his opinion of woman, as either a spiritual or a political creature. He varies his views with the kind of text he writes and the audience he addresses. On the significance of woman's first creation and her spiritual equality to man, he is generally ambiguous. In his colloquy "The New Mother," his feminist character, Fabulla, insists that men have achieved their social superiority not because they possess better souls or intellects but because they have and use physical force to get their way: woman obeys a man, she says, "not as a superior but as a more aggressive person."[60] In any case, she observes, it is only the wife and not the woman who is made subject to man. And she protests the injustice of the supremacy of man on two grounds. Despite their strength and aggressiveness, men are exposed to less danger in war than women in childbirth: "Your kind are stationed in the middle line; another man is in the reserves; another stays safely in the rear; and finally many are saved by surrender and flight. We must engage death at close quarters." And by virtue of the fact that woman, like man, is created in the image of God, which is expressed in "mental gifts," not "bodily form," she is the spiritual equal of man. Questioning Eutrapelus, her

[59]Erasmus is regarded as reformist largely because he places "married chastity" on an ethical par with celibacy and so raises the moral status of the wife, who no longer exists chiefly to ensure that her husband's sexuality be not sinful. By the time of the convening of the Council of Trent, such views were associated with the larger goals of the Protestant writers who popularized them. Despite these differences on the matter of celibacy, I have not been able to discern much difference between Protestant and Catholic attitudes toward the role of the wife. The formal requirements for the performance of marital duties remain the same; the wife is given the same restricted right to disobey in both cases. For a different opinion, see Margo Todd, "Humanists, Puritans, and the Spiritualized Household," *Church History* 49 (1980): 18–34. For images of women in the thought of Luther and Calvin, see Jane Dempsey Douglass, "Women in the Continental Reformation," in *Religion and Sexism*, ed. Reuther, 292–318. For a discussion of the status of reformed women in public and private life in France, see, i.a., Natalie Zemon Davis, "City Women and Religious Change," in *Society and Culture*, 65–95; and Nancy Lyman Roelker, "The Role of Noblewomen in the French Reformation," *Archiv für Reformationsgeschichte* 63 (1972): 168–95. For the impact of Reformation thought on the activities of women in general, see Sherrin Marshall Wyntjes, "Women in the Reformation Era," in *Becoming Visible*, ed. Bridenthal and Koonz, 165–91.

[60]*The Colloquies of Erasmus*, trans. Craig R. Thompson (Chicago: University of Chicago Press, 1965), 271. I have noted the words of the original text, quoted (with column references) from vol. 1 of Desiderii Erasmi Roterodami, *Opera omnia* (Leiden, 1703), in instances where the translation is dubious.

male antagonist, she asks "whether it's granted to men only to be members of Christ [*membri Christi*]" (c. 767), and he replies, "Heaven forbid! That's granted to all human creatures through faith" (271).

Erasmus does not leave Fabulla's position unchallenged. Understandably: it begs the question that most plagued contemporary defenders of women, that is, the extent to which a woman's spiritual (and intellectual) equality with man could sanction behavior that discounted altogether the nature of her physical being. Does the fact that woman is subject to man not as woman (that is, *female*) but only as wife mean that she can behave as if the circumstances in which she finds herself because of her sex have no meaning? Fabulla, the "new mother" of the dialogue, has sent her baby out to nurse, as is the common custom with women of her rank— "vulgo fit," she declares in the original text, with obvious irony (c. 768). Chastising her for failing in her natural as well as Christian duty, Eutrapelus establishes that the practice of wetnursing contradicts not only biological nature but also the connection between mind and body made sacred in Scripture; "the Lord Jesus himself calls his body a 'temple'" (277). In other words, he sees that a woman's spirituality and whatever it implies about her autonomy can never be thought of as independent of her physical being. If Christians are obliged to regard the human body as sacred, the nurturing functions of the female body must enter into any determination of a woman's Christian duty and by extension of the nature of her autonomy. Like the works of Boccaccio and Barbaro, Erasmus's "New Mother" places a woman's sexuality at the center of the controversy surrounding the nature of her nature. The effects of her sexuality do not make her conspicuously guilty (as they do for Boccaccio) or merely salable (as they do for Barbaro), but they do exact the sacrifice of a certain kind of liberty. Not, for Erasmus, valued as generative property, woman is nevertheless bound by her generativity in ways that inevitably affect the conduct of her life.

How far did a woman's nature need fulfillment in married sexuality or, conversely, how far could her spiritual requirements prevent it? In theory, a woman had always been able to elect conventual over married life, although in practice such a decision was often made for her by her parents, who would not or could not supply her with a dowry. By the sixteenth century, monastic establishments for women frequently had reputations for lax morals; in some cases, critics termed them little more than brothels, as Erasmus does here. Most contemporary criticism of this kind comes from writers who do not argue a feminist line. Feminists, particularly those who identify themselves as women, almost invariably praise the life of the woman who sequesters herself from the world, whether formally in an institution or in response to a personal inclination.[61] Erasmus's colloquy "A Girl with No Interest in Marriage" illustrates the main features of the argument against convents and indicates what such reformist criticism might actually signify.

Catherine, a young woman, announces her intention to retire to a cloister. Eubulus, trying to dissuade her, argues that the cloistered life is not what it appears, that Catherine's perception of the nuns' ideal and charming life is actually mistaken. All the advantages she believes she will have in the cloister she can have at home, under the authority of her affectionate parents. He claims that she will exchange the freedom she enjoys by being subject to her parents for the "servitude" of a monastery.[62] "Consider how many advantages you lose along with your freedom," he says.

> Now you're free to read, pray, sing God's praises in your own room as much as you like and whenever you like. If you become tired of your room you may listen to choir chants, attend divine service, hear sermons. And if you see some lady or unmarried woman of outstanding moral excellence, you can improve yourself by her conversation; if you see some man endowed with unusual virtue, you can learn from him what might improve you.

He argues further that her life at home is already a kind of claustration. She can be obedient by obeying her parents; she is already poor because "all [she has] is in [her] parents' hands." And her chastity is as well (if not better) preserved at home. A nun's vows, by contrast, are nothing more than "certain rites that by themselves contribute nothing to religion"; her veil is merely "a linen garment turned inside out" (109–10).[63]

---

[61]For a summary of the quality of conventual life in the late Middle Ages, including opportunities for the exercise of real power under the rules of various orders for those women in authority, see Shahar, *Fourth Estate*, 37–50. For the reputation of growing laxity in conventual discipline after the middle of the fifteenth century in Italy, see Rodocanachi, *Femme italienne*, 239–42.

[62]Erasmus's text has "te pro libera tendis ultro servam reddere": *Opera* (1703), 1:c. 699. Erasmus has earlier qualified the extent to which Catherine is free by having Eubulus remind her that she is to obey her parents except when they command her to violate God's law: "If parents oblige a child to behave with impiety, their authority is to be held invalid" (si nunc parentes adigerent ad impietatem, contemnenda esset illorum auctoritas, c. 699). This was the form under which the freedom of conscience of women was exercised generally, with respect to either a parent or a husband.

[63]Erasmus's attitude toward cloistered life for both men and women was generally negative. See, i.a., James Kelsey McConica: "Erasmus will not see the religious life as the highest form of Christian vocation. It is rather a personal calling which may or may not be profitable. He will advise neither for nor against it. The real lesson is that piety has no external form or specific vocational apparatus; it is an inward state. And it is amply clear that Erasmus expects his reader to be living in the world": *English Humanists and Reformation Politics under Henry VIII and Edward VI* (Oxford: Clarendon, 1965), 22.

For a woman in Catherine's position, however, a decision to remain at home under the authority of her parents as an alternative to the cloister would not necessarily have led to greater freedom. It would almost certainly have entailed an obligation to marry at some point in the future, and probably to a man whom her father had selected, since she is, as Erasmus himself notes, her parents' "possession." She can go against their wishes only if they are "driving" her to "wrong doing and infamy" (109). As a wife, she would be required to transfer her obedience from her father to a husband who would expect to exercise a similar kind of control over her.[64] Moreover, what might be called the sanctification of secular life actually enhances secular authority—whether it is represented by father, brother, or, indeed, civil magistrate—by imbuing it with a spiritual presence. The subordinate is left with few reasons to question it. Such sanctification, of course, later became characteristic of Protestant politics. Magistrates became authorities in spiritual matters (Queen Elizabeth was the "supreme governor" of the English church); husbands and fathers took on the role of priest and confessor. The wife and children had no authority to appeal to outside the context of familial relations.

The prospect of a woman of learning—one who had the "freedom to read" outside the cloister—was not unproblematic either. In his "Abbot and the Learned Lady," Erasmus reveals what a menace she could appear to be. His character Magdalia, usually identified as Margaret More Roper, defends her reading of Greek and Roman authors on the grounds that wisdom is the greatest happiness; the abbot Antronius attacks her on the grounds that women are intended only for pleasure: "It's not feminine to be brainy [non est muliebre sapere, c. 745]. A lady's business is to have a good time" (219). Magdalia's unstated premise is that women are capable of the same intellectual development as men, and that whatever the vocation to which they are called, even that of wife, they can legit-

---

[64]Klapisch-Zuber notes as the situation of Florentine women what may well have been (and on the basis of the literature of feminist protest I suspect was) the case more or less throughout Europe at this time:

> The determination of a woman's identity thus depended on her movements in relation to the "houses" of men. . . . "Honorable" marriages were what regulated the entries and exits of wives, and the normal state, the state that guaranteed the honor of the women and the "houses," could be no other than the married state. Any woman alone was suspect. An unmarried woman was considered incapable of living alone or in the absence of masculine protection without falling into sin. Even if she were a recluse and lived a holy life, even if she retired to a room on the upper floor of the paternal house, she placed the family honor in jeopardy by the mere fact of her celibacy. The convent was the only way out, although terrible doubts about the security of the cloister continued to torment her parents. Among the "best people," therefore, families did not include females over twenty years of age who were not married. [*Women, Family, and Ritual,* 119]

imately acquire and profit from wisdom. "Do you think [a wife] can manage so big a job [as managing a household] without wisdom?" she asks (221). But she also believes that if women continue to be educated, they will be fit to assume positions of intellectual authority—in short, to be in the situation of a Pope Joan: "We'll preside in the theological schools, preach in the churches, and wear your miters." And if educated women ready themselves for such offices, "it will be up to *you* [men] to forbid [it]" (223; *vestrum erit hoc avertere*, c. 746). Magdalia's defense of the intellectual vitality of which women are capable contains a veiled critique of the intellectual sloth afflicting men. Women, she implies, will assume public and ecclesiastical offices only as a sign of the corruption of male clerics and not as a consequence of fundamental social change. Here Erasmus is contesting not woman's capacity for intellectual life but the propriety of giving it institutional rather than merely domestic scope.

The *Institutio matrimonii christiani* (1526) was clearly written for persons in positions of authority, especially the clergy, who might have to explain the principles governing a Christian marriage for the lay public. More precisely than such popular didactic works as the *Colloquies*, it reveals how the issues raised by the humanists' politicization of marriage affected the interpretation of the doctrine of charity as it applied to married life.[65]

---

[65]Erasmus's much briefer and simpler *Encomium matrimonii* characterizes marriage as a condition of life both physical and spiritual, superior to celibacy in that it provides a ground for charitable actions. Marriage is justified by divine law, which—like those "letters" that Paul tells Christians are engraved for them not on tablets of brass, as was the old law, but on the living tables of their hearts (2 Cor. 3:3)—is known only by love: *A Ryght Frutefull Epystle Devysed by the Moste Excellent Clerke Erasmus in Laude and Prayse of Matrymony* (London, 1534), sig. B2–v. Erasmus emphasizes not the duties of the couple but their profound intimacy.

> For what thynge is sweter then with her to lyve, with whome ye may be most streyghtly copuled, nat onely in the benevolence of the mynd, but also in the coniunction of the body. Yf a great delectation of mynde be taken of the benevolence of our other kynsmen, sythe it is an especyall swetnes to have one with whom ye may savely truste, whyche supposethe your chaunces to be his, what felycyte (thynke ye) have the conjunction of man and wyfe, than whych no thynge in the unyversall worlde maybe founde outher greater or fermer?   [C6]

This image of a marriage of "straight coupling" is left without further explanation and so begs the question of domestic order, to be answered at length in the *Institutio*. It is on spiritual grounds, however, that Erasmus argues vigorously against clandestine marriages; he sees them as instances of rape, and invalid because they cannot be founded on any kind of relation between spouses other than a carnal one. Commenting on a case involving the abduction of a young woman from her father's house by a "brigand," he writes: "After carrying her away, the brigand took her where he wished. This crime was applauded by some courtisans as a beautiful act. This is how this lunatic, this rake, this thief, this madman came to possess a wife of good family, of excellent manners, with a considerable dowry, but who suffered constantly because of his behavior and had a hard time observing the rules of piety": *Le Mariage chrétien*, trans. Cl. Bosc (Paris, 1714), 73–74. I use Bosc's

Erasmus bases his entire representation of the relations in marriage on the Pauline dictum that they are analogous to those between Christ and his church. This analogy transforms the husband's authority to a service of love; more important, it leads to a recognition of a kind of equality between the spouses: "One sees that there is something like this [a service of love] in marriage, where all the authority belongs to the husband, who must nevertheless use it not in a spirit of domination but of love and kindness for the weaker sex and in order to maintain a society of equals between them both" (23).[66] This is a union not "according to laws" but between "persons of equal virtue who have the same feelings" (*également vertueuses*, 24; *pares virtutem*, c. 620). Yet in subsequent passages Erasmus gives the authority of the husband so much rigor and scope that an equality between spouses is no longer imaginable in other than purely formal terms. His treatment of the relations of husband and wife suggests that while the notion that woman was the spiritual equal of man was mandated by Scripture, he found that its incorporation as a principle of domestic order was simply too alien to prevailing social practice to receive serious consideration.

Erasmus's wife is not only her husband's political subordinate but also his natural inferior. Like Barbaro's wife, she must conform to her husband's ways: "Marriage requires that the couple share together pleasures, pains, trials, joy and sadness. It is not enough that a wife be virtuous and honest if she doesn't know how to adjust to the temper of her husband; for one has never said that a mirror is faithful because it is decorated with gold and jewels" (159).[67] In subsequent passages, Erasmus continues to

---

translation—evidently the only one of this extraordinary text ever to have been published—as a basis for my own throughout this book. Page references for my translations of subsequent brief quotations refer to Bosc's translation. A complete version of Erasmus's original text may be found in vol. 5 of *Opera omnia* (1704). Dedicated to Catherine of Aragon, it was first published in Antwerp and not reprinted before the Leiden edition of the *Opera omnia*. Wherever possible, I have checked Bosc's translation against this text and noted dubious or important words and phrases. Marriages performed without a "sober and godly consent" are in any case invalid and even grounds for divorce in Erasmus's view, according to a later treatise precisely on divorce: "That whiche chyldyshnes, folishnes, want of wyt and of knoledge and dronkenys hath joyned togyther, that (I saye) whiche the devil hath joyned togither by baudes as well men baudes as women baudes and by whoars which ar hys mynusters and trewe weyghtyng servauntes, that same doth god verye well separate and undo by hys mynysters": *The Censure and Judgement of the Famous Clark Erasmus of Roterodam: Whyther dyvorsemente betwene man and wyfe stondeth with the lawe of God* (London, 1550?), sig. F7v–8.

[66]Erasmus actually uses the word "equal" to describe the relations between married persons; theirs is *societas aequae vitae: Opera*, 5:c. 620.

[67]Against ordinary mistreatment, however, a wife has no recourse: "Remember to suffer patiently a misfortune that you brought upon yourself. If it is not your fault, tolerate it nonetheless, for this pleases the Lord for reasons that are hidden from you" (65).

struggle with the contradiction implicit in his depiction of the wife as equal to and yet wholly dependent on her husband. He insists that the husband "must retain his authority at all time" (214), and also that this authority is shared: "the wife is not so inferior to her husband that she cannot share his authority" (217). She is not to be his servant, but he is not to let her become his mistress. Seeing sexuality as the occasion of a struggle for authority, he worries that a wife may excite her husband excessively, and, conversely, that she may not be sufficiently receptive: "The first fault makes a woman despised by her husband, the second will earn her his hatred" (166). In any case, his well-being is paramount, and to guarantee it is her responsibility. The truly conflicted nature of the equality he has proposed may have driven Erasmus finally to resort to paradox: "a wife is never more a mistress than when she obeys her husband" (224). He concludes, in any case, by insisting on the wife's obedience in highly orthodox terms. The husband is God's representative; he may not deserve to be obeyed, but Christ, who enjoins a wife's obedience, does so deserve. The husband's model is Christ, but if he fails to imitate his master, he does not lose his authority on that account. The reason: "good order," the excuse Erasmus attributes to Paul, who argues for obedience to secular authority, even when unjust, in Romans 13 (297).

The parallel between the family and the state is a rediscovery of humanists, but Erasmus is the first of them to link a wife's obedience to the more general injunction against disobedience to governing authorities which applies to all Christians. Discussing instances in which a wife may disobey her husband, he follows a line of reasoning identical to that of Luther when he argues for the right of Christians to liberty of conscience. So Erasmus counsels a wife: "If he [your husband] orders you to do something that is contrary to faith or good manners, gently refuse to obey him; but if he persists in wishing to be obeyed, remember that it is better to obey God than men" (297). This argument presupposes that the wife is educated to know doctrine and morality. How does Erasmus envisage the education of women, especially in relation to their married lives?

He may be unique in considering how even those women who would do well to have a trade ought to be educated: "As soon as one [i.e., a father] has enough property not to need to work, it is appropriate to educate a young girl in Greek and Latin letters. If one must do manual work because of lack of funds, then she must be taught to read in her language" (234).[68] Who her teacher is to be he does not state; in any case,

---

[68]Cf. Thomas Becon on improving the character of women: "To bring this thing to pass, it is expedient that by public authority schools for women-children be erected and set

for the noble or gentlewoman, tutors were available; for a girl of the "middling sort" who might have to do manual work, elementary schools existed in some communities. For an education specifically in matters of faith and morals, however, Erasmus is explicit. Like Paul, he insists that a woman be instructed by her husband: "If there is anything they [women] desire to know [of the faith], let them ask their husbands at home. For it is shameful for a woman to speak in church" (1 Cor. 14:35). Erasmus's husband is to introduce his wife to the subject of the sermon, "the text and the matter of which the pastor is to speak," before they go to church. When they return home, he is to examine her on what she has learned. "This must not be done with too much exactitude at first; on the contrary, she must be encouraged with praise until she is used to it." After she gains a certain judgment, he can acquaint her with the difference between "good and bad proofs," the "utility of examples and comparisons," and the error in "false and common opinions" (236–37).

What is really extraordinary in this educational program is the assumption that underlies it. Despite his earlier claims concerning the spiritual equality of women, Erasmus sees that their intelligence is inherently defective. In fact, he likens the products of a woman's mind, if not shaped by masculine instruction, to the menses. Only if her thoughts are "fertilized" by the wit of her husband can she bring forth sound and well-formed "children": "for, just as in generation a women does not produce anything perfect without intercourse with a healthy man, and without this she produces nothing but unformed matter that is no more than a mass of bad humors, so also if a husband does not take care to cultivate his wife's spirit, what else can one hope for?" The image (betraying its origins in Aristotelian biology) indicates Erasmus's belief that the obedience of a woman must in practice extend to that privileged order of grace and affect her equality as a member of Christ. Practically speaking, it is difficult to imagine a situation in which an Erasmian wife could successfully obey her conscience. One is even at a loss to imagine what kind of conscience she could claim. Her dependence seems almost absolute. Paradoxically, Erasmus depicts her as fully human only in this condition. Her husband's education of her has shaped her, given her life: "Where would I be if I had not met him to instruct me?" she asks. "I owe to the care you [her husband] have taken to teach me the fact that I have

---

up in every Christian commonweal, and honest, sage, wise, discreet, sober, grave, and learned matrons made rulers and mistresses of the same, and that honest and liberal stipends be appointed for the said school-mistresses, which shall travail in the bringing up of young maids, that by this means they may be occasioned the more gladly and willingly to take pains": *The Catechism* (1560), ed. John Ayre, in *The Works of Thomas Becon* (Cambridge, 1844), 2:376–77.

become reasonable instead of unreasonable, as I used to be, strong instead of feeble, a real Christian not a Pharisee," she further confesses. And from that point, she begins to love her husband as the source of all authority—"to love him as her husband, to regard him as a master, to honor him like her father, to speak with in a more Christian manner, to respect God in her husband" (237–39). In the interest of instituting the ideal of Christian marriage, Erasmus has revived the old myths of a masculine generativity: Zeus producing Athena; Pygmalion creating Galatea.

The most innovative intellectual programs of the early Renaissance are associated with the efforts of humanists to reconceptualize the terms of moral and political life by referring to classical models and modes of thought. In general they reconceived relations between men and women so that they were more overtly political than they had been earlier. The advantage to feminists of imagining that women could assume virtues typically masculine (as Boccaccio did), of stressing the importance of marriage over celibacy (as Barbaro and Alberti did), and of insisting on woman's spiritual equality (as Erasmus did) was vastly reduced by the qualifications surrounding these concessions. Feminists had, however, easier targets in these Italians than in Erasmus, who, more than his precusors, fixed on the difficulty of allowing a woman to experience the meaning of her spiritual equality while restricting her to an inferior and subordinate position in marriage and in society. Feminists struggled to formulate a position from which woman could be both autonomous and dutiful—with little success. Some who felt their dilemma most keenly (notably Marie de Gournay) would finally make woman's spirituality paramount and thus also the justification for political and public activity.

2   *Woman and Natural Law*

During the first half of the sixteenth century, defenses of women exhibited a pervasive concern with doctrine that derived its authority from what were held to be divine and natural laws. Theoretically distinct—divine law recorded in Scripture, natural law in philosophy, especially in that of Aristotle—the two kinds of law merged in thinking that justified existing social and political practices. Because God had created nature, its workings (it was believed) could not be inimical to divine will; because nature as it was known through human experience was always felt to be in some way limited, its true and perfect forms were sought in principles that transcended human experience. Aquinas—whose opinions in the matter are both orthodox and representative of the main elements of Renaissance thought on household government—believed that natural law, which was conveyed as basic forms of human good, could not "as general principles [*in universali*] be eliminated from the human heart." The ability to apprehend natural law was therefore deemed innately and intrinsically human, a feature of human nature as it was divinely created. The law itself was fulfilled by the expectation that if human beings were good, they would be reasonable; and conversely, that if they were not reasonable, they would be neither good nor fully human: "So human virtue, which makes good both the human person and his works, is in accordance with human nature just in so far as [*tantum . . . in quantum*] it is in accordance with reason; and vice is contrary to human nature just in so far as it is contrary to the order of reasonableness." Human society in general and human societies specifically might be analyzed and judged accordingly. Positive law was valid only if it did not violate the general principles of natural law (and therefore by implication divine law): "Every law laid down by men has the character of law just in so far as it is derived from the natural law."[1] So much the more, then, were individual persons supposed to examine their decisions in the light of criteria that devolved from natural law.

Crucial to Renaissance feminism was the fact that there were very few ways to interpret contemporary concepts of natural law that were not prejudicial to woman. Any defender of women, maintaining the spiritual, moral, and intellectual equality of the sexes (and later in the century, in varying degrees, their political and economic equality as well), inevitably encountered two principal challenges. The first is posed by the fact that according to natural law, creation is organized from its beginning as a hierarchy of creatures, with man superior to woman; and that such a hierarchy is justified by virtue of the nature of the creatures it ranks—woman is generically weaker than man in her creaturely and temporal aspect; she is genetically imperfect in relation to him in her biological and political nature. The second challenge is a reflection of the assumption that activity proper to each creature is assigned to it on the basis of its position in this hierarchy—women perform comparatively low tasks because they are inherently inferior to men. To these challenges feminists respond with two main lines of attack.

They show, first, that if there is a law determining an order to creation, it admits of very flexible applications. Pointing to evidence of a historical and proto-anthropological kind (largely quite fictional), they argue that societies express not universal but local and conventional laws (including laws governing women), none of which is more natural than another. Arguments of this kind imply and in some cases actually state that what passes for natural law is no more than a theoretical construct of some imagined good that may (but also may not) have reference to a general human condition. Enhancing the impact of this revisionary notion is an additional and somewhat paradoxical emphasis on that aspect of divine law which most threatens the idea of a hierarchy of creation and hence the natural law validating it: the spiritual equality of woman. What, feminists ask, does this spiritual equality mean? Does it legitimate a freedom of thought? of conscience? What political rights, if any, does it confer? In any case, it is clear that once a degree (however slight) of autonomy is granted the moral and intellectual self—that is, the thinking self—the whole question of natural law is put in another light. For the more natural law is seen to be the *product* of human intelligence rather than the *basis* for human reason, the more what must consequently be represented as "natural law" may be understood as something to be discovered (or

---

[1] *Summa theologica* I–II, q. 94, a.6c; q. 71, a.2; q. 95, a.2c; cited in John Finnis, *Natural Law and Natural Rights* (Oxford: Clarendon, 1980), 30, 35, 285. For the first reference I am indebted to Jonathan Golub.

invented) rather than as something that is divinely revealed. Investigations undertaken along these lines may even conclude that it is within the purvue of every intelligent soul to determine what "natural law" is to be at a particular place and time, whether this soul acts as an individual and risks idiosyncrasy or in a collectivity, in which case what is expressed as natural can be retermed customary or conventional.[2]

In a second and finally subtler attack on natural law, feminists focus on what they claim are abuses. Here their object is to reveal that the hierarchy of creation and its reflection in human society, which is distinguished by its ranks of persons and—more important to them—by their sex, is not natural or divinely instituted. What passes for its justification in natural and divine law is, they assert, no more than the result of the deployment of a preexisting political or economic power. Arguments of this kind often return to a consideration of such questions as the psychology of love and hate; here the tropes of courtly love and of Neoplatonic idealization sometimes acquire new and essentially political meaning. Feminists review the rhetorical strategies of their opponents in order to establish the interests and the interestedness of a particular speaker. The image of the world they seek to establish is socially and politically heterogeneous and philosophically pluralistic.

To return briefly to what I have termed feminism's challenges. To question the hierarchy of creation and its "offices" obviously jeopardizes more than the traditional relations between men and women. It calls attention to the whole question of ideology: the social and political fictions masking the real operations of power, especially (as it is perceived in this literature) of economic power. The feminist effort to analyze the ideology of patriarchy comes to expose the fiction of sex-determined gender, while a study of the economic power that sustains this ideology eventually reveals that equitable social practices cannot be carried on in behalf of women as long as women lack the right to acquire and manage their own property.

---

[2]In his charmingly titled *Concordance of Discordant Canons* (1140), the Bolognese monk Gratian puts divine law in the first and originary position, next natural law (*ius naturale*), then the law of princes (*leges, constitutiones*; i.e., positive law), and finally custom (*consuetudines*), which has to "yield not only to natural law but also to enacted laws, whether secular or ecclesiastical": Harold J. Berman, *Law and Revolution* (Cambridge: Harvard University Press, 1983), 145. Challenging natural law by citing differences among customs, feminists thus violated an established hierarchy within jurisprudential thought. They were not, of course, the first ones to do so; Hiram Haydn, discussing the fate of universal law (i.e., natural law and the *ius gentium*) in the Renaissance, writes that the philosophical skepticism of Machiavelli, Agrippa, Montaigne, and Bruno, among others, expressed itself in critiques of universal law citing cultural differences, among other things: *The Counter-Renaissance* (New York: Harcourt Brace & World, 1950), 131–75.

ITALY

Educating a Subordinate

An obvious and frequent target of feminist protest was the kind of education girls were expected to receive. Boccaccio's histories had expressed what was probably a widely held belief: it was futile to hope that a woman could assume a position of command without risk to her and to her people, or that her fame would ever be uncomplicated by notoriety. Treatises on family life were making clear that when confronted with patriarchal authority and power, the practical significance of her spiritual equality was nil. During the fifteenth century certain noble families had made a practice of educating their daughters with their sons in what were termed humane letters; the Gonzaga family even included provisions for physical exercise. A century later, Alessandro Piccolomini urged that women be taught classical languages "so that through no fault of theirs they not be deprived and ignorant of those habits and attitudes that could make them happy."[3] More common were the educators who recognized the inherent contradiction in such instruction for girls, since it was principally designed for persons who were to participate in civic activities. Lionardo Bruni, in *De studiis et litteris*, writes that a woman should read the classical authors but not be allowed to study rhetoric, presumably because it would permit her to argue with men and make her expert in behavior unbecoming a woman: "Rhetoric in all its forms— public discussion, forensic argument, logical fence, and the like, lies absolutely outside the province of woman."[4] And Matteo Palmieri, in his *Della vita civile* (1526), envisages a woman's life as severely circumscribed by domestic and especially child-rearing duties; he does not entertain the prospect of educating a girl in disciplines for which she can have no use. The conjunction of male and female in marriage and family life is "natural," he claims, but the wife's primary task is only to provide her husband with children.[5] This is her contribution to the commonweal, but it

[3]From an educational treatise of 1550, quoted in Eugenio Garin, *L'educazione in Europa (1400–1600)* (Bari: Laterza, 1975), 156.

[4]Quoted in William Harrison Woodward, *Vittorino da Feltre and Other Humanist Educators* (Cambridge, 1897), 126. On rhetoric as a discipline for women in Renaissance Italy, see Lisa Jardine, "Isotta Nogarola," *History of Education* 12, 4 (1983): 231–44; she cites a passage in Lionardo Bruni's letter to Battista Malatesta which is emphatic in its prohibition of rhetoric in women's education. On contemporary women writers, see studies of Gaspara Stampa, Vittoria Colonna, and Veronica Gambera in *Women Writers of the Renaissance and Reformation*, ed. Katharina M. Wilson (Athens: University of Georgia Press, 1987).

[5]Matteo Palmieri, *Della vita civile*, ed. Felice Battaglia, Scrittori Politici Italiani 14 (Bologna: Zanichelli, 1944), bk. 4, 132. Palmieri's treatise contains four books: on the education of a young man, on the virtues of private life (temperance, fortitude, prudence), on the virtues of public life (justice), and on "useful things" (*utile cose*) for life in the body

reflects her husband's desire for a perpetuity in time. Men wish to "be eternal in their posterity because they cannot be eternal in life," says Palmieri; regrettably, this means they must have intercourse with their wives:

> The end of the act of generation is necessary to the well-being of the human race but in itself it is most disgusting, miserable, and bestial; and indeed the enslavement and burden of every worthy spirit and an animalistic game that deserves to be left to asses. The office befitting a woman is to be solicitous and attentive to the needs of the house, to provide for the needs of the family . . . the commands, habits, manners of her husband ought to be the law a wife follows.   [4.134]

Because the wife's virtue is based entirely on the successful outcome of intercourse, Palmieri's ascetism affects her status more than that of her husband. She has value as a presence through whose almost passive agency children are born and nurtured.

Obviously the behavior of real women, however circumscribed, betrayed such narrow constructions of their nature. The crucial question for those who believed that women were inferior creatures became how to train a human being for a life in which whatever intelligence she possessed was to remain undeveloped without incurring her resentment. Treatises such as Lodovico Dolce's *Della institution delle donne* (1545) show that the answer to this question could entail logical compromises. Dolce opens by making a strategic concession to feminist claims: woman is as intelligent as man. Otherwise, his character Flaminion declares, one could treat them as brutes: "One [would do] well to send our girls back to the seclusion of country estates; and if a spark of wit is found in them, to overlook it, to stamp it out, and to make of them, who are rational animals, real beasts without intellect."[6] He proves his point with the example of Queen Giovanna, the mother of Charles V, who delivers speeches in Latin (without the benefit of notes) to princes and ambassadors "with a more than manly eloquence" (C2). But the education he advocates is actually based on his belief that however intellectually apt, women are feeble, weak-willed, and hence incapable of learning: "they are of weaker constitution than men" (B2v); "their thoughts are more

---

politic. The whole treatise is dedicated to Alessandro degli Alessandri, a fellow Florentine. For Palmieri, see George Carpetto, *The Humanism of Matteo Palmieri* (Rome: Bulzoni, 1984).

[6]Ludovico Dolce, *Dialogo della institution delle donne* (Venice, 1545), sig. B7v. This dialogue, in three books on girls, wives, and widows, is dedicated by its publisher, Gabriel Giolito de Ferrari, to Signora S. Villante da S. Giorgio. The speakers are Flaminio, an instructor who voices doctrine, and Dorothea, his pupil.

flighty, less steady" (B6); and women must not be taught Greek (although he will praise a number who have been), "in order not to put too great a weight on their shoulders" (C5v; cf. C2–3). Girls must be treated more harshly than boys in any case. Of more recalcitrant material, they need more discipline: "It's important that a girl weep often and be sad while she is young, for she can laugh and live happily when she is old" (B4v). Her principal work should be spinning and weaving, no matter what her rank, for even queens need employment (B5); "this is the more true when they do not have family responsibilities. What else would they do? Spend all their time with ladies in waiting and courtiers?" (B6). Dolce's leveling of all women to a single status illustrates how pervasive was the belief that a woman's proper office, whatever her rank, was always to be defined by her relation to man. Her subordination to him is registered symbolically by her constant and even—if necessary—manual labor. A woman so busy has by definition no time to read or reflect. What speech she cultivates is dismissed as idle chatter. Cut off from what Filippo Beroaldo had called "culture"—"conversation, discussion, language, for eloquence is an old and sacrosanct and wonderful regulator of the affairs of state"—a woman remains incapable of contributing to society except as a mother.[7]

Chastity is the virtue that compensates for such ignorance: "In a woman one does not look for either profound eloquence or subtle wit or cunning prudence or the art of living or skill at administering a Republic or justice or anything beyond chastity. If one doesn't find that in her, it is comparable to a total absence of virtue in a man" (D2). To equate the inability to perform the tasks of a citizen with uxorial chastity is to make Barbaro's point in a different way. Dolce's woman has virtue or value only as the sexual property of a man. She must know nothing that would allow her to acquire a human character; she must be fearful of acquiring such a character and shameful if she betrays it: "fear and shame—these are the foundation and the base of the whole structure of virtue [in a woman]" (B5). Concerned here for more than the legitimacy of children, Dolce sees a woman's chastity as indicative of the tacit yet understood agreement she must make with the society in which she lives not to interfere with its patriarchal order. For a woman's reproductive body to remain wholly at the disposal of the men whose diplomacy she serves (as Barbaro so lucidly demonstrates is desirable), she has to remain ignorant, incapable of forming or expressing an opinion of their policies.

Such an agreement was of course demanded of all women to a greater

---

[7]Quoted in Garin, *Educazione in Europa*, 103, who cites Beroaldo in cod. S.5.25 dell' Estense.

or lesser degree, not only those who were young and likely to marry. A widow, though independent in many respects, was nevertheless urged to limit her public activities. Because she was expected to take care of the interests of her minor children, she was allowed some participation in social and economic life, and this freedom marked her as a member of a distinct and atypical group within society: women who behaved in a masculine fashion and were therefore considered virile.[8] Giovanni Giorgio Trissino, in his *Epistola . . . de la vita che dee tenere una donna vedova* (1524), terms a widow "a free woman: . . . such may not be subject to a husband, or a father, or anyone else" (A2v).[9] She is to consider herself a man: "I say that first of all you ought to consider yourself born a man [*nata homo*], in spirit and in body" (A3). His characterization conforms to the legal standing widows possessed at that time in most of Italy; unlike wives, they were entitled to deal in property, to do all kinds of business, and to appear in court.[10] Some feminist protest stresses that a widow's situation is the best a woman can have, an opinion already expressed by Jerome: "Because they have experienced the domination of husbands, widows prefer liberty."[11] Yet Trissino warns that the liberty owed her by virtue of her virility is qualified; there are many masculine activities in which she may not participate. She is to restrict her intellectual interests to moral philosophy and not to concern herself with questions in natural science—"neither in the composition of the world, nor in the defects of the moon, nor in the course of the planets . . . these things belong to the most subtle of philosophies" (A3). She must be devout but not too observant in order to avoid "the vice of hypocrisy" (Bv). She is to practice a decent sociability among men and women; "to be reserved

[8]On the question of virile women and the meaning of androgyny, see chap. 3 passim. Christiane Klapisch-Zuber describes the situation of a widow living in Renaissance Italy as that created by the conflict between the dotal system (which allowed her to take her dowry from her husband's family at his death and live independently or remarry) and patrilineage (which required her to remain in her husband's family if she wanted a part in raising her children). *Women, Family, and Ritual in Renaissance Italy*, trans. Lydia G. Cochrane (Chicago: University of Chicago Press, 1985), 117–31. The legal status of Italian women at this time is covered by Guido Rossi, "Statut juridique de la femme dans l'histoire du droit italien: Epoque médiévale et moderne," in *La Femme*, Receuils de la société Jean Bodin, vol. 12 (Paris, n.d.), 115–34; on property see esp. 125–28. For comments on Alessandra Strozzi, one of the most successful widows of the period, see Lauro Martines, "A Way of Looking at Women in Renaissance Florence," *Journal of Medieval and Renaissance Studies* 4, 1 (1974): 15–28.

[9]Giovanni Giorgio Trissino, *Epistola del Trissino de la vita, che dee tenere una donna vedova* (Rome, 1525), sig. A2v. Trissino's letter is addressed to Signora Margarita Pia Sanseverina.

[10]Trissino is also reminding his reader that a widow is generically human (*homo*), composed of a material and a spiritual being.

[11]St. Jerome, *Ad Eustochium*, quoted in Shulamith Shahar, *The Fourth Estate* (London and New York: Methuen, 1983), 97.

with the bad and presumptuous, and freer with the good and truthful"
(B2). But she is not to discuss (or perhaps even know about) politics: "to
speak of what the Turk is up to in Constantinople, or the sultan of Egypt,
or of what may be decided in the Diet of Augustus . . . nothing is more
inappropriate than to hear a woman speak of war and discuss statecraft"
(B3v). In other words, what Trissino calls her "bitter liberty" (A3) is in
practice no more than a limited license to conduct her business, even if it
requires her presence in public. It is in no sense to be construed socially or
politically.

Galeazzo Flavio Capella's *Della eccellenza et dignità delle donne* (1545)
provides a feminist critique of treatises that (like Palmieri's and Dolce's)
conceive of woman as *naturally* inferior to man—a critique based on the
assumption that what passes for nature is in actuality a cultural construct.
Nature was supposed to offer to the trained mind models of conduct, to
embody a general law. In addition to the scriptural concept of nature,
created and then fallen, were the optimistic accounts of such humanists as
Lorenzo Valla, who asserted that "what nature had made and formed . . .
could not be other than sacred and praiseworthy, like the sky that turns
above us, made lovely by its diurnal and nocturnal lights, and composed
with such proportion, beauty, and usefulness."[12] But whatever the nature of its law, nature in itself, as a concept, was not generally subjected to
systematic criticism. Just such criticism becomes an essential feature of
feminist protest. Capella's defense of women undermines the idea that a
woman's restrictive education accords with natural norms and proposes
instead that it is designed to foster the interests of man, to whom woman
is subordinate.

Capella relies on two kinds of argument. First, the projection argument: women are the victims of male projection (disappointed lovers see
women as evil). And second, the exclusion argument: women suffer
from invisibility (men exclude women from activities they then claim
women cannot perform). The logical force of both arguments derives
from the fact that he attempts to prove the virtue of women not by
disproving the claims of their detractors but rather by framing misogynist opinions with explanations of their causes in social attitudes and
practices. He does not, for example, deny that women are licentious but
rather maintains that because they are encouraged to be lazy and passive,
they hardly have a choice:

Women [are] brought up indolently, confined to dark houses and practically in solitude—all things conducive to amorous pleasure-seeking; and

[12]Lorenzo Valla, *De voluptate* 1, quoted in Garin, *Educazione in Europa*, 87.

they are prevented from many activities allowed to men [such as] hunting, jousting, fighting—pleasures that extinguish every amorous flame; what else [then] remains to women if not with continuous thinking to nourish the fire that consumes them?[13]

He claims women are capable of learning, but blames their reputation for ignorance on men, who ridicule any education that does not conform to those programs instituted for men, "persuading themselves that because women do not go to Pavia to study law, they know nothing and their wit and advice are no good" (D4v). Observations of this sort depend for their rhetorical effect on the ability of the reader to accept a larger and critical frame of reference. In this case, the reader is to see in the status quo the result of attempts by men to gain and retain power by limiting the field of choice for women.

To account for the *origins* of what passes for social stability and growth, Capella examines the projective strategies that protect men. Capella's woman is cast in the role of peacemaker, yet she is not, as she was for Barbaro, a passive link between men but rather the embodiment of an active commitment to stop social divisiveness. Interpreting the myth of the Amazons, Capella argues that their defeat has been misunderstood. It does not signify weakness. Echoing Aristotle's *Economics*, he points out that the physically weaker are actually the intellectually stronger: "Indeed, great enterprises conduct themselves to their desired end more from wit than from bodily strength, and too much strength often makes persons foolhardy" (F2v).[14] Having inverted the customary evaluation of this virtue—courage becomes foolhardiness, timidity prudence—Capella observes that what the state of Venice needs at the moment is precisely a cautiously intelligent—that is, a feminized—citizenry. For the city suffers from vigilantes: "The arms of wicked persons have such power that all good persons must either be victims . . . of criminals or leave their beloved country" (F3); and nothing, he claims, offends justice more than brute force, a feature characteristic, as he has asserted, of the strong, that is, of men in contrast to women. The defeat of the Amazons

[13]Galeazzo Flavio Capella, *Delle eccellenze et dignità delle donne* (Venice, 1526), sig. D4. This treatise, which appears to lack a dedication, was first published in Rome in 1525. Capella also wrote *L'anthropologia* (Venice, 1533), a treatise on history and social life.

[14]The equation of physical weakness with mental strength is a common trope of feminist protest. It is attributed to Aristotle by Elyot's defender of women, Candidus, and was perhaps generally regarded as the logical conclusion of what Aristotle in fact writes in the *Economics*: "For nature has made the one sex stronger, the other weaker, that the latter through fear may be the more cautious, while the former by its courage is better able to ward off attacks; and that the one may acquire possessions outside the house, the other preserve those within": *The Complete Works of Aristotle*, ed. Jonathan Barnes, Bollinger Series LXXI (Princeton: Princeton University Press, 1984), 2131.

is therefore really a concession to a higher form of social life. In the age of iron, when force prevailed, everyone was a killer. To remedy this situation, he declares, women (the Amazons) were forced to give up their arms: "So that not all of us would be ruined by so much evil and become our own murderers, one of the two parties threw down the arms that had been given them at the time of the Amazons in order that justice might be preserved in the world and that the world not again return to an ancient and primeval chaos" (F3r–v). It is, in other words, the absence of *female* aggression that guarantees a society's future through the maintainance of justice in the world. Men, Capella notes, threaten the welfare of states such as Venice by continuing to bear arms and therefore also killing each other. This interpretation of the myth of the Amazons to explain both women's reputation for pacific behavior and the origins of justice, such as it is, differs from comparable accounts of the function of women in society by pointing to its enforced character and to the fact that women are maintained in restricted roles not only or mainly because such roles are natural to them but rather because they are constrained to adopt them by force—a force that is, ironically, a measure of the force that they renounced in order that justice might prevail. As Capella then indicates, what follows is anomalous: offices are not always given to "the most worthy"; for example, he declares, "we see every day that a queen may be without any office at all and yet be more worthy than a thousand other officeholders who makeup the king's court" (G3r–v). Moralists had conventionally deplored the discrepancies between a ruler's virtue (or lack of it) and the high requirements of his public office, and pointed to the moral excellence of persons who had neither authority nor power, but rarely had women as a class been selected as a case in point.

The importance of Capella's *Della eccellenza* lies in its contribution to the notion of history as a scene characterized above all as a struggle for power—a scene in which women have played no part from that moment in mythical time in which they renounced arms, the moment also of the institution of social justice. His work suggests the possibility of a revisionist history in which the doubtful relation of virtue to power—the powerful are not necessarily the virtuous—is scrutinized as a source of other and different explanations of the course of events. Such a revisionist history need not be restricted to feminist perspectives, nor of course was it in practice. Machiavelli and others had suggested that what a society constitutes as justice reflects the conflict and competition among its various members. But Capella's emphasis on history as a record of the affairs of men and not women makes possible another kind of inquiry— the extent to which a historian can be and perhaps is himself an apologist. The writing of history can then be examined as a process by which the record of what is or has been excluded from power is in a sense *permanently* effaced. If the reader understands this, he or she can read history not only to know the mistakes human beings have made but also to discover mistakes in the historian's record. To question history in this way is to begin by regarding the historian himself as suspect, as one who is trying to acquire power by defending a particular party or cause.[15]

Ideal Types

Feminists could find a basis for reconceiving the nature of woman in literature that idealized her; there, as the embodiment of her own kind of virtue, she was the perfect equal of man. Mario Equicola, for example, when depicting love between persons in his Neoplatonic *Libro di natura d'amore* (1526), defends woman as worthy of love and of loving because she, like man, is rational, and reason is the source of love. Analyzing the civic love that binds together a society—Cicero, he notes, posits an "order" to these bonds: relatives first, then friends, guests, and foreigners—Equicola (actually echoing Aristotle) finds that it corresponds to forms of government: "The love of a father for his children is the image of a kingdom; the concord of a husband and wife is similar to the power among aristocrats; the society of brothers and friends conforms to that republic where many good men are in charge."[16] Citing

---

[15]Cf. certain passages in a contemporary history of women, Giuseppe Betussi's *Additione fatta dal medesimo delle donne famose da tempo di M. Giovanni [Boccaccio] fino a i giorni nostri*, with his translation of Boccaccio's *De mulieribus claris* (Venice, 1545). Betussi's history of Joan of Arc, "Gianna donzella francese," records among other things the changes her fame has undergone as a result of shifts in political power. Praising her successful liberation of France, he notes that her fellow countrymen regarded her as divine (sig. X2v). Yet the English accused her of witchcraft, and once in their power she is, accordingly, executed (sig. X3). It is only when a French king, Louis XIII, asks the pope to investigate the case, examine the records, assess the evidence, in effect to try Gianna again, that a different conclusion is reached: "that she was falsely accused and wrongly punished" (sig. X3v). In principle, this passage provides a basis for a new conception of the didactic function of history—one that goes further in its theoretical implications than anything envisaged by the humanist writers of exempla. It is a conception, I think, that has its origins in the perception of historiography as a field of inquiry which proceeds by *excluding* from consideration certain kinds of evidence in order to privilege others. The study of history is educative because the records of history are perennially subject to contestation.

[16]Mario Equicola, *Libro di natura d'amore* (Venice, 1526), sig. N6. This treatise, in six books and first written in a Latin draft, 1495–96, is only occasionally concerned with the status of woman. It does, however, illustrate what kinds of resources a Neoplatonic view of love provides feminists. By representing physical beauty and sexual response to be the basis of a selfless and spiritual love and, finally, a rational vision of creation, it perceives women not so much as ennobled as rational. To the extent that she is also idealized, of course, she succumbs to typing and her defender, like Castiglione's Magnifico, is made subject to feminist criticism. On the *Libro*, see Mario Possi, "Mario Equicola e la cultura

Plato, he then asserts that these "aristocrats" are *equals* and that man and woman possess "equal liberty" (N6). There is therefore no rational basis for misogyny (see especially his discussion of Aristotle and Plato, BB8v–CC). He supports these claims later when, discussing the "end" (*fine*) of love, he examines the circumstances in which bad opinions of women arise:

> And you who claim they are licentious, tell me, what woman ever sought out a man (I speak of a well-bred woman); what woman chose a new lover? Rather they are sought after by importunate lovers with every kind of persuasion. We promise them duty, service, faith; we swear to put ourselves at their disposal. . . . They—by nature compassionate and, as Aristotle says, full of pity—believe themselves to be loved; whence they are constrained to listen, and to believe words partly true and partly false. If we accuse women of love, let us accuse men more, who make themselves prey to women.   [CC]

Equicola refers to the disempowerment of women more directly than Capella did. Men become "prey" to women not because women are aggressive but because, not having been granted the dignity of discourse on honorable or rational terms, they can be perceived to be whatever men want them to be. The fictions women hear actually signify their lack of human identity and agency and, conversely, the power of the men who use them without ever being called to account: "Each insolent act of erotic theft . . . seems honor and glory to a man but to you [a woman, it is] an inexcusable sin and you are often forced to fear death for it" (CC2v). By alluding to a husband's legal right to kill his unfaithful wife, who is not similarly privileged, Equicola makes it clear that a woman's presumed lack of virtue is really a lack of power, and that this lack conduces to her scapegoating.

For other writers who defended woman in ideal terms, her supposed equality with man proved to be problematic grounds for protest. How complex the response to such equality could be is brilliantly illustrated in the third book of Castiglione's *Libro del cortegiano* (1526). Ostensibly devoted to constructing an image of the ideal court lady, the text actually reveals its author's analysis of his courtiers' strategies for controlling all the women of the court, particularly the most powerful of them, Elisabetta Gonzaga, Duchess of Urbino. Not herself a lady of the court, she is rather its governor—at least of its social life—deputized by her ailing

---

cortigiana: Appunti sulla redazione manoscritta del *Libro de natura de amore," Lettere italiane* 32 (1980): 149–71. For an analysis of Equicola's defense of women in Latin, *De mulieribus* (1501), see Conor Fahy, "Three Early Renaissance Treatises on Women," *Italian Studies* 11 (1959): 30–55.

husband, Duke Guidobaldo, who never appears on the scene. Castiglione's rhetorically convoluted discussion of court ladies, women worthies, and queens makes it difficult to know how fully he intended the contradictions that both disturb and illuminate the logic of his argument. His defense fails as a defense; but whether this failure is to be understood as the pretext of a purposeful exposure of male discourse concerning women or merely as an unexaminimed result of his own complicity in that discourse is not altogether clear.

Castiglione begins the third book with an exchange that illustrates the uneasiness an authoritative and powerful woman provokes among his courtiers. The Magnifico's proposal to describe the court lady receives a mixed response. Would it not be better, asks Frisio, to continue to discuss the courtier, since more remains to be said of him? The duchess has already accused the Magnifico of being fearful of the subject of the court lady; and now, responding to Frisio, he deftly defends himself by claims that both praise and demean her—as if to confirm her insight. Were he describing a "queen of the world," he declares, he would only have to name the duchess; as he is describing a court lady, he paints her as he would "wish her to be."[17] By enlarging the scope of queenship in hyperbole, the Magnifico mystifies it; by stating that describing is merely naming, he trivializes it; by portraying the court lady as a hypothetical creature, he dismisses the ability of the duchess to gather around her women of virtue. The duchess warns him "not to exceed bounds," but her contributions to the remaining conversation make clear that however strong her character, her position is indeed weak. The role of the capable Emilia Pia, who might be thought to have supplied a model for the court lady, is made similarly insignificant.

The courtly politics of the first two of Castiglione's four books provides these and all subsequent exchanges in his third book with an analytic context. The ideal courtier of the first two books has been depicted as without authority of his own and effectively powerless. His status vis-à-vis his lord is similar to that of a wife in relation to her

[17]Baldassare Castiglione, Il "Libro del cortegiano" con una scelta delle opere minori, ed. Bruno Maier (Turin: Unione Tipografico-Editrice Torinese, 1964), 340–41. On Castiglione and the subject of women see Dain Trafton, "Politics and the Praise of Women: Political Doctrine in the Courtier's Third Book," in Castiglione: The Ideal and the Real in Renaissance Culture, ed. Robert W. Hanning and David Rosand (New Haven: Yale University Press, 1983), 29–44; and José Guidi, "De l'amour courtois à l'amour sacré: La Condition de la femme dans l'oeuvre de B. Castiglione," in Images de la femme dans la littérature italienne de la Renaissance: Préjugés, misogynes, et aspirations nouvelles: Castiglione, Piccolomini, Bandello, ed. André Rochon (Paris: Université de la Sorbonne Nouvelle, 1980), 9–80. For a study of the work as a whole, see Wayne A. Rebhorn, Courtly Performances: Masking and Festivity in Castiglione's "Book of the Courtier" (Detroit: Wayne State University Press, 1978).

husband; it is mirrored in the observations of Castiglione's own courtiers concerning the life they lead. Their concerns and activities, focused on providing their superiors with pleasure and diversion rather than protection or counsel, might be characterized as effeminate.[18] Their immediate situation is complicated because they are directed by the duchess, aided by Emilia Pia, whom from time to time she deputizes (as she has been deputized) to act in her place. The conversations of the third book bring to a climax the political tension created by what would have been considered an unnatural hierarchy of persons. They are devoted largely to arguments that serve to console Urbino's male courtiers for the degree to which they are subject to the women of the court, who, because of their status (the duchess) and intelligence (Emilia Pia), have a certain control over them, even if it is both indirect and occasional. The Magnifico's ideal court lady, who is so clearly inferior and subordinate to the ideal courtier, is both a repudiation of his subservience to the figure of the *domina*, embodied for the moment in the duchess and Emilia Pia, and a protection against it. That the Magnifico seeks to substantiate the worth of women generally, and thus of the relatively weak figure of his ideal lady specifically, by accounts of the relatively strong figures of legendary and historical queens underscores his vulnerability. In effect, he indicates that the virtue of woman is evident only as an aspect of a past that is in many respects alien to the present he describes. The courtiers' debate on the true nature of woman which follows the Magnifico's idealization and defense reveals the reality of relations between men and women in Urbino's court as Castiglione may have wished to show it. The conversation he reports is in any case conflicted. On the one hand, it is compensatory, guaranteeing the effeminate courtier a part of his masculinity by reserving for him at least some power—over woman. On the other hand, it is self-critical (whether intentionally or not), revealing that ideas concerning the neglible virtue of woman are designed to protect and to flatter those who have conceived them. In his dedicatory letter to Don Michel de Silva, Castiglione has invited his readers to see in his portrait of court life a sincere tribute to the virtue of his courtiers and ladies, and perhaps especially of the duchess. But in his account of their conversation his praise is equivocated by dramatic revelations of anxiety, on the part both of his courtiers, who resist the rule of women, and of the author himself, who depicts with brilliant accuracy the means by which male

[18]On the ancillary and subservient functions of the typical courtier of this period see, i.a., Frank Whigham, *Ambition and Privilege: The Social Tropes of Elizabethan Courtly Theory* (Berkeley: University of California Press, 1984). Trafton, "Politics and the Praise of Women," argues that Castiglione's courtiers are instructed in a female *virtù* by the Magnifico's stories.

subordinates gain and retain control over their female superiors. Here the issue is no longer whether the equality of men and women is desirable in principle but rather why it would be rejected in practice.

Because the Magnifico's purpose—perhaps to protect men from powerful women—is unclear, his peers regard his project, to fashion an ideal court lady, as suspect almost from the outset. Responding to the vaguely bland portrait the Magnifico paints—her qualities may "perhaps [make her] worthy to be equaled to the great courtier [they have been discussing]" (3.6, 346)—Gasparo, playing the part of the misogynist, challenges him on two grounds. He observes that the Magnifico speaks "somewhat in generalities" and that he has described things as he desires them to be rather than explained them as they are (3.7, 346). To examine things as they are means, for Gasparo, not only to observe and analyze them with care but also to dismiss, insofar as it is possible, the wish that they might be otherwise and the evaluative criteria upon which that wish is based. Gasparo's objections here prove to be predictive of the course of Castiglione's entire argument. They force the Magnifico to defend the worth of woman by relating *particular* histories, and so to demonstrate that his type has no prescriptive validity.[19] More important, by analyzing these experiences through the dramatic exchanges of his characters, Castiglione reveals that the Magnifico's typing does not offer women the "freedom" to create the terms upon which they live, as he later declares they deserve (3.16, 357). On the contrary, it restricts them within existing conventions.

Castiglione continues his subtle critique of the Magnifico's project by showing that however readily men discuss what passes for authority on the virtue of woman, they do not permit their exchanges to result in a consensus on the subject. Gasparo, protesting the Magnifico's ideal type, proposes to entertain Aristotle's view that the nature of woman is innately defective. (The fact that he cannot assert it as true follows from "the virtue of the ladies who are present"—he is, after all, nominally under their command.) He reminds his audience that woman can be so considered as a consequence of nature's failed intention, which was to

---

[19]The use of history to invalidate the concept of type and typology in general often results in a challenge to authority. Writers who define and prescribe proper feminine behavior are open to criticism from persons who claim to have experience of exceptions. The prime example of such a critical response, Boccaccio's *De mulieribus claris*, is ironic but other defenses, such as Betussi's *Additione*, are not. The status of the exception is, of course, problematic. In theory, if history yields only a record of differences, then the concept of type is negated. And if women make up a category of persons who defy typing because each individual is unique, then no generalizations can be made about their virtue. Inasmuch as feminists argue in generalities, and notably by reference to "woman," they are themselves subject to Castiglione's critique of typology.

create a man, and also in relation to her composition of elements in nature: she is "matter" rather than "form." The Magnifico is able to reply to these Aristotelian propositions in Aristotelian terms. The physical weakness of woman is negligible, he insists, since strength is the basis for "little perfection"; even in war, the bravest are not the best. Intellectually she is equal to a man. And he reminds Gasparo of the Aristotelian notion that physical weakness characterizes mental strength: "There is no doubt that women, for being weaker physically, are stronger mentally and have an intelligence better suited to abstract thinking than do men." Proposing a second idea of nature, the Magnifico refers to the Aristotelian concept of *telos*: nature has "designed [woman] to a necessary end," which is the generation and rearing of children. This end has its perfection; in fact, "either sex alone shows an imperfection." The Magnifico concludes by referring to Scripture, in which man and woman are both made in God's image by virtue of their part in generation (3.11–14, 351–52, 353, 356). The entire exchange has revealed that even within the work of a single author the idea of woman is controversial. And therefore authorities, insofar as they are supposed to provide certain and definitive truths, are not invariably authoritative.

How men suppress feminist protest, even in some instances while acknowledging its fairness, is illustrated in two subsequent exchanges. Replying to Gasparo's contention that women know themselves to be inferior and consequently desire to be men, the Magnifico declares that the dissatisfaction of women is a function of male abuse: "These poor women desire to be men not in order to be more perfect but to have freedom and to flee from that control which men have exercised over them by their own authority." The subject of freedom does not engage him further, however, and he allows Gasparo to turn the conversation again to the philosophical questions of "matter" and "form" that had earlier been answered inconclusively. Emilia's interruption and complaint—that by speaking in abstractions, he fails to defend women from male detractors, their "enemies"—indicates the social control of women by men which the conversation makes possible (3.16–17, 357–58). Truly contentious and germane issues, if touched on at all, are scuttled in favor of esoteric debate, designed to mask and thus evade what might really cause conflict.

A second instance of such maneuvering (3.20, 363–65) shows that women are aware of its effects and purpose. Continuing his defense of women, the Magnifico rejects the charge that they are not noted for sanctity by criticizing those "accursed hypocrites," the clergy, who take advantage of the fact that women are, for the most part, shut away in houses and convents and hence without a means of self-defense—"for these unfortunates remain shut away without that pompous pride which seeks the name of sanctity"—to assert that they are a threat to Christian virtue. Having secured a scapegoat, such clergy then proceed to commit crimes. They not only try "to corrupt the chaste mind of some woman or another"; they also acquire political and economic power (an action their professed otherworldliness ought to prohibit) and, furthermore, abuse it—"they turn to governing states, to raising up one and overthrowing another, to beheading, incarcerating, and proscribing men, to being the ministers of crime and very nearly the custodians of the thefts of many princes." The reference to the power of the clergy, especially of friars who are committed to poverty yet live outside monastic institutions, contributes to the construction of an image of male authority and power which the courtiers need. For these clergy, who are not supposed to be in a position to gain power, who are politically female inasmuch as they are not supposed to pursue interests in public life, can and actually do succeed in the highest civic ventures. In other words, if friars can acquire control, so, perhaps, can courtiers, that other group of effeminate men. But Emilia again objects, declaring that this conversation about women serves the concerns of men. She contradicts the Magnifico and denies that friars are only evil, reminding him that "if those men did not pray for us, we would have still more afflictions than we do." Her pious point hides a witty reflection on the politics of sex. The Magnifico has correctly observed that it is because women are *shut away* and hence silent that they can be made scapegoats, that the clergy must see to it that women play this role, since the clergy has to dissemble its power in order to avoid taking responsibility for the acts it commits. To some readers, Emilia's piety may have been fraught with a certain irony: when members of the clergy pray, they also are *shut away* and not in a position to "afflict" women by accusing them of sinfulness.

The formal part of the Magnifico's defense—his histories of famous women—subverts the credibility of the concept of type directly by representing only exceptions to it. In fact, unlike his court lady, his famous women demonstrate their virtue in public action. Beyond the question of the feasibility of the Magnifico's project, therefore, lies the question already posed by the conversation as a whole (and raised initially by Boccaccio)—the extent to which the court lady or indeed a female governor or queen can function authoritatively. The Magnifico's exemplary women focus attention on a few women who had real power. How do he and his fellow courtiers respond to them? In what sense is their own political predicament made more acute by these images? Margarita Gonzaga has observed that while women take pride in such histories, men pretend not to hear them (3.23, 369). But Castiglione's courtiers do understand the significance of the Magnifico's examples and react defensively to them.

Frisio, dismissing politically powerful women as "no longer of this world," is easily answered by the Magnifico's example of Isabella of Castile (3.35, 385). Gasparo's challenge is harder to meet. He denies that women in public life can be virtuous in the way men can, not because they lack intellectual or moral capacities but because they bear children. Like Boccaccio, he sees that a woman's sexuality places her in continual jeopardy; morally, she is always suspect. Her sole virtue is chastity, and it has a political reference. Without it, there would be "uncertainty about offspring, and the bond would be dissolved which binds the whole world through the blood, and each man's natural love for what he produces" (3.37, 391). The need to safeguard that bond justifies a double standard: the rigorous rule of chastity for women, who "because of the stupidity of their sex are more inclined to [give in to] their appetites than men," and the "certain liberty" that men have allowed themselves—"because they know that, according to universal opinion, a loose life does not damage their reputations as it does women" (3.39, 392). (Gasparo later inveighs bitterly against the socially divisive effects of women's jealousy and lust, again associating their sexuality with public chaos. Women who are licentious leave the house of the man to whom they are linked by filial or uxorial duty. Once they have done so, their lover's tricks cause dissension: "hatred, animosity, and infinite scandal and open destruction"; 3.74, 439). In short, the "world finds no usefulness in women except the bearing of children." This is not to say that women cannot "rule cities and armies," he concludes, but that "it is enough that they do not do so" (3.39, 392).

These comments elicit a second defense of woman, led this time by Cesare Gonzaga. His argument separates morals from biology (woman's reproductive body) to suggest that if woman is not given a chance to exercise virtue in public life, the reason is not that she is morally defective.[20] Cesare accuses men of immorality, not only of incontinence but also of duplicity. Old men and heads of institutions and states especially, while accusing women, "never grieve for anything more than their lack of natural vigor to be able to satisfy their abominable desires, which remain in the mind, even after nature denies them to the body" (3.40, 395). What virtue they claim is therefore specious. Conversely, women

---

[20]No clearer in Cesare's than in Erasmus's criticism is the proper relation between the biological functions of the female body and behavior that is designated culturally as feminine. A woman's experience is obviously both of her femaleness and of her femininity; Renaissance femininists would also add that she has or can have an experience of masculinity.

who deny men sexual favors are subjected to their "noble revenge": they are accused of what they did not do, and find their reputations ruined (3.42, 396). Their vice is of course trumped up. Concluding his defense with examples of chaste women and of wily lovers, Cesare establishes that with respect to sexual morals, woman deserves to rule man. This seems to be an endorsement of the feminist position that the Magnifico appeared to be supporting when he defended the virtue of woman earlier. What is actually at stake for Cesare, however, is clear in his subsequent comments. To answer Gasparo's assertion that virtuous women do not exist today, Cesare describes two contemporaries—"una donna . . . di bassa condizione" and "un'altra"—who are simply chaste and have no political power. And when he describes the duchess as a woman "who, having lived with her husband for fifteen years as a widow, is not only steadfast in never making this public to anyone in the world, but being urged by her own people to leave this widowhood, chose to suffer exile, poverty, and every other kind of unhappiness rather than accept that which to everyone else seemed the good grace and prosperity of fortune," she abruptly silences him (3.49, 407). Her position is too precarious to permit more of the kind of publicity Cesare's compliment offers. By contrast, the courtiers, Cesare included, stand to benefit from any suggestion that the duchess might take a lover: at the very least, such an action would nullify any claim to authority and power she might make. Hence her sharp rebuke of his apparently gratuitous remark.

Nor does Cesare's picture of a woman's right to govern men go unchallenged by the conversation of Emilia Pia, who lectures her suitor, Unico Aretino, on the proper conduct of a *lover*. Unico, she declares, is to desire what she desires (distance); she is not to desire what he desires (intimacy). If a "single will" is to govern both their souls, she continues, "it is for you [Unico] to do this" (3.63, 427). Their exchange suggests that if woman is to govern, she is to do so not politically in any direct sense but rather erotically, not in court life but in courtship. Gasparo's assertion that woman enters politics only as the guarantor of the legitimacy of man's offspring acquires retrospectively a kind of dramatic ratification. There is a certain irony here too. Emilia Pia, laying down the law of courtship to Unico Aretino, recalls the figure of the medieval *domina*, the queen of courtly lyric and romance, who until the thirteenth century was likely to have taken a large part not only in the "debates of love" but in the activities of her court which extended beyond its actual walls.[21] The

---

[21]The forceful authority of the queen as she is commonly depicted in medieval courtly lyric and romance, in contrast to comparable portraits in Renaissance literature, provides Joan Kelly with evidence that the actual status of women declined during the fifteenth and

image of Castiglione's Renaissance court lady, attenuated and pale in comparison with its antecedent, is further diminished at the end of the book.

Castiglione concludes by showing the power of men to control even the duchess and Emilia Pia, women who have greater social and political status than they do (1.4, 85). Gasparo's last invective against women who exercise their power in love affairs with "ambition," "madness," and "cruelty" suggests how easily even the limited power of women to determine their emotional relations with men can breed resentment. In the final moments of the evening's dialogue, the subject of woman's virtue is effectively suppressed, not only as a subject for further debate but also as one that may have a life in memory. Ottaviano's complaint, that the entire discussion of the court lady has exhibited only extremes— the Magnifico has praised women too highly, Gasparo has criticized them too severely—reveals its latent content when he observes that attention has been diverted from the courtier: By discussing the court lady "we have lost [the opportunity] to understand many beautiful things that remained to be said of the courtier." Emilia Pia calls Ottaviano's objections disingenuous and sees that he remains an adversary; the discussion has proved displeasing to him not because it has been too long or inconclusive or off the main subject but rather because it has concerned the excellence of the court lady. His wish to hear about the courtier is motivated by "an envy . . . of the honor of women." It is the duchess, however, who realizes what Ottaviano's sentiments really mean. She ends the day's conversation by saying sarcastically that when he begins a further account of the courtier on the next day, memories of the praise and blame given women will have vanished from the minds of the company: "They will have left the minds of these men, so that they will be capable [of comprehending] that truth which you [will] speak [concerning the courtier]." She refers to the collective memory of the group she is part of, but she alludes figuratively to what it knows as its past, which (unlike the memories of the transmitters of legend and classical history) does not record and probably is incapable of recording the "onor delle donne." In a gesture symbolic of the invisibility and silence she has

---

sixteenth centuries. See her "Did Women Have a Renaissance?" in *Becoming Visible*, ed. Renate Bridenthal and Claudia Koonz (Boston: Houghton Mifflin, 1977), 137–64. Such a diminution in the figure of the queen is certainly evident in literature, whatever were the circumstances of particular queens. On the other hand, fifteenth- and sixteenth-century epics and romances depict what medieval narratives do not, the virago or lady knight. Historical record suggests that the real power of medieval queens (at least in France) declined during the twelfth century. See Marion F. Facinger, "A Study of Medieval Queenship: Capetian France, 987–1237," in *Studies in Medieval and Renaissance History*, ed. William M. Bowsky (Lincoln: University of Nebraska Press, 1968), 5:3–47.

just identified as the mode of existence proper to women in and of the history of her society, she retires to her "most secret room," and so becomes the dramatic embodiment of the oblivion she has just condemned (3.75–77, 442–43).

As she withdraws to her room, the reader becomes aware that as the book has drawn to a close, its speakers have renounced the argumentative techniques of proof and disproof and have come increasingly to rely on those of persuading, urging, and warning. Cesare Gonzaga has invoked the image of Plato's army of lovers; the Magnifico has cautioned ladies against the deceits of lovers; and finally Gasparo has warned men against ladies who are ambitious and use love to advance themselves in society. The duchess's last word is an action—perhaps an odd way to conclude a text devoted to conversation. Yet it is arguable that this is precisely what Castiglione intended. By moving from attempts to define to attempts to persuade and at last to an enigmatic gesture of protest on the part of a woman, his text in fact exemplifies the very *loss* of control of its subject, woman, that would be the basis for her adequate fashioning, that is, one really designed to achieve the kind of freedom that the Magnifico alluded to earlier. This fashioning could be accomplished, Castiglione may be implying, only by a kind of negative capability, for all the words and images available to his protagonists are inevitably bound up with their male interests. It is not accidental therefore that Castiglione's ladies hardly utter a word throughout this entire defense of their sex. It is only their discomfort that is expressed in the brief comments of the duchess and Emilia Pia.

Castiglione's intentions aside, however, his third book illustrates the logical complexity that can characterize the genre of defense when concessions are made to woman's moral and intellectual equality with man in social and political settings that require her subordination to him. True, in Castiglione's fourth book Emilia finally orders Gasparo to prepare to stand trial for his misogyny (4.73), but the larger issues surrounding the question of woman's nature remain unresolved. Castiglione shows that typology, no matter how ideal, can be vitiated by an appeal to history; history, however, is subject to selective interpretations that have the effect of embarrassing and silencing those categories of persons which the historian has selected to illustrate slight or pernicious characters. And, as Emilia indicates, even complimentary histories are forgotten if their audiences are not disposed to remember them. Castiglione's feminism, if it can be termed such, appears to end in paradox. His retiring duchess reveals that Urbino's male defenders of women can promote the cause of sexual equality only by being silent. His defense of women is represented as an action that he, a male feminist, can only point to but not actually perform.

FRANCE

The Querelle des Femmes

The two principal vehicles for feminist debate in France were the literature of the popular *querelle des femmes* and the courtly doctrinal of princes. In virtually all writing about women, however, the substantive issues and rhetorical tropes of the *querelle* were represented in one way or another. Apart from treatises addressed primarily to questions of education, defenses of women were almost bound to attempt to refute the negative side in the *querelle* controversy. Of its supposedly misogynist texts, Jean de Meung's *Roman de la rose* was the most formidable. His notion of a typical woman, realized in his figure of La Vieille, was a sexually opportunistic, amoral person whose character was traceable to the disobedience of the first woman, Eve. That Jean's *Roman* was also an attack on the coy language of courtly discourse—language that by obscuring the real conflicts of relations between the sexes did little to express the interests of women—was usually overlooked.[22] What was finally at stake in the *querelle* as a whole, and the issue that defenders of women saw as central to their project, was the real power of woman, whether or not it was thought to have a positive (nurturing, conserving) or negative (debilitating, spoiling) effect. How this power was most commonly experienced and expressed is made clearer in works less erudite and even more popular than Jean's encyclopedic poem.[23]

[22]The language of the *Roman* caused Christine de Pisan to protest to her intellectual mentor, Pierre Col. Col argues for understanding Jean's text in relation to its author's intention, which he claims is "good" (*saint*); that is, "to show the madness of those who say that it is wrong to speak of the sexual organs [*les secrez membres*]." Christine de Pisan answers by asserting that no reader can be expected to have complete knowledge of an author's intention, and that texts are understood as their readers wish to understand them. She excuses the "reasonable embarrassment" of women readers and condemns Jean's text and language as "disgraceful with respect to all [categories of] persons." For this correspondence see C. F. Ward, *The Epistles on the "Romance of the Rose" and Other Documents in the Debate* (n.p., 1911), esp. letter 13, pp. 83–111. I cite portions of this text (89–91). For Pierre Col's position, see J. L. Baird, "Pierre Col and the *Querelle de la Rose*," *Philological Quarterly* 60, 3 (1981): 273–86. Useful studies of feminist argument and the status of woman in sixteenth-century France include Lula McDowell Richardson, *Forerunners of Feminism in French Literature of the Renaissance from Christine de Pisan to Marie de Gournay*, Johns Hopkins Studies in Romance Literatures and Languages 12 (Baltimore: Johns Hopkins University Press, 1929). For the medieval background, see also Beatrice Gottlieb, "The Problem of Feminism in the Fifteenth Century," in *Women of the Medieval World: Essays in Honor of John H. Mundy*, ed. Julius Kirshner and Suzanne Wemple (Oxford: Blackwell, 1985).

[23]For accounts of the background to the sixteenth-century *querelle* specifically, see, i.a., M. A. Screech, *The Rabelaisian Marriage: Aspects of Rabelais's Religion, Ethics, and Comic Philosophy* (London: Edward Arnold, 1958), 5–13; and E. V. Telle, *Marguerite d'Angoulême* (Toulouse: Lion, 1937), 9–68. Both critics regard the *querelle* mainly as a pretext for the demonstration of rhetorical virtuosity. But Telle also claims that the misogynist texts of

Les XV Joies de mariage (c. 1425), for example, portrays the wife as the virtual source of power within a family simply because she controls the erotic life of her husband. Setting aside any representation of the actual facts of married life (the repeated pregnancies, the frequency of death in childbirth), the view of marriage in *Les XV Joies* suggests that the negative characterizations of woman—she is a shrew, a spendthrift, a liar, a whore, and so forth—had their origin in the fear that woman might have the means to command men by virtue of her control of reproduction. The wife of *Les XV Joies* controls her husband through her sexuality; stronger than he is, she exhausts him physically and, in return for the sexual favors he would be better off without, gets from him various kinds of gifts that require him to spend more money than he has. Sexuality comes to represent the process by which women deplete the various kinds of reserves men have:

> After [the first months of marriage] the good husband is quite well exhausted and used up, for he always has cares and work and worries and must think of other things. He doesn't participate in the game any more, or just occasionally, to please his wife, and also [if] he can't do it as he would like he gives up altogether. If his wife doesn't do likewise, but is as desirous as she was at first, and [if] the husband's ardor continues to diminish, the pleasures, the delights, the lovely pastimes that they used to have together in youth and when the husband was potent turn to quarreling and contention, and also as his ardor diminishes, they begin to fight. And when her husband's ardor no longer is sufficient for the wife, even though she may be a good wife and wish to do no wrong, she believes that her husband is less potent [than other men] and that she has a good reason to believe it, since she has tried him and he doesn't satisfy her [*il ne lui suffist pas*]. It stands to reason that one man ought to suffice for one woman, or nature has not organized things proportionately, and also I think that if one man is not enough for one woman, God and the Church would have ordered that a woman could have two husbands or as many as would satify her.[24]

Here the wife's behavior inverts the *conserving* function it is supposed to have. A woman's chastity and thrift are two aspects of the same virtue;

---

the *querelle*—essentially reactions to the literature of courtly love—actually affected the status of women: "The result of their repeated attacks was a truly hostile opinion of women that was not exclusively 'literary' but affected the mentality of readers and consequently attitudes between the sexes" (23).

[24]*Les XV Joies de mariage*, ed. Jean Rychner (Geneva: Droz, 1963), 58–59. According to Rychner (vii–lxix), the text was probably written by a cleric in the first quarter of the fifteenth century. Printed editions appear through the sixteenth century. For a brief study of *Les XV Joies* as a historical document, see Madeleine Jeay, "Sexuality and Family in Fifteenth-Century France: Are Literary Sources a Mask or a Mirror?" *Journal of Family History* 4, 4 (1979): 328–45.

both act to preserve her husband's strength and thus to ensure and testify
to his control of her and her activities. By asking her husband for more
sex than he can reasonably give, a wife figuratively opens the door on her
restrictive domesticity. Her strength is anomalous; it even violates the
laws of nature and Scripture, which are predicated on the fact that every
woman can be satisfied by a single man. If she cannot, of course, the case
for a celibate life according to the dicta of Paul is the stronger, since
marriage can lead only to physical, economic, and moral collapse. The
compatibility of the married couple rests in any case squarely on the wife.
Taking seriously the concerns of *Les XV Joies*, Jacques le Grand declares
in his *Livre intitulé de bonnes meurs* (1490): "Both parties [to a marriage]
must be good." But because a husband is often given to doubt, a wife
must be "well behaved not only in her body but in her bearing"; she must
do nothing that would cause criticism, for it often happens that by their
stupid ways wives make their husbands suspicious.[25]

Reaction to the fear of "women on top" explains, in part at least, the
production of a feminist literature that attempts to mediate between a
notion of woman as the daughter of Eve and also as created in the image
of God. Here, generally, an attempt to determine abstractly how the
nature of woman compares with that of man (how is her difference to be
evaluated?) is followed by a discussion of what its devaluation practically
means and has meant to society. A common strategy is to show that a
deficiency of certain attributes, particularly physical strength, is the basis
of great virtue. Because physical strength is associated with acts of
ambition and conquest, it is argued, woman is not given to pride. And in
any case, she cannot be blamed for acts she cannot commit. This line of
reasoning negates the types both of the shrew and the virago. Finally, it
makes a strength of weakness, and celebrates the political constructive-
ness of a kind of Christian passivity that is supposed to characterize ideal
feminine behavior. In other words, it praises women for those submis-
sive qualities that, according to the negative side in the *querelle*, it is most
feared they do not have.

To contradict the idea of woman as degenerate, whose type is the
faithless and disobedient Eve, a writer had to undertake to interpret the
first three chapters of Genesis. Often his first move is to point out that
nowhere in the story of creation is there authority for a type of woman
about which to generalize. The anonymous author of the *Dialogue apologétique* (1516) criticizes such a generalization and everything it comes to
imply through the reflections of his character Femme defendent. To open

---

[25]Jacques le Grand, *Le Livre intitulé de bonnes meurs* (n.p., 1490), sig. g3. This treatise was
printed by Caxton as *The Boke of Good Maners* in 1487.

her case, she asserts that one cannot do as Malbouche, the misogynist, does—"write against all women without making any exceptions" on the authority of Scripture.[26] Her full defense then proceeds in three stages: she comments on the origins of humankind in Genesis 1–3, and on the catastrophic roles of Adam and Eve; she differentiates between the spiritual and legal terms of marriage; and she examines the ways in which vices appear more egregiously in man and in woman. The common point to all her observations is the meaning of woman's first creation in Genesis 1, "that [God] created in his image man and woman." Together these creatures signify human nature, and man's second creation, in Genesis 2, has meaning only as it fulfills the promise of his first: "without woman man was not perceived as good"; not until God fashioned woman could he declare that "human nature" was good (d7v). Femme's immediate conclusion is that woman has the same intelligence as man:

> Man and woman are of one kind, of one essence and substantial nature, and no different except accidentally . . . therefore the woman as well as the man has all that belongs essentially and naturally to the human being, for otherwise human beings would not constitute a single species [une espèce]. Therefore it is certain that the proper and natural condition of human nature is that woman is a rational creature who uses understanding, common sense, and reason. [c8v]

With intelligence comes the ability to choose freely among alternatives. Consequently, Femme can exonerate Eve of Genesis 3 by making Adam as responsible as she is for the Fall. Femme insists that together with intelligence both man and woman have free will, and that Eve did not persuade Adam to sin but that he did so "willingly" (par sa volonté). Moreover, it was he, not Eve, who knew what was at stake: "Adam heard and understood God's commandment that was made to him personally and he saw the danger" (a2v). Their respective punishments indicate the extent of their responsibility. Eve is punished in her own person, but Adam's punishment extends to the whole earth (a6). Femme's interpretation of Genesis is unorthodox but it establishes a point crucial to her subsequent argument: in the relations between man and woman it is the fact of free choice that in itself implies their moral equality. In other words, woman is not, just as Eve was not, the incarnation of irresistible temptation; she does not have the power to provoke man to do things he does not choose to do.

According to Femme, marriage was instituted as a union of man and woman (Adam and Eve), as equals. By requiring the consent of both

[26]Dialogue apologétique excusant ou défendant le dévot sexe fémenin [sic] (Paris, 1516), sig. a1.

parties (which assumes their free choice in the matter), marriage recreates woman as the social equal of her husband, if not of all men: "The husband makes a promise in public to his wife before the church just as the wife to the husband. And because this [promise] is in both cases the same, it obligates the man as much as the woman. For the woman chooses the man by consent and will just as the husband takes the wife for his delight and pleasure" (a7). Then, citing Hugh of St. Victor—"mulier facta equalitate societatis"—Femme goes on to state: "[She] is *equal* in companionship [*est faicte à équalité de compaignie*]," and it is in this sense, too, that she can be said to "serve" her husband: "They are joined by the sovereign virtue of love and pleasure" (a7v). In other words, marriage reenacts the order of the sexes as it is determined in Genesis 1. It is only insofar as it is established "by law" that marriage assigns to man his relative superiority; his superiority functions only in matters that can be referred to law, and is subject to various kinds of legal restrictions. The "rights of marriage" is an aggregate of "conventions, agreements, promises of one to the other, of husband to wife and of wife to husband" (a7). Such rights do not obtain in other domestic relations, as between master and servant or parent and child.

Here Femme reinterprets Genesis 2 and 3 so that the effective meaning of the wife's ontological inferiority and political subordination is relatively restricted. Whereas in the *Institutio matrimonii christiani* Erasmus saw that the wife's spiritual equality was circumscribed by her duty to obey her husband in almost all respects, the author of the *Dialogue* sees that it gives her a choice in all activities except those from which she is excluded by law. If a wife is required to follow her husband's directions, it is only in regard to affairs in which it is conventionally and legally his duty to take charge. Even her legal status is relatively free. Femme, like Aristotle, recognizes three principal relations: those obtaining between master and slave, between parents and children, and between husband and wife. He sees that the first is characterized by a power "of full and complete dominance" (*depositive ou dominative totale*), the second by power "royal or imperial," and the last by power "political or civil" (*politique ou civil*). The power in marriage is therefore essentially that between citizens, and marriage is a "civil and political government in which everyone is a free burgess and not a slave or a servant" (a8).

All this is theory, however. Femme goes on to claim that in practice the principles of equality governing marriage and political life are perverted. Men are in fact on top, women are wrongfully suppressed, and society is the loser. Criticizing government by men, Femme claims that men everywhere and among themselves are driven by ambition and abuse their "seigneurie": "everything is subject to their ambition and pride" (b2v). The consequences are war, sedition, the destruction of cities, and all kinds of crimes against the individual person (b6). Women remain virtuous in part because of the inherent intellectual gifts that derive from their physical weakness—"those that have less bodily strength have more wit, wisdom, and knowledge in their souls." The naturally superior understanding of woman is not developed, however, because she does not receive an education: "Women are not sent to a teacher or master who could give them doctrine and instruction as men are. Were these girls to be as carefully taught as men are, certainly they would acquire as much if not more learning and knowledge." Femme implies that, unlike men, women lack ambition and pride and would not make war, foment sedition, and so forth were their status as "free citizens" realized. Men are more often "démoniacques" than women. Reason is less reliable in them: "Man more often loses his common sense and rational understanding than woman does, as if in him they were easier to lose or not preserve" (d). A feminized civic order is therefore presumably closer to a Christian ideal than are contemporary societies organized according to patriarchal principles. Whereas Barbaro found in woman's political impotence a guarantee of social stability, Femme finds that her disempowerment makes for social chaos.

The *Dialogue apologétique* is unusual in commenting so extensively on the subject of the *equality* between husband and wife, man and woman. More common in the literature that addresses the *querelle* are statements concerning the *complementarity* of man and woman, or the *mutuality* of their responses to life. The person who determines the activities, responsibilities, and duties that constitute such comforting relations, and to whom they are assigned, is tacitly assumed to be the husband. Exemplary of the concern for harmony in marriage is Pierre Lesnauderie's *Louange de mariage* (1523), an extended argument against celibacy and for the active over the contemplative life. The latter was doubtless appealing for many reasons, but aside from such obvious attractions as the accessibility of books and the time to read them, it was doctrinally correct for clerics to believe that it promised a better chance for salvation than did the active life. Questioning this doctrine, Lesnauderie declares that although one serves God in contemplation, one serves the republic in marriage and the active life (b2).[27] In this venture, a wife proves a useful adjunct: "When you have a wife, you can hand over your business and leave your house, for she will take good care of them [both]" (b2v). Nor

---

[27]Pierre Lesnauderie, *La Louange du mariage* (Paris, 1525). In his prologue the author identifies himself as "scribe des privilèges ecclésiastiques de l'université de Caen"; he writes in French "affin que les femmes l'entendent" (b).

is a husband's involvement in the world to be equated with a fall from paradisal and celibate grace. In fact, the reverse is true, Lesnauderie here argues, "for the more difficulty and trial that one has in this world from serving God and suffering, the more merit one has toward God" (b2); and he carefully points out that the pain and tribulation he refers to are not to be understood to come from the woman his reader might marry but from a political character that husband and wife could be said to *share*. If from time to time the active life is the scene of destruction, the cause is not chiefly women but men to whom women respond: "in any case, the principal cause is the activity of men. For Medea killed her children because Jason her husband was disloyal" (b4v). Like Femme of the anonymous *Dialogue apologétique*, Lesnauderie transforms the relative powerlessness of women, the extent to which their actions are responsive rather than initiatory, into a positive sign; but in his case, it is a sign of the couple's common responsibility rather than of the wife's feminine virtue.[28] This idea raises a question that other writers will address, that is, the extent to which a shared life entails a practical equality of persons.

The contention that woman was degenerate by nature could also be examined in light of authorities revered for insights into the law of nature and for the translation of this law into the *ius gentium*, or law of nations. For Renaissance defenders of women, the most formidable texts of this kind were the dialogues of Plato, particularly the *Meno* and the *Republic*. His assertions of the intellectual, moral, social, and political equality of sex and gender served to test Christian doctrine and the scripture upon which it was based. That Plato is not cited more often by feminists can probably be traced to the fact that he advocates the establishment of a commonality of goods, including wives, and is thus in violation of what was held to be a right of property originating with God's gifts to Adam. But Martin Le Franc's dialogue *Le Champion des dames* (1530) refers to both Plato and the *Digests* of Justinian, the great repository of the *ius gentium*.

Franc Vouloir, Le Franc's feminist, arguing against the misogynist Malebouche, claims that Plato wished women to assume powers of government in a number of ways—law, civil administration, magistracies, defense: "He wanted them to study (their wits would thereby not be lost), to argue cases in public, to render reasonable decisions as

---

[28]Lesnauderie also praises the virile woman, presumably as a way of encouraging his reader to marry. He attributes the elevation of Pope Joan to the papacy to the high estimation in which her learning was held, her breach of decorum by cross-dressing and her deception of her fellow clergy apparently notwithstanding: "And she was loved for her knowledge and her literary ability; for when Pope Leo IV died, she was dressed as a man and elected pope and composed musical scores that are still sung in churches today" (f3).

judges, to hold great offices, and in the case of war, to wield bows and slings." Plato, he argues, gives good counsel here, for nature herself gave woman the "wit" to know "justice and law."[29] But like the author of the *Dialogue apologétique*, who distinguishes between what Scripture reveals and what society practices, Le Franc also believes that this ancient vision of a political equality of men and women does not in any way inform present social mores. For Christians, he admits, inequality is in part a consequence of the Fall. "By nature" woman does not deserve subjection to man; it is rather "her forfeit [that] places her beneath him" (188). This forfeit is made more onerous than it should be, however, by the strength of man relative to woman and also by his fear of her lawfulness relative to his criminality. Asking "by what game have . . . [women] lost," Franc Vouloir points to the cause of oppression: "You [men] see quite well that when they govern you, the licence that you have to do evil will be revoked and your condition reformed. You keep them subject, so that they don't dare raise their eyes or speak of any of your deeds." Finally this treatment results in the silence and stupification of the whole sex. Unable to voice their thoughts, women soon lose the power to think. Their pervasive intimidation transforms their "wits" into "very little nothings [*très menues chosettes*]" (186). The most principled of human laws, the *ius gentium*, is no help here, since it has been perverted in practice. God instituted society in the first couple, who walked "arm in arm" so that they might live "as one" (*conjoinctement*), and, Franc Vouloir implies, this ideal is reflected in the *Digests* of Justinian.[30] But it was ignored by the

[29]Martin Le Franc, *Le Champion des dames*, ed. Arthur Piaget, Mémoires et Documents Publiés par la Société d'Histoires de la Suisse Romande, 3d ser., 8 (Lausanne: Payot, 1968), 185–86. The text was written between 1440 and 1442 specifically to answer detractors such as Jean de Meung. It was printed first in Lyon in 1485 and again in Paris in 1530. The title as it appears in the 1530 edition continues: *Contenant la deffence des dames, contre malebouche et ses consors et victoire d'icelles*. The context of Le Franc's debate is courtly, allegorical, and obviously derived from the *Roman de la rose*; it is the most conventional of all the defenses printed in France in this period. In a dedicatory letter to Philippe, duc de Bourgogne, the author (a secretary of the duc de Savoi), praises the duke for his loyal defense of women and asks him to accept his book "with humanity" (*humainement*).

[30]Although the laws of Justinian reformed domestic law in order to ameliorate the condition of married women, especially with respect to property, it did not generally give them a legal status equal to that of men. See Charles Phineas Sherman, *Roman Law in the Modern World* (Boston, 1917), 91–93, 109. But only portions of France, mostly in southern regions, were governed by laws of inheritance that reflected Roman rather than customary law. See Jean-Louis Flandrin, *Families in Former Times: Kinship, Household, and Sexuality*, trans. Richard Southern (Cambridge: Cambridge University Press, 1976), 74–85; and René Pillorget, "Patrimoine, prestige et puissance," in *Le Tige et le rameau: Familles anglaises et françaises, 16e–18e siècles* (Paris: Calmann-Lévy, 1979), 92–104. During the sixteenth century, Roman law appears to be ambiguous in practice with respect to guaranteeing rights and privileges for women; while it enhanced a woman's right to own property, the *potestas patris*, mandating the absolute obedience of wives and children, obviously tended to limit her autonomy. See chap. 3, n. 58.

Romans, who were "proud, haughty," and did not even follow their own rules. The Roman practice of treating woman as inferior is actually not Roman law: "It is not written in any tablet or code or digest; I'm sure of that." Men's indifference to law is further manifest in an unwillingness to take note of or consider woman, who is thereby struck from the records of history, "for these evil men take no more account of a woman than of a nanny-goat" (187).

Le Franc does not propose a return to the practices instituted under Justinian; but by explaining more fully what marriage means, he does suggests that its hierarchical order, consisting of a superior husband and a subordinate wife, perverts the whole idea of walking "arm in arm." Instituted and maintained by force, the relations of man and wife in marriage defy the Pauline rule by which one assigns one's spouse power over oneself. For the purposes of his argument, Le Franc interprets Paul's dictum concerning the sexual life of couples—doubtless originally directed at married Christians who elected celibacy without the consent of their spouse—so that it allusively signifies a more general kind of complementarity of authority and power. Franc Vouloir reminds Malebouche that the sexual life of couples is, according to Paul, an exchange of the powers of their respective bodies, an exchange that conveys a kind of knowledge of the other which is also, at some level, a means of identification with the other. To withhold the power of the body is to deny licit knowledge: "Man does not have the power over his own body and he sins and does evil if woman does not have knowledge of it." "Sexual difference" (*leurs corporelles diversitez*) is, moreover, the basis for spiritual understanding: "Let us turn to an understanding of our bodiless souls," he declares (189). The associative logic of Franc Vouloir's argument represents the empowerment of women as an extension of their sexual power over men, a power that is at once a *congnoissance* of the flesh and the knowledge of the world they have been denied through the force of the male body but which they ought to have gained by virtue of their right to that body. Le Franc's earlier remark that men control women by their superior strength retrospectively acquires additional meaning, for such action misuses the power of the male body against its rightful owner, the female. For Le Franc, Pauline sexual mystery enfolds the image of an egalitarian social order. In marriage, a woman—even of modest rank— can experience equality; his definition adjusts her status in a way that resolves the tensions generated by the *querelle* between woman as sexually powerful and debilitating, on the one hand, and as the object of patriarchal discipline and control, on the other. It gives her a place in a lawful society without recreating the hierarchy of spouses in inverted form—woman on top and governing, man below and governed.

Evaluating Virtue

Whether or not woman was capable of participating in public life was also a practical question. Before the thirteenth century, women of rank had inherited property and therefore rights and offices under feudal law. While everyone recognized that theoretically women in themselves were a class of persons inferior and subordinate to men, the real effects of this categorization could be mitigated by particular circumstances, especially widowhood. Sixteenth-century women of rank, by contrast, were *comparatively* disempowered. In some cases, they could no longer inherit the property upon which rights and offices were entailed; in other cases, new laws superseded the customary arrangements that had allowed them to function as men economically and even to some extent politically.[31] After 1464, the Salic law prevented any woman from inheriting the French crown; this was the culmination of a gradual reduction in the power of the French queen which had taken place over the previous two hundred years.[32] These developments are reflected in Renaissance literature on the education of royal and noble children. The virtues demanded of women in general—silence and chastity, often interpreted broadly to include honesty or lack of deceit—particularly disqualified women of rank for the court politics they could have expected to engage in were they men.

Early in the sixteenth century readers in France could find in print two treatises written to instruct royal and noble daughters: Anne de France's *Enseignements . . . à sa fille, Susanne de Bourbon*, composed between 1503 and 1505 and published in Lyon sometime early in the century, and Jean Marot's *Doctrinal des princesses et nobles dames*, of the same period. A comparison of these texts with those intended for royal and noble boys and men reveals how diametrically opposed are the chief features of the

[31]"From the beginning of the sixteenth century, the success of the renascence of Roman law had the effect, in France, of reinforcing, at least on the strictly legal level, the inequality [between the sexes] in the interests of the man": Pierre Petot and André Andenbossche, "Le Statut de la femme dans les pays coutumiers français du XIIIe au XVIIe siècle," in *La Femme*, 244. This useful and succinct essay gives a comprehensive overview of women and the law in France. For changes in the seventeenth century, see Jean Portemer, "Le Statut de la femme en France depuis la réformation des coutumes jusqu'à la rédaction du code civil," in ibid., 447–97. See also Emmanuel Le Roy Ladurie, "A System of Customary Law: Family Structures and Inheritance Customs in Sixteenth-Century France," in *Family and Society: Selections from the Annales, Economies, Societés, Civilisations*, ed. Robert Forster and Orest Ranum, trans. Elborg Forster and Patricia M. Ranum (Baltimore: Johns Hopkins University Press, 1976), 75–103.

[32]For contemporary discussions of the Salic law, see Claude de Seyssell, *The Monarchy of France*, trans. J. H. Hexter, ed. Donald Kelley (New Haven: Yale University Press, 1981), and François Hotman, *Francogallia (1573)*, trans. J. H. M. Salmon, ed. Ralph Giesey (Cambridge: Cambridge University Press, 1972).

didactic literature intended for girls and women of similar ranks. Erasmus's *Education of a Christian Prince* (1515) and his *Enchiridion* (1504) are devoted to examining the ethically vexed and contested problems of political and public activity in relation to Christian morals. Is a Christian prince or knight, magistrate or administrator, a contradiction in terms? Erasmus's questions are directed at the moral conduct that is both desirable and possible for a governor to pursue in the public interest; their answers have meaning chiefly within the limits of political discourse. He makes no mention of queens regent or regnant and probably did not think that his typical Christian prince could be a woman. Treatises on the education of ordinary children, such as Matteo Vegio's *De educatione liberorum* and Jacopo Sadoleto's *De liberis*, published in French translations in 1513 and 1535 respectively, both drastically limiting instruction for girls, give some indication of the restrictive conventions that allowed Erasmus to assume he need not discuss the education of a princess in political terms. Even some women who managed to participate in public life because they could claim to have a stake in the outcome of a religious conflict showed that they were persuaded of the propriety of such discrimination by using language that implicitly called their own activity into question. Marie Dentière, for example, writing to Marguerite de Navarre in a letter published in Geneva in 1539, speaks of Protestants as "[you] effeminate [*éffeminez*] persons, beside your senses, without fear of God; you are not at all dreadful, for you don't dare to see or understand the truth."[33] In other words, a politically irresponsible and ineffectual person has a woman's character, and vice versa.

The treatises of Anne de France and Marot suggest that the authority and power of queens and noblewomen, although ill defined and (evidently) diminishing, were perceived as dangerous to the welfare of courtly society and ultimately of society as a whole. They can be said to express directly what Castiglione's courtiers only imply. According to most prevailing law and custom, women of rank were subordinate in some degree to those men in their families who had patriarchal authority. Yet practically, by virtue of their status, they might also exert a certain control over men who were their social inferiors. This control might be manifest as a kind of influence or as an overt command. In the first instance, it could be considered an expression of power, whether power was established through force of personality, intellect, or some more

[33]*Correspondance des réformateurs*, ed. A. L. Hermingard (Geneva and Paris, 1874), 4:299. Later literature makes an effective distinction between the feminine and the effeminate, or the womanly and the womanish; such a distinction is implicit in the positive characterizations of woman as peaceful, law-abiding, etc. The relevance of these ideas to Renaissance ideas of gender is discussed in chap. 3.

particular attribute; in the second instance, it could be considered authoritative, issuing from a specific office. Depending on their circumstances,
queens and noblewomen might possess considerable power; they also
sometimes acquired the authority attendant upon an office. The problem
for educators and moralists was that the power of women was rarely
authoritative; it was characteristically informal and ad hoc. Thus it was a
difficult subject to discuss in general terms, and in the absence of rules a
woman of rank was vulnerable to repressive measures, especially those
taken by an irate husband who felt she had behaved insubordinately. The
case of Catherine of Aragon is illustrative of the fate of a queen whose
actual power was thought to have exceeded the limits of her wifely
vocation. (Further down the social scale, the forms of husbandly control
were cruder. Almost every treatise on marriage forbids wife-beating, a
fact that suggests this kind of abuse must have been common. Christine
de Pisan suggests that women ran a greater risk of being beaten when
they exhibited greater competence than men, even in household affairs.)
The treatises of Anne de France and Marot are probably typical in not
revealing just how much authority and power their prospective reader is
or is not to have. What they do make clear is that even a woman of
relatively exalted rank is expected to take account of her feminine weakness and, as a rule, to *decline* to use whatever authority or power she may
have by virtue of her rank. She may need to mask her knowledge of court
affairs and appear to be innocent of intrigue, as Anne de France advises;
or she may be treated in such a way as to make such knowledge impossible to obtain, as Marot prefers. In either case, she cannot function politically.

Many of Anne de France's points of instruction are conventional and
could have been directed at a son. Her daughter, Susanne de Bourbon, is
warned that "the first and main point [of government] above all others is
that with devotion and all your power you keep from doing, saying, or
thinking anything for which God could be angry with you"; and that she
should not trust in worldly things, especially her own understanding:
"Do not trust in anything, [not even] the sense, strength, or understanding that you may think you have . . . live in great fear and be always on
your guard, lest you be deceived."[34] Other points could have been

---

[34]Anne de France, *Les Enseignements . . . à sa fille Susanne de Bourbon* (Moulins, 1878), 2,
7. The text was written between the death of Anne's husband, Pierre II, in 1503, and the
marriage of Susanne, in 1505. It was printed in Lyon, without a date. The printer is
unknown; he was perhaps Geoffrey Tory. Anne de France, also known as Anne de
Beaujeu, "was the virtual ruler of France during the first eight years of the reign of her
brother Charles VIII": René de Maulde La Clavière, *The Women of the Renaissance: A Study
of Feminism*, trans. George Herbert Ely (New York: Putnam, 1901), 25n. Anne figures
importantly throughout this erudite but for the most part undocumented history.

intended only for a daughter. The occupations recommended to Susanne are not designed to instill self-reliance. She is to avoid laziness, to pray, to read the lives of the saints; she may play certain games, such as chess, but not with "too much care," since she might easily become "intemperate": "such things one should use and take in a tempered fashion [attrempée-ment], that is, instead of doing nothing and as a way of passing time" (9–10). The indifference that Susanne must show for intellectual sport matches the diffidence with which she must conduct herself socially. She must avoid above all the impression of *being in command*. If she has to deal with "foolish conduct," she must discipline wrongdoers gently: "Do not seek to reprove or correct them in a haughty manner but in a sweet and gentle way, by proposing new and decorous habits or praising others" (16–17). If she happens to learn what is going on at court, she is to avoid the appearance of being concerned, and not to risk offending wrong-doers: "As far as the court is concerned, it is inappropriate for a young woman to interfere in many things, and wise men say that one ought to have eyes to look at everything and see nothing, ears to hear everything and know nothing, and a tongue to answer everyone but to speak nothing prejudicial" (20). The appearance of innocent circumspection she must cultivate will be enhanced if she actually *avoids* knowing what others are doing: "Take care only for yourself, without asking or seeking to know the deeds or the conduct of others." If information comes her way, she is to pretend ignorance: "If my chance you know something, take care that it is not made public by you; whatever is asked of you, make an effort to avoid knowledge of it" (23). These warnings seem to come from the author's personal experience of court politics; certainly they convey a sense of her own isolation and her fear that her presence at court would elicit envy rather than awe and loyalty.

Jean Marot's brief *Doctrinal* reveals the principal means by which women of high rank were not only counseled but actually educated to be deferential. Astute courtiers (and all persons who did public business) had always understood that to feign a position or attitude was an accept-able mode of procedure under certain circumstances. Humanists who attacked Machiavelli for advocating strategies of deceit rather than open and honest behavior, as did Innocent Gentillet, were more interested in preserving the *image* of the beneficent governor (and thus the possibility of absolute monarchy) than in establishing preferred political practice. Castiglione's *Cortegiano* is a testament to the use to which social artifice may be put, just as the first book of More's *Utopia* is an indication of the risk of its abuse. In Marot's *Doctrinal*, however, women are routinely denied the resources of the mask, the lie, and the ruse. For women who found themselves in circumstances in which they might exert power or be authoritative—that is, for queens and noblewomen—such limitations on their ability to act could prove debilitating.

Marot's views of the speech of women is typical. On the keeping of promises, he declares: "The heart and the mouth of a woman ought to be the same [literally, equal (*égalle*)], for the heart that speaks through a disloyal [*desloyalle*, i.e., hypocritical] mouth is like arsenic in honey."[35] The image inverts the conventional metaphor for beneficent artifice—a "honeyed" art that masks the "bitter medicine" of correction—and suggests that while men can resort to a doubleness of expression (especially for didactic purposes), women must speak only the plain truth. The injunction is an extension of a more pervasive requirement that applies to women of all categories, that is, to be as glass, to mirror a man's will as well as to be transparent to him. In the same vein, Marot warns against violating other conversational norms, specifically by criticizing others: "There is no person more disagreeable than one who bad-mouths others; for the incurable hurt of a false report is much worse than that of a cannon," and by speaking indecorously: "A princess ought to speak neither too much nor too little, for too much detracts from her respectability, and too little shows simplemindedness" (180–81). In short, he urges his princess to restrict her conversation to innocuous pleasantries, a prospect that might seem innocuous itself, were it not that she may actually be required to rule. Only one of his points seems to allude to this possibility. As if to acknowledge that Susanne might actually have to perform some official function, Marot goes on to add that she is to recognize that political power comes from God: "God alone gives him [or her (the ruler)] government" (183). His source is Romans 13:1, a text frequently quoted in contemporary treatises on government: "Let every soul be subject to the higher powers. For there is no power but God: the powers that be are ordained of God." Prospective (and of course male) magistrates were reminded regularly of this condition of rule, which was taken to mean that no officeholder should abuse the prerogatives of his office to behave in ways contrary to divine law. Yet for a prospective *woman* magistrate—however fanciful such a creature might be, at least in France—a reference to Romans 13 would have had a second significance; for it was also and more commonly invoked to warn *subjects* of the dangers of disobedience and rebellion. And because woman was always in some sense subject to man, Susanne must have understood the reference to have a double application. Her authority and power as a holder of

---

[35]Jean Marot, *Le Doctrinal des princesses et nobles dames*, in *Les Oeuvres de Jean Marot* (Paris, 1723), 179. The *Doctrinal* was first published in 1537.

office would have been circumscribed legally by the theoretically higher authority of the man to whom she was, as a daughter or a wife, subject.

Underlying the assumptions that sustained the limited education of queens and noblewomen was a real confusion concerning what constituted the civic virtue of woman. The problem is essentially as Boccaccio expressed it in *De mulieribus claris*: by what means did or could a woman gain public recognition? In simpler fashion, Jehan Du Pré's *Palais des nobles dames* (1530s?) reveals how difficult it was to evaluate activities of women by reference to consistent criteria, and therefore also to conceptualize credible categories of female virtue.

Du Pré's treatise is a response to a complaint by a visional figure, Noblesse féminine, who appears to tell him that women are the objects of libelous writings, "false in everything, denying our virtuous and good deeds."[36] When replying to her request for a history of worthies, however, Du Pré selects his examples according to categories whose common denominator is simply rarity. Thus "ladies ennobled by arms and war" are matched by (among others) "virgins," "women who have lived to a great age," "women who have given birth in an unnatural way," and "ladies for whom the pagan gods, having felt desire, have transformed themselves into members of different species, in order to achieve their pleasure." Du Pré is clearly confused about what virtues he wishes to celebrate; rather than evaluate the actions of women by referring to their social or political consequences, he chooses to focus on their uniqueness. Like Boccaccio, Du Pré regards the fame of women as a kind of notoriety.[37]

The difficulty of developing consistent criteria of value in the *querelle* literature is encountered again in Syphorien Champier's *Nef des dames vertueuses* (1515), a defense of women that illustrates the bias inherent in the author's point of view and hence the inevitably subjective nature of all criteria of value. Champier represents himself as inspired by a female muse and expresses feminist opinions; but, less subtle than Castiglione, he also reveals the anxiety with which he argues for the equality of women. The massive influence of the literature of the *querelle* debate in France made it inevitable that there the literature of defense would exhibit

---

[36]Jehan Du Pré, *Le Palais des nobles dames* (n.p., n.d), sig. a6v. Du Pré's treatise is dedicated to Marguerite de France, probably the sister of François I.

[37]Cf. Vergil's treatment of the *fama* of Dido in contrast to that of Aeneas. For the hero, *fama* designates his reputation, which is celebrated by the poet and validated by his heavenly muse, who helps him unroll the scrolls of war. For Dido, *fama* signifies her notoriety, which is fostered by unreliable rumor. See *Aeneid* 4, 173–94, 298–99. For a study of Renaissance women writers and literary fame, see Ann Rosalind Jones, "Surprising Fame: Renaissance Gender Ideologies and Women's Lyric," in *The Poetics of Gender*, ed. Nancy K. Miller (New York: Columbia University Press, 1986), 74–95.

a greater degree of conventional argument and coded discourse than comparable writing in Italy or England, at least during the first half of the sixteenth century. Like Le Franc's *Champion*, Champier's text is indebted to the tradition of courtly compliment and the medieval *débat d'amour*. Dedicated to Anne de France, it invokes many of the authorities cited in Anne's own *Enseignements*. Unlike these works, however, it represents in dramatic terms the interpretive problem created by the intention of its author to praise what he also reveals he would like to control.

Champier's argument proceeds through two phases. The first is apologetic, the second analytical. His work begins with his account of his audience with a visional Dame Prudence, who complains that virtuous women have not been recognized. He responds by illustrating the mutuality of the relationship of men and women (and therefore the interrelatedness of their moral natures), and he describes history as a scene of feminine heroism. These words of affirmation and praise of woman's virtue are then subsumed under the general caveat, especially pertinent for his royal reader, that all authority and power come from God. But Champier also infuses his text with a critical ambiguity. His points regarding the virtue of woman are framed by observations that indicate a degree of uncertainty surrounding his defense: laws and customs of marriage are culturally variable, and women do not express themselves or their interests because they lack the knowledge to do so. These observations draw attention to the author's role as a visionary. In what sense can his source, Dame Prudence, be said to be authoritative? How can he listen to her, report what is universally and objectively true of prudence, if he is, as by his own admission he must be, merely an exponent of a particular set of culturally variable practices? Practices, moreover, that concern subjects who do not express themselves? The reader who reflects on the implications of Champier's description of his defense may hear the author's voice as less like that of the philosopher whose reveries are informed by an ideal *sophia* figure than like that of the lover whose dream is a projection of his own desires.

Champier defends woman on both ontological and political grounds. In terms of natural philosophy, he sees her as complementary to man. He refers to Plutarch's notion of man as fire and woman as water to describe their physical interdependence. As fire "purges" water, so water "restrains" fire: "So man cannot live in the world well alone and without woman. And woman without man is barren."[38] Women are the vessels of generation; to blame them is also to blame our families and our heritage (cv). Moving to Scripture, Champier states that it is through women and

[38]Syphorien Champier, *La Nef des dames vertueuses* (Paris, 1515), sig. b3v.

their generative powers that the future is guaranteed: "Because man is mortal and cannot live forever in this world, God wanted to give him a companion like himself to bring forth other individual human beings" (15v). These images of complementarity and likeness reflecting an elementary opposition that becomes generative serve as the conceptual basis for Champier's principal point: that legally woman is man's equal in most respects.

Like the anonymous author of the *Dialogue apologétique*, he stresses the relative insignificance of woman's subordination in law and "national custom" (*les constitutions du pais*), specifically by pointing out that such law is not "natural," as is the child's subordination to the father, but civil, determined by positive law: "The wife ought to be subject to her husband not as a child to its father . . . for the father rules the child by natural law and the mother by conventional and political [i.e., positive] law." A father is completely responsible for his child, but a husband is linked to his wife in a union of equals: "And the woman is always and in every respect equal to her husband. And the child is not [equal to the father] and for this reason the husband is to treat his wife well and support her in all cases" (18v). Even less is she to be regarded as a servant; her "service" to her husband, such as it is, originates in an act of will and is the result of a conscious choice. So too her wifely virtues of humility and obedience: "if she serves him it is because she is humble and obedient and not because she is a servant" (k). The language of equality here is, however, not allowed to stand quite unqualified. For Champier later asserts that if a wife is not the servant of her husband, she is certainly the servant of God: "For the lady or the princess is the servant of God and is the governor over many persons and the more power and authority [*domination et auctorité*] she has, the more she ought to thank and love God" (18v). Were the subject of this statement a nobleman or prince, it would convey unexceptionable political doctrine; because a noblewoman or a princess is addressed, it carries the extra meaning that I alluded to earlier in connection with Marot. A wife is obliged to see in her husband the image of God; should she acquire a magistracy, her authority and power to administer the law would be accordingly compromised.

But of greater interest than Champier's defense, as I have suggested, are the philosophical and rhetorical contexts in which he situates it. He prefaces his analysis of the status of woman according to marriage law by pointing out that the place of woman in a society—insofar as it is typified in marriage—cannot be imagined to be fixed by laws of nature because in fact marriage arrangements vary from culture to culture: "But marriages were constituted differently in different places. At first, Moors, Egyptians, Indians, Persians, Garamantes, Parthians, Thracians, and all barbarians had many wives. Some had two, others had as many as their wealth would allow" (15v). The ancient Hebrews had many wives; the Romans could divorce and remarry. Moreover, the basis upon which these practices vary reflects differences in social and economic status more often than divine or natural law: certainly "God's law does not permit repudiation or separation" (16). Champier's opponents could, of course, make a case against pagan practices on the grounds that they violated divine law, but they could not so confidently have claimed that pagan practices could not instance a violation of natural law, which, as Aquinas had demonstrated, was simply the product of human reason. At the very least, such a claim would leave open the question of authority. Culturally variable practices can correspond to a law of nature only if it is very loosely defined (as Montaigne was later to assert). If the subordination of woman is not a fact of societies everywhere, pagan and Christian, then it is unlikely to be able to qualify as natural law. Champier's allusion to the cultural relativity of marriage practices vitiates natural law as legitimating the inferior and subordinate status of women.[39]

As telling in Champier's argument from cultural relativism is his citation of Plato and the historian Strabo as his sources, for it points up the kind of uncertainty in the evaluation of historical evidence which will eventually also implicate him and his discourse. Just as social practices vary from time to time and from place to place, so also does their evaluation by philosophers and historians. His own, he reveals (inadvertently, I think), may vary with what is at stake for him. Like Castiglione, Champier broaches the subject of his authority to defend women; unlike Castiglione, he appears far less aware that an author's apology may not promote his subjects' interests.

Addressing the question of evaluation of social behavior, he observes that women who wish to defend themselves from their detractors are very often unable to do so because they cannot read the evidence in Scripture which would prove their case: "For women are like sheep before the wolf and do not usually consult Scripture in order to defend themselves, and because they say nothing, one attributes all evils to

[39]Champier's comparative method may be an early instance of a critical technique that later was developed for different ends by Huguenot ideologists, who tended to draw "illustrations in a comparative way from the experience and institutions of disparate societies—that is, from the field that corresponded to the old law of nations, the *ius gentium*—and then to infer, by a sort of inductive process, patterns that seemed to be universal and, arguably, in conformity with the 'natural law'": Donald R. Kelley, *The Beginning of Ideology* (Cambridge: Cambridge University Press, 1983), 313. Feminists did not allude to cultural differences in order to discern a general pattern to human behavior but rather saw in their existence the possibility of subverting the very notion of a natural law, at least insofar as it might apply to women.

them" (b4). The statement can serve as a basis for reevaluating the request of the author's Dame Prudence for a defense of virtuous women by one—Champier himself—who has an inner vision of his subject. If Champier cannot claim objectivity, his defense takes on a different character. Like the ideal court lady of Castiglione's Magnifico, it may represent its author's wishes. What may be implicit in Champier's decision to speak for the persons he defends is the fear that they may speak for themselves, a "prudent" decision if women's speech is perceived to be, as it so often was in the various enactments of the *querelle*, subversive of the authority and power of men. It is from this perspective that some of Champier's cautionary remarks about the dangers of sexuality invite comparison with the antifeminist discourse typified by *Les XV Joies*. Warning that too much sex is harmful, Champier declares: "For [sex] *dissipates and kills* [the person through the excesses of] the body because appetite often exceeds power and you see often that men who take beautiful women die young and often suddenly. For their superficial pleasures [*leurs plaisances superflues*] a person is wickedly murdered by his own knife [*il se fait maulvais tuer de son cousteau*; i.e., his penis?]" (k2v). The reference to pleasure, presumably of women, suggests that according to Champier, misogynistic asceticism is justified by the need of men to control female sexuality.

Champier's rhetorically complicated treatise illustrates rather typically the kinds of intentional contradictions that plague many contemporary defenses of women. The assumptions supporting patriarchal society, the authority of men over women, and the superiority of behavior identified as masculine rather than feminine frequently functioned as a counterpoise to whatever feminists asserted in behalf of women as the equals of men. Paradoxically, this is especially the case when one of the most useful tools of feminist protest—the question of authorial position and subjectivity—is at issue. By invoking the relativism of opinions and practices regarding women, their very defenders (with their interests, their assumptions) become the implied subjects of their own discourse. Anne de France and Marot had revealed how limited were the authority and power granted to women; defenders of women such as Champier reveal how difficult it was to come to terms with the ideology of patriarchy, which supported such limitations.

England

Feminist Counterauthorities

The poet's muse singing the deeds of heroes had always been a feminine figure; and, at least since the visional lady Philosophia had appeared to Boethius, men in search of truths by which to live had listened to inner voices that they identified as those of women.[40] The strangeness of this convention must have struck Christine de Pisan, who, considering how to answer the misogynist caracatures of women in *Le Roman de la rose*, invented a feminine muse to sing to her unconvention-ally—not only of the deeds of women but from a point of view that unequivocally assumed their virtue. Her *Livre de la cité des dames* is the result. What distinguishes it from such texts as the *Mulierum virtutes* and *De claris mulieribus* is its treatment of the muse, or, to put it less figura-tively, of historiography. She recognizes that existing discourse on women is prejudicial not by accident but because it is inextricably bound up with the interests of men; that the authorities on this subject identify themselves as men; and perhaps that their language (and hers) is condi-tioned to express a masculine perspective on the world. Her awareness of the ideological dimension of her culture permits her to imagine a history inspired by feminist counterauthorities whose avowed intention is to represent a different truth about the past than that which her contempo-raries know. In this way she attempts to realize what Castiglione (and less consciously Champier) imply is desirable: a text in which the subject, woman, is constructed outside a patriarchal frame of reference. In the conclusion to her work, she reflects on how successfully she has managed her idealistic project.

Christine de Pisan's *Cité des dames* is without doubt the most important feminist text in the French *querelle*. Why no printed edition of it has ever appeared remains a mystery; many manuscript copies were in circulation from 1405 (the date of its composition) through the sixteenth century. It may have been considered too dangerous for the general public (who were unlikely to buy expensive manuscripts): of contemporary and com-parable works in French, it is without question the most radical. All the more reason, then, to ask why in 1521, more than a century after its composition, it appeared in print in England as *The Boke of the Cyte of Ladyes*. Unlike defenses of women published in the 1540s, *The Boke* does not address itself specifically to the question of queens regent and reg-nant; but whether or not Brian Ansley (its English translator) so in-tended, this text would have had a political reference at the time of its publication. The problem that would eventually bring Henry to incarce-rate and then to divorce his queen and the future queen Mary's mother, Catherine of Aragon—the absence of a male heir—had yet to be fully and openly acknowledged (particularly by the royal couple); nevertheless,

---

[40]For a study of such inspiration throughout the Middle Ages, see Joan M. Ferrante, "Allegory," in *Woman as Image in Medieval Literature* (New York: Columbia University Press), 37–64.

the legitimacy of woman's rule was for English readers more than a merely theoretical matter. Catherine of Aragon had before her the example of her mother, the intrepid queen Isabella of Castile; she herself had demonstrated what Aristotle had called the virtues in the mode of command, especially in 1513 at Flodden field.[41] The misogynist slander in the texts Christine de Pisan attacks would therefore not only have perturbed English feminists (as presumably it did French feminists); given the imposing presence of Catherine at the English court, and the distinct possibility that her daughter would become a queen regnant, it would also have been regarded as highly impolitic.

Ansley's printed *Boke* had therefore a polemical dimension that the French manuscript *Cité des dames* lacked. Its readership was intentionally gauged as public, not courtly. As an element in published discourse about the virtue of woman, it performed a double function that closely suited the position Catherine of Aragon was to take regarding her own role as England's queen. It served as the pretext upon which English readers could construct an image of a history in which women were both authoritative and powerful. At the same time, because Christine de Pisan situated her feminist city in the landscape of patriarchy, notably with respect to the wife's subordination to her husband, it also left unchallenged the assumption that men would naturally govern women. It raised by implication the problem first addressed by Boccaccio and later actually solved by the persons responsible for formulating the nature of Mary Tudor's rule—that of the authority of a married queen regnant—but it implied a traditional solution. While Parliament would eventually insist that the political authority of a queen regnant over her husband would be as over any of her subjects, the English people would have regarded such a possibility much before the fact as no less than revolutionary. No previous institution had gone that far.[42] English readers would have perceived in Christine de Pisan's idealism a reason to respect women, especially those with authority and power; they would have seen in her realism a reason not to fear that theirs would be an unnatural and female government. Despite the glorious terms in which Christine de Pisan imagines the virtue of women and its public scope, she does not represent it as the basis for political innovation.

In the opening passages of her defense, Christine de Pisan explains what led her to invent feminist counterauthorities. Having found a book

[41]The best study of the life of Catherine of Aragon is still Garrett Mattingly, *Catherine of Aragon* (Boston: Little, Brown, 1941); but see also relevant pages on patronage at the court of Henry VIII in David Loades, *The Tudor Court* (Totowa, N.J.: Barnes & Noble, 1987).

[42]See my "Woman's Rule in Sixteenth-Century British Political Thought," *Renaissance Quarterly* 40 (1987): 421–51.

on the woman question by one Matheolus, she realizes not only that he is critical of women but that his "slaundres and blames of [them] and of theyr condycyons" are not unique. On this matter, men "speketh as it were by one mouthe and accordeth all in semble conclusyon deter-mynynge that the condycyons of women ben fully enclyned to all vyces." In other words, she recognizes that her experience of misogyny is more than casual. Testing this male vision of woman against what she herself knows, she examines herself and "other women whos companye I haunted; as well of pryncesses and of grete ladyes as of meane gentyll women," and she concludes that men are wrong: "I coude not perceyve that suche jugementes myght be trewe agaynst the naturall condycyons or maners of women." But she also discovers that however wrong men are, their vision prevails in her mind, and even over her own contradic-tory sense of the truth. Finally she cannot controvert the authority of Matheolus or question the social practices he appears to legitimate. The significance of his book supersedes altogether the meaning of her per-sonal experience: "[I concluded] that myne understandynge for his sym-plenesse and ignoraunce ne coude not knowe my grete defautes and semblably of other women . . . and soo I reported me more to the jugement of other then to that I felte or knowe of myselfe."[43] Here she testifies to the immense power of traditional modes of thought, to the persistent vitality of the assumptions underlying cultural practices that can nullify individual judgment.

But the despair that follows Christine de Pisan's acceptance of her supposed inferiority paradoxically provides her with an opportunity to achieve a measure of detachment from the sources that authorize that inferiority, and to discover others that permit another kind of judgment about the worth of woman. Her defensive posture actually develops from her depression. Seemingly convinced by Matheolus and others like him that "god made a foule thynge when he fourmed woman," she

[43]Christine de Pisan, *The Boke of the Cyte of Ladyes*, trans. Brian Ansley (London, 1521), sig. Bb1v–2v. Ansley was Henry VIII's yeoman of the winecellar. Portions of this text have been reproduced in facsimile in *Distaves and Dames: Renaissance Treatises for and about Women*, ed. Diane Bornstein (New York: Delmar, 1978). For a complete translation of Christine's original text into modern English, see Christine de Pizan, *The Book of the City of Ladies*, trans. Earl Jeffrey Richards (New York: Persea, 1982). Studies of Christine de Pisan's works include Charity Cannon Willard, *Christine de Pizan: Her Life and Works* (New York: Persea, 1984); and Diane Bornstein, *Mirrors of Courtesy* (New York: Archon, 1975), 47–62. For the feminism of Christine de Pisan and her contemporaries specifically, see Rose Rigaud, *Les Idées féministes de Christine de Pisan* (Neuchâtel: Université de Neu-châtel, 1911); on the subject of Christine de Pisan and the woman writer, see Sylvia Huot, "Seduction and Sublimation: Christine de Pizan, Jean de Meun, and Dante," *Romance Notes* 25, 3 (1985): 361–73. My own comments on this rich and complicated text are restricted to passages specifically representing feminist positions.

suffers "grete dyspleasaunce and sorowe of courage in dyspraysynge myselfe and all womenkynde so as yf yt sholde be shewed in nature" (Bb3). Nor can she understand why she has not been made a man: "Alas good lorde why haddest thou not made me to be borne into this worlde in the masculyne kynde to that entente that myne enclynacyons myght have ben al to have served the the better and that I sholde not have arred in ony thynge and myght have ben of so grete perfeccyon as they say that men be" (Bb2v). (The authoritative status of this "they" is, of course, what she will call into question.) But, she continues to reason, if God has truly made her inferior as Matheolus claims, then she cannot be expected to make a great showing in the world. "Yet syth it is so that thy debo-nayrnesse stretcheth not so moche towarde me, then spare my negly-gence in thy servyce, good lorde god, and be not dyspleased. *For that servaunt that receyveth leest rewardes of his lorde leest is bounde to his servyce*" (Bb3; my emphasis). In other words, her status as a natural subordinate allows her to maintain what might be called a positive silence concerning the doctrine of her inferiority—a doctrine that is as it were beyond her inferiority fully to comprehend. In this position she can and does hear other voices, now of her own kind—necessarily marginal, interstitial, and (we first assume) heterodox. Three allegorical figures, Reason, Ryghtwysnesse (Droiture), and Justyce, who appear in a vision to com-fort Christine de Pisan, effectively reinterpret history so that it illustrates woman's virtue, not her vice. The brilliance of her argument is evident in her transformation of this collective and feminist muse into one more decisively canonical than any that inspire the misogynist histories she has found so depressing. The process by which Reason and her associates, not the writers who maintain woman's inferiority, are identified with the Logos involves assertions of an unexceptionable orthodoxy. Christine de Pisan bases her defense on an understanding of history that is doctrinally Augustinian and hence beyond reproach.

Her three muses prepare to console her and defend woman by forcing her to notice, first, how indeterminate the whole notion of authority is; and second, how language itself, voicing authority, is given to double meanings: Aristotle contradicts Plato, Augustine contradicts Aristotle, and she must not believe that "al the woordes of phylosophres ben artycles of the fayth of Jhesu Cryst" (Bb4). Nor do poets speak other than "fables" that often admit ironic interpretation, "as one sholde say syth one is a shrewe that is to say that he is good and so by the contrary" (Bb4v). This breach in the wall of authoritative discourse provides the stones for Christine de Pisan's own defense (Bb6r–v). The allegorical city of ladies that is constructed by the words of Reason, Ryghtwysnesse, and Justyce is, as Justyce finally maintains, the true *civitas dei*. Unlike earthly cities, such as Troy, Thebes, and the great city of the Amazons ("women of grete courage whiche despysed bondage," whose queens governed "ryght fayre and well and by grete strengthe maynteyned the lordshyp"), Christine de Pisan's city is suprahistorical and immune to the effects of time (CCv). (There is a certain critical slipperiness to her argument here. Once having called authority into question by pointing to the potential for irony *in language*, as evidenced in the "fables" of poets, she all but invites her reader to assume that the epistemological field is open to a conflict among multiple authorities of which hers may be merely the newest. In her conclusion, she claims that her feminist contribution to knowledge is a necessary complement to Christian orthodoxy, the "artycles of the fayth," and that it supports rather than denies the virtue of woman. But her readers may wonder on what basis it is to be accepted over the old orthodoxy, inasmuch as it too must be "fable.")

Christine de Pisan constructs her city in three stages, each corresponding to a level of insight into history which her muses successively provide. Their contributions to the final structure indicate her own commitment to what might be called fair-mindedness, specifically to an account of the past which, having demystified its patriarchal assumptions, tries rigorously to avoid speaking from positions adopted by reference to other kinds of privilege. Thus Reason, whose mirror is a sign of both reflection (on history) and self-awareness (especially of her own interests), must admit that some men rail against women with "god entente, that is to knowe for to drawe agayne these men that be out of the waye by the hauntynge of dyvers women that ben vycyous and lyght" (Dd2). But (like other defenders), Reason also allows for male projection. Men whose sexual powers are failing blame women: "For nature is waxed colde in them whiche suffreth theym not to put theyre courage to effecte after theyr wyl that the appetyte wolde without puyssaunce . . . they knowe not howe to put away theyr sorowe but to blame women" (Dd3).[44] In general, however, Reason's words bear out the earlier claim of Justyce, who asserts that her own "measures" are rarely observed as far as women are concerned. A fraudulent justice erroneously covers for her in worldly affairs: there are "men of the worlde [who] have other mea-

---

[44]Augustine regards the failure of the male "member" to respond to "volition" as proof of the essential sinfulness of "lust:" *The City of God* (New York: Random House, 1950), 465. Misogynists blamed women for both provoking and discouraging male sexuality; that is, they identified the uncontrollable nature of the male sexual response with the "irrational" nature of woman. Christine de Pisan is elsewhere critical of women who do not respond to the kind of moral instruction she provides here: she speaks of those who are "wild and hard to control," who must be "roped into her structure, the cage of [her] glorious city [*trèsbuchées en nos latz . . . fichées en la caige de nostre glorieuse cité*]": *Le Trésor de la cité des dames* (Paris, 1536), sig. a4v. For this reference I am indebted to Hope Glidden.

sures whiche they say dependeth and cometh of myne. But falsely they measure often tymes under shadowe of me and there theyr measure is not alwaye juste" (Cc3v).

Reason's defense begins with claims that were to become commonplace in later treatises: a woman's body is not deformed, nor is the soul that inhabits that body defective (Dd6v); her weak body signifies strong intelligence, and makes violent crime difficult if not impossible.[45] And because her whole nature is capable of virtue, and not, as one "auctor" has it, of "yll courage . . . as [if of] chyldren," her speech also has "auctoryte"—otherwise Jesus would not have chosen Mary Magdalene to tell of his resurrection (Ee2, 3v). Reason must contend with the fact that woman's authoritative speech is restricted to private life, for women "holde noo pleadynge in the courte of Justyce nor they knowe not of the causes ne dothe no jugement." But the reason is not, as men claim, that a woman "that sytteth in the place of justyce governeth her shrewdly"; it is rather (and here Reason is very discrete) the nature of public "offyces" (Ff). The administration of justice entails the power not only to rule but to punish wrongdoers, and punishment requires physical force: "[Magistrates] sholde make them [wrongdoers] to obeye by force of theyr bodyes and by puyssaunce of armes and that the women may not do" (Ffv). In fact, in "science" or the knowledge of government, women have "naturall wytte," and "wydowes . . . have kepte good governaunce in all theyr doynges after the dethe of theyr housbandes" (Ff2). True, women know less of the world, "for that they haunte not so many dyvers places ne so many dyvers thynges but they holde them within theyr houses and it suffyseth them to do theyr busynesses and there is nothynge that techeth a creature reasonable so moche as dothe the experyence of many dyvers thynges." And like her numerous imitators, Christine de Pisan believes that education would go far to remedy the ignorance of woman: "Yf it were the custome to put the lytel maydens to the scole and . . . to lerne the scyences as they do to the man chyldren . . . they shulde lerne as parfytely" (Kk5v). To conclude, Reason observes that inexperienced and uneducated men, such as farmers and mountaineers, are as ignorant as women; logically, this is an important point: it introduces to feminist debate the concept of a control. The statement "women exhibit a certain behavior" can have meaning only in light of the behavior of men in similar circumstances.[46]

---

[45]This is chronologically the first instance of an argument from the equation "weak body, strong mind," often attributed to Aristotle in the *Economics*, that I have found in Renaissance literature, as well as the first instance of it in print; see n. 14 above.

[46]While reflecting an essentialist view of the sexes, the analysis of misogyny by way of

Christine de Pisan's Reason cannot make any of these observations, however, without attesting to the feelings of privation that accompany them—in a sense, her remarks give renewed meaning to the despair earlier induced by Matheolus. For Reason has done no more than point out that woman has a *natural* wit that under favorable circumstances can function as does a man's educated wit. By Reason's own admission, a typical woman resembles persons (men, presumably) who, "for defaute of lernynge," seem "as bestes they be so symple," however much "nature hath made them as parfyte in . . . body and understandynge as . . . the wysest people . . . that ben in good cytees" (Kk5v–6). Reason does not claim (as other defenders often do) that the intellectual achievements of women are easily comparable to those of men, for she sees them as too circumscribed by time and place. They are the product of a ready "wytte," not learned "scyence":

> For this naturall wytte maye not endure but durynge the lyfe of the persone that hathe it and when he dyeth his wette dyeth with hym but the scyence that is goten endureth perpetualy for ever to theym that hathe it for to knowe in praysynge and it profyteth unto many people in soo moche that they do teche it unto others and maketh bookes unto theym that ben to come.   [Oo3]

And pointing (with what may have been a certain irony) to the authority most commonly cited by misogynists, Reason observes that Aristotle's science is worth more "to the worlde" than "all the prudence without scyence goten of all the men passed or those than ben." She has to conclude, therefore, that the question of woman's intellectuality, which has to be characterized as the operation of a natural wit that lacks the education that would make its products known, "draweth not to the purpose of the strengthynge of our cyte" (Oo3v). Reason, it seems, is adequate only for faulting male authority. Because she refers to actual and historical truths, rather than to moral and spiritual ones, she cannot imagine and thus become the voice of a feminist counterauthority. On the contrary, her rationality, at a certain point, can even discourage such a

---

the idea of a control tends nevertheless to focus attention on behavior that men and women share, and hence on human nature as both determined by sex and developed by an experience of gender. For studies of the schooling available for Ansley's women readers, see J. W. Adamson, "The Extent of Literacy in England in the Fifteenth and Sixteenth Centuries: Notes and Conjectures," *The Library*, 4th ser., 10 (1929–30): 163–93; Josephine Kamm, *Hope Deferred: Girls' Education in English History* (London: Methuen, 1965), 15–51; and Rosemary O'Day, *Education and Society, 1500–1800* (London: Longmans, 1982), 179–95. On literacy in this period, see David Cressy, *Literacy and the Social Order* (Cambridge: Cambridge University Press, 1980).

discourse. According to intellectual criteria, the virtue of woman must remain in a sense conjectural; history has yet adequately to test it.

Ryghtwysnesse must establish the virtue of woman by criteria unknown to Reason. Emblematically, she brings to Christine de Pisan's defense a ruler, a measure by which to reassess the events of the past. Her project entails the refutation of charges of licentiousness and inconstancy by an exposure of the effects on women of male physical force and the social system it creates. To refute the charge that woman is naturally licentious, Ryghtwysnesse must challenge the belief that rape is the fault of woman. If it can be proved (as Vives will later assert) that male force is never decisive in cases of rape, then woman can be termed innately lustful. If not, then male lust must at least be admitted and male force condemned. Ryghtwysnesse not only denies that woman is innately licentious—"it is noo pleasaunce . . . to be ravyshed"—but also asserts that woman is generally more constant than man (J5). Like Reason, Ryghtwysnesse appeals to experience to prove her point, but in her defense (unlike Reason's) it is experience that has already been interpreted as history. Her reference to history permits her to develop a context for the misogyny she wants to invalidate which goes beyond explaining rationally why there is prejudice, and permits a *rewriting* of experience as it has been recorded for posterity.[47] By far the most brilliant of Ryghtwysenesse's revisionary texts is that describing the life of Dido, who "loved moche better Eneas than he dyde her."

> For not withstandynge that he had gyven to her his faythe that he sholde never take other woman but that he sholde be hers ever more, he departed after that she had refresshed hym with good and ease, his shyppes full of treasoure and goodes as she that had not spared her goodes there as the herte was holly sette. [He] wente away without takynge leve by nyght ryght *traytourously* without knowynge of her and thus he payed his hostesse. The whiche departynge was to her so grete sorowe of hym that she loved so muche that she wolde forsake all joye and her lyfe also. . . . Thus pyteously ended the noble quene Dydo that whiche had ben so gretly worshypped that she passed in renowne all other women in her tyme. [N5; my emphasis]

Ryghtwysnesse might have represented her heroine according to the well-established Boccaccian tradition, in which her constancy to Syc-

---

[47]Ryghtwysenesse's rewritten histories are preceded by several instances of feminist defense that depend on the idea of a control: there is no reason for parents to rejoice over the birth of a boy rather than a girl; a boy takes more than a girl and gives less (II, 7; sig. B3v–4); both men and women play tricks in love and should be warned (II, 54; sig. N4); and men love clothes as much as women do (II, 62; sig. Q).

haeus finds a political correlative in the security of her city. For Christine de Pisan's purposes, however, the story Ryghtwysnesse actually tells—a revision of Vergil's dramatization of the ethical choice that Aeneas must make between *pietas* and *eros*—is more effective. Her Aeneas never hears the Vergilian Mercury's message; in fact, Ryghtwysnesse suppresses Vergil's imperial theme altogether. She chooses rather to make an explicit and central feature of the story what Vergil never even implies, that is, that Aeneas's pledge of love actually included a promise of fidelity. Given chivalric norms—every true hero promises fidelity to his lady—her reasoning is sound. And given her premise—that Dido had a valid claim on Aeneas's loyalty—her conclusion is correct. The hero betrayed his love.

By these and other examples of women in history and story, Ryghtwysnesse makes a double contribution to the concept of a feminist authority. By rewriting texts that she finds prejudicial to woman, she contests the apparent male consensus on the question of her inferiority, not by denying it in the terms established by those with a stake in proving that inferiority—that is, by accepting their versions of the past—but by writing new ones. And she reveals how thoroughly the misogynist society Christine de Pisan knows and has complained of is actually described by written (rather than yet to be rewritten) texts. Again Dido's case is illustrative. Ryghtwysnesse has represented Dido as morally wronged, but the principal (Vergilian) tradition in which that queen figures has it that her "betrayer" is *pius* and principled. Thoughtful readers may reflect upon the meaning of the discrepancies in these two stories. To what extent does Christine de Pisan's retelling challenge Vergil's account and, more important, what it stands for politically and ideologically? Having left Dido—ostensibly for patriotic reasons—Vergil's Aeneas goes on to "inveigle" (*ambire*) Latinus, the ruler of the Latins, to give him Lavinia, his daughter, who is already promised to the indigenous Turnus. The act clearly has prophetic meaning: the protesting Juno expresses Aeneas's appropriation of Lavinia as his *men's* appropriation of Latin property, presumably to include its women; "the sons of Aeneas" (*Aeneadae*), she claims, will be permitted "to beseige the borders of Italy" (*Italos obsidere finis*; *Aeneid* 7.333–34). In effect, Aeneas's betrothal authorizes the appropriation or rape of women as the commencement of a civil society and thus posits this kind of brutality as acceptable.[48] What, then, are the moral dimensions of the hero's *pietas*? If the Trojan conquest of Italy proceeded as Vergil tells it, Christine de Pisan's version of the story

[48]Cf. the legendary rape of the Sabines by Romulus and his men, the descendants of Aeneas: Livy, *Ab urbe condita libri*, 1.9. See also my comments on a comparable action by Boccaccio's Dido in chap. 1.

of Dido and Aeneas is the more credible. Together the two stories, read intertextually, suggest that orthodox history and story, here represented by Vergil, celebrate a special civility—exemplifying "unjust measures"— in which the subordination and even the objectification of woman are taken for granted. Of all Rightwysenesse's revisions of the past, this one most closely approaches history's correlative form: prophecy. (Ryght-wysenesse has begun her defense by praising the words of the sibyls.) By establishing a comparative basis for reevaluating history, as she does by repeatedly rejecting misogynist histories for her own, Ryghtwysnesse also provides a fairer model for human society now and in the future.

The last of Christine de Pisan's allegorical figures, Justyce, epitomizes a feminized Logos: she is the "synguler doughter of god and [her] beynge procedeth purely of his propre persone" (Cc3). Her voice is therefore angelic and her insight holy. As an authority, she transcends both Reason, who interprets experience, and Ryghtwysnesse, who rewrites history and story. Justyce carries a "vessel of gold" that measures out to each his rightful portion; an extension of Reason's mirror and Ryghtwysenesse's ruler, it depends upon reflection and comparative assessments to deter-mine what kinds of action to take. Justyce constructs the last portion of Christine de Pisan's city by establishing the excellence of women saints, virgins, and martyrs, and, more important, names the character of the whole structure. It is nothing less than Augustine's *civitas dei* rebuilt, "of the whiche one maye saye (Gloriosa dicta sunt de te civitas dei)" (Z2). The claim engages moral and theological considerations that refer to the author's vision of history at the opening of the defense. There Reason has declared that when women suffer from mistreatment by men they are like "the golde the more it is in the fornayce the more it fyneth hym, whiche is to understonde that the more they be blamed wrongfully the more encreaseth theyr meryte" (Ddv). Obviously this concept of merit has nothing to do with a classical virtue that thrives upon prospering in this world. Rather it guarantees salvation in the next. It means that a lady of Christine de Pisan's city, who through affliction is morally ennobled, is like Augustine's saintly pilgrim who by his *contemptus mundi* gains a place in the heavenly city.

As a defense against misogyny, however, this allegorical city proves to be only partly effective. Reason has argued that woman is naturally as well endowed with the capacity for intellectual virtue as man, but that owing to her subordinate status in society she has been historically misrepresented. Ryghtwysnesse has maintained that she is morally as virtuous as man, but that male force overcomes her; Ryghtwysnesse rewrites the records of the past accordingly. Justyce does not—as might be expected—envisage a system of social reform but rather insists that

woman is divinely favored because of this neglect and abuse. Her histories are of female saints and martyrs, who triumphed through tribulation, and, we are to suppose, would not have rejected their earthly fate
had they been able to do so. Their sacrifices are intended to be seen as
imitationes Christi, a reminder that Justyce's vessel of gold formally points
to the cup of the eucharist, as all just measures are doctrinally superseded
by acts of charity. How much consolation this essentially Pauline paradox—to suffer is to prevail, "for my strength is made perfect in weakness" (2 Cor. 12:9)—afforded Christine de Pisan or her readers is another
matter.[49] In any case, she herself is aware of the problems her paradox
cannot solve. In closing her defense, she warns against lewd love.
Women are to "fle it," for its end is always to their detriment: "And
thynke not the contrary for otherwyse it maye not be. Remember howe
they [men] call you frayle and false and alwaye they seke engynes right
strange and deceyvable with grete payne, and travayle for to take you so
as one dothe to take wylde beestes" (Z3v). Her alarm clarifies the connection between blame (as by detractors of women) and assault (as by lewd
lovers). If woman is perceived as both false and frail, evil and weak, as she
is in fact perceived by men, there is virtually no reason not to wish to
take, possess, and control her. If, however, the premise itself is erroneous, it can be seen as the rationalization for an illicit desire and a valid
object of protest. But whatever the case, this feminist realization cannot
change a social order in which male force is always decisive. Christine de
Pisan urges wives to accept their subjection not because they deserve or
can use it but because "it is not some tymes beste to a creature to be free
out of subieccyon" (Z3). Here she alludes to an intractable reality that
sustains the patriarchal privileges she has theoretically invalidated. She
may also be admitting that her city offers in the present only a psychological defense.

Christine de Pisan's celebration of woman's and women's virtue cuts
two ways. Her heroines, especially those martyred or victimized, demonstrate their virtue but also the utterly intransigent power of patriarchy;
they embrace their suffering as a means to triumph, painfully and paradoxically. But if theirs is the way to virtue, who among ordinary women
will feel encouraged to follow them? And, of more concern to the

---

[49]Christine de Pisan's sense of justice, even in its feminist character, is obviously
conditioned by a valorization of suffering that, from our point of view, may appear to
jeopardize her defense of women. To appreciate fully her belief that suffering confers
power, to reject entirely the notion that (perhaps from a latent feeling of guilt) she *wishes*
women to suffer, may be beyond our capacities as post-Freudian readers. For a brilliant
study of some ways out of such an ideological impasse, see—on a different but related
subject—Caroline Walker Bynum, *Holy Feast and Holy Fast: The Religious Significance of
Food to Medieval Women* (Berkeley: University of California Press, 1987).

English polity, what kind of protection can Christine de Pisan's city offer the two prospective queens regnant in the coming decades? The debates on gynecocracy which took place in the next years challenged Christine de Pisan's essentially Gallic vision of society, and established that in England woman could prevail politically by virtue of holding royal office; more important, they also established the theoretical grounds for woman's rule in all public offices.

Woman's Rule: The Tudor Queens

The institution of gynecocracy—the command of a woman over men—had been recognized as indefensible by virtually all authorities known to commentators on politics of the period. Boccaccio's Dido, the Renaissance *dux femina*, was a figure of ironic proportions (her political virtue constrained by her sexuality), and Aristotle's unfavorable assessment of a woman's capacity for constructive public behavior had persuaded humanist writers on government and the household that restrictions on her activities were biologically justified. Most telling were Paul's injunctions against a woman's speaking in public. Subsequent patristic and clerical commentators frequently linked them to Eve's misguided conversation with Satan, which led to the loss of paradise. Nor was there any well-known precedent for woman's rule in English history before the accession of Mary in 1553; Maud or Matilda (1127–1135), daughter of Henry I, does not seem to have been considered a true queen regnant and is never mentioned in treatises on the subject.

But the dynastic problems implicit in the reasons for Henry VIII's divorce made vital a consensus on the legitimacy of a queen regnant, and in fact in 1544 the successions of both Mary and Elizabeth were provided for under the terms of the Third Act of Succession of Henry VIII. Their successions were not, however, given any legal justification other than what this act could be understood to confer. Commentators who argued both for and against gynecocracy focused on those crucial topics already discussed in Christine's *Boke*: the supposed ontological inferiority of woman, in theory a problem all women who participated in public life had to confront, and the political subordination of the wife, crucial to a married female magistrate. What actual evidence was there for woman's inferiority? And if domestic order required a hierarchy of command, how far did the obedience rule bind a woman to carry out her husband's orders? Were she a magistrate, was her official conduct also under his control? Those who argued for gynecocracy did not necessarily have to defend women per se, although some did—Elyot, Agrippa, and Aylmer, for example; they had only to find a way to legitimate woman's rule over men, that is, to transform woman's "nature" so that its supposedly inherent debility would be superseded by the qualities of the male.[50]

For Juan Luis Vives, who wrote his *De institutio foeminae christianae* in 1523, later translated by Richard Hyrde as the *Instruction of a Christen Woman* (1540) at the request of Catherine of Aragon for guidance in the education of Mary, no such transformation was possible, much less desirable. His advice to these royal women indicates the scope of the resistance to woman's rule. He builds his case on the premise that woman is feeble by nature; not only is she to be subordinate in marriage, she is also not to attempt in any way to regard herself as fit to direct affairs of state. Whatever her rank, a woman is to guard her chastity above all, to avoid idleness even if she must engage in manual labor to do so, and not to think in terms reserved for men. She is specifically not to consider such challenging questions as the nature of vice and virtue, "a large feelde to walke in," since she "may be enfourmed by few wordes"—she "hath no charge to se to but her honestie and chastyte."[51] Like Bruni, Vives believes that she does not need eloquence, the art of persuasively com-

---

[50]For the debate on gynecocracy in this period, important historical studies are Mortimer Levine, *The Early Elizabethan Succession Question: 1558–1568* (Stanford: Stanford University Press, 1966), and *Tudor Dynastic Problems, 1460–1571* (London: Allen & Unwin, 1973). A useful study of some of the persons involved in the controversy as it developed in the 1570s is Dennis Moore's "Recorder Fleetwood and the Tudor Queenship Controversy," in *Ambiguous Realities*, ed. Carole Levin and Jeanie Watson (Detroit: Wayne State University Press, 1987), 235–51. In addition to those studies already mentioned, some recent surveys of the literature on and by women in the English Renaissance are Elaine V. Beilin, *Redeeming Eve: Women Writers of the English Renaissance* (Princeton: Princeton University Press, 1987); Katherine Usher Henderson and Barbara F. McManus, *Half Humankind: Contexts and Texts of the Controversy about Women in England, 1540–1640*, (Urbana: University of Illinois Press, 1985); *Silent but for the Word: Tudor Women as Patrons, Translators, and Writers of Religious Works*, ed. Margaret Patterson Hannay (Kent, O.: Kent State University Press, 1985); and Suzanne W. Hull, *Chaste, Silent, and Obedient: English Books for Women, 1475–1640* (San Marino, Calif.: Huntington Library, 1982).

[51]Juan Luis Vives, *A Very Frutefull and Pleasant Boke called the Instruction of a Christen woman*, trans. Richard Hyrde (London, 1540), sig. B2. In his preface Hyrde suggests that Vives presents the education of women in a positive light, an interpretation not borne out by a reading of the text. Hyrde relates that he gave his translation to Sir Thomas More for his perusal; More was made "very glad" by its contents (A3). On the subject of "honestie and chastytye," Vives is later draconian, actually denying rape: the woman "is an evyll keper that canat kepe [the] one thyng well commytted to her kepyng . . . and specially whiche no man wil take from her agaynst her wyll nor touche hit excepte she be wyllynge her selfe" (G4). For Vives as a humanist, see, i.a., Robert P. Adams, *The Better Part of Valor: More, Erasmus, Colet, and Vives, on Humanism, War, and Peace, 1496–1535* (Seattle: University of Washington Press, 1962); for Vives on women's writing in the *Instruction*, see Valerie Wayne, "Some Sad Sentence: Vives' *Instruction of a Christian Woman*," in *Silent but for the Word*, ed. Hannay, 15–29; and for reading Vives, see Janis Butler Holm, "Struggling with the Letter: Vives's Preface to the *Instruction of a Christen Woman*," in *Contending Kingdoms: Historical, Psychological, and Feminist Approaches to the Literature of Sixteenth-Century England and France*, ed. Marie-Rose Logan and Peter L. Rudnytsky (Detroit: Wayne State University Press, 1989).

municating with other persons, presumably her peers: for her to be "eloquent of speche" is tantamount to babbling and "a token of a lyght mynde and shrowde conditions" (S4v). She must learn for "her self alone and her yonge children or her sisters in our lord," since it does not behoove women "to rule a schole nor to lyve amonge men or speke abrode" (E2v). Should she actually imitate a man in manner and dress, she would demonstrate her lack of chastity: "Hit can nat lyghtly be a chaste mynde that is occupied with thynkynge on armour and turney and manne's valiaunce" (E3, E3v). She must not dress in man's clothing, "els . . . she thynke she hath the manne's stomake" (K4). But she must take the terms of her intellectual discourse, her vision of life entirely from men; they must interpret the world for her, in both its past and present form: "Nor the woman ought nat to folowe her owne jugement" (F2).

Vives's instructions to Mary make it clear that he does not think that she, a woman, can function as a monarch. For she cannot produce an heir to the throne without marrying, and she cannot marry and govern, since for a woman of any rank whatever not to be subordinate to her husband in all respects is to violate the laws of nature and thus to lose the "worship" or respect her rank entitles her to: "The woman is nat rekened the more worshipful amonge men that presumeth to have mastrye above her husbande: but the more folisshe and the more worthy to be mocked: yea and moreover than that cursed and unhappy: the whiche tourneth backewarde the lawes of nature, lyke as though a sodioure wolde rule his capitayne" (Y3). Far from assuming command, she was to be servile and self-effacing; in effect, to follow rules set for all wives and in some instances of exceptional rigor. Like Erasmus's ideal wife, she should mirror her husband's moods. She may reprove him gently, but "if he begynne to waxe angrye, stryve nat with hym." If he beats her, she is to think that this is God's punishment of her; if he grows "wytles," she "wyll handle wysely inough and neither provoke [him] to angre nor take from [him] the honour belongyng to the man, but bryng hym in good hope that all thing shal be done after his wyll" (b2v–3). She is to excuse her husband's adultery, for he is not as bound to be chaste—"by the lawes of the worlde"—as she is (f2v). In short, Vives's woman (like Erasmus's) is to live in two ways, presenting herself as one who is choosing and willing her destiny, and at the same time observing those immutable proprieties that attend her state of life.

That state was never to include magistracy, much less royal office. Citing Thucydides—who believes that women should not "be as moche praysed with a comen voyse and moche less dispraysed," but remain "clerely unknowen, neither the comon fame to make any mention of her" (h2v)—Vives outlines the fate of a woman who dares to violate the injunction to limit herself to familial duties:

Therfore you women that wyll medle with comen matters of realms and cites and wene to governe people and nations with the braydes of your stomackes you go about to hurle down townes afore you and you light upon a harde rocke. Where upon though you brouse and shake countres very sore, yet they scape and you perysshe. For you knowe neyther measure nor order, and yet whiche is the worst poynt of al you wene you knowe veray well, and wyll be ruled in nothynge after them that be experte. But you attempte to drawe all thynge after your fantasye without discretion. Wene you it was for nothynge that wyse men forbad you rule and governaunce of countreis and that saynt Paule byddeth you shall nat speke in congregatyon and gatherynge of people. All this same meaneth that you shall nat medle with matters of realmes or cities. Your owne house is a cite great inoughe for you. [h2v]

Crude in its representation of details, Vives's condemnation of woman's rule would have found favor with the Marian exiles of the 1550s, who argued that because Scripture forbids woman authority in the public arena, God's providence will prevent her rule from prospering. In Vives's words, such a woman is doomed to light upon a hard rock. For him the archetypal figures of Deborah and Judith, who incarnate the virile virtues as they are represented in antiquity according to Scripture, can no longer serve as models, since the love of Christ supersedes their justice (h3v).

Sir Thomas Elyot's *Defence of Good Women* (1540) functions (whether intentionally or not) as a refutation of Vives's *Instruction*. Without actually addressing the question of woman's rule, Elyot argues the feminist point that a woman is *capable of governing*, if only or primarily when no legally or politically suitable man is available. The terms of his defense suggest that he composed his treatise around 1532, when supporters of Catherine of Aragon were soliciting works in her behalf and against the divorce. The text itself represents a model queen, Zenobia of Palmyra, first as a consort and then as regent for her young son, whose circumstances in certain respects resemble those of Catherine after 1530, when Henry ordered that she live apart from him as a virtual prisoner of the state. Elyot shows in Zenobia all the qualities canonically attributable first to a princess, second to a married queen, and third to a queen regent. More directly apposite to a comparison with Catherine, Zenobia is, at the dramatic moment of her appearance in Elyot's dialogue, also a captive queen; her movements are restricted and she is obviously without authority or power. What she is able to demonstrate in spite of her misfortune is her ability to take charge and govern if the need arises, precisely the ability that Catherine's supporters sought for her in the final years of her life, and particularly in 1532 and 1533, when plans were in place for the deposition of Henry (in favor of Mary) by the invading forces of Charles V. These points of comparison suggest the possibility that Elyot intended his *Defence* as political propaganda in favor of the Catholic and imperial cause in England.[52] The crux of the treatise is, in any case, the extent to which a married woman is obliged to obey her husband. How it is solved obviously bears on the situation of a queen consort, and, more remotely, also on that of a married queen regnant.

The conceptual basis of Elyot's text is his assertion, made specifically against Aristotle's *Politics*, that "in armes women have been found of no lyttel reputation" and that "the wyttes of women are apte . . . to wisedom and civile policie"—both arms and arts are essential to the governor.[53] These claims are supported in the first part of the text by a dialogue between a detractor and a defender of women, Caninius and Candidus, respectively. Elyot supports the latter's position by referring to Aristotle's *Economics* (as Castiglione and others had done), in which a woman's physical weakness is said to indicate her strong wit—the principal quality needed by a ruler. In other words, he denies that the superior strength of a man is necessary to ensure the proper administration of the law, a point that, in contradiction to Christine de Pisan's reservations concerning a woman magistrate (who is not physically strong enough to punish wrongdoers), is important to later arguments in defense of the rule of Elizabeth Tudor—hers was to be a government of law, not of a person. These claims are further developed in the second part of the text by Zenobia, who, speaking in her own defense, not only demonstates dramatically her fitness to rule but also attacks inferentially the notion of authority as enshrined in canonical texts rather than the product of a historical moment and with a relevance to it. In a certain sense, she is her own authority. The significance of the fact that all texts, and in this case those that define the nature of woman, are historical and therefore susceptible to change and contradiction will also be central to later defenses of gynecocracy which base their position on cultural relativity of written law and custom.

Zenobia's account of herself includes the most important features of the ideal woman of contemporary defenses. She is educated in the humanist tradition, she is chaste, even Dianaesque in her skill in the hunt, and thoroughly deferential (although also actively helpful) to her husband. Her capacities for government, realized when she becomes regent

---

[52]For a discussion of the possible political references in Elyot's defense, see my "Feminism and the Humanists: The Case of Sir Thomas Elyot's *Defence of Good Women*," in *Rewriting the Renaissance*, ed. Margaret W. Ferguson et al. (Chicago: University of Chicago Press, 1986), 242–58. See also Stanford E. Lehmberg, *Sir Thomas Elyot: Tudor Humanist* (Austin: University of Texas Press, 1960; rpt. Westport, Conn.: Greenwood, 1969).

[53]Sir Thomas Elyot, *The Defence of Good Women* (London, 1540), sig. C6v. Elyot dedicates his treatise to Anne of Cleves. It also exists in a modern edition by Edwin Johnston Howard (Oxford, O.: Anchor, 1940).

for her young sons (E5), are earlier demonstrated in her behavior toward her husband. While true to the rule of obedience, she also demonstrates her right to an independent judgment on moral matters: she obeys her husband, but only to a point. "Justice," she says, taught her to give "due obedience" to her husband and restrained her from "anythynge whiche [was] not semely." But she also insists that a wife is exempt from those constraints on her freedom if what her husband wishes "may tourne them bothe to losse or dyshonesty" (F2). Elyot's representation of uxorial obedience echoes but also reinterprets that of Erasmus in the *Institutio matrimonii christiani*. Erasmus, when advancing a similar notion of a wife's right to disobey her husband, placed the action in the context of the woman's duty to obey God before any person in matters of morality and faith—a position also common to early Protestant reformers, most notably Luther, who used the argument to justify a Christian liberty of conscience against civilly instituted authority. By setting his dialogue in classical Rome, however, Elyot emphasizes the philosophical rather than the theological context of his representation of the notion of obedience. Disobeying her husband in the interest of morality, the pagan Zenobia is obeying not the Christian God but her own reason; she therefore refers her decision not to the behavioral norms of the *vita contemplativa* but rather to those of the *vita activa*. Elyot's humanist defense is thus to be distinguished from that of Erasmus and texts in the tradition of radical Protestantism, which were then in the process of formulating a concept of "passive resistance." These texts had, initially at least, an exclusively spiritual application; Elyot includes, or does not exclude, political and social applications.[54]

[54]Obedience to various kinds of authority was, of course, routinely enjoined of every political subject in virtually all jurisdictions in Europe and England. In England specifically, William Tyndale's *Obedience of a Christen Man* (1528), which went into numerous editions throughout the sixteenth century, is perhaps the most representative of popular treatises on the matter. Tyndale likens a father, a husband, and a master to God; he commands the absolute obedience of children, wife, and servant. For the homiletic tradition on the conduct of wives, see Carole Levin, "Advice on Women's Behavior in Three Tudor Homilies," *International Journal of Women's Studies* 6, 2 (1983): 176–85. Martin Luther's claim that temporal rule is limited to political and not moral or spiritual matters, published initially in a series of sermons in October 1522 and then as a text titled *Von welltlicher Überkeytt wie weytt Man yht gehhorsam Schuldig sey* (1523?), grants the political subject the freedom of conscience that had always been granted a wife, at least doctrinally. It is tempting to speculate that the whole concept of a legitimate resistance to political authority was developed by analogy to the wife's traditional right to disobey the unrighteous orders of her husband, although as far as I know there is not the slightest evidence for such a conclusion. For a translation of Luther's text, "Temporal Authority: To What Extent It Should Be Obeyed," see *Luther's Works*, ed. Walther I. Brandt (Philadelphia: Muhlenberg Press, 1962), 45:81–129. For an analytic survey of ideas of obedience in England throughout the sixteenth century, see Richard L. Greaves, "Concepts of

Any final assessment of Zenobia's exemplarity must, however, take account of the circumstances in which she is represented at the conclusion of the dialogue. As regent, she has attained public virtue for a time (always in the name of her sons), but she is at last defeated and dies a captive. Elyot may have intended this feature of her condition to parallel Catherine of Aragon's in the early 1530s and so to rally his readers around the queen, but the image has a thematic impact that goes well beyond this possibly topical reference. By showing that Zenobia ends her days among Roman matrons, Elyot implies that her virile virtue, though required by her situation as regent, is in the longer term to be constrained by patriarchal norms. If Zenobia figures Catherine's strengths and potential, as well as those of all good women, she also tragically represents that queen's actual powerlessness and by extension the precariousness with which all Renaissance women exercised a civic virtue. Unintentionally perhaps, Elyot has concluded his *Defence* with an image that recalls the caveats of Boccaccio and Christine de Pisan.

Agrippa of Nettesheim's *De nobilitate et praecellentia sexus foeminei* (1509), translated as *Of the Nobilitie and Excellencie of Womankynde* (1542), is the most explicitly feminist text to be published in England in the first half of the century. It served further to focus opinion opposed to the rigorous Vives. Dedicated in its original form to Margaret of Austria, Agrippa's defense compliments her regency by celebrating the intellectual, political, and martial achievements of women. His English readers, on the other hand, would almost certainly have seen in it a topical reference to the two young princesses whose succession to the throne was in jeopardy, in part because they were female. Like many later feminists, notably Marie de Gournay, Agrippa bases his entire argument on a broad interpretation of Genesis 1. Making the crucial distinction between biology and psychology which was to determine so much of the subsequent discourse on sex and gender, Agrippa asserts that men and women differ physically only "in the sondry situation of the bodily partes," and spiritually not at all—"The woman hathe that same mynd that a man hath, that same reason and speche, she gothe to the same ende of blysfulnes, where shall be noo exception of kynde."[55] The common belief that woman is naturally inferior to man is a result of cultural forces.

Political Obedience in Late Tudor England: Conflicting Perspectives," *Journal of British Studies* 22 (1982): 23–34; and Patrick Delana, "True Obedience in Early Tudor England: Mirrors-for-Subjects, 1485–1558" (Ph.D. diss., Claremont Graduate School, 1985).

[55]Agrippa, *Of the Nobilitie and Excellencie of Womankynde* (London, 1542), sig. A2r–v. Agrippa's text is translated by Thomas Clapham. For Agrippa's work as a whole, see Charles Garfield Nauert, *Agrippa and the Crisis of Renaissance Thought* (Urbana: University of Illinois Press, 1965).

Agrippa opens his critique of patriarchy by asking the question that so preoccupied Castiglione and Christine de Pisan: To what extent are women the victims of their own silence and enforced domestication? He observes that they can neither make laws—that is, write the rules by which society lives—nor write history, which justifies these rules. They are therefore without the means to contribute to or criticize the intellectual bases on which they are categorized as inferior. If it had been lawful for women "to make lawes, too wryte histories, how gret tragedies (trow ye) wolde they have writen of the inestimable malice of men" (D8v). This is all the more evident when it is realized that women are as intelligent as men; they lack only education.

Like Le Franc and Champier, Agrippa represents the ideal woman as a product of the culture of antiquity, far superior to that experienced by his female contemporaries. Sensitive to arguments that derive woman's subordinate status from her physical weakness and stress the importance of male strength in keeping her in her place, he notes that both Lycurgus and Plato believe that even in the most physical sense women are capable of contributing to the commonweal, specifically by performing "all feates perteynynge to the warre." The martial skills they possess in ancient Greece are matched elsewhere in the ancient world by other physical powers that actually function to give them "virile" vocations: in Getulia, Bactris, and Galatia, men are idle and women "plow and tylle the fields, . . . buylde, . . . bye and sel, . . . ryde, . . . go on warfare, and . . . do all other thynges which nowe amonge us the men do" (F7r–v). But the decisive determinant of a woman's equality is her economic power, which Agrippa links to her ownership and management of common marital property, and defines according to what he claims are Roman practices following the *ius gentium*.

Legally, in England as in many places on the continent, a couple's common property was totally at the husband's disposal. He could not touch his wife's dowry, or the property that was provided for her in their marriage contract: otherwise he was in charge of everything she brought with her as belongings or inheritance.[56] But Agrippa confers upon the wife an economic status equal to that of her husband: "And it was by the

[56]Useful studies on customary and legal arrangements for the control of property in England include Pearl Hogrefe, "Legal Rights of Tudor Women," *Sixteenth Century Journal* 3 (1972): 97–105; Pillorget, "Patrimoine, prestige et puissance," 81–115; Alan Macfarlane, "Economic Arrangements," in *Marriage and Love in England: Modes of Reproduction, 1300–1840* (Oxford: Basil Blackwell, 1986); Lawrence Stone, *Sex, Marriage, and the Family in England, 1500–1800* (New York: Harper & Row, 1977), 85–93; and more comprehensively, Courtney Stanhope Kenny, *The History of the Law of England as to the Effects of Marriage on Property and on the Wife's Legal Capacity* (London, 1879).

Romaynes' assente decreed and wrytten in the common tables, that women shuld not grind at the quyrne, nor drudge in the kytchen; nor the husbande shulde not say: wife I give the this; nor the wyfe: husbande I gyve you this; bycause they shulde knowe that every thynge betwene theym was common" (F3v–4). Here there is at least the presumption that a wife has the right to manage the couple's common property, although how far that right extends Agrippa does not say. Furthermore, because a wife is neither a drudge nor in any sense earning a livelihood as a wife, since she cannot be paid by a person whose wealth is already her wealth, Agrippa goes on to claim (as Le Franc had done) that under Roman law women had the same legal rights as men. According to the Roman civil code, they were permitted

> to judge, to arbytrate and decyde matters, to doo and take homage and fealtie, to keepe courtes and mynyster justyce amonge theyr tenauntes. And for this pourpose, the woman may have covenant servauntes of her owne, as well as the man may: and a womanne may be judge, yea amonge straungers. She maye also gyve name to her familie and kynred; so that the chyldern shalbe named after their mother, and not after their father. And in dyverse places of the law cyvyle, womenne have touchynge theyr doweries, many great privileges graunted them.   [F6]

In his own time, Agrippa maintains, women exist in a captive state. Like the writer of the *Dialogue apologétique*, who represented the contemporary status of women as having degenerated from an originary standard of fairness set forth in Scripture and the law of nations, Agrippa uses the notion of a just legal standard in antiquity to criticize the indefensible practices of his own people:

> Thou wylte saye, that [political equality of woman] is nowe forbydden by lawes, abolished by custome, extincted by education. For anon as a woman is borne even from her infancy, she is kept at home in ydelnes, and as thoughe she were unmete for any hygher busynesse, she is permitted to know no farther than her nedle and her threede. And than whan she cometh to age, able to be maried, she is delyvered to the rule and governance of a jelous husband, orels she is perpetually shutte up in a close nounrye. And all offyces belongynge to the commonweale, be forbydden theym by the lawes. Nor is it not permitted to a woman, though she be very wise and prudent, to pleade a cause before a juge. Furthermore, they be repelled in jurisdiction, in arbiterment, in adoption, in intercession, in procuration, or to be gardeynes or tutours, in causes testamentary and criminall. Also they be repelled from preachynge of goddes worde, agaynst expresse and playn scripture, in whyche the holy gost [is] promised unto them by Johel the prophet. . . . And thusby these lawes the women being subdewed as it wereby force of armes, are constrained to

give place to men, and to obeye theyr subdewers, not by no naturall no divyne necessitie or reason, but by custome, education, fortune, and a certayne tyrannicall occasion.   [F8–G]

Agrippa dissociates existing social practice from what he considers legitimate authority (i.e., divine or Roman law) and links it to what he calls custom, a notion that had yet to acquire all the connotations that English common lawyers, arguing for the status of the constitution of their government as "immemorial," would later give it. For Agrippa, custom has no inherent authority; he conceives of a tradition of social practice that has grown steadily more corrupt. Rather than justify the position of women, custom tends to invalidate it.[57]

He is therefore able to give new significance to terms and concepts common in patriarchal discourse. "Ydelnes" becomes anything (but particularly work with a needle and thread) that is not directed at full participation in public life; marriage and the convent become forms of incarceration; the concept of a subordinate vocation for women becomes an unnatural denial of natural abilities; the prohibition against preaching becomes a violation of Scripture; and the subordination of women is traced to the possession of superior physical force; "armes" are denied legal justification. The association of the political authority of man with "tyrannicall occasion" is especially significant because it describes the status of woman within a society in terms of the rights of a subject. A tyrant was by definition above the law—the question was whether or not he was entitled to be so. Husbands were clearly never to be allowed such entitlement, since they were bound by divine law. Thus their position as "head" was subject to various requirements—chiefly the duty to love— which in effect prohibited domestic tyranny. Fathers were under a similar injunction: to protect and foster the interests of their daughters. But whatever the circumstances of a particular family, Agrippa maintains, the general practice of denying woman economic and political equality is illegal. In his eyes, woman could perform any kind of public office, execute any kind of public charge.

---

[57]Lawrence Manley describes Agrippa's view of a similar process of degenerative change with respect to the law of nature, which was commonly held to be both immutable and accessible to human beings generally. The law of nature, Agrippa writes, "is altered at every chaunge of time, of the state, and of the prince, which tooke the firste beginninge of the sinne of our first parent, whiche was cause of all our miseries, from whence the first lawe of corrupt nature proceeded which they terme the lawe of nature": *The Vanitie and Uncertaintie of Artes and Sciences*, quoted in Manley, *Convention, 1500–1750* (Cambridge: Harvard University Press, 1980), 119. The idea of the law of nature as a kind of fiction is a feature of two later defenses of women; cf. the treatises arguing for the claims of Mary, Queen of Scots, by John Leslie and David Chambers, discussed in chap. 3.

The broad spectrum of opinion on women, ranging from Vives's conception of their inferiority to Agrippa's insistence on their equality, represents directly the various ways in which patriarchal domestic and political order was experienced. Contemporary misogynist satire illustrates yet another aspect of this form of government; by suggesting that an inversion of the usual hierarchy of the sexes is justified when a man is impotent (both sexually and politically), it can contest the whole idea of the natural inferiority of woman.

Edward Gosynhill's *Scholehouse of Women* (1541), for the most part overtly critical of woman, also creates an image of a wife whose crude assertions of her independence of the usual marital constraints are motivated by a wish to escape her husband's anxious bossiness. Gosynhill opens his treatise by declaring that despite his apparent criticism of wives as shrews and strumpets—his contradiction of a book "all in prayse of the femynye"—he actually "nothynge purposed of yll intent/ That shulde prohybyte the sacrament"—presumably of marriage—and that his dialogue is simply "somwhat to jeste" between the "masculyne" and the "feminy."[58] His apology indicates the general tenor of his work. A jest can occur only between persons who are, however hypothetically, social equals (as fool and king are at the moment of their exchange), and Gosynhill's fictional wife is a victim of abuse rather than actually insubordinate.[59]

To explain if not excuse charges of sexual misconduct, Gosynhill relates his "lewde" wife's complaints of her husband's behavior to her friend the Gossip:

> And be the daye never so longe
> He doth nothing but chyde and braull
> Yeye gossyppe, the more is my wronge
> Hore and herlot he doth me call
> And byddes me, gossyp, scrape and scrall
> And for my livyng, labour and swete
> For as of hym no peny I gette. . . .
> Ware not, gossyp, these chydren thre
> I wolde not tary, ye maye be sure
> Longer with hym, daye ne houre. . . .   [A4v–B]

---

[58][Edward Gosynhill] *The Scholehouse of Women: Wherin every man may rede a good prayse of the condicyons of women* (London, 1541), sig. D4v. Portions of this text are reprinted in *Half Humankind*, ed. Henderson and McManus, 136–55.

[59]I am suggesting not that jests cannot serve to make their targets victims or scapegoats, but rather that jests *shared* by two parties have the effect of making them equals, if only momentarily.

Gossip replies with reasonable advice:

> Be sharpe and quycke with hym agayne
> Yf that he chyde, chyde you also
> And for one worde, gyve you hym twayne. . . .
> Cherysshe yourselfe, all that ye maye
> And drawe unto good companye
> Caste not yourselfe, gossyp, awaye
> Because he playeth the churle with the. . . .   [B]

The women's exchange in fact covers some of the principal points in Agrippa's defense: the wife is subject to a kind of tyrant; he brawls, makes her work hard for nothing, and she cannot leave him. Her only recourse is therefore to a form of self-defense, since in the absence of care from her husband, she must care for herself, or give as she gets, chiding for chiding. Her resistance to his mistreatment acquires a certain justification, however much it violates the rule of uxorial decorum. That she hears this advice from a gossip indicates the possibility that a woman's real identity may derive from a process of mirroring *between women* exclusive of men. This idea is of course doctrinally heterodox (since a woman ought to mirror her husband) and practically forbidden by rules against uxorial idleness and extradomestic activity.

Gosynhill terms his wife's words "tordes" but their filthiness becomes suspect in light of what he reports of his own sexual anxieties in a facetious aside. Like the author of *Les XV Joies*, he imagines a wife whose sexual appetite is stronger than her husband's. He first warns his reader not to "prayse no other man's instrument/ Better then thyne owne," for then his wife "wyll not spare/ Were he never so naturall a foole/ Tylle she have assayed the selfe same tole" (C2r–v). He next observes that if her lover shows her the "game that they love beste/ And wyll not do it" (since it is a game they both love, the implication is that he cannot do it), "then well [she] jeste." But this good humor is only apparent, for in fact she "wyll never love hym afterwarte" (D). These accusations mask a double fear that this husband's tool is deficient (provoking praise of a better one) and that this lover's game is only pretense (explaining why he does not actually play it). The implied diffidence of husband and lover is consequently recast as female lust; male shame is expressed as female inconstancy. In any case, male sexuality establishes a moral and physical norm to which female sexuality must conform. The woman cares only for an impressive tool and hates a man who fails to use it. If her husband's tool is admitted to be less than impressive or her lover finally reluctant, it is she who is both licentious and fickle.

With the death of Edward VI and the imminent accession of his half-sister Mary Tudor, literature on woman's rule became overtly political. Henry's divorce had made Mary a bastard and hence unfit to govern, and she had to establish her legitimacy and thus the legality of her monarchy by an act of Parliament. This act allowed her (and any other female monarch) to rule with all the political powers normally reserved for a male monarch.[60] It addressed only her status in positive (statutory or customary) law, however; she found that even as queen regnant she still confronted a challenge in what was referred to as divine law, which, according to traditional interpretations of Scripture (especially Deuteronomy 17 and 1 Timothy), forbade government by a woman. Because the critics who expressed their objections in print were all Protestants in exile in Europe, their antifeminist protest was also a means to condemn a Catholic monarchy. They interpreted Scripture to prohibit the Godless rule of both popes and women.

Thomas Becon in his *Humble Supplicacion unto God for the restoringe of hys holye woorde unto the churche of Englande* (1554), Antony Gilby in his *Admonition to England and Scotland to call them to repentance* (1558), and Christopher Goodman in his *How Superior Powers Ought to be Obeyd* (1558) declared that gynecocracy is outlawed by Scripture. Goodman, focusing on what was to him the real weakness of Mary Tudor's rule, objects that hers is a tyrannical government because she has rejected the religion established by Edward VI.[61] John Knox's case against gynecocracy is the most developed and cogent. His *First Blast of the Trumpet against the Monstrous Regiment of Women* (1558) represents woman's rule as a violation of all three categories of law—divine, natural, and positive—which he describes as the foundation of "good [political] order."[62] True, he acknowledges that Scripture records women governors, but they are justified by God's grace and exceptional. History itself exemplifies natu-

---

[60]The act states that the "supreme Governor and Queen of this realm" is to have all kinds of "regal power" in as "full large and ample manner" as "any other her most noble progenitors, kings of this realm": *Tudor Constitutional Documents: 1485–1603*, ed. J. R. Tanner (Cambridge: Cambridge University Press, 1948), 123.

[61]For an analysis of these texts, see my "Woman's Rule." For a study of the Marian exiles, with biographical notes on Aylmer, Gilby, Goodman, and Knox, see Christina Hallowell Garrett, *The Marian Exiles: A Study in the Origins of Elizabethan Puritanism* (Cambridge: Cambridge University Press, 1938); and for the role of religious radicals in fashioning a sixteenth-century political theology, see Michael Walzer, *The Revolution of the Saints* (Cambridge: Harvard University Press, 1965).

[62]John Knox, *The First Blast of the Trumpet against the Monstrous Regiment of Women*, in *The Works of John Knox*, ed. David Laing (Edinburgh, 1855), 4:373–74. For Knox's views on the legitimacy and consequences of Elizabeth's rule, see Richard L. Greaves, *Theology and Revolution in the Scottish Reformation: Studies in the Thought of John Knox* (Grand Rapids, Mich.: Christian University Press, 1980), 163–64.

ral law; it reveals that women rulers are typically "monsters." Queens who are more than consorts are invariably disruptive and so testify to the error that allows those who apologize for gynecocracy to see in the "long consuetude" or the "custome" of such governments a lawful precedent. Nor can convenience serve as a justification, as might be claimed in the case of a queen regent (413). In short, any positive law that sanctions gynecocracy invites disorder.

Knox's treatise provoked defenses of woman's rule for the next quarter of a century. Most important, largely for its representation of the concepts underlying the act of Parliament that gave Mary Tudor the authority of a male monarch, was John Aylmer's *Harborowe for Faithfull and Trewe Subjectes* (1559), written in behalf of the new queen. It also covers new ground; first, by attributing to Scripture the character of a *historical* document and hence permitting a certain flexibility in interpretation of divine law; and second, by denying that nature itself is constitutive of a law or laws.

Scripture, Aylmer claims, does not provide a basis for constructing models of government; it teaches one thing only: obedience. (Aylmer does not describe under what conditions this obedience is to be observed or enforced.) Since Knox and his allies regard Scripture as legislative, and base their objections to woman's rule on it, Aylmer's point, if undisputed, would undermine their entire argument. Aylmer, by contrast, sees that Scripture is not concerned with law or "cyvill pollycie," and that when it addresses matters of public behavior it is often reflecting upon a particular historical situation. Refuting Knox's interpretation of 1 Timothy, he declares:

> [The third reason of his argument] is oute of Saint Paule, wherby women be forbidden to speake in the congregacion, for it is an unsemely thinge for them to speake. This is mervelouslye amplefied and urged, as thoughe it were so sounde as no faulte nor cracke could be founde in it. This is the Hercules clubbe that beateth all downe before it. . . . [But] I laye this foundacyon whiche I laide before, that Saynt Paule, nor none of the reast of Christe's garde, meddle not with cyvill pollycie, no further then to teach obedience, nor have no commission thereunto in all the whole scripture. And this beinge a great matter of pollicie . . . it can not be within the compasse of Paul's commission, and so followeth it, that Paul either in this place [1 Timothy] ment no such matter as they gather; or if he did, he did it wythout the compasse of his commission, but that is unlike.[63]

[63]John Aylmer, *An Harborowe for Faithfull and Trewe Subjectes* (London, 1559), sig. G4v. Aylmer specifies that his text is an answer to the "late blowne Blaste concerninge the Government of Wemen." It is dedicated to the Earl of Bedford and Lord Robert Dudley, whom Aylmer asks to defend his "pore treatise, which is the defence of them by whome

According to Aylmer, Paul's restrictions on women in church were prompted by the unruliness of those in a *particular* congregation: "For the avoydinge whereof, Paule mente to bridle them; as withoute doubte he wold have done the men also if they had prophecied unorderly" (G4v). This way of reading Scripture prohibits an interpretation of its prescriptions as absolute. In this respect, Aylmer's practice conforms to that of apologists such as Champier, who consider the status of women in light of social expectations and cultural norms.

Aylmer also attacks the idea of nature as constitutive of a kind of law. He sees nature as inherently given to slight variations of type and of experience—most women, for example, have one baby at a time, but some women have twins. Within certain limits, then, what Knox terms monstrous exceptions to nature must be reclassified as simply uncommon; thus twins are uncommon but not monsters. Such is the case, Aylmer argues, with the woman ruler. And not only have women ruled, he adds, they have ruled in great numbers "in the chefest empires and monarchies, and not only in them but in the common wealth of the Jewes" (Dv–2). In other words, Aylmer redefines nature so that it can be thought to provide not laws but only indicatations of the general patterns into which certain kinds of events tend to fall. The concept of a "rule" against gynecocracy, sanctioned by a law of nature, gives way to Aylmer's idea of a magistracy that predominently favors men but does not exclude women, an idea established by a consideration of historical evidence.

These interpretations of divine and natural laws open the way for the proposition on which Aylmer will base his support of Queen Elizabeth's sovereignty: though neither Scripture nor nature is decisive in denying the legitimacy of woman's rule, providence can be seen to support it. He establishes that the English succession is determined by "enheritaunce and lyneall discent" and then asserts that in the absence of a male, God, "for some secret purpose," must have "[minded] the female should reigne and governe" (B3). "Placeth he [on the throne] a woman weake in nature, feable in bodie, softe in courage, unskilfull in practise, not terrible to the enemy, no shilde to the frynde, well, *Virtus mea* (saith he) *in infirmitate perficitur.* . . . If he put to his hande she can not be feable, if he be with her who can stande against her" (B2v–3). As proof that this principle has not been challenged, he notes that many men who are weak or enfeebled by extreme youth or age have governed without any dis-

we be detended all" (A4v). In his historicization of Scripture, Aylmer is preceded by John Colet; see Colet's *Exposition of St. Paul's Epistle to the Romans*, trans. J. H. Lupton (London, 1873; rpt. Ridgewood, N.J.: Gregg, 1965), esp. 91–92.

qualification being urged against them. This proof is, of course, an essential element in any formulation of the theory of the monarch's two bodies—physical and political—and as such it is a feature of arguments in defense of absolutism and divine right. Aylmer merely includes female-ness as another form of weakness that is overcome in the body politic; as such, it cannot be discriminated against. In sixteenth-century political thought, gynecocracy is more easily justified by appeals to providence and divine right than by arguments for an equality of virtue.

Aylmer's notion that the monarch, any monarch, is supported by God in the performance of royal duties permits him to discover a solution to the problem of the married queen regnant—a solution implicit but not fully described by the act of Parliament that gave Mary, as a married queen regnant, the kind of authority and power she would have had automatically if she had been a male monarch. His solution clearly is indebted to the notion that the monarch possesses a mysterious and politically effective second body.[64] Just as accession to the monarchy by right of inheritance puts right the infirmities of old men, baby boys, and women, strengthening them with God's hand, so it alters the relationship of husband and wife, insofar as affairs of state are concerned. Refuting Knox, Aylmer says: "Yea say you, God hath apoynted her to be subject to her husband. . . . [T]herfore she maye not be the heade. I graunte that, so farre as perteineth to the bandes of mariage, and the office of a wife, she muste be a subjecte; but as a magistrate she maye be her husband's head" (C4v). In short, a queen regnant is two persons politically: a wife who is subordinate to her husband in marital affairs and a magistrate who is superior to every one of her subjects in affairs of state.

The distinction between the queen's two bodies and their proper func-tions finds its precedent in parliamentary law. But how convinced Ayl-mer was that this legal fiction would find acceptance among his readers is partly to be inferred from his conclusion. There, endorsing proto-constitutionalist theory, he claims that Parliament and not the monarch is the final authority in the realm: "If the parliament use their privileges, the King can ordein nothing without them. If he do it is his fault in usurping it and their follye in permitting it"; and since Parliament commands the country, a queen regnant is no more dangerous than a king: "It is not she that ruleth but the lawes" (H3r–v). She runs no more risk than a king in appointing inept persons to execute those laws; she is no more likely than

[64]For a discussion of the concept of the monarch's (and specifically the queen's) two bodies, see Ernst Kantorowicz, *The King's Two Bodies* (Princeton: Princeton University Press, 1959), and Marie Axton, *The Queen's Two Bodies: Drama and the Elizabethan Succes-sion* (London: Royal Historical Society, 1977).

a king to be ignorant about a particular law. His protest here contradicts his earlier admission that men are inherently more "mete" for governing than women: if God's strength makes a "feable" woman strong, she is no more likely to need restraining by Parliament than any of her male counterparts. Aylmer's nervousness on these points may indicate an awareness of contemporary opinion: in theory, a queen regnant was to be a prince; in practice, she was to appear subject to a higher (male) author-ity.[65] In any case, his recommendation that the monarch in her legislative role be subject to Parliament is unusual in light of the political discourse of this period. It would limit the royal prerogative in a way that was supported only by the most radical of parliamentarians and their com-mon lawyer allies in the next century.[66] Aylmer might not have conceded as much to Parliament had the monarch he defended been a man.

The feminists who defended women in the earlier half of the sixteenth century had initially to engage and refute those authorities who by invoking absolute truths maintained that woman was not fully a human being—not, at any rate, as fully human as man. Divine law, inscribed in Scripture, was fortunately ambiguous; writers from Christine de Pisan to Agrippa and Aylmer found in it support for the intellectual, moral, and hence even social and political equality of woman. They all expanded on the meaning of the first creation. Aylmer, crucially, gave the hitherto decisive pronouncements of Paul a historical context and so denied their application to general situations.

The supposed law of nature proved to be more difficult to refute, largely because it appeared to be so much in tune with the physical realities of sexual difference. Aristotle's notions of domestic government seemed to be the realization in political terms of biological givens: wom-an's soft, weak, moist body was merely the palpable manifestation of her impressionable and vacillating mind. Such writers as Barbaro, Palmieri, Dolce, Marot, and Vives described to readers how to contend with such a problematic creature. They insisted that in order to consolidate their families' wealth and legitimate their social status, men had to have docile and tractable wives and daughters. When natural law was subjected to

---

[65]Elizabeth's refusal to marry seems a logical product of the dilemma Aylmer describes here. Her half-sister had not functioned successfully in her double role as wife and queen, evidently incapable of exploiting the male political persona that law and custom had given her. For further speculation on the imagistic and political possibilities open to Elizabeth as a prince, see my "Representing Androgyny: More on the Siena Portrait of Queen Eliz-abeth I," in *The Englishwoman of the Renaissance (1500–1640)*, ed. Anne M. Haselkorn and Betty S. Travitsky (Amherst: University of Massachusetts Press, forthcoming.)

[66]Francis D. Wormuth, *The Royal Prerogative, 1603–1649* (Ithaca: Cornell University Press, 1930), 47–68.

feminist scrutiny, however, it proved to be less than monolithic. Such writers as Capella, Castiglione, and Agrippa, taking a historicist and proto-anthropological line, pointed to societies in which wives and daughters did not behave according to the theoretically universal patriarchal model. Marriage arrangements, the education of girls, and the role of the sexes in the public arena varied with time and place: so feminists claimed. No matter that many of their examples of cultural difference were fanciful and beyond reasonable proof. Feminists were felt to be on the mark in alluding to them; certainly arguments from relativism were dramatically amplified in the second half of the century.

The attack on natural law had the effect of setting aside the case for maintaining absolutely the inferiority and subordination of woman. Attention was subsequently to be directed to an analysis of human behavior which no longer depended so heavily on the idea of man and woman as distinct though complementary types. Such defenders of women as Elyot, who celebrated the virile woman of classical history (and perhaps allusively in his own century), provided later feminists with a crucially important concept: the idea of androgyny. This idea was to allow speculation on the meaning of sexual difference in establishing patterns of behavior; it was to admit a discussion of the extent to which (if at all) sex did or ought to determine social roles; and, dramatically, it was to permit a recognition that cultural concepts of gender, what constituted masculinity and femininity in a given society, were to be separated from sexuality, the fact of being male or female.

3   *Sex and Gender*

AN emphasis on the spiritual equality of woman encouraged feminists to imagine that this aspect of her being might be the basis for a reevaluation of her whole person. Their project had initially to confront the problem posed by Erasmus's "New Mother"—how far the femaleness of woman was to determine her activities in general. To what extent did her sex provide a natural basis for calling her to certain offices and not others? Were the behaviors or roles assigned to women and therefore gendered as feminine altogether dependent on the fact of her being female? Certainly some activities characterized as masculine or feminine could be performed by either a man or a woman. K. D. M. Snell's research on female apprentices demonstrates how widespread was the employment of women outside the home in all the standard trades. Correspondingly, the employment of men in household tasks—in theory designated as the duty of women—was also common (although far more so among persons in the lower ranks of society than among the gentry).[1] Given the similarity of work performed by male and female farmers, artisans, and tradespersons, it was only logical for some feminists to argue either directly or by implication that sex and gender were different. Sex, they believed, was *innate*; gender was *assigned* by cultural expectations to forms of behavior, and in some important cases to qualities of mind, and was *variable*, in that a person of one sex could exhibit behavior and attitudes characteristic (by cultural definition) of both genders. Obviously, to be female was not necessarily to rule out masculine behavior and vice versa. These distinctions represent a refinement of the typologi-

[1]K. D. M. Snell, *Annals of the Labouring Poor* (Cambridge: Cambridge University Press, 1985), esp. 270–77, 295–314.

cal thinking that was derived from the concept of a "naturally" constituted man or woman. The ability of feminists in a patriarchal culture to
introduce such distinctions in an argument that actually *valorized* femininity depended on an analysis of the meaning of gender which was, I
think, new to the debate on women.

The difference and relation between sex and gender had already been
represented allusively in the philosophical literature of antiquity and in
Renaissance epic and historical writing that drew on ancient sources.
Patristic literature had quite clearly established that there were two aspects of personhood: that comprehended in the universal category *homo*
or humankind, and that restricted to the categories of sex, *vir* and *femina*.
Strictly speaking, as I have mentioned, the first category is fully evident
only to the spirit; on the other hand, life in time is conditioned by a
person's place as male or female. This orthodox view was everywhere
undermined by representations of androgyny, both as a phenomenon
proper to human history, exemplified most frequently by the figure of
the virile woman or virago, and as a symbol of the union of two opposing
abstractions—the *coincidentia oppositorum* of feminine love and masculine
war in cosmic harmony, for instance. Of these two kinds of oxymoronic
gender, certainly the first, drawing as it did on legend and history, was
the more important for feminists, especially in the initial stages of their
protest. Persons who were sexually distinct were seen to be capable of
being behavioristically androgynous; the more carefully their androgyny
was described, the less close seemed the link between sex and gender.

Discussions of behavior as gendered were not, however, generally
carried on by reference to the complex question of bisexuality or transsexuality, that is, of a single human being who was amorphously male
and female or who had been female and then had turned into a male. This
subject had its own discourse. Galenic medicine claimed that the female
genitals had contained within them inversions of the male's: in themselves the female genitals were essential for procreation but they were of a
lesser quality, in that they were "cool" rather than warm. If sexual
frustration made a woman sufficiently hot, her male genitals would
appear.[2] So Jacques Ferrand declares: "[It may be] that a woman, being
inflamed with the violence of love, may put forth those genitall parts
which are not other then those of a man reversed or turned inward." The
condition could be prevented by avoidance of celibacy. In itself it was
considered "monstrous," and fear of it quite obviously strengthened the

---

[2]For a discussion of the Galenic view of sexuality, see Thomas Laqueur, "Orgasm,
Generation, and the Politics of the Reproductive Body," in *The Making of the Modern Body:
Sexuality and Society in the Nineteenth Century*, ed. Catherine Gallagher and Thomas
Laqueur (Berkeley: University of California Press, 1987), 1–41.

case for marriage: a woman, it must be supposed, was likely to agree to sex in the interests of avoiding monstrosity through overheating.[3] Bisexuality or transsexuality of this kind—manifested, that is, as a departure from a *physical* norm—was referred to sometimes as hermaphroditism, sometimes as androgyny; and both were dreadful.

To interpret Renaissance attitudes toward women, however, it is useful to reserve a term to designate that mystical form of masculine-feminine union or continuum as the positive valence of androgyny. Perhaps symbolic androgyny will do. As a figure representing the spiritual (and intellectual) dimension of human experience, it has a long history. Linda Woodbridge has usefully distinguished the two principal sources establishing both positive and negative aspects of the hermaphrodite/androgyne: and as an image of debile sexual confusion it appears in Ovid's *Metamorphoses*, as an image of sympathetic generativity it is described in Plato's *Symposium*.[4] Marie Delcourt, writing on the hermaphrodite in classical antiquity, considers its prominence in the literature of mysticism and cosmology; Edgar Wind has revealed the extensive representation of androgyny in the culture of Neoplatonism.[5] In search

[3]James Ferrand, *Erotomania, or A Treatise Discoursing of the Essence, Causes, Symptomes, Prognosticks and Cure of Love or Erotique Melancholy* (Oxford, 1640), sig. A7. This is a translation by E. Chilmead of Jacques Ferrand's *Mélancholie érotique*, published in Paris in the sixteenth century. A transformation of this kind, which results in a hermaphrodite, a person who is half-male, half-female—in contrast to an androgyne, who is mysteriously fully masculine and fully feminine—obviously does little to advance feminist arguments for the feminization of society. It does, however, destabilize the system by which male and female—and hence masculine and feminine—are set off from each other, rendered mutually exclusive and categorically opposed. On this text see Massimo Ciavolella, "Métamorphoses sexuelles et sexualité féminine durant la Renaissance," *Renaissance and Reformation/Renaissance et Réforme* 24, 1 (1988): 13–20. For more on androgyny and hermaphroditism, see Ian Maclean, *The Renaissance Notion of Woman* (Cambridge: Cambridge University Press, 1980), 38–39.

[4]Linda Woodbridge, *Women and the English Renaissance* (Urbana: University of Illinois Press, 1984), 140–41. Woodbridge considers the meaning of the hermaphrodite in relation to the question of cross-dressing. Transvestism was obviously the point at which the difference between biological sex and psychological gender which supported feminist demands for equality narrowed considerably. Dress concretized what could otherwise be understood as amorphous and fluid. A woman blacksmith was socially acceptable; a woman in breeches was not. The former would have been classed as a virile woman, the latter as woman faking maleness. She could be doing so because she needed her breeches in order to behave in a virile fashion (Shakespeare's Portia), or because she wanted to contest conventional gender signifiers (the *hic mulier* character). The latter case was perceived as socially harmful by persons concerned to preserve privileges of sex and rank. Cross-dressing is discussed further in chap. 4.

[5]Marie Delcourt, *Hermaphrodite: Myths and Rites of the Bisexual Figure in Classical Antiquity*, trans. Jennifer Nicholson (London: Studio Books, 1956); Edgar Wind, *Pagan Mysteries in the Renaissance* (New York: Norton, 1968). For a discussion of the two kinds of androgyny, see Lauren Silberman, "Mythographic Transformations of Ovid's Hermaphrodite," *Sixteenth Century Journal* 19, 4 (1988): 643–52; and Carla Freccero, "The Other

of a way of promoting the concept of the human, of the *homo* that subsumes *vir* and *femina*, in the interest of claiming equality, feminists turned to androgyny because in its mystical expression it appeared to explain so suggestively what they regarded as a wholly obvious and demonstrable social fact: that men and women shared common behaviors, attitudes, experiences.

The idea of (positive) androgyny also had currency in contemporary political affairs. Sixteenth-century Europe was governed by powerful women regents; England had two queens regnant, Scotland one. Elizabeth I was responsible both directly and through her apologists for an extensive rhetoric of political androgyny. As important as the actual theory of the queen's two bodies was the elaborate symbolism establishing that her rule was both just and equitable. Spenser conveys her political excellence in the multiple perspectives of his *Faerie Queene*. Sidney's *Arcadia* demonstrates that the best form of justice embraces the feminine element of equity.

In herself, of course, the virile woman tended to reaffirm patriarchal values. Her excellence is seen in her masculinity—that is, her rationality, courage, and physical strength. Her parodic counterparts in myth (the uxorious Hercules) and popular satire (the little cuckold) usually further confirmed the valorization of the masculine. Their weakness is termed effeminacy. What these portraits most pointedly lack is an affirmation of the positive character of woman, of femininity as opposed to effeminacy. To see femininity in a positive light, to detach it from its negative reflection in the effeminate male or in the misogynist caricature of woman as vain, capricious, self-indulgent, garrulous, and stupid, feminists had to consider the origins and the meaning of symbolic androgyny, particularly as it was represented in myths of justice and politics. By representing woman as a type in whom are incarnate virtues specifically associated with femininity—mercy, patience, temperance, and so forth—feminists began to argue not only for the worth of woman but also for the feminization of society as a whole. Correspondingly, they spoke of a degenerate kind of masculinity—the cruelty (typically gratuitous) of the bully and tyrant—and its deleterious effects on the family and the state.

---

and the Same: The Image of the Hermaphrodite in Rabelais," in *Rewriting the Renaissance*, ed. Margaret Ferguson et al. (Chicago: University of Chicago Press, 1986), 145–58. See also the discussion by Jerome Schwartz, "Aspects of Androgyny in the Renaissance," in *Human Sexuality in the Middle Ages and the Renaissance*, ed. D. Radcliffe-Umstead (Pittsburgh: Center for Medieval and Renaissance Studies, University of Pittsburgh, 1978), 121–31. A seminal discussion of androgyny in relation to literary feminism is Carolyn Heilbrun, *Toward a Recognition of Androgyny* (New York: Knopf, 1973).

ITALY

A Life Apart from Men

Ortensio Landi's *Lettere di molte valorose donne* (1549) pur-
ports to be the collected correspondence of literate women of the nobility
and gentry in the Veneto and neighboring districts. In Landi's words,
they were to prove that women are not "inferior to men in eloquence or
learning."[6] As a group, the writers are clearly not of the *cortegiana* type;
they write no love letters and they perceive their social situation in terms
of marriage or conventual life. Recognizing the vocational limitations
they confront—in part because they have thought so seriously about
humanist representations of virtue—they respond by evoking humanist
myths of denial, entertaining comic fantasy, and rewriting the humanist
history from which they have been excluded. They exploit the resources
of their spiritual equality in fictions that express their own empowerment. By imagining themselves in male roles and performing in situations usually closed to women, they exhibit strengths identified as both
masculine and feminine and assume an androgynous character.[7]

Much of the correspondence of Landi's "*valorose donne*" shows how

---

[6]Ortensio Landi, *Lettere di molte valorose donne, nelle quali chiaramente appare non esser ne di
eloquentia ne di dottrina alli huomini inferiori* (Venice, 1549), sig. A. Landi's collection is
dedicated to Sigismondo Rovello; it is, in his words, prompted by the fact that ladies need
a protector, "so that the wicked tongues that are enemies of women's honor will be
shocked into refraining from maligning women" (A2r–v). The letters themselves appear
to be the work of women of the nobility and gentry in the Veneto and neighboring
districts. How much editing Landi did is unclear; it has been asserted that he was in fact the
author of all these letters as well as of those of Lucretia Gonzaga (cited in n. 7). See S.
Bongi's introduction to Landi's *Novelle* (Lucca, 1851); also "Lando," in vol. 20 of *Enciclopedia italiana* (Rome: Istituto dell' Enciclopedia Italiana, 1933). On Venice as a locus of
feminist sentiment, especially later in the century, see Patricia Labalme, "Venetian Women
on Women: Three Early Modern Feminists," *Archivo veneto* 112, 152 (1981): 81–109. For a
study of the sexual mores of Venetian culture in general, see Guido Ruggiero, *The
Boundaries of Eros: Sex Crime and Sexuality in Renaissance Venice* (New York: Oxford
University Press, 1985), esp. 163–64, on the relative freedom of Venetian women.

[7]The innovativeness of Landi's *Lettere* can be gauged by comparison with a second
collection, also edited by Landi: the *Lettere della molto illustre . . . donna Signora Lucretia
Gonzaga* (Venice, 1552). The collection, dedicated to Pietro Paulo Manfrone, governor of
Verona, contains letters that are undated but seem to range over ten or fifteen years and to
chronicle the end of Lucretia's unhappy marriage to Gioanpaulo Manfrone, a nobleman
who was imprisoned at Ferrara by the Estes. Her elegantly formal correspondence reveals,
among other things, how easy it was for an educated woman to employ the standard
tropes of humanist discourse: Lucretia evinces enthusiasm for the military life as evidence
of civic virtue; praises logic and rhetoric as useful to the statesman; argues that work forms
the man; celebrates a glorious death in battle for liberty; warns of the perils of courtiership;
and pronounces the poems of Gaspara Stampa wonderful for a woman. Her social
criticism is restricted to the way she has been required to live as a wife; once a widow, she
resolves not to forgo her new "liberty": "A M. Andriana Trivulza," sig. O3v.

well accepted were the notions of proper wifely conduct even by such feminists as Landi. A lady identified simply as Lodovica uses conventional terms to chide a friend for her garrulousness: citing Sophocles, she says, "Silence is the ornament of women" (A8v). Apollonia Rovella blames a wife whose husband is strict and niggardly; she has been disobedient and disagreeable: "As far as I can see, this is your fault, because you disobey him and you never try to do anything to please him" (H5v). And Paula Castigliona warns Leonora Forteguerra that although her husband beats her for no reason, she is to refrain from responding in such a way as to provoke him further (L3). A few writers discuss the alternative of the convent. Portia Melita complains to her aunt Ginevra that she is being married much against her will to a horrible man: "He's crazier and more maniacal than Ajax, than Pisander; moreover his body stinks more than Ruffino's did." She weeps and tears her hair, for she has had more attractive suitors: "Does it seem to you, dear aunt, that such a man is right for me, who has had such gracious and handsome suitors?" (E5r–v). But Emilia Solcia advises Fulvia Rossa that marriage is in general better than convent life, since the latter tends to corrupt morals: "With a thousand ploys and secret wiles [the priests] confuse your brain, and once it's confused they make you deaf, so that it would have been better for you to go to Hell" (G4v). None of these writers seems interested in her husband as a person; few describe the companionship that is supposed to characterize marital union, according to treatises on marriage. For the most part, they see marriage as a condition to be accepted, certainly imperfect but marginally preferable to any alternative. Their realism does not, however, inhibit their willingness to imagine the attractions of a single life apart from men, or—even more boldly—of life as a man.

The result is not always unproblematic. By reading Vergil, for instance, Isabella Sforza confronts the same moral exempla that instruct her male contemporaries: "I, for my part, never read the divine Aeneid of Vergil that I do not seem to be reading a perpetual hymn in praise of virtue" (B4v). She longs to imitate the hero, to arm herself against love, to reject "desire" (*concupiscibil appetito*; B5). She wishes to become a Diana-like version of Aeneas, both to deny and to discard her sex as her hero did his Dido.

To Lucretia Masippa, the hero Ulysses provides a means by which to revise and rewrite her own experience of exploring the world in the ways a woman could, that is, in the imagination. She begins her account of herself as a Ulysses by revealing that a short trip from Venice to Cremona and Piacenza has created in her "a longing to travel forever seeing the world." She is held back, she says, by concern for her daughters and for fear that she will be regarded as "flighty and irresponsible" (*vagabonda e instabile*). And she speculates that were she to adopt the course of Ulysses, she might experience the consequences that he did: "Who knows whether traveling would perhaps not have the effect on me that it did on Ulysses? . . . that is to make me much more prudent than I am, [by] seeing so many different customs of the world" (M2). But it is pleasure, not prudence, that she stresses next; she could wish to be a man in order "to travel where I pleased"—specifically to encounter the virtues as they are represented in women, whether they be typically masculine (courage) or feminine (temperance):

> I would like first to see the beauty of the ladies of the Thomas More family. I would like to see the good manners of the women of Holland, and to learn from them how to make such wonderful cloth. I would like to see whether the German women are still as brave as they used to be when they shamed their men by resisting the enemy. . . . I long to see the graceful bearing of the women of France and to pay my respects to the virtuous and courteous Queen of Navarre, who has so captivated me that I think only of following in her sacred footsteps.   [M2r–v]

But in conclusion, perhaps remembering the prudence of her hero, she begs her reader to teach her to satisy her desire "without spotting or damaging her feminine reputation." She determines to "travel" through and in books—Ptolemy, Strabo, Pliny—and so to imitate not Ulysses but the virtuous ladies of Sforza. Her deference to custom and what she sees as her office clouds her vision of a feminine world of adventure.[8]

The frustrations of a life lived according to patriarchal norms could also be met by excursions into the realm of the comic. For Aurelia Verdella, this realm is a woman's world in which all the male parts are played by women who are larger, stronger, and more acute than any man could be. Encouraging her friend Sulpitia Biraga not to fret over the departure of her bailiff, Aurelia observes with disdain that she and other "modern women" are pusillanimous because "we [think we] can do nothing without the help of men." In fact, she asserts, the opposite is true. And were it possible to perpetuate the human race without men, she would be happy. Reflecting on her wish for a life among women, she imagines managing her friend's estate: "I promise you I would rather see Satan [there] than a man. May the Amazons be blessed." Her vision includes a celebration of her ability to conduct her affairs shrewdly: "Let me go to the markets to be a buyer, for I don't worry that anyone will cheat me. If we have to buy oxen for plowing our fields, won't I know

[8]The pursuit of knowledge was not, of course, a problem only for women; for Dante's Ulysses, see *Inferno* 26.

that their limbs must be hairy, their eyes black and large, their chests also black, their ears laid back, their foreheads large, their nostrils open, their thighs heavy and separate from their necks?" And she dismisses the possibility that they will ever need to call on a man: "Agree not to marry again or to litter the house with men," she demands of her friend Sulpitia. To do their work, she will import strong women: "I shall summon twelve large Slavic women who will seem as twelve Colossi; they will plow, harvest, and cook, I promise you, so that each one of them—even the most feeble—will substitute for four men" (O2–3). Her fantasy compensates for actual experiences of the real or enforced helplessness of women, already the subject of commentary by such critics as Agrippa and, most poignantly, Christine de Pisan. It suggests that in Italy, as in England, peasant and artisanal women regularly did heavy work, that a woman of the gentry believed she could do business. In Aurelia's comic perspective the contribution of men to the well-being of women becomes trivial and physical size of no importance; consequently, too, their much-vaunted sexuality (a reason for the claustration of women) becomes no more than what is biologically necessary for the continuance of the human race. In the process, the social order is inverted; the supposedly superior sex becomes brutal; and, by implication, the inferior sex is reconstituted as civilized. Remarkably, this vision lacks animus; Aurelia does not enslave men, she simply rejects them in order to make more room for women.

The feminist projections of both Masippa and Aurelia exhibit a certain deference to the patriarchal structures of their societies. More direct forms of protest allow other writers to formulate positions that, while in no way giving women an equal place in society, provide them with an opportunity to identify themselves as unjustly victimized. Why, asks Ippolita Crema, do men think that only they are "born to letters": "Why do they insist so brazenly that all wit belongs only to them? that all strength belongs to them and finally also all value?" And she urges her daughter to pursue her studies so that men will at last "be constrained to be silent and admire womanly virtue" (C). Obviously inspired by humanist histories of famous women, Lucietta Soranza insists that it will be through a literary life that women will recover "their former honor and traditional reputation," and that this recognition will permit them to escape from "the tyranny of men and to guard against their trickery [insidie]" (D8). How this literary life might affect the place and reputation of women concerns Livia d'Arco, who follows Christine de Pisan in believing that history must be rewritten to expose the injustice of patriarchal society. Her protest differs from its earlier instances of expression because it is so self-critical. She asks for a moral change in women, that they acquire all the virtue proper to men, so that men cannot fail "to commemorate them," but she realizes that such an act of self-creation will not in itself achieve the re-presentation of womankind that she looks forward to. That will entail a confrontation with history, a rewriting of the past so that what has appeared to be the weakness of women can be recognized as the vice of men. She further determines to expose the process by which the ideology of patriarchy has come to be established, to reveal its origins in a systematic terrorization of woman, and, most important, to demonstrate that in patriarchalism there is a kind of incivility that destroys men as well as women. She advises her women readers:

> Let us strive to be good, of a true and perfect goodness, and let us not fear their pens, let us study eloquence together with wisdom, and even we may write blaming men, how they have been against us for so long, and even to this day: let us show them by clear examples taken from the heart of the truest histories that from the time of Adam men were always foolhardy, quarrelsome, deceitful . . . let us show them that they were always thieves, torturers . . . that they were always weak in suffering adversity . . . how many evildoers have been men, how much damage have they wrought, and for how much harm have they been responsible in the world. [R4r–v]

Courageous as her request is, however, Livia also understands how unlikely it is to be granted: "O Lord, why aren't all women of my mind?" (R4v). In essence, her whole argument—her protest as well as her doubts—inverts the arguments of the critics who had insisted that the virtue of women is proved by their actual powerlessness. Her analysis of extant history suggests that if women are morally better than men, their superiority cannot be demonstrated by history, since women not only have had practically no part in deciding the affairs of the world, but also—more telling—now remain for the most part reluctant to record the truth of their own innocence. She effectively identifies the women who are "not of her mind" as promoting the interests of men. Thus she represents women as feminist or conventional; the former character is strong, the latter weak. As the literature of protest develops throughout the remainder of the century and into the next, the strength of woman will be further discriminated so that it will be understood as embracing qualities positively valued both as masculine and as feminine.

For some writers, the struggle to come to terms with patriarchalism resulted in an evaluation of the physical nature of women which contested what education and culture held was the inherent frailty of the sex. To Beatrice Pia, for instance, humanist exempla were of interest chiefly because they celebrated all the masculine virtues that were associated with male strength. As she interprets these accounts, she suggests that for a woman to act like a man is for her to experience the virile dimension of her person. Were all women to do so, they would "awaken," as she puts it, from their "profound sleep." The heroines of the classical past are important to her less for their moral qualities than for the feats of physical endurance that "permitted them to govern and rule over others in a more than masculine fashion." She even describes an existence in which the most imposing of biological demands on a woman—childbirth—is met by energy that is both demonstrably of the female and also, by virtue of what it achieves, clearly masculine. This effort defies processes of acculturation which have persuaded women to see themselves as weak:

> The Gaditane women have been praised by historians because immediately after giving birth, they rose from their beds and proceeded with domestic tasks, and they did not customarily lie in bed thirty or forty days as we do, emptying the larder of delicacies, robbing the henhouse and eating a ton of boar's meat. Because of this we do not know how to do such wonderful deeds as did the German women, who restored to battle order the army that was in flight from the enemy.   [R8]

The reference is a powerful one in that it associates the rituals of modern—in contrast to barbarian or mythical—childbirth with a negative sort of creativity: in bearing children her female contemporary is also forced to bear the burden of helplessness, of ignorance—"[it is] because of this [helplessness] that we do not know how to do such wonderful deeds." And not because childbirth is itself debilitating—it is not, as the Gaditane women prove—but because it is perceived as an instance of female frailty and feminine impotence. As Beatrice Pia's contemporaries pointed out, it is the relative physical weakness of women, associated as it is with their sexual vulnerability, that renders them not only morally suspect but also easy targets for male scapegoating. The uncivilized and uninhibited German women who turn around an army in retreat symbolically recover the physical strength that would make them invulnerable to such abuse.

Sex, Gender, and Social Status

The revisionary notions of sex and gender proposed by Landi's correspondents may have been provoked by the continued acceptance of conservative doctrine generally. If anything, notions of the nature of woman became more prescriptive during the second half of the century. Treatises on the family focused on the education of the young girl (and prospective wife), the kind of work she must do (physical or intellectual), and her status within the family (how subservient to her husband's management she must be, the kinds of attention and affection she could expect or claim from him). This very specificity indicated how contentious doctrine had become. Writers persist in maintaining the necessity for a strictly hierarchical order in the household, but they also try to explain why it is natural (and therefore not subject to alteration) and in the best interests of women. Feminist critiques of such conservatism seek to reassess these interests and to show that when they are correctly formulated, men are not correspondingly disadvantaged but actually benefited by sharing them.

How thorough patriarchal rule ought to be was of course subject to qualification, especially in light of Christian teaching. Nevertheless, some treatises on domestic government which stress parallels between the family and the state claim that a father has *absolute* control over his dependents. Nicolò Gozze, in his *Governo della famiglia*, a fictional dialogue between the author and a companion, declares that man is born first to govern himself and then "to govern others, principally those who are naturally closest to his household and family."[9] The office of the father is first to love his children and then to safeguard the affairs of the family; in any case, "everything depends on the government of a wise and prudent father of the family." The relationship of man to woman—in which he takes care of public and she of private affairs—is universal, "used by all the people of the world," and has "always been held to be natural, as Aristotle has noted" (B3v). Like Gozze, Paolo Caggio, in his *Iconomica* (1552), insists that the father's authority is total and not to be delegated to subalterns, as authority is, for example, in a republic, where "more hold office than in a family . . . thus all who are magistrates in a city to whom obedience is owed can be said to rule. . . . But it is not so in a family in which the government belongs to a single head; and that is the father of the family. He alone has the power to command."[10] He is in fact "a king in his kingdom"; and if he is also to have the "greatest respect" for his wife, it is because she is "only one level beneath [*un grado di manco*]" him (B6v).

Resentment of such restrictive attitudes is evident in other treatises. Alessandro Piccolomini, in his *Della institutione di tutta la vita dell' huomo*

[9]Nicolò Gozze, *Governo della famiglia* (Venice, 1589), sig. Av.

[10]Paolo Caggio, *Iconomica* (1552), sig. A4v. Caggio identifies himself as "gentil'huomo de Palermo"; Girolamo Ferlito, writing from Venice, dedicates this work to Bernardino Sanseverino, Duke of Somma.

nato nobile e in città libera (1552), makes a Neoplatonic distinction between a man's beloved and his wife: the first is a person with whom he is spiritually united in a *"unione d'animi"*; the second is his *"consorte."*[11] A wife is ordained by God for the propagation of the species, a beloved for inspiration and delight. The wife is at a disadvantage, and Piccolomini anticipates her protest. Destined to her domestic office by her weak nature, she may envy her husband's freedom "as he is at liberty to leave and remain away from home at will" (bk. 10, I4v). But she is not to be glum on this account: wives should not, "for fear of being held too bold . . . or [for] some other reason," be reluctant to smile; and they should take care not to "show themselves with a perpetually harsh and bitter expression" (I5v). Nor should a man's beloved repine at his absence but rejoice "that the most virtuous business [*quelli virtuossissimi uffitii*] belongs to a really civic-minded man" (H7v). In any case, a wife is to mirror her husband, that is, to exist only as the reflection of his desires and wants. To Piccolomini, she is his "Eco" (I6); for Pietro Belmonte, writing for his daughter in his *Institutione della sposa* (1587), she is to be remade in his image: "in sum, I wish you to transform yourself totally in him, to follow entirely his way of doing things . . . and as a new kind of chameleon take from him the color that he shows you" (Bv).[12] She, too, is not to grumble at her situation but "to know that just as the great deeds of heroes [*atti egregi e eroici*] are more praiseworthy than an existence of ordinary ease, so also are the manners of a gentle person, graceful ways, and noble reflections" (I4v). Belmonte attempts to forestall his daughter's complaints by equating her compliant conduct with heroic action.

A woman's education was obviously crucial to her future success as a human chameleon. Both Dolce and Vives had pointed out that she was chiefly to be taught how to preserve her chastity, the foundation of all her other virtues. The position might have been regarded as reactionary: the previous century had seen the development of different humanist conceptions of education for women, at least for those of noble rank. Palace schools, such as the one run by Vittorino da Feltre in Mantua early in the

---

[11]Alessandro Piccolomini, *Della institutione di tutta la vita dell' huomo nato nobile e in città libera* (Venice, 1552), bk. 9, sig. D3 and D2v, respectively.

[12]Pietro Belmonte, *Institutione della sposa* (Rome, 1587), sig. Bv. Belmonte's treatise was composed for his daughter on the occasion of her marriage. Doubtless his precepts are harsh. How uncompromisingly were such precepts enforced? In a review article, Anthony Mohlo sensibly cautions against underestimating "the extent to which ideology and practice may not always have been in harmonious synchrony with each other" during this period: "Visions of the Florentine Family in the Renaissance: An Essay on Francis W. Kent's *Household and Lineage in Renaissance Florence: The Family Life of the Capponi, Ginori, and Rucellai*," *Journal of Modern History* 50 (1978): 309.

fifteenth century, provided the daughters of their patron's family with the same classical education that their sons had.[13] Some humanists in the next century (Erasmus, for example) had favored educating women of means, and, however contradictory that education on occasion proved—as what they read tended largely to enforce ideas of their weakness and inferiority—it did at least permit a degree of intellectual sophistication. In general, although women of the urban gentry or "middling sort" do not appear to have seen whatever education they had as a means of understanding their situation—of rewriting their history, as Christine said—feminist writers continued to plead for more education for women on revolutionary grounds. Conservatives, such as Giovanni Michele Bruto, registered their opposition to such appeals.

Bruto's *Institutione di una fanciulla nata nobilmente* (1555) makes a conventional case for a girl's instruction by moral exempla (but forbids corporal punishment),[14] which is subsequently developed into a doubly paradoxical argument: the education of a woman is to consist in limiting her access to education; her consequent ignorance is actually the highest wisdom. Condemning fathers who are unwise enough to give their daughters erotic verse to read, which makes them "lazier and more effeminate" (*effeminate*) than they are by nature (B6v), he answers a more general question: "I cannot make myself believe by any argument that [for a woman a literary education] could be good" (C4). His defense of his position, based on an inversion of the terms of the usual moral argument for education, not only of women but men—"the misapplication of literature has more often been harmful and inconvenient that useful and commendable" (C4v)—reveals his real concern when he deals with the education of a wife.

Study, whose end is "delight" and "profit," is for her entirely inappropriate because she is given to man "by nature" only "for domestic work": "thus [a wife] has only actively to attend to our [*sic*] welfare and that of the family." Study can only hurt "the beauty and innocence of her spirit." In any case, "the government of states and republics is not given

[13]On the schooling of the Gonzaga and Nogarola women, see William Harrison Woodward, *Vittorino da Feltre and Other Humanist Educators* (Cambridge: Cambridge University Press, 1897), 73–92, 224–25, 247–50.

[14]Giovanni Michele Bruto, *La institutione di una fanciulla nata nobilmente* (Anvers, 1555), sig. B6, is perhaps a companion piece to Bruto's *Praeceptorum coniugalium*. This edition of the *Institutione*, dedicated to Signor Silvestre Cataneo for the education of his daughter, Marietta, appears with a French translation on facing pages. An English translation was published in London in 1598; for an earlier unacknowledged translation, see Janis Butler Holm, "The Myth of a Feminist Humanism: Thomas Salter's *The Mirrhor of Modestie*," in *Ambiguous Realities*, ed. Carole Levin and Jeanie Watson (Detroit: Wayne State University Press, 1987), 197–218.

to women" (D4; Mary Tudor had acceded to the English throne thirteen years before the publication of this treatise). That a woman's merit derives only from her application to uxorial duties is clear when Bruto speaks of the danger of ambition. She must not, above all, aspire above her office (D4v); nor must she be "so proud [*ambitiosa*] that she disdains to pitch in when the laundry is being done; she must participate in all the household work" (E8v). Her education in ignorance is, however, compensated for by a corresponding virtue, because, as Bruto maintains, she is in fact "wiser" than the man who is educated: "whatever the knowledge and understanding of all those men who in antiquity attended the Lyceum, the Porticum, and the Academy with applause and renown for wisdom, it is little or nothing compared to that of the person who knows God" (D8v). Bruto's assessment of learning recalls the warnings of Paul and Augustine on the relative uselessness of learning *when spiritual matters are at issue*.[15] Bruto transposes the Pauline justification of a spiritual ignorance—the wisdom of the world as spiritual folly—into the realm of pure secularity and implies that the woman who does domestic work is sanctified.[16]

When a woman's virtue is analyzed with reference to her situation *outside* as well as within the family, however, it may be subject to new and finally more complex assessments; in any case, her status as inferior and subordinate is not invariable. Tasso's *Discorso della virtù feminile e donnesca* (1572) represents the woman as a wife and also as a person with moral standing or *virtù*. His model is his dedicatee, the Duchess of Mantua,

[15]See St. Augustine, *Confessions*, 10; and Petrarch, *De ignorantia*, in his *Prose* (Milan: Ricciardi, 1955).

[16]Not all who saw the household as a diminutive state accepted the legitimacy of the idea that woman (and especially a wife) was wholly subordinate to man within it. Fausto da Longiano's *Delle nozze* (Venice, 1554) uses the relatively privileged status of the Roman matron under Justinian as an entry into a proto-anthropological argument against the politicized marriage as a natural and universal condition. Most important, he relates that a Roman wife was protected by law, rather than by moral or religious precept, against abuse from her husband: "Law gave the wife the right to bring an action against her husband for mistreatment" (Bv). He devotes much of his treatise to establishing the high legal status of women in other parts of the ancient world. Obviously he did not intend that contemporary practice be prescribed by these points, although he does urge that current abuses be reformed "to a better use" (B3v). What he does establish is that ideas and social practices related to sex and gender are culturally constructed. Examples from economic life could also serve to undermine patriarchal structures. Giacomo Lanteri's *Della economica* (Venice, 1560), a dialogue on household government dedicated to Renée de France, represents a wife functioning like an urban artisan; her economic productivity is a guarantee of her autonomy, at least with respect to certain activities: "In the city, artisans may exercise their crafts without interference [on the part of the authorities] so that the city may be provided with food and other necessities; so you, my wife . . . taking from me a general direction, will see to it that the family will undertake such work according to my plans initially, and yours secondarily" (K8v).

whose "inner beauty" inspires him. Marriage no longer serves wholly to define her; she has another mode of existence that Tasso defines as "ladylike" (*donnesca*) in contrast to "feminine" (*femminile* [*sic*]).[17] The line between her two characters is precise. For although, as Tasso remarks, Plato states that men and women have the same virtue naturally and become different only by "experience" (*operationi*), Aristotle's analysis of the different virtues of men and women has effectively determined the arrangement of authority and power *in the family* (A3r–v). Following Aristotle, Tasso claims that woman is capable of rational activity but only insofar as it is directed at controlling her emotions: "but of the other virtues—which are situated in the intellect—a woman ought scarcely to know anything; for intellectual speculation does not suit her" (B). Nor does she need prudence, the virtue associated with positions of authority and power and "the rule [or basis] of the other virtues"; in a woman prudence only "serves the prudence of man and ought not to exceed that which is necessary [to that end]." It follows that she must obey her husband. At this point, however, Tasso interrupts himself and contradicts his source: in fact, Aristotle fails to consider all cases. There are circumstances other than domestic in which a woman functions. She may, if she is a queen or noblewoman, be called to an office other than that of a wife, in which case her genetic inferiority is wholly eliminated. Since, as he notes, he writes for the Duchess of Mantua, who is neither a "citizen" nor a "private gentlewoman" nor a "bourgeois matron" (*una industriosa madre di famiglia*), he must consider the woman who is "heroic." Her special virtue is *donnesca* (literally "of the female governor"), not the "thriftiness" of the wife but the "grace" of the "royal lady." And such a woman is judged with men, by a single standard. Indeed, for the heroic woman, the virtue of the wife is entirely inappropriate: "In heroic

---

[17]Tasso's more popular work on marriage, *Il padre della famiglia* (1580), does not mention *la donna donnesca*; it does, however, suggest that a woman of noble birth may have a public and political authority over a husband of lesser rank: "When it happens that by some accident of fortune a man marries a woman of higher rank, he must—without, however, forgetting that he is a husband—honor her more than he would a woman of equal or lesser rank; and have her as a companion in love and for life, but as a superior in activities that are manifestly public." She, on the other hand, must remember that as a woman she is invariably subject to man: "She must think that no distinction of rank can be as great as that difference which nature has made between men and women, and by which women are naturally made the subordinates of men": *Tasso's Dialogues: A Selection, with the Discourse on the Art of the Dialogue*, trans. Carnes Lord and Dain A. Trafton (Berkeley: University of California Press, 1982), 82. (This edition has Italian and English on facing pages; the translation here is mine.) Recent studies of Tasso include Fabio Pittorrie, *Torquato Tasso: L'huomo, il poeta, il cortigiano* (Milan: Bompiani, 1982). For a study of Tasso's discourses on poetry especially in light of his attitudes toward family relations, see Margaret W. Ferguson, *Trials of Desire* (New Haven: Yale University Press, 1985).

ladies is a heroic virtue that compares with that of the man, and for women gifted with this virtue modesty is no more appropriate than courage or prudence, nor is there any distinction between their deeds and offices and those of heroic men" (B2–3).

Tasso concludes by complimenting "the present Queen of England," who despite her separation from the church is nevertheless dear to every "high-minded spirit" for "the heroic virtue of her spirit and the loftiness of her remarkable genius" (B3v). If this conception of woman as both wife and heroine is indebted to the idea of the queen's two bodies, as seems likely, it is broader in its reference. Unlike a monarch, Tasso's *donna regia* is privileged not because she has a mystical second body but rather because of her rank. Although linked to blood, her qualities are nonetheless human. The forms of empowerment Tasso terms *donnesca*, in contrast to *feminile*, are those that depend on a conflation of attributes conventionally identified as masculine and feminine; his ideal woman is thus behavioristically androgynous. Since her feminine attributes are assessed positively, her portrait supports the fundamental distinction between the feminine in contrast to the effeminate which defenses of woman are in the process of establishing during this period. As Nicolao Granucci observed, commenting on two attributes commonly gendered as feminine: "In the tender breast of a woman, linked to great beauty, can be found the prudence and fortitude of mind, together with all the other virtues, that the sternest men possess."[18]

Tasso's specification of the heroic woman also serves to illustrate the relative weakness that other writers assigned to a comparable figure who might appear similar but actually is not: the court lady. Any Renaissance author attempting to fashion such a person was bound to confront contradiction, for the rules governing a woman's conduct in public and thus at court—whatever her rank or social abilities—prohibited her from speaking her mind or taking decisive action. The difficulty of her position is illustrated in two treatises describing manners for women at court: Ludovico Domenichi's *La donna di corte* (1564) and Stefano Guazzo's *Civil conversatione* (1575). Domenichi makes clear that a woman is wholly unsuited to the challenges of self-representation intrinsic to court life; Guazzo points out how fragile are the actual relations of power between men and women, and consequently how gravely a woman who attempts to participate actively in public life can threaten the stability of the system that sustains those relations, whether in the court or in the family. Both

---

[18]Nicolao Granucci, *La piacevole notte et lieto giorno: Opera morale* (Venice, 1574), sig. H4v.

treatises demonstrate that the literature of courtiership, or, in Guazzo's case, of civic life, is a poor vehicle for the defense of women.

Domenichi's reasoning is categorical. Woman cannot participate in court life because she never attains adulthood: "A male who is a child is not always a child but becomes a man with time: but the lady is a child all her life."[19] Just as "a child is not up to court activities . . . so a woman cannot meddle [in them]." She does not have the "prudence" and "wit" that would enable her both to be "urbane" and "to play the fool": "Jokes, games, and gestures designed to make people laugh are inappropriate to women" (A4). In other words, she lacks, or is forbidden to use, the intellectual and social resources needed to prosper at court. She is handicapped by the very sincerity that Marot had argued earlier was essential to the virtuous woman who had to appear in public because of her noble birth, but also to refrain from participating in public life because of her sex. Hence her double bind. Without sincerity, a virtue Domenichi terms "simplicity," she is socially unacceptable: "although urbanity is a virtue in men, it is not a virtue in women" (A4v). Yet her simplicity is incompatible with the self-defensive behavior needed for social success: "simplicity . . . is spoiled by lying, or indeed by simulation and dissimulation" (A4). "Purity" is "natural," Domenichi claims, and therefore the court lady's "agreeableness" cannot be "faked" (*simulata, finta, immascherata*; C2v).

Guazzo's concept of women at court and in public is both subtler and more exhaustive. He makes clear that the "conversation" he describes is more than a means of communication. It is both a way to self-knowledge and a tool for self-advancement. "Civil" conversation is a mirror of the self and essential to its further development, as Guazzo's character Annibale asserts: "The estimation that we have of ourselves is not our own but taken almost on loan from others."[20] In politics, it gets the speaker a position; in the marketplace, it earns him wealth. Conversation is the medium in which a person acquires his reputation, not the value he has but rather what his society gives him. The speaker Cavaliere declares:

---

[19]Ludovico Domenichi, *La donna di corte* (Lucca, 1564), sig. A3v. Domenichi's *Nobiltà e eccellenza della donna* is a translation of Agrippa of Nettesheim's treatise, discussed in chap. 2.

[20]Stefano Guazzo, *La civil conversatione* (Venice, 1575), bk. 2, sig. I2. The text is dedicated to Signor Claudio Peschiera. For Guazzo see J. L. Lievsay, *Stefano Guazzo and the English Renaissance* (Chapel Hill: University of North Carolina Press, 1961). For a study of the language of courtly society with reference to Guazzo, see Frank Whigham, *Ambition and Privilege* (Berkeley: University of California Press, 1984); especially important for literature on women is the chapter "Tropes of Social Hierarchy," 63–87, which discusses the kind of rhetoric that attempts to make "an absolute ontological distinction between the ruling class and its subjects" (63).

Of this you can be certain if you once enter a prince's court, where you will see an infinite number of courtiers gathered to deal with many things; to learn news of deaths or of the confiscation of goods; to entertain ways of begging a prince for honors, clothing, favors, grace, or privileges, either for himself or for others; to converse with stewards and secretaries and ushers before making their requests. Nor are their allies absent, assembled in a beautiful circle in secret counsel, discussing the way to disgrace some official and put another in his place.   [I3v–4]

It is a conversation from which woman, and especially the court lady, is excluded. She is necessary to court society, but only as an ideal presence. As Aleramo, another of Guazzo's speakers, observes, all court gatherings would be insipid "without the participation of women" (R8v). But if the lady fails to follow rules of self-effacement, she is dangerous. When men converse with "men of bad reputation," they are, in a sense, in their element. They can protect themselves from imitating criminal actions. In conversation with a chaste gentlewoman, by contrast, they are moved by "lascivious and ungoverned appetite" (R6).[21] The conversation of the court lady must therefore attempt to achieve the inverse of that of the courtier. Rather than rhetorical expertise, she must exhibit verbal restraint and avoid representing herself as a person of feeling and action. If she speaks, it must be with a kind of "majesty" (*maestà*; S4)—she is to be neither provocative (endangering a man's self-control) nor virile (a possible rival) nor austere (inducing feelings of guilt). The moral and aesthetic framework within which she is expected to function is remarkably small.

Guazzo recognizes the possibility that a woman could wish for and even seek to secure a public role and recognition, but he believes that were she so distinguished, she would destroy society. Like many other

---

[21]Guazzo confesses that he does not restrict the activities of the court lady in light of *her* moral deficiencies; dicta against women "are not pronounced to blame women but proposed in light of the deficiencies of the man, who is more likely to sin when conversing with a woman of good reputation than with wicked men; for conversing with loan sharks, thieves, adulterers, blasphemers, and other reprobates, it is easy to resist wickedness, while conversing the ladies, even decent ladies, one feels oneself moved by lust" (R6). The court lady thus faces a moral paradox: the more chaste she is (or appears), the more sexually tempting she becomes. The meretricious *cortegiana*, by contrast guarantees a certain courtly morality. A commoner response to the chaste woman may have been anger and loathing. Repulsing a man's advances, she signifies his undesirability; rather than the scorning subject, however, she is transformed into the scorned object. Prodicogine Filarete, in his contemporary *Difesa delle donne* (Padua, 1588), writes that the vilification of women is caused by male frustration: "Men, knowing that they have been rejected as vile and abjectly horrible persons, don't know how to respond other than by vilifying the entire female sex. . . . And this response is so far off the mark that women are marked with vices that they altogether lack; [on the other hand] men, who falsely attribute these vices to women, are themselves far from honorable" (Bv–A4v; the signatures of this book are out of sequence).

writers, he discusses the possibility of a kind of equality between husband and wife, perceived largely in terms of age, rank, wealth, and especially consent to their union; both husband and wife should desire marriage. Finally, however, these images give way to others that specify the unacceptability of equality of the sexes. Cavaliere admits that a woman desires fame, especially if she can achieve it by actions that win public acclaim; in this respect she resembles a man: "Just as if I were not to be content with being a good man according to my own conscience but wanted to testify to it with action, so that the world would recognize me; so ladies moved by this ambition want to be part of court life and try . . . to inscribe themselves in the register of good women" (X7v). But Cavaliere's *donna famosa* is no more attractive than Boccaccio's. Annibale, a conservative, alluding to the notions of a woman's virtue expressed in humanist histories, notes that a woman of his own time cannot expect praise for this kind of thing, "nor does it happen that such ladies boast of their prowess, for the race of Spartan women is extinct today" (X5v). Were a lady to violate this decorum, she would be unfortunate because her husband, whom he now terms a "little husband" (*maritello*), would be known to be a fool (X5v). The unstated intention of all these passages on court life is twofold. They are designed first to convince the reader of the wisdom of preserving a woman's capacity to symbolize the moral and social ideals—and chiefly those based on the virtues of restraint and self-abnegation—that men, while required to honor in women, are not expected to imitate or achieve themselves. (Men are both inspired and tempted by a good woman; they see other men merely as competitors and feel less need to fear being corrupted by the criminals among them.) And second, these passages are intended to convince the reader that although a woman can be "ambitious," it is better for her and for society if she is not.

There was of course one mode of discourse in which a woman's desire to prove her virtue in public might be acceptably expressed. In his dialogue "Della dignità della donna" (1596), Sperone Speroni makes use of Petrarchan conventions to transform the passive ideality of woman—even in her role as wife—into a force that works actively to promote her husband's virtue. He gives her a place in the social order in which she can act as her husband's "inspiration," the *éminence rose* that directs his civic life. By transposing the terms of courtly and domestic discourse, Speroni is able to invent for woman a kind of autonomy that she does not ordinarily have. Danielo, Speroni's feminist, begins the dialogue by asking the question typical of courtly debates of love—whether "the man is governed by the woman"—while discussing the more usual claim that she is "at the service" of the man. Indeed, he goes on to ask, apparently addressing the institution of marriage, what the nature of the woman's service to the man in fact is. Is she a "servant" (*serva*) or a "slave" (*schiava*; D3v)? And finally, what force moves a man to be governed by a woman who is at his service? He discovers the answers to these questions in the formulation of a paradox similar to the one Erasmus had proposed to explain the position of the wife in the *Colloquia*: it is because a woman shows love and puts herself at the disposal of her lord that she rules him. And it is because she shows love that her lord's reciprocating service to her is not, like most forms of service, "from lack of spirit," but rather a just recognition of her worth: "you [the lady, are] worthy of my service."[22] Danielo is able to develop these tropes beyond the conventions of courtly discourse when he—unconventionally but deliberately—assimilates the principal features of the courtly *domina* to those of the wife.

Claiming that the beneficent domination of woman over man (according to the courtly equation) is destroyed at the moment of marriage, which is instituted by a male "force" analogous to the force of a mob against a lawfully governed republic, Danielo sees that love, a kind of counterforce, can in time reinstitute a wife's lawful and benign order of government. Having obtained his wife by forcing her into an unnatural and illicit submission, love converts the husband into her law-abiding subject: "I tell you . . . that every woman [*donna*] by nature . . . is the governor [*signora*]; if custom is contrary, it is because we men, tougher and made with greater strength than you women, force you with violence and tyrannize over you, perhaps in the very way that Roman armies used to elect an emperor in contravention of the laws of the republic." Man's usurpation of power is or ought to be, however, momentary: "for such violence . . . often yields to duty that clearly shows itself in acts of love, a love that (*once our laws by which you are unjustly made to serve us have*

---

[22]Sperone Speroni, *Dialoghi* (Venice, 1596), sig. D3v. This collection of dialogues is dedicated to Cardinal Aldobrandino by Ingolfo, Conte de Conti. The extent to which wives were, or might be, regarded as servants or slaves is not wholly a matter of courtly or Neoplatonic rhetoric. E. Rodocanachi notes that in this period Italian households frequently employed slaves, the vast majority of whom were in fact women: *La Femme italienne à l'époque de la Renaissance* (Paris: Hachette, 1907), 211–21. Wives who supervised or worked beside those slaves and under authoritative males might well feel that in practice there was little to distinguish between themselves and their helpers. Speroni's companion dialogue on the nature and status of women, "Della cura famigliare," reveals no comparable interest in revising concepts of a wife's duty. The tone of the dialogue is set by its principal speaker, Peretto, an aged father who is about to give his daughter in marriage. He counsels her to renounce the exercise of her own free will and to consider that without her husband's direction she is merely a lifeless body: "abandoned, cold, and dry, she collapses without breath or words" (H2v). Should her husband require redirection, she should proceed discreetly, "without accusing her husband, [so that] he will recognize his own shortcomings, and in a very gentle manner, almost as if he were reproving himself for them" (I4v).

been broken), living in your faces, makes you lords of our hearts" (D3v). This situation is later attributed to the fact that "Reason" controls the actions of men and "love" the actions of women. The usual values of the concepts are inverted. Love is recognized as a superior reason: it "curbs" desires better than reason does in its ordinary manifestation (D4v). The term "wife," Danielo concludes, means a "natural and general governorship" (F). His analysis of the affective relations between spouses sets legally recognized relations of authority and power in marriage against what is imagined idealistically to be their actual modification in practice. The customary rule in marriage is set aside, and the rule of the courtly and Petrarchan *domina* becomes the rule of the wife.

The literary conceitedness of Speroni's analysis of the paradox of wifely service and lordship may not have encouraged his contemporaries to see in his new model of marriage more than a psychological reference at best, and in fact his notion of the wife's rule does not require an alteration in the forms of marriage at all: her power is influential rather than authoritative. Resorting to the imagery common to descriptions of marriage, Danielo reports that he has heard his friend "il Padovano" describe the husband as a sun, his wife as its intelligence—"a mystery hid to common persons." This feminine influence inspires the good works by which men restore and preserve the republic (to be imagined, perhaps, as the real equivalent of the hypothetical one destroyed by the act of male violence that made woman a wife): "Our spirit made pregnant by the virtue of the woman will bring forth many good deeds: for as for the business of the republic, our end is the state" (F2). Speroni's "mysterious" revision of relations in marriage nevertheless goes at least some way toward demystifying the vapid ideal of a sincerely honorable and passively majestic woman which Domenichi and Guazzo have earlier sketched.

When the social position and role of woman were understood to be the products of *cultural processes*, the virtues deemed properly or typically hers had the greatest chance of being reassessed as valuable to *human beings*, regardless of sex. The proto-anthropology of such writers as Champier had questioned the notion that the subordination of woman was a universal phenomenon, changeless and impervious to historical or local pressures. Other feminists had attributed the position of men to their superior strength (for Capella, expressed in an originary moment in which women handed over their arms), which was subsequently translated into laws and customs prohibiting women from acquiring equality with men. Bernardo Trotto's *Dialoghi del matrimonio e vita vedovile* (1578) illustrates the economic interests that often seem to be at stake in this disempowerment, especially of wives—a subject already broached by implication by Barbaro and Alberti—and concludes by suggesting that these interests have been miscalculated. He implies that the authority and power that men and women *share* are more conducive to their prosperity than whatever drives men to attempt complete control of women. More generally, he shows that the ideas of prudence, clemency, and legitimate political resistance are often closely associated with ideas of the feminine and its valorization. His examples suggest that a rationale for a constructive politics of self-restraint can be traced at least in part to an experience of privation that is identifiably that of women. This is to say not that he is concerned simply to show that women are socially, politically, and economically oppressed—his interests are not so practically oriented—but rather that if the sign of oppression is in his culture feminine, it is not without its resources.

There are four principal speakers in Trotto's dialogue: the widow Hippolyta, who argues for the "freedom" of the unmarried (in her case widowed) women; Astemio, who represents the case for the traditional forms of marriage; Antonio, a skeptic and misogynist; and Aleramo, who defends women as persons as well as wives. His contribution to the dialogue is comprehensive and includes long set pieces that function as separate dramas within the larger drama represented in the treatise itself. It is in some measure because of the cogency of the remarks of the first three speakers that Aleramo's reply carries so much weight.

Hippolyta concentrates on establishing that marriage is a form of servitude for women. Challenging the notion of complementarity in marriage, she claims that in marriage its constitutive elements, male and female, are not made mutually compatible. Rather, these elements, indeed each person, has his or her own kind of perfection, which is expressed in activities that are undertaken and need to be assessed independently: "And the man and the woman, however unified they are [in principle], are always busy in different activities, in which it is much better, most of the time, that they are alone than together to no purpose."[23] And to explain why women perform better when they are not in the company of men, she asks: "Who freezes our hearts in greater fear and bondage than the husband with his will that is always at odds with our own?" (C). For her the concept of marriage as a harmonious complemen-

---

[23]Bernardo Trotto, *Dialoghi del matrimonio e vita vedovile* (Turin, 1578), sig. B3v. Trotto dedicates his work to Hippolita Scaravella Castelliera, who, by virtue of her own *bellissimi discorsi*, was its chief inspiration. In his letter to his readers, he identifies some of his speakers: Hippolyta is the image of his dedicatee, the widow of the senator; Antonio is identified as Antonio Bello; Aleramo as Aleramo Becchuti. His story of Livia derives in part from Seneca's *De clementia* 1, 9.

tarity screens a harsher reality of domination and subservience. In having to obey, a wife becomes a servant, whatever else she may be called. This relationship is not natural but rather circumstantial: "it is not the fault of nature that we obey but rather the bad luck of the draw [*disgratia della sorte*]." When a wife becomes a widow, she is released from this obligation: "she is no longer subject to a man's bestiality" (D4). Her complaints on the whole reverse the usual terms of the relation of marriage—man is the rational head, and so forth—and point to what is for her its fundamentally erroneous supposition, that men are in charge because they are reasonable. In fact, she argues, it is simply that they are stronger.

Astemio's comments defending marriage are intended as ironic responses to Hippolyta's complaints. His most memorable statement (a reworking of Proverbs 31) compares the family to a cargo ship freighted with its master's goods, with the wife as skipper. The image illustrates the uxorial condition to which Hippolyta has objected and implies its economic basis: the woman may be in charge of the family vessel, including its goods, as Astemio says, but she is not in any case its owner. Her duty is as Aristotle defined it: "to conserve the riches already acquired by the husband" (K4). Indeed, according to Antonio, who argues against marriage as too demanding on the husband, a wife not only labors to enhance the value of her husband's property; she is herself property. Recalling Alberti's picture of male friendship as predicated on the gift of women for sexual purposes, Antonio—defying Aleramo—insists that a husband must be able to show his wife in a state of undress to others, "to show in one way or another the parts of her body"; that is, to place his wife's sexuality on public display in order to maintain his authority over her. He will lose his authority if he cannot treat her as an object, a possession—"if he cannot please himself by playing with his wife" (Bb).

Hippolyta's objections to marriage are answered by the reforms implicitly advocated in Aleramo's criticism of marriage. Contesting the view that marriage requires the objectification of the wife, Aleramo asserts that if the sexes are to live together in concord, they must have equal status: "thus all knowledgeable persons have said to each other, and philosophers have agreed, that equality is the mother of concord and of friendship, and that inequality leads to hatred" (V2). Woman's creaturely identity to man makes her his double in "all things," even in "the knowledge of government" (V2). Images illustrating relations of equality in marriage make its practical effects more explicit: a couple is like two brothers, like right and left hand, like lord and vassal—"if the prince does not cause his vassals grief but governs them well, he is loved, served, praised, and his state grows great." In fact, according to chivalric norms (as Trotto's readers probably knew), the monarch is only as powerful as his vassals make him: "the king appears much greater when his lieutenant is more honored" (Y4v). Of all political relations, only those of feudalism separate power and authority so decisively; without the support of vassals, royal authority is impotent.

Aleramo makes a special point of emphasizing the value of woman's work. When Antonio asks rhetorically how one can value "feminine virtue" when a woman is constantly occupied in "low matters"—"in being silent, tolerating her husband, taking charge of four sacks of grain [and] two hens, nursing children and telling them stories . . . stitching a couple of shirts while twisting a poor spindle all day, making soup, and roasting meat . . . ; the hour a man loses in wooing a woman is more valuable than all the work she does in a lifetime" (Bb3)—Aleramo replies that these are valuable tasks that need to be done; they actually contribute to the economic welfare of the family. What is clear to Trotto's reader, however, is that a woman's labor is for persons other than herself, and because she can make no claim upon it herself, it is undervalued.

The subtlest part of Trotto's defense reflects his understanding of the way a culture assigns values to sex and gender. One might even say he has a sense of how men and women come to figure certain values— which then take on conventionality—to themselves and to each other. To illustrate these processes, he recalls two instances in which a woman has stood for a specific political program. In both, her counsel and position are seen to be wiser and more effective than those of the men whom she confronts.

His most dramatic example is the British queen Buidica (Boadicea), whose speeches encouraging her subjects to rally against the larger and superior forces of Nero stress the value of a "freedom in poverty" (*una libera povertà*) over an "affluent enslavement" (*ricca servitù*). She argues that the Britons are themselves the cause of their own misfortunes. "Having let [the Romans] set foot on this island, [we ought] to have chased them out" (Dd4v). She reminds her army of the other Romans they have expelled from their island, including Caesar, Augustus, and Caligula. And she concludes by deriding Nero, calling him a woman and herself a man. As Aleramo observes on the quality of martial combat undertaken by women in general, "by neither strength nor courage nor bodily form was there any way to tell the males from the females" (Eev)[24]

---

[24]Of contemporary feminists, Trotto is as knowledgeable as any about the important women of his century. He cites as examples of virile women several sixteenth-century queens: "The name of Catherine Queen of England is outstanding; she achieved victory (only a few years ago) on that terrible day on the banks of the Tweed, where more than ten thousand Scots died, together with their king. And who does not know of the courage and

But this traditional role reversal, in which a virile woman reaffirms masculine values, is less significant than the drama of which it is a part. In the person of a barbarian queen who opposes the imperial army of Rome, an army that his readers would have identified as civilizing, Trotto has devised a symbol of the spirit of liberty triumphing over forces of conquest. His androgynous female general, who advocates political freedom over material well-being, not only implies a limit to the effects of force (here associated with the civilizing Romans in contrast to the barbarian Britons), suggesting that a weaker nation can be moved to fight and win to preserve its independence, but also a skeptical view of what passes for civilization. Her appeal suggests that the obvious advantages the kind of society Rome can offer its colonies do not necessarily outweigh a people's need or desire for autonomy. Here civility and barbarism are gendered (conventionally) as masculine and feminine, but the value of each is reversed by a crucial association of *libertà* with British barbarism rather than with Roman civility. The independence of the barbarian female who (like Trotto's Hippolyta) cannot be persuaded to accept a comfortable subservience is valued more than the aggression of the ostensibly civilized male.

Aleramo's description of Livia, the wife of Augustus, is similarly subversive of patriarchal norms. Like his portrait of Buidica, it demonstrates that whatever his culture idealistically construes as feminine can on occasion serve to focus criticism on those norms. Livia's role within the drama Trotto contrives for her is to argue for a benign and flexible rule rather than an absolute autocracy. It is important that she not argue for a republic, for to do so would destroy the implicit parallel between her situation and that of Augustus's subjects. She deals with the concept not of a ruler under law but rather of a ruler who is himself the law. Clearly the lines of argument along which this notion of a benign ruler will be developed are already implicit in the configuration of the drama: Livia protests a political abuse that appears to have a close correlative in marital abuse. Once again, the subordination of women within patriarchal society is perceived as justifying criticism. I report this exchange at some length, as it is both rich and complex.

Livia begins her advice to Augustus by pointing out that no degree of power can guarantee a magistrate's (specifically an emperor's) safety:

---

fortitude of Margaret of Austria, daughter of the emperor Maximilian, and regent for Charles V. She, having been repulsed by Charles VII, king of France, gathered such a huge army and gave such manly help to the English that France suffered an extraordinary defeat. And to show herself no less the mistress of peace than of war, she then made a treaty with the most prudent Louise of Savoy, mother of Francis I, king of France, termed the peace of Cambrai" (Ee2). See also his treatment of literary women, sig. Ee2v–ff. By the end of the century, encyclopedic information on contemporary women is not unusual in defenses.

It is no wonder, Augustus, that you live in so much danger. For one cannot govern such a great empire without offending many, nor does the luck of human beings permit a single prince to please everyone, even if he is most just. Forthe greater part of even virtuous men aspire to wealth and glory. Unable to satisfy their greed and envious of the preferment of others, they blame the prince and embark on treacherous behavior, not so much to him as to his state. And this viciousness is common to all subjects, but especially to powerful and rich ones, and it is so fixed in their hearts by nature that it cannot be eradicated by counsel or laws or any kind of strength. [Bb4v–Cc]

Livia depicts human society as inherently divisive, its struggles for power predicated on an innate selfishness and greed that no virtue on the part of subjects or justice on the part of magistrates can fully overcome. Her characterization subverts idealized schemes of a social and political hierarchy based on the nature of creation and posits instead a human nature that is typically lawless. Augustus concurs, observing that a prince would truly seem divine (*simile a Dio immortale*) were "he never to have to deal with ordinary men." He implies that the very idea of a hierarchy of persons is in the order of a political fiction; reality admits no such gradations. It is, moreover, precisely among those whom a magistrate would expect to be naturally loyal, "his family and kin," that sedition is most common. "Against open enemies we can make use of friends: but against these others we have no help at all" (Cc). His admission is significant in its demystification of the notion of royal power; like Machiavelli, Trotto sees that there is no magic in royalty—or, one infers, in a husband. The nearest kin of which a magistrate could be afraid might well be his wife.

In answer to this problem, Livia argues that violent retribution, spurred by a fear of dissension, only exacerbates the magistrate's predicament; its solution lies in clemency: "Thus the desire for revenge, to punish all those who do evil, only brings forth disaffection and disgrace. Take therefore another way and let us conquer with pardon. For mercy is more profitable than cruelty" (Ccv). She advocates what appears to be a policy that, while supporting a rule of law, is nevertheless based on a concept close to that of equity: in the interest of peace, retributive acts, even though legitimate, may need to be forgone: "All violent deeds, although they may be most just, disturb the spirits [of the people]: by contrast, loving actions quiet them." But clemency is not to be exhibited indiscriminately.

It does not seem to me that one has to pardon all evildoers. Those who are arrogant, restless, wicked, and perverse . . . I would like you to cut away [from the body politic], as one does a part of the body that is not susceptible to medicine. But the others who commit crimes because of youth, little experience, ignorance, or for some other reason, willingly or not, I would have you correct with words and warnings . . . without taking their lives.   [CcIv–2]

The figure of woman is here identified with irenic and conservative action and illustrates in a manner more subtle than Astemio's skipper the ways in which women can have and use power. Finally, both Buidica and Livia are exemplary of a politics represented from the point of view of the female and as informed by feminine values—Buidica, the subject who is female, refuses wealth in the interest of liberty; Livia, the feminine magistrate, advocates clemency in the interest of the whole society.

The Female and the Feminine

For some feminist writers, beliefs that sustained a hierarchical notion of sex and gender proved especially open to question. Their strategy of defense was, first, to propose reasons for altering the symbolism associated with the female and feminine; and second, to suggest ways in which women might be regarded sympathetically. Christine de Pisan, Castiglione, and others had earlier attacked the assumption that woman was inferior to man by virtue of divine and natural law, but without an appreciation of a methodology that might be adequate to studying the formative basis of such an assumption (and of others like it) apart from certain simple techniques: they pointed to conflicts between authorities and differences of time and place. Approaches later in the century were capable of a greater degree of self-reflexivity; they concentrated on establishing the nature of and sources for the supposed evidence for misogyny. In this criticism, the figure of woman sometimes acquires a new kind of symbolic value. Because it is by examining the terms of woman's meaning as a symbol that the conventionality—rather than the naturalness—of her social position is made clear, she comes to stand for the potential of a society to change. In a sense, she becomes the symbol of the socially self-reflexive act, the image of a constructive form of doubt that qualifies the significance and usefulness of traditions, habits, and customs.

Girolamo Ruscelli's *Lettura ove . . . si pruova la somma perfettione delle donne* (1552) asks the most fundamental of questions concerning methodology: On what basis do we arrive at determinations of value? Or, to put it another way, what must we do or ask if we want to move beyond ignorance of what is and is not good? Ruscelli implies that we can establish what we know as true and valuable only by examining the logic behind praise and blame, which reveals nothing more than the non-verifiability of opinion in general. Why or what one praises or blames is never a wholly uncontroversial affair. Ruscelli's defense indicates that in the last analysis attention is to be directed to the person who is doing the praising and blaming. What are his motives, his concerns? What is at stake for him?

The philosophical context of Ruscelli's treatise is a Neoplatonic celebration of love; as its title indicates, its overt intention is to prove "with new and clear reasons . . . the high perfection of women." He is more immediately concerned with discovering the correct criteria for establishing this "perfection," however: he argues that the humanist practice of establishing a thesis to interpret events of the past by collecting illustrative examples is misleading. History offers a virtually limitless store of exempla, each of which can be used to illustrate a historical position, and those who praise by exempla invite others to blame by exempla. Praise and blame are themselves relative; a person or thing is always no more or less than some other person or thing, and the determination of absolute and certain worth eludes us: "if therefore we say that men are vile, wicked, and villainous and assert that women are worthier than they," he asks, "what have we really proved, except that women are less imperfect than men?" And he asks that "sound reasoning" not be based on generalized opinions but be directed to specific issues. If men are to be blamed for accusing women, let it only be "for the clearing of particular false charges against women."[25]

Ruscelli's insight into the nature of opinions derived from comparisons is of greater importance to the defense of woman than any of his later claims of her worth because it directs the reader's attention to the methodological weakness of defenses that depend only on such claims (as Christine de Pisan had already noticed): without reference to a control, no comparative opinion is sound. Ruscelli himself notes that when ordinary women are denigrated, it is because some paragon of male humanity is assumed to set the standard: "we presuppose that we are speaking of naturally true and perfect men" (D4). Assessments of women are meaningless unless the criteria used to determine them are also applied to assessments of men. *Failure* to see things as they truly are, and so to avoid opinionated assessments, does not actually affect the things so misjudged. Certainly it does not detract from their real value. But it does

---

[25]Girolamo Ruscelli, *Lettura . . . sopra un sonetto dell'illustriss. signor Marchese della Terza alla divine signora Marchesa del Vasto ove con nuove et chiare ragioni si pruova la somma perfettione delle donne* (Venice, 1552), sig. D3v. Ruscelli dedicates his treatise to Giovanni Battista Gavardo, whom he identifies as "Gentil'huomo Bresciano"; in his address to his readers, he represents it as a "tempio" to Giovanna d'Aragon.

reflect the intellectual debility of the person who can do no more than make comparisons. "Ignorance or little wisdom, in whomever you wish, in discerning gold as gold, jewels as jewels, beauty as beauty, goodness as goodness [i.e., the thing itself] does not take the beauty, goodness, or perfection from those things that have them but rather signals the imperfection of those who are ignorant [of them]" (Ev). The burden is on the judge to prove that his judgment is more than opinion. In a sense, Ruscelli's argument provides in a rather circuitous fashion substantiation for a position long familiar to defenders of women who, like Castiglione and others, had claimed that those who blame women reflect their own inadequacy. It differs in supplying, for the first time, an analysis of why such blame cannot be taken as definitive.

Luigi Dardano's brilliant *Bella e dotta difesa delle donne in verso e prosa* (1554) takes as its point of departure instances in which particular women who have been judged blameworthy in history defend themselves. He is less concerned about the mechanisms by which we assign praise or blame than about the extent to which we inherit or have imposed upon us attitudes and values that make such opinions practically inevitable. Unlike most of his contemporaries, he directs attention not at the decisions that are made about women but at the range and quality of the choices that define and limit the decisions it is possible to make.

His defense is constructed as a series of retrials of famous women whom history has condemned. The stories reflect the antagonisms between the sexes as they are expressed in historiographical bias: the claims of history are represented by misogynist men, the women to be retried by women defenders. The conflict between the two positions is therefore similar to the difference between readings of the past that aim to justify patriarchalism and those that intend to reveal it as unnatural and unjust. In the course of his argument, Dardano proposes two new principles of historical investigation: the principle of uniqueness and the principle of the paradigm. By the first, he demonstrates that historical events need to be considered unique and unrepeatable; by the second, that the behavior of any individual actor in the drama of history is in some measure (and how much is unclear) conditioned by ideology; in short, that behavior is not entirely an expression of personal feeling or conviction. His two principles exist, obviously, in tension with each other. An event that is considered to be unique in its causes and effects must at the same time be understood in relation to a system of values of which it is a manifestation. Like Ruscelli's notion of the meaningless comparison, Dardano's principles are clearly incompatible with humanist historiographical practice, according to which events are understood both in typological terms— that is, in terms of likeness and difference—and as expressions of human will.

The retrials that form the substance of Dardano's second book are conducted by a lawyer for men, Fulvio Stello; his feminist opponent, Hortensia; and three judges: the emperor Trajan; Carondo, prince of Tyre; and Seleuco, lord of Locrensis. Each defendant tells her own story, interrogated from time to time by both lawyers. Fulvio's opening apology for the prosecution suggests that the earlier convictions have been in error, the result of prejudice rather than an impartial assessment of evidence. He adduces various authorities who have testified to the wickedness of woman *as a sex*—Bernard: "Nothing arouses a man more than the tricks of a woman"; Augustine: "No one can be completely with God in his mind and still be linked to the passions of women"; Jerome: "Woman is the gateway of the devil, the path of iniquity, the strike of the scorpion"; Pope Gregory: "The safe thing is not to listen to woman"; and Origen: "Woman is the arm of the devil, the mother of sin."[26] Such dicta indicate that Hortensia's clients may have been (and may continue to be) judged guilty merely because they are women; implied is the possibility that not they but a misogynist society is on trial.

Eve's retrial, the first, exemplifies the workings of the principle of uniqueness. It is especially important that it is Eve who assumes this role, since she is typologically the woman in whom all future women are shadowed. To declare her history to be a manifestation of "uniqueness" is effectively to free all subsequent women from a typological tyranny, to eliminate the possibility that their individual histories can be identified with a fixed and hierarchical order of nature and history. Eve speaks in her own defense, asserting first that when a sin is confessed and repented of it cannot continue to be held against the sinner. She invokes the Psalmist: "Blessed are those whose sins are forgiven" (G2). Nor can the sin of one be passed down to others: "the son does not bear the sins of the father," because "the soul that has sinned will itself die" (G2v). She and Adam have suffered and paid—"we have suffered long and bitterly"— and that atonement is sufficient for humankind and for her female descendants (G2). On the principle of uniqueness itself Eve is quite specific: "Therefore, considering the sayings of holy men, the proposition [that woman lacks virtue] is false with respect to their kind if not to a specific example, if we really are the same in each being unique. The evil life of one in some many ought not to deny the goodness of others" (G5). Superficially this might appear to be a rephrasing of arguments from exception, so common in feminist literature. But because it is Eve who

[26]Luigi Dardano, *La bella e dotta difesa delle donne in verso e prosa* (Venice, 1554), sig. F6. The dedication is by Dardano's nephew Hippolyto to Francesco Veniero. Dardano's Proem criticises "the ill will of certain men, who for no reason vilify women." He wishes to defend the sex, "for if the virtue of women is not greater than that of men, at least it is no less" (A3).

speaks, Dardano can be seen as criticizing the practice of describing historical events in general terms, of finding behind them a typological order. Not only is it wrong to apply moral judgments to the kind rather than to the individual woman; no concept of "kind" has moral validity.

Iole's retrial is devoted to demonstrating the relevance of a second principle of historical interpretation, that of the paradigm. As a defense, it is rhetorically complex, in that Iole alludes to a second history—of Mariana, the wife of Herod—to justify the action for which history has wrongly condemned her, Iole. Mariana's case exemplifies human thought and action that clearly derive from conventional concepts of revenge; they are closely linked to the interests of men. Iole's treatment of Hercules, by contrast, exhibits a respect for social peace and concord, ideals that in the literature of feminist defense are attributed to the social thought and activities of women.

The betrayal of Hercules by Iole, while typologically close to that of Samson by Delilah, is nevertheless distinctive in its reference to a heroic and purely classical *virtus*, the basis in humanist thought for the moral development of the civic hero. The lines along which the myth was usually explicated were familiar to most sixteenth-century readers. Hercules, who symbolizes the excellence of the *vita activa*, is seduced from his role as protector of the polis by a woman; he submits to uxoriousness and is made effeminate as a result. No longer able to perform deeds of valor, he is transformed into a mere storyteller, one who re-presents in words the great actions of the past. His weakness can be (and often is) attributed less to a moral failure in him than to the fatal charms of Iole, whose sexuality is regarded as entirely debilitating to male strength and initiative.[27]

Dardano's is a subtler interpretation of the myth. Implicit in it is a relationship between doing and telling—that is, between action and reflection, and, yet more imposing, between conquest and civilization. A focus on these oppositions opens the way to a subversion of accepted meanings: Hercules becomes a figure of human lust for power, Iole a figure of pacification, of self-control through self-reflection and self-representation. This is precisely what Dardano makes of her. Iole represents Hercules' virility not positively, as the basis for action benefiting the polis, but rather negatively, as a license for rape and conquest. She describes him as violent, as inhumanly cruel, as bloody-handed: "Hercules . . . with his superior forces took the city, destroyed and ruined it

---

[27]The mythological status of Hercules as figure of earthly glory was well established by the time Boccaccio wrote *De genealogia deorum gentilium*. As *hera* means earth and *cleos* means glory, Hercules is fame (13.1).

entirely with inhuman cruelty and unheard-of impiety. Having seized everyone, [his forces] put them to a cruel death and stole their treasures. He seized me and took me to his kingdom as his consort" (K8). Now in her eyes a veritable antihero, he is subsequently transformed into a civilized creature of discourse by her artful pleasures. Fulvio's accusation of Iole is rendered ironic by its assumptions: "You made him sit among your maidens and tell stories . . . of his marvelous deeds; . . . and spin . . . without respect for his greatness, known to the ends of the earth from his youth, until he fell into your treacherous hands and [was betrayed by] your vicious and fraudulent faith as a wife" (K4). But by her own account, Iole had accomplished what force of arms could not. Exhibiting "a unique kind of patience in the face of an intolerable injury," she had achieved, as she says, "what no mortal knew how or was able [to do]: with study, wit, science, wealth, and arms I was able to do it without violence and avoiding bloodshed, death, ruin, and the destruction of kingdoms. By pleasures, delights, and benign artifice, I succeeded in conquering the whole world because I conquered Hercules, who himself conquered the whole world" (L3v–L4). Iole's words here specifically recall her accuser's earlier charge that she has "effeminized" the hero (K3v): "You made him put down the terrible iron club with which he slaughtered so many persons . . . you made him lay aside the bow, the quiver, and the arrows with which he wounded and killed innumerable valiant men" (K4). Iole has, in other words, overcome a figure who threatened civilized human life, not by a superior kind of violence but rather by its antithesis. Like Bernardo Trotto's Livia, Iole becomes a symbol of a policy—of conquest by civilizing rather than making war on the enemy—that is gendered as feminine because it makes use of qualities conventionally associated with women.

By her example, Iole questions the humanist conception of the hero's *virtù* and identifies the civilizing and stabilizing agency in history—one that is, moreover, politically decisive—as the benign pleasures that characterize relations between women and feminized men. She thereby introduces to Renaissance historiography a feminine point of view similar to those of such earlier defenders as the writer of the *Dialogue apologétique*, Capella, and Trotto: woman's weakness is not only innocuous in that it prevents antagonism, strife, and war; it is actually constructive in that it allows her to find occasions for reflection. Thus it can provide her with the self-knowledge necessary to control the ambition already deplored in her enemy, Hercules.

Methodologically crucial is Iole's reflection upon Hercules' strength: "Hercules by his great strength made me his consort against my will, [an act] for which he had no authorization" (K7v). It is important to her case that Hercules' action is illicit and unauthorized, because it illustrates that she can have been condemned earlier, and therefore be in need of a retrial now, only by reference to a system of values that did not need formal authorization. By defending her counterconquest of the hero by the example of Mariana, a victim of similar violence but without the effective recourse available to her, Iole establishes that the culture she describes, fictionally of antiquity but actually Dardano's own, is one in which male violence toward women receives implicit sanction. In the case of Hercules, Iole's story implies, such violence is obscured by the covering myth of the hero as a secular saint. Here Dardano insists on what I have called the principle of the paradigm—that is, the extensive power of the system of thought to which a person is introduced when he or she begins to communicate with others, and probably never abandons unless moved into some other system by a profound alteration of moral and intellectual attitudes.

Iole's story of Mariana functions as positive evidence of the benign nature of her own so-called crime: Iole might have done to Hercules what Mariana tried to do to Herod—"I did not do what she did, with the greatest approbation"—but in fact she did something quite different. Iole relates that Herod had murdered his wife's brother, Jonathan, who closely resembled her, and then, when on a trip to Rome, anticipating his own death, ordered her murdered also. Having discovered his plot, Mariana attempted to use her wit to kill Herod on his return from Rome: "she used all her wit and knowledge to effect a revenge." But her methods were less adept than those of Iole: Herod avoided her trap and the death he "so richly deserved," and she was executed after all (L). Iole claims that Mariana preferred execution to living unavenged, and implies, I think, that this preference is to be deduced from the drastic nature of Mariana's behavior toward Herod. The story as a whole is intended to distinguish between Iole's and Mariana's responses to violence. Iole's case is enhanced by her representation of Mariana's action as characteristically masculine, conducing not to the amicable settlement of differences but to continued divisiveness and destruction. Not only does Herod kill Mariana's male relatives, including the sons they share, after he has killed her; she is herself indistinguishible from her brother—"they were both so beautiful and of a similar complexion that no one could tell one from the other" (K8v–L)—and so passes for male (at least in this account). Mariana's desire to murder Herod may be explicable and excusable both as revenge and as self-preservation. But it is also representative of an essentially ironic process in which justice that is purely retributive, and therefore in the case of violent crime necessarily violent, destroys the very things that it seeks to preserve: social order, stability, continuity. That retribution is a gender-specific goal is implied by the masculinity of its perpetrator, the female Mariana. Its revelation of a negative or aberrant aspect of masculinity—the equivalent of effeminacy in relation to femininity—is suggested by the destructive violence of the action. The entire episode's paradigmatic reflection of the ideology that has condemned Iole's constructive solution to the violence she has suffered—that is, the feminization of its perpetrator—now requires a feminist reevaluation.

An examination of custom often reveals a connection between forms of social behavior and the presumptive values that sustain them. In the first half of the century, a few defenses of women were concerned with evidence of a proto-anthropological kind and as a consequence could suggest that social behavior was unrelated to what was considered natural. Domenico Bruni da Pistoia's *Difese delle donne* (1559) represents an advance on arguments of this kind. Looking at contemporary customs, especially as they find legal formulation, Bruni suggests that the disempowerment of women has its origin not in principles of natural or divine law but in misogynist opinion. More important, he is able to imagine as an alternative to the patriarchal social order, conceived as a hierarchy of persons whose status reflects their natures or essences, an *economic* social order in which place and value are determined by a person's work and by how well he or she does it. Thus he entertains notions that could justify a new and nonpatriarchal society.

Bruni begins by listing the conventional complaints against woman, which he terms "slanders," in order to make explicit how comprehensive are the psychological inhibitions women as a class have to suffer. Foremost is the doubt cast on their very humanity. Bruni notes that Aristotle asks whether women are not "imperfect animals," and "many" place them among the "brute beasts" rather than "rational animals." More generally they are termed "vain," "inconsistent," "mean-spirited," "untrustworthy," "proud," "irrational" (if they are crossed they become like beasts), "licentious," "treacherous," "greedy," "weak," "envious," and "vindictive."[28] Like Dardano's citations of patristic authority, Bruni's list of vices popularly attributed to woman testifies to the pervasiveness of assumptions sustaining male privilege.

Her supposed vices are followed by a discussion of legal restrictions on her activities. This strategy allows Bruni to connect misogynist opinion with contemporary law:

---

[28]Domenico Bruni da Pistoia, *Difese delle donne nella quale si contengono le difese loro, dalle calunnie datele per gli scrittori e insieme le lodi di quella* (Milan, 1559), sig. A3–5. The signatures from H forward are out of sequence.

> By civil law woman is prohibited from all public offices and also from all
> magistracies that are reserved exclusively for men. . . . Second, by the same
> prohibition, she cannot judge or pass sentences or intervene in these kinds
> of affairs. Third, she cannot testify in another's behalf before a magistrate.
> Fourth, she cannot defend anyone in court or act as a solicitor for someone
> else in any court or tribunal. Fifth, she cannot act as a mediator or arbitrate
> among parties to a dispute—again according to civil law. Sixth, she cannot
> adopt children as a man can; this may be because she is expected to have
> children naturally and not by legal arrangement.   [A5v–6]

These restrictions apply to a woman's ability to use the law as an instrument by which to guarantee her own rights and to safeguard her own
interests. Bruni goes on to describe restrictions on her exercise of economic privileges which determine even more decisively her social status
in general. She cannot provide collateral for anyone; she cannot make a
will; she cannot be the guardian of any child but her own; she cannot
accuse anyone in a criminal case; she cannot participate in any public
activity of a political kind (*"usare alcuna attione populare"*); she has no
paternal authority over children; she cannot borrow from the state, a
privilege reserved solely for men; she cannot be a banker, propose any
kind of legislation, or inherit property—"thus men succeed in reserving
all rights of property to themselves alone" (A6–8). According to canon
law she is also denied many privileges, including the right to administer
the sacraments. In conclusion, Bruni observes that these restrictions,
codified by "writers," have done as much as popular opinion to discredit
a "worthy sex." In fact, his account of law and popular opinion suggests a
relation between the two: that law is the legalization as well as the
validation of opinion. A misogynist can find his opinions the basis of law
because legislators and judges have written and interpreted law in light of
misogynist opinion.

Bruni has no evident interest in the reform of actual social or legal
practice; his concern is to analyze what appears to be prejudicial treatment of women in relation to the way they are called upon to function
within a society rather than to some specious concept of their *natural*
inferiority to men. He claims that the Italian woman is barred from
taking legal action because "public decency" (*publica honestà*) needs protection (H4).[29] But such a matter of decorum has nothing to do with

---

[29]Though Bruni's idea that female *honestà* affects the capacity of woman to go to law in
no way casts doubt on her status as an adult human being, it appears to be a direct
evocation of the juridical concept of *pudor sexus*. In effect, it reconstitutes a woman's
incapacity at law so that it becomes a positive benefit to her; because of her natural
infirmity (*infirmitas sexus*), she is not liable for many kinds of wrongdoing. In practice, of
course, Bruni's benefit constituted a form of discrimination. Guido Rossi notes: "Under

nature. Women are restricted to domestic activities not "because of lack of judgment" but "according to ancient custom," which varies with the requirements of the situation and the country (H4). Bruni reminds his readers that although jurists usually prohibit women from participating in public life, they admit "on hereditary grounds" that a woman may succeed to a kingdom and govern it (H3). And in Egypt and Thrace, according to Herodotus, men remain at home "to do housework" without suffering a loss of status (I). Women in Italy are not allowed to engage in financial activities because custom forbids them to do so; "but if the custom were otherwise, as it could have been, and as in some regions it is, it would not be judged reasonable to assume that men are of less account and perfection than women are" (H8v). In other words, custom functions as natural law although it is demonstrably unnatural: the claim that women are naturally unbusinesslike simply means that in the society of the speaker, custom dictates that women shall not do business. In theory, Bruni admits that in other societies a woman's chastity might not be sufficiently jeopardized by her participation in public life to warrant her sequestration at home.

In any case, he asserts that a better guide to a person's status and worth in society is the work he or she does. A brewer, for example, is not by virtue of being a man a more valuable human being or more naturally suited to govern than a woman of any rank or vocation. Brewing does not develop civic virtue, and the brewer is in this respect as virtuous as the wife who helps him in the shop.

> Every woman in her rank does as well as a man in looking after her affairs and organizing her life . . . according to her talents. We see that a shoe-maker, a tailor, a blacksmith, a gardener, or others occupied in similar manual trades work only at the things that properly concern them, and pay no attention to affairs of state, or public festivals, or honors, or awards, or things that concern the government of republics, or anything else of this kind. The very same thing is true of women workers, who according to their rank are occupied with spinning, cooking, weaving, or performing some other domestic task, together with managing the household, bringing up the children, and caring for the family.   [C3]

---

pressure from new ideas of law created as elaborations of old principles, the incapacity of women to go to law [ester en justice] was in part justified as a privilege. After the thirteenth century, in effect, it was thought that *pudor sexus* required that a woman should not be obliged to go to law. She ought to be represented there by her husband, her parents, or a deputy. In reality, however, the famous privilege was nothing more than a prohibition to go to law, sometimes limited to wives, at other times extended to all women": Guido Rossi, "Statuts juridique de la femme," in *La Femme*, Recueils de la Société Jean Bodin, vol. 12 (Paris, n.d.), 131–32.

Bruni's picture of artisanal life not only eliminates sex as a criterion of worth; it rules out the possibility that merely being a woman is itself an office to which one may be called and expected to conform. The offices open to Bruni's hypothetical woman are similar to those open to men. They are both social and economic; performance in them calls for particular *skills* that are subject to objective evaluation rather than for behavior that conforms to rules of deference. In conclusion, Bruni asks us to evaluate women in terms of social rank, economic function, and political office; and to substitute these categories for that of sex as the basis of social and moral criticism:

> And if we wish to speak of country women, we will see they are in no way inferior to their husbands. For they are intent on the same basic rural tasks as their husbands . . . clearly we see that whatever the rank of the woman, whether noble, or middling, or low, or rural, she is not to be judged as of lesser rank, less worthy, or less perfect than men.   [C5r–v]

Bruni indicates the way in which custom and the behavior it mandates function as expressions of ideology and not of nature. He also insists that sex cannot correctly be considered to be an index of either virtue or office: a female farmer is as good as a male farmer; a woman acquires virtue as a farmer, not as a woman.

Bruni's analysis of an economy that was probably foreign to many of his readers raises the question of the relation of rank to feminist conceptions of sex and gender. If the results of K. D. M. Snell's research on English labor in the sixteenth century hold also for Western Europe generally—that is, that women routinely worked beside men in manual trades and on farms[30]—then Bruni's feminism was derived in part from an observation of actual economic conditions. He was basing a theory of gender on evidence that must have been deliberately overlooked by apologists for patriarchy, who constantly separated the work of women from that of men, in accordance with the ancient Aristotelian model. At the same time, he demonstrated what is also clear in feminist apology generally: the conception of society as a hierarchy of rank, whether attention is focused on offices at the high or low end of the scale, can promote feminist argument because it makes possible comparisons of male and female performance within the same rank-determined offices, and thus brings into focus the ideological factors that serve to discriminate against women who hold those offices and do exactly what men do or something very comparable. As feminist literature developed into the

[30]Snell, *Annals of the Labouring Poor*, 270–75.

next century, an understanding of work became increasingly important to arguments for equality.

The persuasiveness of any defense of women depended to some extent on its treatment of historical evidence. Such feminists as Christine de Pisan and those in Landi's collection, dismayed that the history they read generally left unexamined the conviction that the prerogatives of men were validated by divine and natural law, urged the creation of new histories that could present the case for maintaining that woman was as virtuous as man. Some saw the point of beginning with an investigation of the *empirical* basis of existing histories, that is, with an investigation of what passed as historical evidence.

The defense of Lodovico, the feminist speaker in Stefano Guazzo's 'Dell' honor delle donne" in his *Dialoghi piacevoli* (1587), is really predicated on his awareness of how difficult it is to interpret such evidence. He contradicts the misogynist Annibale, who represents women as less honorable than men because they have achieved less in history. Lodovico, advancing a familiar claim, states that "honor," like fame, eludes women because they are prevented from leading the kind of life that conduces to its achievement. Women would not only equal but be superior to men were it not that "men, whether out of tyranny or envy, have decided to allow women to be occupied only with spindle and thread; hence it is no wonder that from lack of instruction and practice the acuteness of woman's intellect remains unremarked." He further declares that the scarcity of the evidence supporting the honor of women is not an indication of their "nature" but simply "circumstantial" (*per fortuna e per occasione*).[31] This explanation is straightforward enough, but, as Guazzo proceeds to reveal, it is at best no more than hypothetical. It suffers from the failing of analyses that depend on selecting the relevant counterfactual: if the activities of women had not been restricted to household affairs, would they have chosen a public life?

Lodovico's examination of the effects of enforced domesticity provides a sounder basis for estimating women's virtue. Enlarging on his statement that woman lacks honor in the ordinary sense of the word, Annibale asserts that she really does not want it. She aspires only to earn a good reputation by living a private life. Lodovico replies that "if chastity and an intelligence of household affairs made a woman honored, a peasant could be as honored as a queen, with respect to these two virtues." Moreover, were "modesty" the only true ornament of the feminine character, no woman (his example is the Queen of Sheba) would have

[31]Stefano Guazzo, *Dialoghi piacevoli* (Piacenza, 1587), sig. Aa.

troubled to learn wisdom. In fact, all the examples of feminine virtue that appear in historical record demonstrate the falsehood of Annibale's position. They show women struggling for recognition for more than good housekeeping: women would not have exercised themselves in this way "if they had not thought that they would so make themselves glorious and immortal" (Aa3r–v).

Finally, in his most successful move, Lodovico subverts the very criteria by which "honor" is established by analyzing the social situation perhaps most perplexing and at the same time most characteristic of the relations between the sexes—the separation of authority and power, the former the man's, the latter the woman's. He addresses Annibale's objections to cross-dressing and his contention that feminine "chastity" includes respect for the social and conventional forms of recognizing sexual difference. In the last analysis, Lodovico claims, *all* outward forms are simply misleading, and it is simply irrelevant whether women wear men's clothing in public. The more impressive fact is that they actually share with men the conduct of public life and affairs of state. The real deployment of power within the framework of publicly instituted authority is virtually hidden. If the exercise of such authority were carefully examined, it would reveal itself to be as much in the hands of women as in those of men: "women have today so much power over men that they can rejoice that they remain in houses, governing the city and public affairs as they wish . . . for women govern the governors as governors govern the state" (Aa6). Lodovico's vision of the *éminence rose* is more acute than Speroni's Neoplatonically derived image of an idealistic marriage. Its immediate reference is both to such actual histories of women in positions of unauthorized power as Tacitus's *Annals* and to the formidable power of such regents as Catherine de' Medici. More important: it raises the question of the status of historical evidence itself. If authority and power are separate, and indeed can even be deployed to antagonistic ends, then it can be misleading to focus chiefly—as histories generally do—on activities that take place in the spheres where authority appears (but may not actually be or have been) decisive. And if women not only can but also do wear men's clothing, literally as well as figuratively, then any history based on the selection of evidence that is wholly or in part determined by conventional notions of sex and gender is immediately subject to question. In a sense, Lodovico points in these remarks to the precarious nature of writing history and perhaps even to its fundamental unknowability, a feature of the past that in these Italian defenses seems to be closely bound up with the image of woman both as an unattainable ideal and as a reality so intimate that it cannot be made public.

FRANCE

Women Writers

The profession of letters was legally open to women in the sixteenth century, however difficult of access it was in practice. Nevertheless, the restrictions on a woman's education, the demands of domesticity on her time (and often from an early age), the widely held assumption that her best eloquence was in holding her tongue, and the limited extent to which she could converse with persons outside her immediate family must often have achieved what the law did not. Obviously, the conditions of underprivilege in which most women lived presented real obstacles to any authorship to which they might aspire.

Women who wrote in France appear to have responded to these circumstances differently than their counterparts in Italy did. Feminist protest, especially to various kinds of abuse in marriage, was common in the letters collected by Landi, but the persons who wrote them, identifying themselves as noblewomen or at least of the propertied class, were not professional writers. On the other hand, such women as Veronica Stampa, Olimpia Morata, and Tullia d'Aragona published works in verse and prose and acquired authorial reputations in their own lifetimes but did not engage in overt protest. This was not the case for Louise Labé, Helisenne de Crenne, and the Mesdames des Roches, each of whom represented women as the intellectual equals of men and saw a clear need for feminist polemic, particularly to be addressed to women as a class of persons that had yet to realize its potential. They saw, moreover, that such encouragement was crucial to their own success as authors: without a female readership, their positions could only be precarious. Louise Labé writes an apologetic preface to her *Euvres* (1555), Helisenne de Crenne writes several "epistolary invectives" in her *Oeuvres* (1560), and the Roches women write defiant odes and epistles in their *Oeuvres* (1578). In all of these works certain concerns are central: the act of writing must be justified in opposition to the rule of silence; the life of the mind, exempted absolutely from the restrictions governing social and familial life, must be shown to provide woman with her only real experience of freedom; and literary composition must be recognized as shaping a feminine and heroic (or masculine) self. Most important, in virtually all this protest women as a class of persons are represented not only as abused by men, especially their husbands, but also by the whole cultural system that relegates them to positions of inferiority.

Louise Labé opens her preface by observing that women are no longer prevented by "the severe laws of men" from applying themselves "to [the acquisition of] knowledge and intellectual discipline," and that they must strive to profit from the new "honest freedom" that they have so long desired. Thus they will demonstrate the "wrong" men have committed in the past by denying education to women.[32] Labé appears to be referring here to law, both as the custom of excluding girls from schools and as discriminatory practices within the home which may have been determined by factors less legal than economic and technological, primarily the relative scarcity of books before the widespread establishment of printing houses. Her principal concern—that women gain personal honor from their literary activity—is certainly linked to the development of a popular press. She distinguishes between women of the past, who derived their social status entirely from their husbands and expressed it in the quality of their clothing and other personal adornments, and the educated woman of the future, who will be acknowledged for her own accomplishments. *That* woman will no longer be significantly clothed in gold chains, jeweled rings, and sumptuous dresses, which she cannot really consider hers except by "convention" (*usage*), but rather will be uniquely valued: "the honor that knowledge will give us will be entirely ours: and it will not be taken from us by the thief's skill, or by the strength of foes, or by the passage of time" (41). The image testifies to what must have been a common experience for women—the recognition that their society perceived them as reflections of men, that (as Barbaro had noted) a woman without a man was in a certain sense invisible. By contrast, Labé represents the woman writer whose self-promotion is by way of self-discipline, an index of virtue, and not conferred wealth, an index merely of social rank. In her writing, she is known as a man might be known in similar circumstances: a human being who defines for his or her readers the meaning of such things as social rank.

Labé's insistence on the need for women to cultivate an educated self, in distinction to what might be called the personality of an object, allows

---

[32]Louise Labé, *Oeuvres complètes: Sonnets-élégies, Débat de folie et d'amour*, ed. François Rigolot (Paris: Flammarion, 1986), 41. This edition reproduces the title page of the original edition, printed in Lyon in 1555. For recent studies on Labé, see the editor's preface and bibliography; see also Enzo Giudici, *Louise Labé: Essai* (Rome: Ateneo, 1981), esp. 58–62; Jeanne Prine, "Louise Labé: Poet of Lyon," in *Women Writers of the Renaissance and Reformation*, ed. Katharina M. Wilson (Athens: University of Georgia Press, 1987), 132–48; and Madeleine Lazard, *Images littéraires de la femme à la Renaissance* (Paris: Presses Universitaires de France, 1985), 48–57. For the rhetorical strategies of Labé and some of her contemporaries, see Ann Rosalind Jones, "Assimilation with a Difference: Renaissance Women Poets and Literary Influence," *Yale French Studies* 62 (1981): 135–53, and "City Women and Their Audiences: Louise Labé and Veronica Franco," in *Rewriting the Renaissance*, ed. Ferguson et al., 299–316. Labé's preface is dedicated to M.C.D.B.L., who has been identified as Mademoiselle Clémence de Bourges of Lyon.

her to focus attention on the forms of dependency that might impede such a program. She asks her friends who are virtuous to "raise their spirits beyond their spindles," and imagines that although women are not "fit to command," they may be the "comrades" of men in "civic as well as domestic affairs" (42). Her reference to women's spindles gives her remark an economic context and raises a further question: How is this person who is perceived typically as engaged in servile tasks to be accepted as a comrade in civic actions? Whether or not women actually performed domestic tasks, of whatever variety, matters less, I think, than that they were supposed to be doing them, however symbolically. And the more symbolically, perhaps, the worse, for activities merely symbolic are clearly irrelevant economically; they indicate that a woman cannot use her labor to get rich any more than she can earn a reputation in public life.

Labé in fact confronts a kind of crisis of a collective female identity. She is asking that women drastically alter their ways of seeing themselves. As a consequence they must be prepared to confront the peril of success as well as the disappointment of failure. To indicate what success might mean, Labé asks women to achieve intellectual "honor" so that men may be forced to return to their own endeavors for the public good: "and beyond that reputation which our sex will receive, we will be of value to the public in that men will take greater pains to acquire knowledge out of fear that they will be surpassed by those to whom they have claimed to be superior in almost everything" (42).[33] The passage conveys both Labé's sense of the intimidation women feel at confronting a literature by and for men and her wish to engage the writers of this male literature in a kind of rivalry, one perhaps destined to contest the very superiority men are supposed to have. The remark, both an encouragement to women and a warning to men, reveals Labé's understanding of the risks that attend women's acquisition of "honor," which, as she would have it, supports but finally also threatens patriarchy. To succeed "in such a praiseworthy

---

[33]Labé limits the public activity she would have women engage in to intellectual matters. Curiously, she herself is reported to have fought "against the Spanish at the siege of Perpignan. The probable truth is only slightly less colorful: she may well have taken part in a tournament in 1542, the year of the siege, or perhaps later, in 1548": Prine, "Louise Labé," 133. What is certain is that following the conceits of epic romance, and specifically of Ariosto's *Orlando furioso*, Labé represents herself in her poetry as androgynous, insofar as she bears arms and fights battles. See "Elégie III," ll. 37–42, where she claims she can be recognized as a Bradamante or a Marfisa. Defenders of women had frequently instanced women warrior figures (usually taken from such histories as Boccaccio's *De mulieribus claris*) as proof that woman's virtue is equal to or the same as man's, and the example of Joan of Arc was widely recognized as historically factual; but to my knowledge, Labé is the first woman writer so to characterize herself.

enterprise," she adds, "we must encourage one another" (42). Here Labé's specific concerns are different from those of her Italian counterparts, largely because she envisages a feminist literature intended to be public and professional rather than private and occasional.

Labé concludes her preface by reconsidering the subject of history for all women, whether educated or not. Her analysis clarifies her earlier remarks on the "severe laws" that deny women an education by indicating how crucial is literacy, particularly writing, to the process by which a person conceives of himself as having a certain unique worth, and, conversely, how deeply implicated is the system that limits female education in the failure of women to achieve an "honor" that is neither uxorial nor conventional. She observes that to live an unrecorded life is to have no past. Memory serves us ill, she declares; it gives us only the vaguest sense of where we have been and hence of what we have become. The greatest of pleasures is this recovery of the past through a personal literature that at the same time is an awareness of the self extending through time, changed by experience and yet also changeless in its continuous exercise of self-reflection:

> But [the recreation] provided by study leaves one with an enduring contentment with oneself. For the past makes us happy again and in a better way than the present. The pleasure of feelings is lost immediately and never returns, and sometimes even the memory [of them] is as troublesome as the actions were delightful. Moreover, other kinds of pleasures are such that when a remembrance of them occurs, we cannot recover the frame of mind that we were in when we enjoyed them: however vivid the image of them that we have, we know that it is only a shadow of a past that fools and deludes us. But when we put *our thoughts* into writing, no matter how busy our brains are subsequently with an infinity of business and constantly shifting, and we take up that writing again after a long time, we return to the same point and the identical frame of mind [that we first had]. Then we double our pleasure: for we rediscover the pleasure that we had in the matter we wrote about or in the knowledge that had been given to us. And beyond that, the judgment that our second thoughts make of our first thoughts offers us a special joy.   [42–43]

The process of literary composition and recomposition of a personal past which Labé envisages here constructs a history and a subject that must be complex. A mind contemplating second thoughts is engaged in the task of revision that makes impossible a notion of the subject as simple and consistent. Nothing could more obscure the image of the ideal woman and wife than this sketch of a literary woman, who through self-representation has gained the power to reflect upon herself, to take note of change, to imagine that she might not be restricted by "law" from attempting to construct a multifaceted personality that might actually use the resources of fiction to gain social and political advantages. Such complexity was of course precisely what earlier commentatators wanted to discourage.

The effects of this kind of revision are, for Labé, remarkably heartening. What she testifies to is her delight in the freedom to change, to move through time, in short, to be a person who is capable of invention and play rather than a cipher figuring some lifeless abstraction. Because she confronts a written past, this literary woman moves out of the time-free zone in which decisions appear to have no causes or effects but to relate only to questions of obedience to God or to his supposed representative on earth, the next male kin. In a sense the literary woman becomes the "comrade" to man whom Labé had described earlier—not because she directly challenges his authority to command but because, having enlarged the concept of authority to include an authorship of the self, she has available to her the same intellectual resources that he does.

Labé's conception of the literary woman who is educated to a knowledge of herself as historically complex, a privilege her culture for the most part restricted to men, was not of course widely shared. Some feminist writers do nevertheless testify to the struggle women confronted on precisely this score. The protests of Helisenne de Crenne, for example, focus primarily on the creative independence owed her authorial as opposed to her domestic self. The latter may be constrained to obey her husband, but the former is free to invent images of women exempt from this kind of control. Crenne's feminist writing is logically complicated in part because she brings to it a variety of concerns. But its context as a whole is relatively simple: a profound dissatisfaction with men—as husbands, lovers, critics, and readers. She sees her work in part as a warning to other women to avoid the snares of love; in her prefatory remarks to her readers, she sets herself their example: "Be always on your guard . . ./ I shall act as your scout [*avant garde*]/ To my own expense, grief, and suffering."[34] And in her dedicatory letter, "épistre . . . à toutes honnestes dames," she confesses to regrets so great that writing, for her

[34]Helisenne de Crenne, *Les Oeuvres de Madame Helisenne de Crenne* (Paris, 1560), sig. Av. The earliest edition of Crenne's polemical works, titled *Les Epistres familières et invectives*, was published in Paris in 1536. Crenne appears to be the nom de plume of Marguerite de Briet, the wife of Philippe de Fournel, seigneur de Crasnes in Picardy. For a brief study of Crenne and a translation of her letters, see *A Renaissance Woman: Helisenne's Personal and Invective Letters*, trans. and ed. Marianna M. Mustacchi and Paul J. Archambault (Syracuse: Syracuse University Press, 1986). Crenne's major work is a romance titled *Les Angoysses douloureuses qui procèdent d'amours* (1538); portions of it are translated with an introduction by Kittye Delle Robbins-Herring in "Hélisenne de Crenne: Champion of Women's Rights," in *Women Writers*, ed. Wilson, 196–218.

the only really therapeutic activity, is virtually impossible: "[it is] a sorrow that is greater than all others in that my shaking hand is immobilized" (a2). It is the question of *how* rather than what she writes that elicits from her a feminist response.

The exemplarity she chooses to give her miserable relations with men involves her in a methodological problem particular to the woman writer—that is, the extent to which her readers will see in her literary subject a sign of who she really is and what she has lived through. Her literary stance is frequently confessional: "Alas when I recall the afflictions that [in] my sad heart were and are still provoked by great desire and the pricks of love [*infiniz desirs et amoureux aguillonnemens*]," she exclaims in her opening letter (a2). But when she replies to her husband's accusations of infidelity on the grounds of evidence in her writing, she claims that as a writer she is entitled to create purely *fictional* characters and situations that cannot be understood as reflections of a personal reality. She takes refuge behind a literary persona, in a sense to be construed as the shadow of her divine image, her first creation. The terms of her protest suggest that in the spiritual autonomy given woman as a consequence of her possession of an immortal soul, Crenne sees the basis of an intellectual and artistic autonomy—even insofar as the effects of that autonomy may be transcribed in writing. She insists that her mind provides her with the sole domain in which she experiences freedom, and that this freedom, in all its consequences, including even the construction of pure fiction, is legitimate. Her claim is revolutionary in its implications. Doctrine governing the conduct of women in public held that the resources of the imagination—feigning and fictionalizing—ought to be denied them. Treatises on uxorial behavior insisted that a wife both mirror and be transparent to her husband; if she could not actually be like him, she was never to be other than what he thought she was. Crenne's authorial privilege would violate these rules.

Feigning and deceit were, in any case, strategies that Crenne regarded as essential to the life of every woman, as none could avoid situations in which her own desires were thwarted. Like several of her Italian counterparts, Crenne represents conventual life as a refuge from male abuse. In her first "épistre familière," she speaks of the "saintly ways" of religious life and confesses that she would have remained in a convent but for obedience to her parents. It is as a repository of memories that the convent is chiefly of value, however; when she recalls this life she is compensated for the privations of the present: "because I am prevented from enjoying the real thing [the convent], I find it useful to turn to its representation in the mind [*à la mentalle me conviendra avoir recours*]" (H2).

Her mental life is, in fact, the only life that permits her to confront her authentic self. Her remarks to a young friend suggest that since a woman's feelings of dissatisfaction will have habitually to be transformed into a pretended agreeableness out of deference to her husband, she will do well to cultivate a sense of the difference between who she is and who she must appear to be for the sake of her own peace and security. Mindful of the necessarily duplicitous nature of woman's behavior, Crenne advises a young friend, Clarice, "to deny by your appearance what you most wish for [within yourself] in order to avoid irritating those who because of you [and your behavior] could pass judgment on you" ("épistre familière viii," Kv). She suggests that a husband or father can rebuke a woman for having certain feelings (desire, frustration), although his authority may rightfully extend only to what a woman does on the basis of those feelings.

As a woman writer, Crenne realizes that she lives precariously in two worlds, demarcated by the limits of marital authority and power. In the first she is bound by law and convention to behave as her husband wishes; in the second she is at liberty to do what she pleases in her imagination, restricted only by the law of God. When, however, she attempts to include in the second world her literary work, an expression of her mental life and yet one that can be shared by others and hence also public, she discovers that she again confronts law and convention. She explicitly protests her husband's charge that in writing of love she has been unfaithful: "the hasty flight of your heart to such imaginings has made you believe that what I wrote to avoid idleness actually commemorates an adulterous love [amour impudique]. And moreover you think that I experienced this love [lascivété] in my own person. . . . You said that the words that issued from my mouth were the proof of my crime" ("épistre invective i," M4–5). She maintains that what is done in her writing has nothing to do with her own behavior—indeed, she remarks, what is done by her literary characters is on the whole complicated, varied, and in many cases contradictory; hence no single moment of action she describes can be made to indicate the sum of her moral and social thought.

She even goes so far as to claim that words themselves have no necessary connection to factual truth or reality. When she earlier confessed to adultery, she claims, it was only because she was terrified. Her statement was pure fiction: "indeed I admit that angered by the numerous abuses with which you have tormented, I lost patience. I gave way to passion [fureur]. These abuses drove me beyond reason: and this was the reason that my words indicted me for something that my complete innocence [*ma clere innocence*] was never actually tainted with."[35] And she goes on to assert that she will continue to speak of love, "not because I have learned about it through experience but in literature" (M5). If she has earlier claimed that the subject of her writing is not to be considered purely mimetic of a personal reality, here she declares that as a writer she be allowed to read fiction as supramimetic. Like Labé's imaginatively complex woman of letters who has a sense of herself as *historical*, Crenne's literary woman who asserts the right to fictionalize a self by writing and through literature violates patriarchal rules against any representation by a woman which involves feigning or playing with the whole truth.

Crenne must know that the literary license she asks for will not be granted. Deploring the fact that her husband will misjudge her despite her protests, she invokes two examples of calumny against women, neither of which suggests that within her contemporary culture a woman accused of viciousness can be cleared of blame easily if indeed at all. Her first example, referring to Socrates' understanding that Xantippe stands for all women, shows how typological thinking conduces to prejudice: "he [Socrates] was one of those men—exhausted [by his querulous wife]—for whom everything they see that bears a certain image, resemblance, or suggestion to that which angers them they think capable of producing the same reaction" ("épistre invective iii," N7v). She links typological thinking to a notion of history as repetitive and thus changeless; in effect she points to the error that Dardano's Eve had protested against earlier when she endorsed what I have called the principle of uniqueness. Crenne's second example, the virgin Tuccia and her sieve, reveals how hard it is for a woman to maintain her reputation as chaste. If she is accused of licentiousness, she is as good as guilty—real proof of innocence is inadequate to clear her name; only a miracle will suffice. So, she claims, Augustine celebrates the exculpation of Tuccia, accused of fornication: "to demonstrate that the accusation was false, she miraculously carried water in a sieve, a sign of purity and virginity." Evidently aware of the implications of the example—what man would be called upon to prove his innocence by occasioning a supernatural event?— Crenne declares: "When I call to mind all these things, I cannot refrain

[35]Anne R. Larsen notes that this passage reinterprets episode 5 in *Les Angoysses*, in which Crenne confesses to having a lover, Guenelic: "The Rhetoric of Self-Defense in *Les Angoysses douloureuses qui procèdent d'amours*," *Kentucky Romance Quarterly* 29, 3 (1982): 235–43. Here in her letter to her husband, Crenne is less concerned to debate the question of uxorial morality than to assert the creative independence of the writer and the supramimetic status of literature.

from calling on several goddesses to know whether one moved by my pitiful exclamations will consent to help me justify myself. . . . Juno ought not to be reluctant to help wives who have faithfully kept her chaste laws" ("épistre invective i," M8).[36] By invoking *Juno's* help, Crenne implies that there are no effective ways to clear her name in a (Christian) culture that represents a woman's vindication of her own moral status as miraculous.

I know of no other instance in the feminist literature of this century in which a writer has insisted particularly on the autonomy of artistic expression for women. The assertion is potentially revolutionary: written expression is free from the constraints placed on social behavior and it may reach audiences its author does not know or have intended it to reach. The act of writing is, in a certain sense, an action that takes place in the public arena. Literally voiceless and linked with liberty of conscience and of mental life, in theory an aspect of every Christian's spiritual equality, it is also (paradoxically) voiced in print and stands a chance of being prohibited to those who are socially subordinate. When such persons claim the liberty of the pen, therefore, they are, in effect, claiming something like social equality, at least by virtue of the fact that they are being heard.[37]

The feminism of (Madame) Madeleine Fredonnoit Des Roches is conveyed in her description of how she might enjoy authorial freedom *within* the constraints of patriarchy. On what they are, she is, if anything, even more explicit than Crenne. In her first ode she describes her transformation from maid to wife as if from a (relative) intellectual liberty to a professional and entirely unnatural enslavement: "Nature wants education and study/ To produce a perfect work," she observes, but, ironically,

> Our parents have the praiseworthy custom
> Of making us unused to reason,

---

[36]Tuccia was widely recognized as a symbol of virginity during this period; see, i.a., Roy Strong, *Portraits of Queen Elizabeth I* (London: Oxford University Press, 1963), pl. 20.

[37]Crenne later complains of a hostile critic, one "Elenot," who has ruined her chances for literary fame: "Nothing bothers me except the displeasure I feel when I remember that my cruel fortune requires that if there is one stupid and malicious person in the famous city of Paris, my books will come to his blind and bigoted attention. I am certain that no good will come of it." She is later willing to forgive him if he acknowledges his fault: "If you are willing to forgo your perversity, I will persuade the ladies to forgive you": "Epistre invective iv," sig. O7. Who "Elenot" was is uncertain. A misogynist critic frequently mentioned by feminist writers is Gratian Du Pont, whose *Controverses des sexes masculin et féminin* went into several editions during the sixteenth century.

> Of keeping us shut up in the house
> And giving us a distaff for a pen.   [Av][38]

Despite the trade of pen for distaff, however, her childhood was privileged in comparison with married life. Then the wings that allowed her flights of fancy were strong; now the quill of authorship, plucked from those wings, is broken by the cares of her "profession":

> In the happy times of the past season
> I had my wings fixed to my side:
> But losing my youthful liberty,
> My pen was broken before my flight.
> I wanted to hover over a book
> And breathe out my grief on paper:
> But some duty always pulled me away,
> Telling me that I had to follow my profession.   [A2][39]

Like Labé and Crenne, she sees in what her refuge consists, but more acutely than they how difficult of attainment it is. Adversity is transcended, she claims, by mental exercise; it is even the precondition for attaining the most excellent of intellectual visions:

> To tolerate the evils of life,
> God gave us a powerful mind

---

38   Noz parens ont de louable coustume
        Pour nous tollir l'usage de raison,
        De nous tenir closes dans la maison
        Et nous donner le fuzeau pour la plume.

Mme and Mlle Fredonnoit Des Roches, *Les Oeuvres de mes-dames Des Roches* (Paris, 1578), sig. Av. The work lacks a dedication and is addressed simply "aux dames." The authors are mother and daughter, Madeleine and Catherine, respectively. For studies of the Roches women, see, i.a., Anne R. Larsen, "Les Dames des Roches: The French Humanist Scholars", in *Women Writers*, ed. Wilson, 232–59 (containing a selection of verse and prose in translation); and Tilde A. Sankovitch, *French Women Writers and the Book: Myths of Access and Desire* (Syracuse: Syracuse University Press, 1987), 43–71. Both studies provide useful bibliographies.

39   Au temps heureux de ma saison passée,
        J'avoy bien l'aile unie à mon costé:
        Mais en perdant ma jeune liberté,
        Avant le vol ma plume fût cassée.
        Je voudroy bien m'arester sur le livre,
        Et au papier mes peines souspirer:
        Mais quelque soing m'en vient tousjours tirer,
        Disant qu'il fault ma profession suivre.

So that it would return to the creating mind
In spite of death, fortune, and envy.   [A2v][40]

But this mind, described as the "Amaranthus-like flower" that "blooms" in the "winter" (of evil, i.e., hardship; A2v) in which the woman writer is forced to live, appears to have been the most delicate of hybrids.

The work of Madeleine Des Roches's daughter, Catherine, hints at the constraints she experiences as a writer because, like her mother, she is supposed to have a "profession." Her witty "A ma quenoille," an ode in which her spindle is both the subject of her complaint and her defense against complaining, illustrates that for a woman writer domestic duties prove to be a curious burden. Addressing her spindle, her "care" (*souci*), Catherine declares: "I swear to you . . ./ Not . . . to exchange/ Your domestic honor for an alien good/ That wanders constantly and lasts only a short time" (Qv). For her spindle must know that if from time to time she writes, it is her spindle she celebrates; it and nothing else protects her from the "abuse" that a woman who writes risks incurring:

> With you beside me I am much more secure
> Than if ink and paper came to be scattered
> All about me, for to avenge me
> You can much better respond to abuse.   [Qv][41]

Catherine's image—the making of poetry on a spindle—is of course densely allusive. Weaving as subterfuge and the representation of historical truth by way of the construction of defensive fictions coalesce in the work of the legendary Penelope, who, by deploying her wit in circumstances of political impotence, provides a model for the woman writer that Catherine actually aspires to be. Catherine's "spindle" is not therefore entirely a *domestic* subject but rather a sign promising the realization of a poetic vision of heroic dimensions. By covering her creativity with the fiction of womanly duty, Catherine (like Penelope) avoids incurring critical abuse—although it also seems fair to ask what scope that creativity will in fact have.

---

40   Pour supporter les maux de nostre vie,
         Dieu nous feit part de l'intellect puissant
         Pour le réduire à l'intellect agent
         Maugré la mort, la fortune, et l'envie.

41   Vous ayant au costé je suis beaucoup plus seure
         Que si ancre et papier se venoient à ranger
         Tout à l'entour de moy, car pour me revanger
         Vous pouvez bien plutost repousser une injure.

Madeleine Des Roches has earlier apologized for her literary work by insisting, like Labé, on the importance of writing to the composition of a self and its recognition by others. Writing "gives a certain indication not only of the richness of the spirit and its natural and acquired qualities, but also of the native character of those who speak or write" (a2). She dismisses the much-recommended virtue of silence as the form of elo-quence appropriate to women: "And if . . . you tell me that silence, the ornament of woman, can cover faults of the tongue and of understand-ing, I will answer that it can very well prevent shame but not give honor, since it is speech that separates us from animals without reason" (a2). And finally, she tells her daughter in "Epistre à ma fille," writing is the only way in which a woman can achieve honor, since heroic endeavour as men know and experience it, for the benefit of the state, is not open to women. If ancient authority requires all persons to honor God and their country, it (tacitly) limits the obligation of women: "For my country I have no power/ Men have all the authority/ Against reason and equity" (a3),[42] she declares in words reminiscent of Christine de Pisan, who also claimed that she was exempt in some degree from doing her best in a society that saw her as inferior. Consequently she recommends that her daughter's attention be directed at acquiring a virtue of another kind: "knowledge of divinity." This knowledge will not vanish with her death, like the unrecorded wit of Christine de Pisan's good but illiterate women, but by being recorded as the "effect" of her thought it will bear witness to her honor in the future (a3v).

Nevertheless, it is at least arguable that insofar as Catherine's spindle is *not* a covering fiction but rather an indication of the *kind* of subject she believes she really can treat, she will not get very far toward the literary heroics her mother has urged her to pursue. Her mother's quill, broken by the cares of a professional domesticity, provides a clearer image of her own authorial condition. Catherine's ode touches on the pathos of any writer who works from an experience of deprivation and at the margins of her or his culture. The great and obvious subjects are for such writers primarily those that treat a heroics of a future time, necessarily perceived from a present that knows practically nothing of what they might mean. The very futurity of the subject makes its artistic realization problem-atic.[43]

---

[42]"Pour mon pays je n'ay *point de puissance,*/ Les hommes ont toute l'autorité,/ Contre raison et contre l'équité." The concept of equity is of great importance to feminist discourse in this period and subsequently. A legal term, it refers to a jurisprudence not strictly retributive and literalistic but rather casuistical and informed by a concern for circumstance.

[43]Renaissance epic poetry is of course typically prophetic, at least in part; other genres,

Husbands and Cuckolds

The contradictions already inherent in the position of a wife may have been exacerbated during the second half of the century by the Tridentine ruling against clandestine marriage. Parental control over the marriages of their children, mandated by the council, must have made a marriage for personal preference more difficult for both men and women but affected men disproportionately, as they had previously enjoyed at least some measure of freedom of choice. It is not too hard to imagine that a reluctant bridegroom, unsure of himself and even less so of the woman his parents had selected for him, would have to be encouraged to obey their wishes by descriptions of a married life made easy by the kind of uxorial devotion and obedience celebrated in marriage treatises, the spiritual equality of woman notwithstanding. In any case, it is against this literature, committed to the continuance of the politicized marriage and the idea of the family as a diminutive state, that ideas of sexual difference and shared gender had to take shape.

In René Benoist's *Catéchèses* (1573), contradiction takes the form of a concession that is effectively rescinded: a woman's virtue is granted but its agency is shown to be vicious. While she is more able than man "to achieve the perfection of Christianity, which is love," it is precisely this capacity to love and to inspire love in others that attracts Satan. "Envious of the perfection of women," Satan provides women with tricks to seduce men: "he is so much against them [women], and has so far prevailed, that he has made of their tricks the snares and devices to fool, seduce, and corrupt men as holy Scripture reveals."[44] Their natural gifts make women the more dangerous: "the more they have of the graces and gifts of nature or art, the more dangerous they are, especially to wellborn men." For this reason "one must take much more care for the education

---

such as pastoral, project their subjects into a future time. But the future this literature describes is not only history in a literal sense. It is also the product of a rich tradition of such kinds of representation, a repository of themes and tropes made more or less readable by virtue of established codes and the discourses upon which they draw. Catherine Des Roches betrays her awareness that her future as a poet will depend only tangentially on this tradition; in a sense, her spindle is not the poet's tool (a pen) but a real spindle. Few writers before the nineteenth century (Defoe perhaps excepted) consider any kind of productive labor a fit literary subject. Cf. Sankovitch on the poem's conclusion: "In the last two lines, the spindle occupies again the dominant place of the husband, as 'care' adorned with 'merit' now usurps the substance of any possible prospective writing, becoming its only permissible subject, and in effect eliminates the joys of free creativity": *French Women Writers*, 5.

[44]René Benoist, *Catéchèses* (Paris, 1573), sig. A4r–v. Benoist dedicates his work to "la royne mère du Roy," and specifies that it offers "instruction concerning the ornaments, dresses, and jewelry of Christian women." In fact the treatise is largely devoted to the duties of a wife.

[of women]" (A6), who have (predictably) greater need of the "friend-ship of Christ" (A5v).

What appears to be at stake here is less a woman's nature as affectionate or charming (even to a dangerous degree) than the only power misogy-nists ever grant a woman: her sexuality or, as Benoist would have it, her openness to Satan. Conventionally, of course, a husband combats the Satanic element in his wife by having her serve as a licit outlet for his own sexuality. Benoist conveys this notion allusively in his comments on uxorial obedience. A wife must follow her husband, "from whom God wishes her to take instruction not only in the Christian religion but in all other things" (Er–v). This rule is interpreted more precisely elsewhere to suggest that it is through obedience to her husband that a woman speaks to him of God: "I would like women to be obedient to their husbands so that, in case some do not believe by the word, they will be won over without [a, the?] word by the honest conversation of women [i.e., their wives] . . . undertaken in fear of the Lord" (B3; cf. 1 Pet. 3:1–2). Logically, however, Benoist's dictum leads to an anomalous situation. Women must obey, he has insisted, in order that their husbands be converted by their honest conversation. But one cannot be converted to a new or different spiritual course by a person to whom one can dictate what decisions of this kind must be. Benoist is actually concerned to establish the doctrinal correctness of quite a different kind of relationship: the inherently reflexive nature of the wife's behavior, which is *sanctifying in itself*. By her obedience she sanctifies—by analogy with the church—whatever course of action her husband takes. The real model for this reflexivity is not the church but the wife's conventionally passionless but receptive sexuality. Benoist's closing reflection on the necessity for a wife's modesty puts an even finer point on his case. He is concerned lest the husband's authority be placed at risk because of her power as a seductive woman. He closes with this unequivocal warning: "It is ob-vious that Christian wives or daughters who dress carefully [*curieuse-ment*], or dissolutely, or in a bizarre fashion are destined to go to hell [*sont reservées au feu d'enfer*]" (C3v; cf. 1 Pet. 3:3–5).

Benoist here raises a fundamental question about a husband's authority which finds various answers elsewhere in secular treatises. Concepts of political (as opposed to marital) authority were in the process of being reformulated throughout the century. Generally speaking, absolutists took a position similar to that of Benoist, insisting that the obedience of the subject was a sacred obligation. Others, like Guillaume Budé in his *Institution du prince* (1547), maintained that while the monarch's preroga-tive was legislative, the monarch was himself under divine law, which functioned to level all social and political distinctions and rank: "according to divine law, all men are equal without distinction or exception as to the obedience they owe that law." Hence monarchs, who are not obliged to obey positive law, ought in fact to honor it: "and it is a statement worthy of a king to wish himself subject to the law according to his own will and also to proclaim and maintain it publicly in order to give reverence and authority to his edicts, constitutions, and ordinances."[45] When one assesses the extent of marital authority, however, it is important to remember that husbands, unlike monarchs, were never constrained by anything comparable to positive law: marriage, unlike civil government, had no *legal* regulation apart from matters of property, ordered by customary arrangements for the management of the dowry, and prohibitions against various degrees of consanguinity. The kinds of commands a husband could issue were therefore largely indeterminate, governed only by his duty to love his wife.

Several contemporary treatises illustrate this lack of definition. Claude Baduel's *Traicté . . . de la dignité de mariage* (1548) begins by contesting the assumption popular with some (especially early) humanists that marriage is incompatible with a life of letters, and, by extension, a life in politics.[46] On the contrary, he writes, "we will show that the good manners and dignity to which a man is born cannot be better acquired . . . than by the reverent conversation and companionship of the wife in whose society the educated man can live honestly, seriously, modestly, and with great temperance" (C7r–v). But how the conversation and companionship that will contribute so significantly to civic life are to be conducted is a deep mystery. Baduel later declares that a wife not only is to be absolutely subject to her husband but also must remain silent in his presence: "when the husband is present it is indecorous [(*une*) *chose layde*] for a wife to speak, whether or not he is himself speaking." As Baduel explains, the very sound of a wife's voice suggests her insubordination. If she speaks, she seems "to wish to usurp her husband's authority and steal the dignity of his position and power" (F5).

Jean de Marconville's *De l'heur et malheur de mariage* (1571) entertains similarly incompatible positions. Early in his treatise, he speaks of the "conjugal friendship" that requires husband and wife to be "equal." In fact, marriage is the only relationship in which friends can be equal: "All

---

[45]Guillaume Budé, *L'Institution du prince* (Paris, 1547), sig. B4v. He continues: "And it is a saying worthy of a king to wish himself willingly subject [to the law], and also to say so publicly in order to give reverence and authority to his edicts, statutes, and ordinances."

[46]Claude Baduel, *Traicté très utile et fructueux de la dignité de mariage et de l'honneste conversation des gens doctes, et lettréz* (Paris, 1548), sig. B. Baduel's treatise is dedicated to Madame Jehanne de La Haye, who is identified as the widow of "Maistre Anthonie arlier [*sic*], Docteur en droict, conseillier du roy en son parlement de Thurin."

friendship is out of line [*impropres*] except conjugal friendship, which consists in a certain equality [*parité*] of persons, for love cannot be perfect where there is inequality [*inegalité*] and in all friendship there is inequality except in that which is gained [*conciliée*] in marriage."[47] This condition of parity means that a husband must "govern" a wife sweetly and in the process of gratifying her. He must never use physical violence against her (A7v). Their actual relations, as Marconville depicts them, are more complex.[48]

Like Italian humanists of the previous century, Marconville sees that marriage, the exchange of women between men, functions to stabilize social order: "by means of the wife the disputes, dissension, and controversies that could have arisen because some [men] desired natural beauty do not occur; if wives were of uncertain status, other men, wishing to enjoy themselves, would accordingly abandon themselves to pleasure" (E). A woman who clearly belongs to a man does not jeopardize the peace unless, as Marconville then notes, she herself has economic power and enters the marketplace. He specifically warns against the disruption caused by a rich wife: "But if it happens that a man marries a rich and ambitious wife, she will want to govern him [*le maistriser*] and take the position of lady and mistress, and he will always be a scorned husband and have to struggle to keep her in subjection. And for this reason there is a big difference between marrying a poor woman who will be subject and in servitude to her husband and a rich ambitious one . . . who only wants to supplant him [*le suppediter*]" (I2v). In the interest of keeping the peace, Marconville overlooks the repeated injunctions against treating a wife as a servant and, taking flight from the problem in fiction, concludes his advocacy of the poor wife by celebrating the patient Griselda. Clearly both fascinated and horrified at the possibility of inversions of power in

[47]Jean de Marconville, *De l'heur et malheur de mariage* (Paris, 1571), sig. Av.

[48]Did such benign pictures of marriage in fact mask social conflict? Pierre de La Primaudaye's chapter on marriage, "Du mariage," in his immensely popular *Académie françoise*, which went into many editions during the century, both in its original form and in translation, hints that wives (and probably husbands) could and did frequently disregard doctrine. In correct patriarchal fashion, La Primaudaye's vision of creation places man at its apex with woman; the basis of their marriage tie is a "true and not feigned friendship" (*amitié*). Thus a husband must command his wife "graciously, as if she were a free person" (*ainsi qu'à une personne libre*): *L'Académie françoise* (Paris, 1587), sig. H5v, H2v. Finally, however, she is his possession, originally an element in the distribution of property and power authorized in scripture and therefore "immutable" (G4v). Hence she is to submit "willingly" to her husband (H7v). If she assumes command, they both lose honor. Nothing here would be remarkable if La Primaudaye had not also condemned wives for "games, dancing, play-acting, hunting, shooting, and other activities highly unsuitable for their sex" (I2). Rarely does what is represented as the social reality of the lives of (at least some) women so directly challenge contemporary marriage doctrine.

marriage, he contradicts his earlier picture of "conjugal friendship" by insisting on the wife's absolute subjection.

The conflicted arguments of these and comparable treatises on marriage in France are easier to describe than to explain. However much they profess a wife's equality, their real concerns center on the figure of the husband, especially in his authoritarian role of domestic governor. Their persistent reference to political ideas and models could, however, result in feminist attacks in kind: writers protesting marital abuse used these very sources to further their own arguments. Claude de Taillemont's *Discours des champs faez à l'honneur et exaltation de l'amour et des dames* (1551), for example, categorizes the rule of the husband as *tyrannical*. The basis of Taillemont's own sense of a just relation between the sexes (delivered to him in a dream by Athena) is the identity of man and woman as both rational and spiritual beings, to be derived conventionally from their common creation.[49] Such a relation does not exist in contemporary life as Taillemont sees it; and he imagines its absence emblematically, as a world where things are "so backward that one can see nothing . . . ; everyone errs and abuses his status and rank" (a4r–v). The image obviously signals the writer's interest in redirecting the prevailing system of sex and gender relations.

The most novel of the points Taillemont rehearses deal with aspects of patriarchal economy, from the disposition of dowries to government expenditures on war. Not only, he says, are women used as household labor after they are married; their fate as prospective wives depends on the state of the marriage market as a whole. If a father has sufficient means to supply only one of his daughters with a dowry, he sends the others off to convents, excusing his conduct with the trumped-up charge that his daughters are given to licentiousness. In fact it is men (including ambitious fathers) who need reform: "in order to justify themselves, they want to blame someone else" (c7v). But marriage is not, in any case, a happy state for a woman, especially if her father's plans have succeeded

---

[49]Both sexes have souls in which the image of God is imprinted. "It is understood that God gave to each of them the same nature [*essence*] and an equal portion of intellect": C[laude] de Taillemont, *Discours des champs faez à l'honneur et exaltation de l'amour et des dames* (Lyon, 1551), sig. e5v; see also d7. In fact, Taillemont goes on to claim that woman is superior: "As far as human weakness is concerned . . . it is . . . common to both sexes: but more . . . to the man than to the woman" (d8v). She is overcome by Satan, man by her: "The corruption of the woman seemed to Satan to be sufficient for conquering man" (e). On the marrying off of daughters for money, Taillemont is particularly explicit: young girls "are shut up in cloisters and nunneries by their cruel relations as if they were wild animals who frighten men. . . . And I find it very strange that most of these girls come from good and rich families, and [they are] so well brought up that with little or no dowry a good place could be found for them. Hence it is obvious that avarice or the desire to marry them off to a very rich man and not lack of means is the cause of this abuse" (e8r–v).

and she is married to a rich and powerful husband: "However honest and perfect [such wives] may be, their husbands esteem them as much as pigs do daisies; there are no caresses but rather continuous screams and blows and hence a perpetual dissension and enmity between the two and finally the destruction of the family" (fv). Indeed, as Taillemont's feminist Philaste reports, the practice of scapegoating woman extends beyond the limits of the household, since she is also blamed—unjustly—for the disorder and bankruptcy of the state. He asks:

> Is it not men who hold royal and civic offices? manufacture and trade? get into debt? disturb the peace, living with their spouses not like two in one flesh but as two entirely opposed entities? who would now want to ask from whence proceeds the ruin of families, if it is clear that woman do not hold offices or have status? that they do not go to law, judge, or accuse? and even less receive public funds? or ever go to the Levant to deal in merchandise? It is not they who go to war, wasting their substance and that of others, pillaging the poor, murdering, blaspheming—even though all these things would be possible were custom to permit them, witness the republic [*sic*] of the Amazons and the prudent government of various queens.   [f3v–4]

Implied here is the extraordinary possibility that women might undertake the full range of public and civic activities, including executive government and international trade. Note, too, that nothing more than "custom" prevents them from doing so. Taillemont's invocation of the first creation of woman is grounds for his rejection of customs of this kind; they do not give men a "prérogative" upon which to construct a "government" (*seigneurie*) over women (d7). By the end of the treatise it is clear that he regards patriarchy as a "tyrannie" of the kind he had previously deplored (e3).

Protests reflecting political thought, such as Taillemont's *Discours*, expressed the opinions of a certain segment of society. Certainly a more extensive audience existed for literature representing misogyny and, more broadly, conventional views of woman and society. But as I suggested earlier, domestic satire is often an ambiguous element in this diverse literature. Such treatises as *Les XV Joies* and the *The Scholehouse of Women* are biperspectival in their representation of the married couple. Their typical wife is shrewish and fickle; and readers disposed to see in a woman a figure conventionally docile must have condemned her. But her husband is suspicious and abusive, self-centered and impotent; for other readers was it quite reprehensible of his wife to resist mistreatment, even if her style was low? Doctrine concerning appropriate forms of resistance to marital abuse was contested throughout the century in any case. Most writers condemned wife-beating; others, early in the next century, would provide for legal action on the part of the wife in cases of this kind. To regard these texts as *simply* misogynist is therefore, I think, to overlook their interrogative function. Rabelais's *Tiers Livre* (1552), in which the position of the woman and especially the wife is constituted ambiguously, from (at least) two points of view, illustrates some of the principal features of this kind of mannerist satire.

Rabelais did of course represent the quintessential misogynist to most feminists of his time, and rightly so in many respects. The Panurge of *Pantagruel* exemplifies the curious mixture of moral vulgarity and philosophical sophistication that marks so much contemporary clerical writing on women. A participant in the sixteenth-century *querelle des femmes*, Rabelais was linked with such precursors as Jean de Meung, whose character La Vieille in his *Roman de la rose* epitomizes the kind of moral degeneracy that clerics often (sometimes facetiously) attributed to women; and with such contemporaries as the lawyer André Tiraqueau, whose *De legibus connubialibus* justifies the prejudicial treatment women received at law by invoking what its author considers to be the immutable verities of divine law and the *ius gentium*.[50] François Billon, in his *Fort inexpugnable de l'honneur de sexe féminin* (1555), particularly castigates Rabelais for his portrait of the physician Rondibilis in *Le Tiers Livre*, pointing to the description Rondibilis gives of a woman's genitals as the locus of "an animal, something interior and alive, irritating, biting, bristling with a tickling sensation, that ravishes all their senses."[51] Rondibilis, according to Billon, attributes to the presence of this animal all the natural fragility, inconstancy, and imperfection of woman. To recent readers, notably Wayne Booth, Rabelais continues to qualify as a writer who disparages women.[52]

[50]For a study of *Le Roman de la rose* in the context of the *querelle*, see especially Eric Hicks, *Le Débat sur "Le Roman de la Rose": Christine de Pisan, Jean Gerson, Jean de Montreuil, Gontier et Pierre Col* (Paris: Champion, 1977); for Tiraqueau, see references in Maclean, *Renaissance Notion of Woman*.

[51]François Billon, *Le Fort inexpugnable de l'honneur du sexe féminin* (Paris, 1555; facs. rpt. The Hague: Mouton, 1970), sig. E3v. Cf. François Rabelais, *Le Tiers Livre*, in *Oeuvres complètes*, ed. Jacques Boulenger and Lucien Scheler (Paris: Pléiade, 1959), chap. 32.

[52]Wayne Booth argues that Rabelais's *Oeuvres* should be charged with sexism. His book is written for men; "voices of women . . . never enter [it], even by remote implication. . . . The truth is that nowhere in Rabelais does one find any hint of an effort to imagine any woman's point of view or to incorporate women into a dialogue." That Rabelais wrote within the culture of patriarchy is no "excuse": "Rabelais and Feminist Criticism," in *The Company We Keep: An Ethics of Fiction* (Berkeley: University of California Press, 1988), 404, 407, 412. I have tried to identify in the spoken objections of Hans Carvel's (admittedly) nameless wife a woman's voice; I think it registers a feminist point of view on marriages that are based on economic considerations. History is of course no "excuse" for anything; critics go to history for explanations.

If, however, the Panurge character in *Le Tiers Livre* is regarded from the perspective of sixteenth-century marriage doctrine, the distinction between misogyny and feminism is less clear. Panurge's dilemma, and the dilemma of so many of the male readers of treatises such as Benoist's and Baduel's—whether or not to marry—is explored in a manner that is highly prejudicial to *his* case. He is revealed to be the sexually feeble, unnerved, and jealous man (whether a prospective or actual husband) of satirical treatments of marriage in which the wife's vigor both terrifies her husband and mocks the natural law that decrees her subordination to him. In many respects, the Panurge of *Le Tiers Livre* is a development of his earlier incarnations. In *Pantagruel* he was an exponent if not of male sexual power at least its rhetorical expression.[53] Having asserted his indiscriminate, promiscuous, and infinite potency as a young man in *Pantagruel,* the elderly Panurge of *Le Tiers Livre* reveals not only the actual weakness of the *senex* as lover but also the latent debility of his earlier type, the boasting chauvinist: impotence, and consequently the threat of his wife as his master sexually and in every other way as well. Both Panurges are, I think, the result of Rabelais's critical sensitivity to the extremes of clerical fantasy. If on the one hand such fantasy can take a compensatory satisfaction in picturing as empty the rhetoric of the secu-lar male who claims he is capable of all the sexual pleasure the cleric must deny himself (Panurge in *Pantagruel*), on the other it can satirize the defenses of the cleric who, by picturing marriage as the condition of cuckoldry, may be willing himself to think he is well rid of the obligation to marry and produce children (Panurge in *Le Tiers Livre*). The Panurge of *Le Tiers Livre* dramatizes what Rabelais saw as the unattractive features of the typical male reader of marriage treatises: unsure of his own sex-uality and hence given to boasting; suspicious of others in the event that he be proved unsatisfactory; and calculating in order to guarantee success in a venture—marriage—that is notoriously susceptible to failure.[54]

[53]For Panurge's use of the rhetoric of sexuality, especially in *Pantagruel*, I am indebted to Hope Glidden, "Rabelais, Panurge, and the Anti-Courtly Body," forthcoming in *Etudes Rabelaisienne*.

[54]Rabelais's satire of Panurge as the *senex* does not in itself constitute a defense of women or specifically of wives, although like comparable if less compelling works, such as *Les XV Joies*, it does give the figure of the young wife a vitality superior to the *senex* and perhaps to men in general. M. A. Screech notes that Rabelais's typical woman is imagined according to the "Platonico-Hippocratic" model as described by Rondibilis; that is, unlike the typical man, she has no will or self-control sexually—she requires satisfaction. See his *Rabelais* (London: Duckworth, 1979), 247. Her desire is, however, for procreation and against a sterile pleasure—in contrast with Rabelais's male characters, who are concerned chiefly with the conservation of their own resources, and the control of dependents, whether women or children. Considering questions of style, expression, and language, Elizabeth Chesney Zegura sees that throughout *Le Tiers Livre* Rabelais's "extreme phallocentrism" is

Panurge's mock encomium on debt has many references, among them the relations between man and women in marriage, a subject Panurge investigates throughout the book. The image of cosmic borrowing and lending as the basis of universal harmony and generativity has its origins in the ancient concept of creation as a system in which elements and substances undergo beneficial transformations in the cycle of life and death. Hence Panurge can speak of debt as the "great soul of the universe" (341);[55] and of the debtor as lender and hence someone to be preserved, since both his needs and his resources will eventually be called upon to produce new activity and life. In fact, Panurge's apology for cosmic debt is actually an apology for the cosmic *exchange*. Significantly, he imagines an ordered exchange, for this strategy allows him to claim that without exchange the need for such resources would not disappear but rather would be expressed in a disruptive manner: "men would behave as wolves to other men . . . assassinating thieves, poisoners, wrongdoers, evil thinkers, evil watchers, each person wishing everyone ill" (342).

The entire elaborate and intriguing image begs the question that the book itself will attempt to answer. In the literature defending marriage, what has stopped men from fighting is the ordered exchange of *women,* and it is they who are the occluded referent in Panurge's discourse. The debt that is crucial to the maintenance of social order is not—as he claims—cosmic or to be generalized in abstract terms (appropriate only to philosophical discourse), but rather marital. This debt has two aspects: social and sexual. Because a husband is said to owe his wife his sexuality, and thus to stand perpetually in debt to her, a social order that depends on the discreet proprietorship of goods and women is maintained. As a *social* phenomenon, the marriage debt does not proliferate into an infinite cycle of borrowing and lending of women throughout the system as a whole. The exchange of women may be a precondition of harmony among men,

---

in part a "literary ruse": "instead of blindly seconding the myth of male superiority, as he first appears to do, the androgynous Rabelaisian narrator in fact interrogates the mainsprings of patriarchal culture": "Toward a Feminist Reading of Rabelais," *Journal of Medieval and Renaissance Studies* 15, 1 (1985): 132.

[55]Rabelais, *Tiers Livre*, 341. On the figure of debt here, see Screech, *Rabelais*, 225–31. Screech notes that Panurge uses the fashionable idea of cosmic exchange as a smokescreen: "the debts that he is really defending are common or garden money ones" (227). Camilla Nilles argues that "debts and conjugal bliss are inexorably linked in Panurge's mind"; for him "the creative force of debts will be replaced by the procreative force of marriage": "The Economy of Owing: Rabelais's Praise of Debts," *Etudes de lettres* 2 (1984): 81. Rabelais's treatment of various forms of debt is actually quite complex. On one level, Panurge wishes to pay the marriage debt and not be a cuckold; on the other, he fears that such an expense is beyond his means. Frère Jan attempts to console him with the assurance that if he marries and proves sexually impoverished, cuckoldry will bring him material riches.

but as a transaction involving particular persons it occurs infrequently and under highly controlled circumstances. As a *sexual* phenomenon, however, the marriage debt is continuously self-generating. Panurge alludes to it in this sense when he describes the generation of children as a lending of the self to the future of the human race: "everything proceeds by lending and borrowing to and from one another: hence one refers to the debt of marriage" (346). This lending is also of something that is owed; or, to rephrase the concept, what is owed is also lent. What belongs to the wife in the form of her husband's indebtedness is also his to lend to her; she is therefore also in his debt (recall Le Franc's treatment of the Pauline concept of marital exchange). Generally speaking, the meaning to tease out of the concept of the marriage debt, as it was known to Rabelais's readers, concerns the constraints it imposes on spouses. What one owes to a spouse cannot be paid to a person to whom one has no indebtedness: adultery is forbidden. And if what is lent to a spouse is actually the payment of a prior debt, in marriage one is never entirely the owner of a whole self. One cannot call in what one has lent if the loan is actually what one owes.

To Panurge the significance of these constraints is complicated by a consideration of his earlier character. As a young man, he represented himself as a womanizer, that is, as one who paid no debt of his own but rather borrowed from the husbands whose women he supposedly took and in whose debt he could be said to stand. Is he prepared now to renounce the license to contract this illicit form of debt in favor of the legitimate debt of marriage? If he does marry, can he actually pay the debt of marriage? If he cannot pay the debt of marriage now, do we know that he ever really borrowed from other husbands? Pantagruel has forgiven Panurge's financial debts incurred in the consumption of his Dipsodian property, but Panurge begs to remain indebted for "a few hundred" (*quelque centurie*; 348). Does this request indicate a wish to marry, or to revert to the illicit economy of the womanizer, or simply to keep as much property to himself as possible? The question reflects the standing of the woman in marriage and on marriage itself as a condition of life. For in marriage what is borrowed and lent is the couple's shared sexuality. In adultery what is borrowed and lent (however unknowingly) is the woman. (In celibacy nothing is either borrowed or lent.) In the first instance woman is a person; in the second she functions as property. (In the third she does not exist in a sexual capacity.) As Rabelais will show, each of these states is differently conservative but only the first is truly generative. Pantagruel has dismissed Panurge's encomium with hard words concerning the *economic* aspects of debt—"Owe nothing to anyone (says the holy Apostle) except love and mutual delight" (347)—but he also describes allusively Rabelais's notion of a proper sexual indebtedness.

Panurge's initial exchange with Pantagruel indicates that he thinks in contradictions that recall, at times with inversion and irony, the terms of the arguments in treatises on marriage. He begins by describing the first year of marriage as exhausting for the husband; however pleasurable, it leaves his "spermatic vessels" so "dried up" that he is completely "unmanned" [*évirez*] (350). When Pantagruel later urges him to marry, he describes first his friendship with cuckolds (an allusion to his past life) and second (more important to his present dilemma) his fear of being one: "I like cuckolds a lot and they seem to be good guys and I am happy to be with them but I would rather die than be one" (358). But the alternative, a virtuous wife, "some honest and prudent woman," is not attractive either: "if . . . God willed that I marry a woman of good repute, and she beat me, unless I were a Job raised to the third power I would go crazy. They have told me that good women usually have bad tempers" (359). In fact, he worries that his wife may be unchaste or disobedient, and so take control of him—both conditions that husbands are warned to guard against. Marriage, indebtedness, illness, and cuckoldry are associated when Panurge claims that if he falls ill his wife will of course care for him, but because he is ill she will also be unfaithful to him: "free and unmarried, I have no one to care for me or feel that love which they call conjugal. And if by chance I fall ill from paying the marriage debt, my wife, tired of my passivity, will give herself to someone else; not only will she not care for me, she will make fun of my calamity and (worse) rob me" (360). Why will he fall ill? It was a medical commonplace that too much sex made a man unhealthy. And, he argues later, women think only of sex: they imagine that "whatever gestures, signs, or attitudes one shows them refer only to screwing" (*belutaige*; 396). Citing Aristotle, he later says that women are insatiable. His protests of rude good health are excessive and so take on a defensive and ironic significance: "I have an indefatigable tool . . . ; my member . . . is the best in the world" (427).

The moral effects of Panurge's sexual anxiety are figured in his monkish garb. Eliminating the codpiece, which he claims is the sign of the virile warrior, he passes off his brown serge robe (*son robe en bureau*) as a toga. It functions, however, as a sign of his intention to *calculate* the advantages and disadvantages of marriage, to try to arrive at certainty regarding its outcome.[56] His *bureau* is both a robe and an office: "I want

[56]On Panurge's quest for an answer to the marriage question and its relation to the action of *Le Tiers Livre* as a whole, see, i.a., Thomas M. Greene, *Rabelais: A Study in Comic*

to keep an office from now on and look closely at my affairs." He believes his *bureau* has an "occult property" that will make him sexually potent. Putting it on, he declares, "I itch to be married and to work like a brown[?] devil on top of my wife [*en diable bur dessus ma femme*]," the near pun revealing the close connection he makes between sex and not spending but acquiring money. As a married man, he will be a "great householder" and not a cuckold; so his accountant will not turn his sols to francs on his *bureau*: "sus cestuy mien bureau ne se joue mon argentier d'allonger les *ss*" (353). Actually afraid of being sexually spent by paying his marriage debt, Panurge here boasts that he will make money on the transaction. His notion of the economy of marriage is subsequently contradicted by the notion that its real wealth derives from spending (begetting children) rather than saving (letting others borrow one's wife and so stand in one's debt). Actual money, as Frère Jan later explains, is what a cuckold receives.

Rabelais's satire of Panurge as a figure representing extremes in the repertory of clerical images of marital behavior becomes a feminist critique of the transactional element in marriage when he shows Panurge consulting the most astute of his friends, Frère Jan, an unironic version of what Panurge pretends to be—a sexually potent male in clerical costume; he thus also embodies a principle of reality in scenes otherwise characterized by fantasy. When Panurge approaches him for advice, once again asserting his potency, Frère Jan calls Panurge old (between the publication of *Pantagruel* (1532) and *Le Tiers Livre* fourteen years have elapsed), notices his gray hair, and warns that "time wears out everything" (*le temps matte toutes choses*; 428). When Panurge then expresses a fear that he may be cuckolded, Frère Jan agrees but consoles him with monkish (facetious) logic. From Frère Jan's point of view, cuckoldry is paradoxically advantageous, and in precisely the way Panurge has imagined his marriage would redound to his credit. For as a cuckold, Frère Jan tells Panurge, he will be well treated, he will have many friends, he will be saved, he will be rich. "You will be worth all the more, you sinner, You will never have been so comfortable. You will find nothing diminished. Your wealth will increase . . . you withered ball bag" (429). In other words, by not paying his debt to his wife but by having others in debt to him because they have borrowed (taken) his wife, he will spend nothing and even grow rich from their expenditures. To reason the way to

---

Courage (Englewood Cliffs, N.J.: Prentice-Hall, 1970), esp. 59–63; on Panurge's resistance to knowledge, particularly self-knowledge, see Edwin M. Duval, "Panurge, Perplexity, and the Ironic Design of Rabelais's *Tiers Livre*," *Renaissance Quarterly* 35, 3 (1982): 381–400.

marriage by calculation in (or on) a *bureau* is in fact to reason the way to being a cuckold, for marriage—requiring sexual expense—must be disadvantageous in the economy of sexuality unless it admit cuckoldry. Monkish logic aside, Frère Jan and the reader know what Panurge cannot acknowledge, that according to a truer calculus sexual indebtedness signifies the power to lend and indicates potency whereas sexual credit is the inverse, a sign of a *couillon flatry,* a faded (and empty) ball bag.

Frère Jan's remedy against cuckoldry, the outrageous ring of Hans Carvel, the "great gem merchant," further contradicts Panurge's claims to trust in his *bureau*. It implies that if Panurge marries, he will be a January-like husband who is sexually impotent, and, more important, that his wife will not submit to commodification or subscribe to an idea of marriage as an arrangement dependent on the possession and exchange of property. Frère Jan's example of the cuckolded husband, the old and learned Hans Carvel, shows him attempting to educate his young and lusty wife in the dangers of adultery in the manner prescribed in treatises on marriage—by lecturing on the evils of such sin, reading lives of chaste women, and, an extreme measure, giving her a sapphire necklace, that is, reminding her of her economic dependence on and value to him. Driven at last by fear to take the devil's advice, Hans Carvel decides that he can ensure his wife's fidelity only if he puts on his finger the devil's ring, in fact his wife's "*comment a nom*" or vagina. Ridiculing the effectiveness of such a solution, Frère Jan observes in conclusion that the young wife declines to have her sexual organs function as her husband's ring—in short, to be his precious object—and continues her pursuit of a suitable consort: "I forgot to tell [account for: *compter,* i.e., *conter*] how [Carvel's] wife, feeling him [his finger inside her], pulled back her bottom as if to say, 'Dummy, that is not what to put there'; and then it seemed to Hans Carvel that someone had wanted to rob him of his ring" (433). She thereby not only indicates her dislike of her old and impotent husband's evaluation of her as a sexual *object*—a vaginal ring—but also alludes to what might be considered her true potency (in contrast to a masturbatory satisfaction) through the generation of children. Paid in truth only by the expense of semen, the husband's marriage debt is of course not finally an expense at all, since it results in the new life of a child, an extension or increase in the lives of its parents. It is important that Hans Carvel's *wife* is the character who is supposed to correct Panurge's perspective on marriage. The point of view of contemporary discussions of marriage was invariably that of the prospective bridegroom, and their tone is, as I have shown, frequently one of calculation. Rabelais protests the relative narrowness of such concerns by showing that the canonical end of marriage, the generation of children, is achieved by sexual passion. Hans Carvel's wife is after all not persuaded to remain faithful by his gift of a sapphire necklace or by masturbatory pleasure, nor can she accept her status as merely ornamental. Her notion of increase is of a different sort.[57]

Rabelais concludes his critique of contemporary marriage doctrine by reflecting on the actions of other figures who play a part in bringing about a marriage: the parents (and especially the fathers) of the couple, who regard their daughters as commodities that they possess and hence may sell. In this case, the youthful Pantagruel appears as the prospective bridegroom. Certain of his virility and hence of marriage as a possible way of life, he has rather to fear that the exercise of parental authority will forbid him to choose a particular woman as wife (and she him).

By his representation of Gargantua's authority over Pantagruel in the matter of matrimonial choice, Rabelais appears to support an Erasmian position against clandestine marriage and for the necessity of parental consent; he seems to see a marriage without such consent as a form of economic exploitation. The profit of such unions all goes, Gargantua warns his son, to the priests in whose presence the couple's vows are exchanged: "such marriages are all to the advantage of their priests [mystes] and not at all to the good and profit of the spouses" (495). He complains that the parents who are absent from the ceremony are absent also from any discussion of their children's welfare or the propriety of the match. Applauding his son for his dutiful regard for his father's wishes, Gargantua describes the grief of parents whose healthy and well-educated daughter has been "raped" by a sickly and poverty-stricken stranger. "What kind of spectacle do you imagine this is?" he asks the company. Sufficiently agonizing, he thinks, to warrant violent retribution. A father is justified in murdering such a suitor and his cohort, the conniving priest, if he catches them in the process of abduction, "even if his daughter has agreed to the match [quoyqu'elle en feust consentente]" (498). Would Gargantua allow a daughter of this kind to escape the same punishment? His wording on the point is in any case ambiguous: the father "ought to put them ignominiously to death." Gargantua has earlier observed that a father would rather see his daughter dead than dishonored, an opinion reminiscent of Vives's typical father in his Instruction, and the reader therefore has some reason to think that the persons Gargantua refers to as "them" include this carefully cherished daughter.

The old king's program for such a Draconian revenge suggests that his condemnation of clandestine marriage, ostensibly undertaken by both priest and husband for real gain, hides a second and opposing danger that

---

[57]Spenser's Malbecco (The Faerie Queene, III.10.15) shares many of Panurge's traits; specifically he regards his wife as property.

Rabelais intends to illustrate: that of abusive patriarchal power over marriageable children, especially daughters. He was not alone in this regard. The lawyer Jean de Coras, who explained for his countrymen the importance of Henry II's edict on marriage incorporating Tridentine doctrine into civil law (1566), was careful to say that the responsibility of parents toward their marriageable children did not include the ancient Roman *potestas patris*. In other words, by forbidding clandestine marriage, the state did not give a father the power to incarcerate or murder children so married.

> It is true that civil law has established new laws, for [but?]—mitigating [*amolissant*] the extremely bitter rigor and severity, and in view of [*prévoyant*] the unnatural [*desnaturée*] austerity of a kind of parent too ready and inclined to hate and destroy his own flesh—it does not permit or wish the power of the father to consist in atrocious and brutal cruelty but rather [insists that it be expressed] in love and faith, and [it does not give] a father . . . the right to kill his child, however perverse, wicked, or miserable. It is enough that a father can accuse his child and present him or her to a judge for punishment.[58]

Gargantua's threat, implying that the Roman *potestas patris* remains in effect, is therefore in clear distinction to contemporary opinion. Moreover, if a father had the rights Gargantua claims, the consent that was doctrinally the basis for marriage would become in every case purely formal and perfunctory. (What daughter would fail to obey a "Roman" father?) The existence of *potestas patris* would in itself create the possibility of marriages of the Hans Carvel type.[59]

[58]Jean de Coras, *Paraphrase sur l'édict des mariages clandestinement contractéz par les enfans de famille contre le gré et consentement de leur* [sic] *pères et mères* (Paris, 1572), sig. c6. Screech notes that marriage as the giants conceive of it "derives from Roman law"—that is, a marriage is not valid without the consent of the couple's parents. Gargantua's position is, Screech believes, also Rabelais's: *Rabelais*, 282–86. It contradicts Tridentine canon law on clandestine marriage in one important respect. While the Counter-Reformation church could not be held to authorize marriages made without parental consent, it did not actually invalidate them; in this stance it was joined by Henri II, who deplored and forbade clandestine marriages but nevertheless recognized those that had taken place. Gargantua's essentially Roman position on the *extent* of parental control clearly exaggerates what both post-Tridentine civil and canon law required. Rabelais, who wrote before these laws were promulgated, balanced his support of the principles on which they were to be based by an equally forceful condemnation of the ghastly excesses they appeared to legitimate by seemingly reinstating the ancient *potestas patris*. Rabelais was concerned not to justify the *potestas patris* but rather to show its limits in a Christian society.

[59]Rabelais's depiction of woman in *Le Tiers Livre* found imitators as well as critics. In "De l'inégalité de l'age des mariéz," Nicolas de Cholières returns to the image of the *senex* as husband who, far from assuming direction of his household, is scorned by all its members. According to his character Fulgence, his failing sexuality is ridiculed: "The sum

Woman in History

François Billon's *Fort inexpugnable de l'honneur du sexe féminin* (1555), like many other feminist histories, provides a rudimentary chronicle of famous women as the basis of a defense of the sex, in form if not in style a continuation of Christine de Pisan's *Cité des dames*. More effective as social criticism are the points that Billon raises to justify such a revision. By revealing that the historical reasons for the disempowerment of women are without foundation, he is able to urge his readers to create a new history critical of patriarchy, and to sketch its beginnings from a time immemorial. The tone of Billon's *Fort* is admittedly difficult to categorize. Like Rabelais, whom he ostensibly refutes, Billon is given to facetious exaggeration; unlike Rabelais, he appears at times to exaggerate in order to belittle his subject and decry its seriousness. Dedicating his treatise to the queen, Catherine de Médicis, he may have thought that to her and her court feminism had come of age, that to speak of it without a certain *sprezzatura* was to rule it out of civilized discourse. At the same time, his readers cannot have failed to take account of the fact that in his *Fort* feminism *is* discussed, and at some length. Billon repeatedly associates the acquisition of political power by women with their opportunities to speak, to voice grievances, to assert new and feminist principles of justice. Describing his own purpose in writing, he declares that he is moved by "a just regret and pity for the unworthy and general servitude of the women of this age."[60]

For Billon, God is himself androgynous: he created male and female in his image; the difference between them "is recognized only in those bodily parts that are necessarily different for the purpose of generation." As God has no body, it is his spirituality alone that they imitate, and there no difference of sex is relevant: "between these souls there is no difference of sex." This view of sexuality implies what all notions of androgyny admit: that human behavior exhibits a range of characteristics, masculine and feminine, which do not depend on sexual—that is, biological—differences. Billon stresses that man and woman have the "same" understanding and reason; they both "equally" aspire to an angelic state in which "there will be still less difference." Billon even manages to make

---

total of what the good man could sow on the grass would amount to a grain of millet in the throat of an ass": *Les Matinées* (1585), in *Oeuvres du Seigneur de Cholières*, ed. E. Tricotel (Paris, 1879), 1:254. His lusty young wife can only mock him, and with justice, for nature is on her side: "The authority of the prince is nothing [*ne peut rien*] compared to the rights [*ce droit*] that nature has given this female" (257).

[60]Billon, *Fort inexpugnable*, sig. A2v. Billon dedicates his work to Catherine de Médicis and other noblewomen of France. For a brief sketch of Billon's approach to the *querelle des femmes*, see the introduction by M. A. Screech in the Mouton edition (n. 50 above).

positive Aristotle's account of woman as "something miscreated or naturally defective" (*une chose occasionée ou deffectueuse en nature*), and argues that it is true only in the sense that for Aristotle man is "active" and women "passive"; passivity in her is not, however, a defect. In fact, human "perfection" or wholeness is to be found not in either sex alone but only in the union of their attributes and qualities: "therefore it must be that for her part she is no less whole than he who is without woman only half a person" (Av–Bv). Here Billon both Platonizes and Christianizes Aristotle, understanding sexual difference as that between the two aspects of an original androgyne, in whose wholly spiritual form (that of the creator or God) this difference is entirely effaced. His revision of Aristotelian doctrine allows him to maintain that it promotes woman's education in that her softer constitution permits her to gather and retain information better than a man's ("les femmes sont plus aptes à souvenance, plus vigilantes, plus sobres et plus constantes"; B3).

Because Billon asserts so forcefully the equality of men and women in everything but the narrowest physical sense, he is able to challenge the practice of subordinating women to men socially and politically. If one agrees that intellectually women are equal to men—"where the intellect of one can penetrate there also can the intellect of the other"—it follows that were the education of men and women the same, even to their physical training, they would be capable of the same activities. What prevents women from such comprehensive education is merely envy: "considering that it is beyond a doubt that were young girls like boys regularly instructed in knowledge and morals, and required to take physical exercise, there would be as many learned, virtuous, and strong women as there are men." Were women to be so educated, men would not see them as radically different from themselves—in short, "some strange monster" (B3r–v). Billon's commitment to the physical training of women permits him both to criticize the enforced inactivity of the housebound or cloistered girl and to extol the marital accomplishments of certain queens (B4, C3r–v). These observations suggest that he accepts virility as a principle of normative and not exceptional behavior for women.

Billon also supports a woman's right to participate in public life. He terms the idea of a hierarchy of creation merely theoretical and hence not in itself the basis of a political order. While there is indisputably "an order necessary in all things" which is maintained by recognition of degree, "by a superiority and inferiority of the sexes, of estates, and of persons," this order cannot determine a "wise government" unless at the same time the fallibility of human beings as political creatures is also acknowledged. He refers to the virtue of "humility," desirable in a person holding office, and seems to envisage a justice predicated on a magistrate who is himself not only law-abiding but also equitable in his judgments. Government and especially justice established strictly by reference to rank is misconceived "unless in one's soul and by the judgment of reason one is willing to show humility (however elevated one's rank) toward those who are of the least status" (B4). In other words, the practice of government ought to be regulated with a certain flexibility; a magistrate (or superior) who governs a subordinate with humility reduces the distance between them, and adjusts the claims he has on that subordinate in acknowledgment of his own fallibility. By entertaining these ideas, Billon separates the speculative realm of metaphysics, where perhaps he locates abstract justice, from the real domain of practical politics, where equitable justice must predominate.

The context of Billon's statement is Christian and moral, and he seems intentionally to avoid implying anything that could be construed as support for the notion of a constitutional monarchy under law. As I have mentioned, political feminism, insofar as it was expressed by arguments for gynecocracy, found its advocates among monarchists who tended to reject the legitimacy of constitutional restrictions on royal authority and power, and not the more liberal monarchomachs. Yet Billon's next remark reveals how closely feminism could be associated with the concept of fundamental liberty for human beings generally. Because, as he believes, all political persons regardless of rank should function with "humility" in public affairs, the very basis for interparty wars, and specifically the war between the sexes, is nullified. Therefore his society should end "that old and hateful war between the sexes" and "the disputes and bitter restrictions of feminine liberty cited above" (B4). When he discusses the arrangements of power within a marriage, he is even more explicit. God intended not that husbands should have "all authority" over women but rather that spouses should respect each other's liberty: "For liberty is a heavenly gift that God wants equally to give to all living persons, a liberty that a virtuous man ought not to usurp over a wife as virtuous as he. And in cases in which a husband is inferior to her in this respect, she can the more have control over him, in the humility of a loving heart" (yv).

Billon's notions of reform are implicit in the evidence he gives of woman's virtue in the public arena. Like Capella, he imagines a time when women had political power because they knew how to wage war. Assyrian women, he notes, regularly went to war riding astride, but Alexander prohibited this practice, "to make them forget the business of war." In the future, he declares, women will again ride astride, although in this instance they will be fighting not the enemies of their country but "the stubborn enemies of their sex." For Billon, the practice of the Assyrian women becomes symbolic of a much more comprehensive feminist struggle: it seems "that for a purpose to be revealed only in the future women could well assume again some form of masculine dress; at an opportune time (and it would not be so strange if this were the present) to equip themselves for the cavalry, booted and spurred, to wage again the war as Amazons against the old stubborn enemies of their sex" (Q). The tone of burlesque in this vision of renewed Amazonian warfare does not quite obscure the significance of Billon's subsequent reference to Mary of Hungary, who in his eyes reincarnates the ancient woman warrior. He pictures her leading an army of the Low Countries to attack and repel the Picardians to help her brother, Charles V. But, he adds, reflecting on the figurative dimension of the action, let all the "enemies of women" be aware that Queen Mary's forces may at the same time be secretly deployed against *them:* "all the adversaries of women . . . ought now to fear that under the guise of dealing a blow against the Picardians with her forces from the Low Countries . . . she may come secretly here instead with royal and worthy princesses, with the intention of making cruel forays" (Q). His warning indicates more of the nature of "the war of the sexes" he has mentioned earlier, and especially of the way in which this conflict, expressed in social and psychological rather than military and material terms, will be carried on under the cover of ordinary diplomatic and political activities. No matter what the ostensible purpose of a woman's activity, its hidden purpose is the overthrow of patriarchy.

Billon also sees that *no* historical evidence of women in public or any other sphere of life carries weight unless it is interpreted in an account of the past that gives it meaning. Like Christine de Pisan and others, he calls on women to rewrite history, and to reveal that the most fundamental struggle history records is not between nations or people but between men and women. His new and unorthodox muse is a powerful earth goddess whose very being, the feminine earth itself, has been violated by men:

> What would it be like, O readers, if women were once permitted to make laws and histories for the space of a year only? Oh, what tragedies and abominable acts would come to light, what rapes, what adulteries, and how many husbands would be exposed. . . . If the Grandmother of All [the earth] took notice of the least part of what men did on her face, she would swell her old veins against the heavens, and there would be so many earthquakes that the order of the elements itself would be perverted. [Yr–v]

It is, of course, precisely such a perversion or inversion of the elementary order of patriarchy that a feminist history would bring about. Elementary, indeed, not only because by privileging men it begins by being a violation of the very face of the earth, but also because this earth is the "Grandmother of All." A feminist history would record a different history from the first hour of creation.

But how subject to its own kinds of bias does Billon imagine such a feminist rewriting would be? Does he, in other words, escape the rhetorical predicament already entered by such feminists as Champier? To defend his request he returns to consider the image of an androgynous deity, in this case one who presides over the truth of the past, a Clio who represents fairly the interests of male and female. It is she who will support this new history, not because she is for women but because she is committed to fighting error: "For this Lady Truth who holds on high the sword of paternal justice will be on your side [i.e., that of the feminist historian]. Thus do not hesitate to express her wishes with regard to all love that is painted with a worldly masculinity." Nor should the feminist fear incapacity, neglect, or ridicule, "for if ever since the great flood all the transient power of evildoers cannot efface the traces of your characters and letters . . . it is the more certain that those who wish to appear virtuous (as imitators of their God, who so loved Lady Truth that he is Truth itself) will not be scandalized by your words and will not attack you" (II). If Billon has earlier challenged the outward forms of Christianity with his image of a vengeful goddess of the earth, he here reminds his readers of the orthodoxy of the image of Christ as the (feminine) Word, *la propre Verité,* illuminating for the virtuous their past and history. By conceiving of the Word as androgynous (and so returning to his opening image of God), Billon clarifies the nature of a literary defense of women in a culture privileging males and the masculine. It requires an altogether new "order of elements," linguistic as well as physical, a second creation in and of language.

The visionary impulse implicit in Billon's call for a rewriting of history is made explicit in Guillaume Postel's defense of women in public life. His *Très Merveilleuses Victoires des femmes du nouveau monde* (1553) develops a theory of salvation history whose central principle is the dramatic interaction of male and female. This dynamic is regarded not literally but at the symbolic level of Neoplatonic analyses of the relation of form or idea to matter. Postel avoids a wholly idealistic account of history only by finding an exemplification of his theory in the figure of "la pucelle Jehanne." Equating masculinity with Platonic reason and femininity with its material or historical realization, Postel argues that it is to women that men must look for the government and rule of states in the new world that is unfolding. The two sexes are analogues of the superior and inferior worlds, represented by the Animus, or "l'Anime," and the Anima, or "l'Ame."[61] The Animus, like the eye, allows us to perceive the truth, while the Anima, functioning like visual space (the word Postel uses is *l'air*) allows those truths to become visible. The two sexes are thus inextricably linked in the generative act that is both cognitive and historical, a recognition of the truth as transcendent and also as manifest in the actual space and time of history: "the one [the male] that imprints in us a knowledge of the truth, as a light on the eye makes things visible; the other [the female] who looks at it after it is imprinted, as space is the locus of things represented by the light, such that it is impossible without this space to make a thing visible, however strong the light and healthy the eye that may be united in one or the other." The Animus is also pure reason, which seeks the Anima, or its realization in deeds: "it is not enough to know reason but one must act it out in deeds" (Br–v). Translated into practical terms, these mystical notions of world order become arguments for government by women. Men are inspired by divine truth, but it is women who provide the means by which this truth is made historical.

Postel sees the epitome of the female governor in "la pucelle Jehanne." She has acted as the temporal magistrate who organizes the state, "temporal monarchy," so that it expresses the will of God and the ideals of the church. She will be superseded by a powerful "mother of the world," who will be the perfect executrix of the Providential design—"the true accomplishment of divine power, according to both religion and policy, as Jehanne of Vaucouleurs was the consummation of the corporeal and civil force for the king, for whom she revived the French monarchy" (C3). Postel's celebration of the historical Jehanne makes it impossible to regard the concept of a "mother of the world" in purely symbolic terms. In his unusual cosmology, this "mother" functions as an antitype to the Virgin; while the latter intercedes in heaven for the souls of the faithful, the former commits herself to the progressive realization of God's will on earth. Put another way: Postel feminizes the significance of the Holy Roman emperor as he was conceived by the imperialist party, in contrast to the papal, from the late Middle Ages and the investiture controversies.

[61]Guillaume Postel, *Les Très Merveilleuses Victoires des femmes du nouveau monde et comment elles doibvent à tout le monde par raison commander et même à ceulx qui auront la monarchie du monde vieil* (Paris, 1553), sig. A8v. The signatures in this edition are out of sequence. Postel's treatise is dedicated to Marguerite de France. On Postel, see William James Bousma, *Concordia mundi: The Career and Thought of Guillaume Postel (1510–1581)* (Cambridge: Harvard University Press, 1957), and Marion Leathers Kuntz, "Journey as *Restitutio* in the Thought of Guillaume Postel (1510–1581)," *History of European Ideas* 1, 4 (1981): 315–29.

Postel's thesis is tenable only if women can be relieved of the guilt of the Fall so that they can be seen as the principle of historical creativity, and he devotes a considerable part of his treatise to a discussion of Eve. As a type of womankind she cannot be the source of evil in history, for as many men as women have committed sin: "one ought to accuse those who are most, not least, blameworthy" (A3v). Moreover, it is an indication of Eve's excellence that Satan took her for his enemy—a choice that eventually leads to a manifestation of the real importance of the feminine in history. For it is from the "materiality" of a woman (that is, from the Virgin's womb) that God's redemptive power is revealed and Satan destroyed: "hence the feminine sex is the reason for showing all the world that Satan, the prince of the world, is extremely powerful . . . and his great power notwithstanding, the generative and material part of the woman [*la semence et partie materielle*], which was evidenced to show that God was more powerful than Satan, conquered him." The divine fecundity of the Virgin is therefore the true sign of diabolical power, in that it indicates the moment at which he is mastered; it is, moreover, a sign elicited by Eve, whose purely human and natural weakness first established his strength. To conclude his analysis of the Fall, Postel refers to the drama of salvation history to suggest that marriage is good because the Virgin has overcome Satan; her victory compensates for Eve's defeat. "It is for this reason that it is written that it is not good that man should be alone" (A6v). Postel's logic is obscure, but he clearly means that woman should function as man's helper in the largest possible sense. She is the agent of the incarnation of all his ideas, without whom they would remain wholly theoretical. Such an eccentric interpretation of history may not have found many sympathetic readers. It nevertheless served to demonstrate how easily a different set of assumptions—in this case associated with Neoplatonism—could feminize a patriarchal vision of history without destroying its providential and heroic character.

Many defenses of women attempted to offer a critique of patriarchy by examining what their authors considered to be the history of women's disempowerment. Some, such as Capella and Billon, saw the subordination of women as originating in a symbolic moment in which they disarmed, either voluntarily or by force. A return to their primal status as men's equals and, paradoxically, an end to the war between the sexes was imagined as a rearming. Others took a more analytical view. They spoke of the structures of discrimination in law and custom, structures that they saw as originating not in or even according to natural and divine law— that is, as having a kind of absolute justification—but rather as the consequence of male power, whether it was understood literally as superior physical strength or more generally as economic control. Their historicism did not posit a different and truer origin of human society in a state of sexual equality but rather questioned the notion of origin itself. Both Nicolas de Cholières, in his *Guerre des masles contre les femelles* (1588), and Alexandre Pont-Aymery, in his *Paradoxe apologétique où il est fidellement demonstré que la femme est beaucoup plus parfaicte que l'homme en toute action de vertue* (1596), develop a concept of natural and divine laws as metaleptic, that is, as the result of what they are supposed to have caused or made possible. Opinions, practices, and positive law are discovered to be not the expressions of eternal principles of justice, but rather their provocation, the pretext for their enunciation.

Cholières's treatise takes the form of dialogues between three principal characters—Nicogène, who supports the notion that women are inferior to men; Alphonse, who claims that actual instances of women who have been active in the public arena prove the contrary; and Ginécophile, who argues certain points concerning the legal basis for the Salic law. The discussion as a whole focuses on two principal points: the extent to which a positive law can be said to vindicate by appeal to divine or natural law the political or social practice it legitimates or brings into being, and also the extent to which such a positive law can be made to seem irrelevant in view of the social and political practices it forbids but cannot abolish. Cholières suggests, although for obvious reasons he cannot prove, that the law respecting the public activities of women is an instance of a metaleptic reversal and therefore without a basis in divine and natural law; and that it is observed in such an inconsistent fashion, and so differently from one society to the next, that it cannot be made to support a notion of gender as determined by biological sex. His proto-anthropological critique of custom is framed by his more comprehensive analysis of law in general, which effectively divorces all sanctioned practices from any connection with an absolute authority.

Nicogène's misogynist position is legalistic and based on the assumption that "women must be well subordinate [*bien basses*] because legislators have not wished to free them from the power of their fathers, parents, and friends, and finally of their husbands."[62] In proof, he cites various laws, "as divine as they are human" (D4v), that guarantee that women will remain without significant public rights, and in "perpetual wardship," which he identifies as the creation of Demosthenes, and its extension in "the Attilien [?] law," according to which the ancient Ro-

---

[62]Nicolas de Cholières, *La Guerre des masles contre les femelles* (Paris, 1588), sig. D4v. The dialogue is prefaced by a mock dedication to Mademoiselle Penthasilée de Malencorne, Infante d'inébile, Dame de la Croulée, etc. The signatures in this edition are out of sequence.

mans placed women under the men in their family, "to control [their] very flighty and willful nature" (E1–2). These laws are designed, in other words, to reform defects in the female character. The power of the husband, he declares, is universal, "common to all peoples"; the obedience the wife owes him is expressed in the absolutely unexceptionable law preventing her from bringing him to trial (E4v). The claim of universality is clearly crucial to his argument; if a law or custom can be shown to be universal, it can be seen as an element of the *ius gentium,* the law of nations, a category associated with the law of nature.

It was to be the claim of the English common lawyers, arguing later in the sixteenth century for the primacy of the English constitution over the monarchy (and therefore against the divine right of kings), that common law was universally recognized among the English and had been law from time immemorial. That is, they claimed for it a kind of changelessness. They were able to do so, in large measure, because they were dealing with a law that in its earliest form was unwritten and merely a matter of generally accepted practice. But law that had been written and codified was not so impervious to challenge on the grounds of inconsistency, as Cholière's Alphonse reveals in his reply to Nicogène. He points out that the classical form of wardship written in Roman law is no longer in force, and, more generally, that the subordination of women is never to be equated with their enslavement (as the practice of wardship might seem to justify), at least in France, because slavery of any kind is inimical to French society: slavery "would un-free [*desaffranchir*] the French from the freedom [*franchise*] that they have gained over all other peoples, insofar as French laws discriminate against slaves in this kingdom" (F2). In short, one cannot be French and a slave, no matter what one's sex.

The evidence of history denies both the universality and the wisdom of the subordination of women: "there are many gynecocratic states where women have governed and they have not plunged into chaos through misadventures." Alphonse does not carry his argument to the next step and question precisely on what basis laws are enacted (as Pont-Aymery will do later), but his discussion of the general subject of legislation suggests that they derive from social opinions that reflect the interests of the legislators. As he says, legislators relegated women to a position of inferiority "for their own profit" (G2). Cholières crucially restricts the application of the idea of projective blaming to the mechanics of legislation—the particular profit of men sponsors a general law against women—and in this way exposes the fundamental interestedness that underlies the establishment of what has passed for a divinely sanctioned social order.

In his analysis of the basis for the Salic law, which forbids women the

succession to the French throne, Ginécophile argues a similar line, pointing out that this law is illogical from a practical point of view, because if
women have the skill to be successful regents, they also have the ability to
be queens regnant: "if women are charged with a regency why do you
deny them the benefit of the succession?" (G6v). This objection obviously reflects Ginécophile's entertainment of realistic criteria to evaluate a political performance on the basis of the real use of power within
defined structures of authority and his rejection of contemporary theories
based on the notion that kingship is a mysterious office. It exposes as
anomalous the political situation in which rich and intelligent royal or
aristocratic women sometimes found themselves—in possession of a
considerable (and perhaps even a decisive) amount of power but without
the authority to use it. The mystery necessary to assume the offices that
were denied them was simply maleness. Alphonse then makes explicit
what Ginécophile has implied: "women ought to be given public offices
in both aristocracies and democracies, for you see that they hold their
rank in both kinds of government, for a princess and a great lady does not
give place to a knave or a low common person" (L7v–8). There is
therefore no reason they should not also have the authority and power
that is vested in the actual political offices that are reserved for men of
rank, according to rank. When Nicogène invokes Hotman on the Salic
law, Alphonse mentions cases from medieval monarchies in which the
authority of a queen was needed for certain kinds of political and legislative action.[63] As he relates, queens were required to countersign edicts
"for their full force and effect"; they sat in the king's council, "they were
made to attend parliaments and estates" (presumably for the same reason); and they could create peers and free prisoners "as well as kings"
(O4v). These remarks draw attention to the inconsistency of considering
women-in-themselves as subject to men-in-themselves when in fact as
individuals they are often the superiors of men. Why is such inconsistency tolerated? Why, indeed, does the whole question of the interests of
the powerful remain unasked?

   Like Cholière's *Matinées,* however, *La Guerre* has also a facetious side;
its polemic turns in on itself and its author rejects a serious conclusion.
Alphonse has asked early in his defense whether, if the man is the head of
the family and the woman its heart, the head can in fact function without
the heart: "I confess that the head is higher, but tell me whether it does
not remain lifeless if the heart stops?" (G2v). The question neatly relativ-

[63]Alphonse is in fact correct. For medieval queenship in France, see Marion F. Facinger,
"A Study of Medieval Queenship: Capetian France, 987–1237," in *Studies in Medieval and
Renaissance History* 5, ed. William M. Bowsky (Lincoln: University of Nebraska Press,
1968), 3–47.

izes the importance of "place" in hierarchical terms—what is higher is not necessarily superior. This view is reinterpreted along satirical lines at the end of the dialogue when a new speaker, Boniface, who seems to take Alphonse's part, declares that he will continue to fight against Nicogène's misogyny. He notes (with obvious irony) that because courtisans have commanded "the greatest philosophers of their times," thus demonstrating the power, through sex, that women have over men, it would be wrong to deny them complete authority: "one would do wrong to women not to allow them to govern men, for men govern bears and other beasts that they have in their power" (P8v). This observation confirms the new hierarchy of Alphonse—the heart once again dictates to the head—but only by restoring traditional stereotypes. The sovereignty of the heart is a way not of valorizing conciliation over confrontation, mercy over justice, and hence femininity over masculinity, but rather of acknowledging the relative weakness of reason in the face of passion. The allusion to the philosopher's government by the courtesan calls into question any incentive to reform society on the basis of a critique of patriarchy and its law.

Pont-Aymery's *Paradoxe apologétique* (1596) belongs conceptually with Cholière's *Guerre* because it also entertains the notion of law as metalepsis. It indicates that in the case of legislation on women, the law follows and does not precede actual practice; indeed, it reflects the concerns of those who possess the means to dominate others. His analysis depends upon a reevaluation of Aristotelian notions of feminine softness and masculine enterprise; the first is understood to indicate a propensity toward exercising the functions of the "soul," the second to express "greed," a vice that specifically destroys the soul.[64] Elaborating on his paradoxical assessment of gender, he claims that the fluid and flexible virtue of woman is "much more effective" than that of man; it depends on "thought and imagination" (*la ratiocination, la faculté imaginative*)— skills that are needed in statecraft (A8). Jehanne la Pucelle is commended for her constancy (C6); Clotilde, the mother of Clovis, for her piety (E3). He also remarks on the emotional correlative of the physiological characteristics of woman, a "sadness" that makes her "wise, cautious, and prudent"; a man, by contrast, is passionate and often moved "to many frivolous and flighty considerations" (E5r–v). Worse, a man suffers from acquisitiveness, an attribute entirely negative, "the only instrument by which are constructed all the devices that do violence to our soul" (G3).

[64] Alexandre Pont-Aymery, *Paradoxe apologétique où il est fidéllement demonstré que la femme est beaucoup plus parfaicte que l'homme en toute action de vertu* (Paris, 1596), sig. A7, G2v. See also the author's views of generosity (*libéralité*), which he sees exemplified more in women than in men (G5r–v).

"Greed, plague of humankind, it's with good reason that you live among men, who are naturally enemies among themselves. You disturb the brain; you hinder rationality" (G2v). Implicit in this portrait of man as passionate, greedy, and irrational—all negative qualities associated traditionally with woman—is a type still relatively new to the literature of defense: the man who is womanly but in a vicious way. He stands in contrast to Pont-Aymery's earlier portrait of the wise and prudent woman who is virtuously feminine, as well as to her male counterpart, the man of compassion. The concept of womanliness has here acquired a positive and a negative value; one could say that feminine behavior is to be distinguished from effeminate behavior. Neither behavior is restricted to women.

In what, Pont-Aymery next asks, does the pretended superiority of men really consist? Were men superior, it would be manifest in their behavior, which is actually not at all superior. (To be true to his early analysis of gender, Pont-Aymery should concede that men are no better or worse than women.) In fact, he claims, men achieve the reputation they have by manipulating the terms of moral judgment to their advantage; "they approve in themselves what they find reprehensible in women, as if virtue and vice were the simple toys of their own designs and had nothing to do with their manner of living." To reduce the categories of his society's moral discourse to mere verbal toys designed to promote the status of men is to undermine utterly the basis of patriarchy—that is, the notion that woman is naturally inferior—and to direct attention to the *actual behavior* of persons of both sexes. In truth, Pont-Aymery sees, the law requires women to adhere to different rules not because they are different but because it has been made and interpreted according to feelings that are closely bound up with self-love and, paradoxically, a profound fear of powerlessness. "These profane [men] oblige the female sex to observe laws that they themselves cannot observe: laws based on their [own] jealousy, suspicion, weakness, greed, depraved consciences, and pride, thinking that it is good to forbid to others what they cannot keep themselves from doing. In this they have a care for their own particular defects and not the law of nature" (G4v–5). The much-cited law of nature is, in other words, no more than a cover for the imperfections of men.[65]

[65]How strongly a defender of women might feel compelled to reinterpret the *texts* that served to sacralize laws designating the superiority of men is indicated by the *Deffense en faveur des dames de Lyon* (Lyon, 1596) by a writer who identifies himself, or herself, only as "Le Delphyen." Neither learned nor elegantly written, this treatise is clearly polemical. Its argument—that God actually prefers, defends, and blesses Eve, while he merely gives laws to Adam—seems to derive from a passionate sense of the injustice of misogyny. Le

French feminists who argued their case from history frequently found that their opposition drew on the fruits of that discipline at least as often as they did. In Bodin's magisterial *Six Livres de la république* (1576), for example, the writer's arguments *against* woman's rule nicely illustrate the process of metaleptic reversal which Pont-Aymery will later expose. Bodin himself could not be more emphatic in ruling out the possibility that woman has a place in government—an opinion he supports with references to philosophy (natural law) and history (the examples of Isabella of Castile and Mary Tudor). For Bodin, as for Barbaro, political patriarchy follows domestic patriarchy. The household, he declares in the first of his six "books," "Du ménage," is "the true image of the republic," and the distribution of power in the household is the model for that within the state.[66] Within the household, the liberty of any of its members is controlled by the authority and power of his or her superiors: "the natural liberty that each person has to live according to his pleasure is experienced under the power of another" (b2); that is, it is constrained by obligations to obey a higher power. Nor can any private agreement, oath, or marriage contract that stipulates "that wives will be in no way subject to their husbands" alter this allocation of authority and power, which is sanctioned by "divine and positive law [*droit divin et humain*]" (b6v).

Delphyen begins by complaining that the ladies he or she addresses ("les dames de Lyon") fail to respond decisively to the attacks of a detractor: "you never take him to court" (*vous n'employez jamais le bras de la justice*) but rather expect to convert him through Christian charity: "you combat vice with virtue" (A4). It is this Christian charity that Le Delphyen questions. In fact, the author reconceives of the deity, imagining a feminist and judgmental God who could not have condoned the victimization of women, even in order to show mercy to the men who abused them. From the very beginning God loved the woman he had created and wanted to defend her [*de la femme . . . prendre la cause en main*]. Strictly speaking, Le Delphyen maintains, Eve violated no law in eating the apple; when God gave this command, it was to Adam only, as Eve was safely ensconced in the spirit of God (B4). And consequently Adam alone is to be blamed. The privileged treatment God gives Eve he also gives to other women. In fact, Scripture does not record that one woman went to hell (C). The real significance of this extraordinary defense lies, I think, in its representation of justice not only as a legitimate weapon for feminists to use in defense of women but in a certain sense as the *only* weapon that will be truly effective. Appeals to fairness, decency, morality—in short, charitable forms of criticism—have not worked. To make the point, Le Delphyen, rewriting Scripture, has to imagine that as a class of person women epitomize justice and, almost by definition, cannot exhibit mercy to those who attack them.

[66]Jean Bodin, *Six Livres de la république* (Lyon, 1594), sig. a6. Preceded by his *Methodus ad facilem historiarum cognitionem* (1566), a treatise on history as a source of knowledge, Bodin's *Six Livres* was the most formidable work on political thought of his century. See, i.a., Julian Franklin, *Jean Bodin and the Sixteenth-Century Revolution in the Methodology of Law and History* (Westport, Conn.: Greenwood, 1977); and Donald R. Kelley, *The Foundations of Modern Historical Scholarship: Language, Law, and History in the French Renaissance* (New York: Columbia University Press, 1970).

Bodin's reasoning with respect to woman's rule in Book Six is a simple extrapolation of his statements on the household. Just as persons within a household do not have the right to agree to modify their positions in that household, so no people can alter the fundamental inferiority of the woman by allowing a particular woman to accede to the throne: "Gynecocracy is squarely against the laws of nature that give men the strength, the prudence, the arms, and the power to command and takes [these things] away from woman" (R5). In theory, at least. Bodin must admit exceptions (women have had political office) even as he condemns them as disruptive. His principal example is the queen regnant, who he sees is beset with difficulties that a king simply would not confront. Not only is a queen regnant more subject to criticism, which can lead to civil unrest; she also more readily risks the disaffection of her courtiers in the dispensation of royal favors. For her to marry is not a solution; if she marries a subject, she creates jealousy; if a foreigner, either he lacks the military power that guarantees his safety or he has it and can promote his own people to offices, "a thing insupportable to every nation of the world" (R8v). Bodin's case in point is Philip II, but he was doubtless also mindful of the prospects of a French marriage for Elizabeth. In any case, he illustrates the predicament of the married queen regnant as that queen saw it; she could not govern with a consort, for if he accepted her superiority, he would be in danger, and if he did not, her people would be subject to a government by aliens.

Bodin realizes, however, that the English parallel is remote and saves for his concluding remarks a concern that is closer to home: that the unofficially powerful woman, whom I have earlier characterized as the *éminence rose,* is in her own way as disruptive as the legitimate female magistrate: "In truth, it is all one whether women command as sovereigns or men who are sovereigns obey women, as Cato the elder declared, following Aristotle" (S3). His alarm ironically indicates what Pont-Aymery makes explicit, that laws restricting the activities of women have their origins in the interests of men. In this case, objections to woman's rule reflect men's fears that were they to renounce their exclusive rights to political authority, they would have no check at all on the subtler forms of subordination they risk by being uxorious. Bodin's English translator is even more direct: the real danger is that "emperours and kings bee themselves obedient unto women's pleasures and commands."[67]

---

[67]Jean Bodin, *Six Bookes of a Commonweale* (London, 1606), 753. It is remarkable that no translation of Bodin's work was published during the reign of Elizabeth.

ENGLAND

Protestant Families

The doctrine of Elizabethan marriage treatises reflected Elizabethan political realities. While conservative opinion on marriage in Italy and France rested on the assumption that patriarchal marriage was the necessary basis of the state, similar opinion across the channel was motivated by an additional need to validate a theocratic government. To this end doctrine governing the forms of marriage was altered in a way both more and less favorable to feminist sentiment: more in that a wife is frequently considered as *homo* (a human being with a conscience and intellect), and less in that English Protestantism conflates priestly and magisterial functions in the family and the state. (The queen was, if not *caput ecclesiae*, at least its "supreme governor"; the secular and religious arms of her government were in a sense one.) The tendency of reformers to sacralize the role of the husband in marriage and the household was already evident in Erasmus. For English Protestants later in the century, the obligation to see in marriage an opportunity to sanctify rather than merely to further the lives of ordinary persons increasingly determined the nature of marital doctrine. The wife's capacity for a spiritual life seems to have elicited somewhat more flexible interpretations of the rule requiring her obedience, although this rule was itself never abrogated. And while not a sacrament, as it was for Catholics, marriage was recognized as a state optimally requiring the consent and goodwill of both parties to it. Many treatises insist that the affective lives of spouses are implicated in the performance of their marital duties, and it is not too much to claim that they reveal a self-consciousness absent from the literature on marriage before this time. Put another way, the concern to establish rules of conduct and to justify them by reference to divine and natural law gives way to an emphasis on the diverse forms of behavior that are most conducive to familial harmony and happiness.[68] Spouses are urged to develop a greater understanding of each other's ways.

This moral and psychological flexibility is not, however, evident ev-

---

[68]Economic factors were probably also important to the development of a notion of marriage as a relationship of persons more or less equal. Alan Macfarlane has pointed out that, in contrast to persons on the continent, English property holders could assign during their lifetimes movable property in testaments without restrictions regarding primogeniture or the sex of the persons in question, and that women as daughters and widows often possessed such property through gifts as well as dowries: *The Origins of English Individualism: The Family, Property, and Social Transition* (Oxford: Blackwell, 1978), esp. 80–93. Susan Dwyer Amussen notes that women were much more likely than men to make bequests to other women: *An Ordered Society: Gender and Class in Early Modern England* (Oxford: Blackwell, 1988), 91–93.

erywhere. In treatises in which marriage remains largely politicized and regarded as a form of government, a wife, like a subject, is instructed in the virtue of obedience and the dangers of rebellion. Discussions of the duties of inferiors emphasize that the consequence of disobedience is social chaos. In *The Second Tome of Homilees*, published in 1570, a wife is told that the pain she experiences in childbirth is a sign that she has relinquished "the libertie of [her] owne rule";[69] if her husband beats her, she is not to take it "heavily but [to] suppose . . . that thereby is layde up no smal rewarde hereafter" (Hh5). A sermon published the year before in *Certayne Sermons Appointed by the Queen's Majesty* clarifies the need for such obedience in conventional terms: "it is not lawfull for inferiours and subjectes in any case to resist or stande against the superior power"; to dismiss authority is to invite "al mischiefe and bitter destruction both of soules, bodies, goodes and commonwealths."[70]

The kind of education advocated for girls could also be severe. Becon had urged that schools be established for girls as well as for boys, and Richard Mulcaster, in his *Positions Concerning the Raising Up of Children* (1581), speaks of the girls who are "ordinarily trained" in "the first elementarie" as indicative of "the manner and custome of my countrey."[71] Apart from what he claims is their natural "towardnesse," he argues the case for prudence; if women should get power, they could accuse men of not having prepared them properly to wield it: "if we tender not their education duetifully, they maye urge that against us, if at any time either by their owne right or by our default, they winne the upper roome and make us stand bare head" (169). His warning suggests what several treatises on marriage corroborate: marriage doctrine had increasingly to entertain questions of rank. That the wife who was of a station higher than her husband could retain the privileges and the habits of life acquired by virtue of birth and training was a possibility that, though not new, at least was relatively novel. Equally emphatic were treatises that discouraged any kind of privilege for women, and especially for wives. Bartholomeus Battus (Bartholomew Batty), in his *Christian Man's Closet* (1581), argues that a girl should be instructed only in morals (traditionally suited to woman) and certainly not for a commanding social role: "Let her learne to heare none other thing . . . but that which may appertaine to the feare of God." She is to be underfed so that she will not feel lust: "Let her not eate openly . . . in the feastes and banquetes of

[69] *The Second Tome of Homilees* (London, 1570), sig. Hh2v.
[70] *Certayne Sermons Appointed by the Queen's Majesty* (London, 1569), sigs. K, I7.
[71] Richard Mulcaster, *Positions Concerning the Raising Up of Children* (London, 1581; facs. rpt. New York: Da Capo Press, 1971), 167. Mulcaster dedicates his treatise to Queen Elizabeth.

her parentes, lest shee see such meats as shee might desire. . . . Let her so eate as that shee may alwayes be an hungred. . . ."[72]

Nor do most writers who stress the importance of religion, and specif- ically of Protestantism, enhance a wife's opportunities for autonomy within or outside the household, as their commitment to a person's right to conscience might suggest. For Andrew Kingesmill, in his *View of Man's Estate* (1576), a woman who does not "marry in the Lord" seizes a dangerous "libertie" that will soon turn into a "streyght bondage" be- cause she will be forced to obey her husband's irreligious authority.[73] Henrie Smith's *Preparative to Marriage* (1591), making a similar point, demands mutual affection from spouses ("they may be called . . . a paire of friends") and compatibility in their vocations. To the prospective husband he advises: "If thou be learned chuse one that loveth knowledge; if thou be martiall, chuse one that loveth prowesse; if thou must live by thy labour, chuse one that loveth husbandrie: for unlesse her mind stand with thy vocation, thou shalt neither enjoy thy wife nor thy calling."[74] Their partnership is to extend to their joint management of their affairs. The husband

> must divide offices and affaires and goods with her [his wife], causing her to be feared and reverenced, and obeyed of her children and servaunts like himselfe; for she is an under-officer in his commonweale, and therfore she must be assisted and borne out, like his deputie, as the prince standeth with his magistrates for his owne quiet, because they are the legges which beare him up. To shew this communitie between husband and wife, he is to maintaine her as he doth himselfe, because Christ saith, they *are no more two but one.*"   [E2v]

Yet in matters of faith she is not to have a hearing. She is to be "meete as God said"—that is, she is not be a Catholic—for "how is she meete, if thou be a Christian and she a Papist? We must marrie in the Lord . . ." (D4r–v). She is also to be instructed by her husband. Smith's concern for the religious life of the family leads him eventually to the contradiction that confounds the ending of Erasmus's *Institutio matrimonii christiani*. Despite a woman's claim to affectionate treatment, her husband must attempt to "reclaime [her] from her faultes," and she, responding to this education, must not "examine whether he be wise or simple, but [know] that she is his wife, and therefore they which are bound must obey, as

---

[72]Bartholomeus Battus, *The Christian Man's Closet* (London, 1581), sig. T3r–v. This work is dedicated to Thomas and Brian Darcie.

[73]Andrew Kingesmill, *A View of Man's Estate* (London, 1576), sig. K3.

[74]Henrie Smith, *A Preparative to Marriage* (London, 1591), sig. C5v. Smith dedicates this work to William Cecil, Lord Burghley.

Abigaill (I Sam. 25.3) loved her husband though he were a foole . . ."
(E7). Her obedience must be unquestioned because her husband "in his
familie hath all the offices of Christ: for he must rule, and teach, and pray;
rule like a king, teach like a prophet, and pray like a prist" (F3). The case
of Katherine Stubbes vividly illustrates a wife's categorization as perpetual neophyte. Praised by her husband, Philip, for "her singular wis-
dome" in his *Chrystal Glasse for Christian Women* (1630), her skill at
preaching allows her "most mightily to justifie the truth of God against
. . . [the] blasphemous untruths [of papists and atheists]." But the doctrine she pronounced was essentially his:

> You could seldome or never have come into her house, and have found her
> without a Bible or some other good booke in her hand. And when she was
> not reading, she would spend her time in conferring, talking and reasoning
> with her husband of the Word of God and of religion: asking him what is
> the sense of this place and what is the sense of that? . . . she obeyed the
> commandement of the apostle who biddeth women to be silent and to
> learne of their husbands at home.[75]

Other treatises depict the conflict that occurs when customary expectations of a wife's obedience are set against the requirement that she be
allowed a certain autonomy. Robert Cleaver, in *A Codly [Godly] Form of
Householde Governement* (1598), sees the household conventionally, as "a
little commonwealth," whose government, both "civill and righ-
teous"—that is, political and spiritual—is to be in the hands of the
husband, who is "cheefe," aided by his wife, who is "fellowhelper."[76]
But he emphasizes that her obligation to obey her husband derives from
her "consent of the heart" to the marriage when she marries him.[77] If she
does not wish the marriage to take place, her parents ought to break off
arrangements for it (I2r–v). After marriage, Cleaver would further protect a wife's autonomy. He declares that an equality of estate in marriage
is to be expected (that is, it is to be wished for), but he indicates that a wife
of "higher estate" than her husband must be recognized as his superior in

[75]Philip Stubbes, *A Chrystal Glasse for Christian Women* (London, 1630), sig. A2v. A
pamphleteer for the Puritan cause, this Stubbes is perhaps the brother of John. In any case,
he is associated with the Marprelate faction: his *Anatomie of Abuses* (1583) was attacked by
Thomas Nashe in the *Anatomie of Absurdities* and defended by Gabriel Harvey in *Pierce's
Supererogation* (1593).

[76]Robert Cleaver, *A Codly [Godly] Form of Householde Governement* (London, 1598), sig.
B5. (This work went into numerous editions.)

[77]Cleaver's emphasis on heartfelt consent suggests that the wife obeys by choice rather
than out of her nature as a creature subordinate to man. Cf. Gordon Schochet's distinction
between the patriarchal and contractual conceptions of political oligation in his *Patriarchalism in Political Thought* (New York: Basic Books, 1975), 7–8.

"divers actions of publike appearance." Whether or not this distinction reflects a knowledge of the theory of the monarch's two bodies, it demonstrates that Cleaver recognizes in practice a relaxation of the usual restrictions governing the public behavior of married women. More important is Cleaver's contention that a wife's contribution to her husband's "headship" could be considerable. Commenting on her "dutie" to "admonish" her husband, he cites the example of Naaman, who took the advice of his servant: "so . . . when [a husband] faileth in dutie, he is to heare her good counsell and admonition, either concerning heavenly matters or earthlie affaires: she notwithstanding considering her estate and condition under him, and in humilitie confessing herselfe to bee the weaker vessell. 1 Pet. 3:7" (N2v–3; for Namaan, Cleaver cites 2 Kings 5:13–14).

Conflict becomes overt, however, when Cleaver attempts to make rules governing instances of uxorial disobedience. Following the reformers' formula for so-called passive resistance, he states that a wife "should obey her husband in good and right or else shee doth not obey him as the Lord but as the tempter" (Q6v–7). He implies what he has already suggested by his treatment of the subject of admonition and a wife's "good counsell," that a husband does not invariably represent divine authority. He may be of the devil's party. Hence marriage cannot *compel* a wife's obedience; it is not a "tiranny" in which the husband's will functions as the monarch's absolute prerogative (P5). But how a wife is to know enough to judge whether her husband follows the tempter is a question answered with a contradiction. A husband is, after all, a "pastor" in his house, and women are not to possess "eloquence, great witte, ordering of the common-wealth, [or] prudence" (Aa5).

The more flexible a writer's treatment of the rule of uxorial obedience, however, the more frequent his representation of protests against it or exceptions to it. In such cases, the image of the household as a government tends to lose its prescriptive force, and relations within marriage are seen to depend not on a rule of reason or the headship of the husband but on a complex set of arrangements between spouses who are acknowledged to be more feeling than thinking creatures. Dudley Fenner, whose *Artes of Logike and Rethorike* (1584) had many printings, indicates the way an interest in affective life could be expressed in the language of domestic government. His wife has a special duty; it is "to bee an image of the authority and wisedom of her husband, in her whole administration . . . and from a meeke and quiet spyrite in al her behaviour of words, deeds, apparrel, countenance, gesture, etc. to signify plainly she hath feeling of him in her hart as of the image of God's majestye, glory, and perfection."[78] Here the husband's headship is acknowledged as a "feeling in the heart" of his wife, a condition that depends on the same kind of "consent" that Cleaver saw as basic to marriage. In essence, of course, relations between spouses are what they have always been: although the wife has internalized rather than mirrored her husband's will, she remains the image of his authority.

George Whetstone's *Heptameron of Civill Discourses* (1582) addresses the question of affection in marriage by examining why couples do or do not live in "unitie," that is, as one. Faliero, who among the characters in this dialogue is an authority on marriage, when asked to explain what causes some marriages to be "hell," answers that "the advantage of reason . . . is the onelie cause thereof." For if a couple is "divided in desire, differ in life, and delight in neither's love, reason, that findeth out this contrarietie, soweth contention." When there is "no difference in love," on the other hand, "reason that delighteth in unitie maketh the joyes of mariage innumerable."[79] Traditionally, of course, reason had been as-signed to the husband as "head," in contrast to the wife as "body," and it was his superiority in this respect that justified his government and created the "unitie" within marriage. Faliero's assertion makes sense only when reason is considered to be a faculty common to both sexes, used to give a certain articulation and meaning to the emotions. If reason no longer is the privilege of the male but rather shared with the female, the case for a functional equality of husband and wife is strengthened. Their "unitie" is guaranteed by cooperative rather than authoritative relations.

Indeed, according to the *Heptameron*, reason alone is no longer a ground for contracting marriage. Although suitable marriages may con-tinue to benefit the state and so find political justification, no one can (or ought) to enter marriage because his reason tells him that it is prudent or economic to do so. The calculating attitude that Rabelais ridiculed in the hapless Panurge is here again at issue, as Falerio asserts that "the office of free choise is the roote or foundation of marriage which consisteth onely in the satisfaction of fancie, for where the fancie is not pleased, all the perfections of the world cannot force love, and where the fancie de-lighteth many defects are perfected or tollerated among the marryed" (Y). While such observations are by no means new—English readers would certainly have known of the dicta of Chaucer's Wife of Bath on the

[78]Dudley Fenner, "The Order of the Housholde," in *The Artes of Logike and Rethorike . . . togeather* [sic] *with examples for the practise of the same, for methode in the government of the familie prescribed in the Word of God* (Middelburg?, 1584), sig. B6v.

[79]George Whetstone, *An Heptameron of Civill Discourses* (London, 1582), sig. E4. *An Heptameron* is dedicated to Sir Christopher Hatton.

subject of forced love—they do alter the conception of marriage as an institution primarily civil and economic. How alien to traditional discourse on the household they still were is indicated by the remainder of Whetstone's dialogue, which returns to a traditional view of the household as a commonwealth governed by the husband (Y1v–2v).[80]

Androgyny

The second version of Sidney's pastoral prose romance, published as *The Countess of Pembroke's Arcadia* in 1593 after editing by the countess, Sidney's sister, contains a powerful exposition of the notion of androgyny as the foundation for a defense of woman and more especially of woman's rule. Sidney may have composed his work with his virgin queen regnant in mind; his impolitic letter condemning the prospect of her marriage with the duc d'Alençon was the occasion for his exile from court and consequent leisure to write.[81] In any case, the behavior of

[80]Emphasis on the wife's emotions could also lead to concessions that depended on acknowledging her supposed frailties. So William Vaughan's *Golden Grove* (London, 1600) states that marriage is a "communion and fellowship of life betweene the husband and the wife," and he forbids a husband to "injure his wife by word or deede," because she is a "feeble creature and not endued with such a noble courage as the man." Any punishment, moreover, will cause a grievous reaction, "as if hee should spit into the aire, and the same spittle return backe upon his own selfe." He must even refrain from educating her in better manners, and "suffer [her] to be merrily disposed before him otherwise (a woman's nature is such) shee will by stealth find out some secret place or other to tattle in, and to disport herself": sigs. M7, N4v. Vaughan's unstated premise, that a woman is inherently infantile and less "noble" than man, finds its political analogue in the pure patriarchalism of such thinkers as James I, whose *True Law of Free Monarchies* had appeared three years earlier. James I regarded his subjects as never more than children politically. See James I, *The True Law of Free Monarchies*, in *The Political Works of James I*, ed. Charles H. McIlwain (New York: Russell & Russell, 1965), 55–56.

[81]For an account of Sidney's relations with Queen Elizabeth, see, i.a., A. C. Hamilton, *Sir Philip Sidney: A Study of His Life and Works* (Cambridge: Cambridge University Press, 1977); for a comprehensive study of the *Arcadia* as an expression of the tensions in Sidney's political life, see Richard McCoy, *Rebellion in Arcadia* (New Brunswick, N.J.: Rutgers University Press, 1979). Two recent studies contribute to an understanding of the *Arcadia* as influenced by the author's experience as a courtier attempting to challenge monarchic practices: Arthur F. Kinney, "Sir Philip Sidney and the Uses of History," in *The Historical Renaissance: New Essays on Tudor and Stuart Literature and Culture*, ed. Heather Dubrow and Richard Strier (Chicago: University of Chicago Press, 1988), 293–314; and Annabel M. Patterson, "'Under . . . Pretty Tales': Intention in Sidney's *Arcadia*," in *Essential Articles for the Study of Sir Philip Sidney*, ed. Arthur F. Kinney (Hamden, Conn.: Archon, 1986), 357–75. Few writers of his period were as adept as Sidney was at disguising the authorial voice in the chorus comprised of his many characters. Despite the risks that attend an interpretation of a work of fiction as a vehicle for political and ideological debate, I shall offer a reading of the *Arcadia* that I hope does justice to its representations of sex and gender, especially as they relate to theories of government and the state, without unfairly overlooking Sidney's delicate and manifold uses of irony or the literary effects of his skill at

Sidney's various royal characters—his two principal kings, Basilius of Arcadia and Euarchus; Basilius's queen, Gynecia; the two Arcadian princesses, Pamela and Philoclea; and the two princes, Pyrocles and Musidorus, son and nephew, respectively, of Euarchus—conveys an extended feminist critique of various aspects of patriarchy. Sidney portrays dramatically the psychological consequences of shared gender, especially in courtship and mature sexual relations; he also establishes what in his view is the significance of virtues conventionally represented as masculine or feminine to a theory of the state and its justice. As a result, he discovers that the concept of the feminine, as it describes private and moral as well as public and political action, has a greater and more impressive scope than any other writer of the century discerned.

Sidney's genius was to see that the conventional analogies between marriage and the state, between relations of sex and gender and political relations, allowed certain major features of marriage and political doctrine to be elucidated. He understood that the true point of comparison between both orders—the ethical, embodied in the personal relations between man and woman; and the political, embodied in the civic relations between magistrate (typically, the monarch) and the people—was in their exemplification of the figure of oxymoron. In marriage and the family, the union of husband and wife, reflected initially in their experience of androgyny within their own persons (as Breton was shortly to notice), was the basis for domestic harmony. In the state, the union of the monarch and his or her people, between nobility and commoners, reflected initially in their shared respect for law, was similarly the basis for political order. In both cases, differences that Sidney regarded as innate, even as biological givens—namely, sex and social rank—are contained within the ample flexibility of a *coincidentia oppositorum* that is actually

---

manipulating the tropes of pastoral and courtly discourse, often in a facetious or parodic mode. My text is the 1593 edition, emended in light of the 1590 revised *Arcadia*, edited by Maurice Evans (Harmondsworth: Penguin, 1977). The status of the 1593 text—actually a hybrid composed of the revised 1590 text (brought to public attention after Sidney's death by his sister, the Countess of Pembroke), plus the (largely) unrevised 1580 text—as entirely Sidney's own and a true reflection of his last intention in writing has long been the subject of critical debate. I am aware that in considering the 1593 text as a unity, especially with respect to its final chapters, which recount the judgment of Euarchus, I am assuming that Sidney would not have substantially altered what he had originally written in the 1580 text; Euarchus's judgment is discussed below. For a close study of the two texts and their differences, see William Leigh Godshalk, "Sidney's Revision of the *Arcadia*, Books III–V," in *Essential Articles*, ed. Kinney, pp. 311–26. The evidence has suggested to some critics (although obviously not to me) that the editions of 1580 and 1593 are actually two texts. A. C. Hamilton writes: "The 1593 *Arcadia* remains two separate works, one work which is essentially complete as it stands, even though unfinished, and a fragment of a different work": *Sir Philip Sidney*, 171.

experienced as a constant process of identification of self and other in the functional—that is, behavioristic—terms supplied by the concepts of gender (always androgynous) and law (always sovereign). Sidney's text is feminist to the extent that it gives a positive value to the feminine aspect of male behavior in private life: it is Pyrocles' womanish behavior that allows him to approach Philoclea, literally but also in spirit. The romance is feminist too in its analysis of the monarch's public role as judge, demonstrating that the virtues of equity and mercy, regularly represented as feminine in the iconography of justice, are consonant with providential restorations of the body politic.[82]

Throughout the *Arcadia*, the roles of father and magistrate, fundamental to understanding patriarchy and hence also feminist resistance to it, are conflated in the figure of its principal monarch, Basilius. The initial mistakes he makes in both capacities get Sidney's plot under way and establish by inference norms of domestic and political order. They are the result of a single interpretation of an oracular enigma and in a sense are mirror images of each other. Seeking to protect himself from the adverse fortune the oracle seems to him to prophesy, Basilius has both sequestered himself from public life by retiring to the *otium* of a pastoral world, governing through magistrates, and forbidden his daughters, Pamela and Philoclea, to entertain suitors or the prospect of marriage, at any rate during his lifetime. In other words, he attempts to control his own destiny by moving into timeless zones. Pastoral is the locus of a recreative repose from the *negotium* of the city; his daughters' celibacy signifies his refusal to allow the crown its dynastic evolution, to enter into the processes of generation that history itself comprises. Sidney's attention is focused initially on the effects of these privations on the princesses and, through the words of Basilius's chief minister, Philanax, he actually defends the need to allow woman experience of the world. Declaring "unnatural" Basilius's determination to keep his daughters unmarried, Philanax notes that a human being "restrained" from certain activities will inevitably come to think them desirable. Nor—and here he

---

[82]The gender identities of justice (masculine) and of equity and mercy (feminine) are established in antiquity. For the iconography of Dike (justice) and Dikeiosune (righteousness or equity) and of Osiris (the sun, justice) and Isis (the moon, equity), see James Nohrnberg, *The Analogy of the Faerie Queene* (Princeton: Princeton University Press), 388. Nohrnberg considers the representation of equity throughout Spenser's bk. V, 372–94. See also the comments of Jane Aptekar on Spenser's Jove and Litae in *Icons of Justice: Iconography and Thematic Imagery in Book V of the Faerie Queene* (New York: Columbia University Press, 1969), 16–21. It is important to realize that women characters do not necessarily exemplify persons who judge with equity; because equity is symbolically feminine, men can show it as well as women. The relationship of justice, equity, and mercy in the *Arcadia* is discussed below.

implicitly attacks such educators as Vives, Bruto, and Battus—will "ig-norance" (personified in Pamela's shepherd guardian, Dametas) in itself maintain virtue, particularly in the face of misfortune. "Oh, no, he cannot be good that knows not why he is good, but stands so far good as his fortune may keep him unassayed; but coming once to that, his rude simplicity is either easily changed or easily deceived; and so grows that to be the last excuse of his fault which seemed to have been the first foundation of his faith."[83] Philanax links humanist concerns with the *vita activa*, in which fortune assays human beings, to the reformers' belief that untried virtue is no virtue at all and, without referring to gender, applies his morality of trial to his master's daughters. In principle his argument is feminist: man and woman have the same virtue and it requires the same exercise.

His point takes on a dramatic reality when the princes Pyrocles and Musidorus become suitors of the princesses. Both young men disguise themselves in order to gain access to the ladies they love. To court Philoclea, who is in the close custody of her parents, Pyrocles appears as a virile maiden, Zelmane, whose "device," inscribed in a jewel, is "a Hercules made in little form, but set with a distaff in his hand, as he once was by Omphale's commandment, with a word in Greek but thus to be interpreted, 'Never more valiant' " (131). To pay suit to Pamela, who lives as a shepherdess supervised by the rustic Dametas, Musidorus is dressed as Dorus, a shepherd. As Sidney's narrative will show, both young men impersonate their other and opposite self, the man Pyrocles a woman, the prince Musidorus a commoner. In disguise, they signal the oxymoronic union of self and other which Sidney will demonstrate to be the basis, first, of the stability of the couple, and thus the family; and second, of the state. Neither Pyrocles nor Musidorus denies his sex or rank, but both show that sex and rank do not necessarily govern their behavior. By their disguises they suggest that these fundamental elements of self admit a wide and even self-contradictory experience of their opposites or others, and that this experience constructs two beneficent unions: the "one flesh" of marriage and the body politic of the state. Those figures traditionally identified as the "head" of a particular body, the man in marriage and the monarch in the state (here exemplified by Pyrocles and Musidorus, respectively), have a particular need to understand the terms on which they may be said to govern the larger entity of which they are a part. These prove to be terms that by valorizing the

[83]Sir Philip Sidney, *The Countess of Pembroke's Arcadia*, ed. Maurice Evans (Harmondsworth: Penguin, 1977), 82.

feminine give persons categorically subject to the "head" a major if not technically equal claim on the fate of the body in question.

Sidney's understanding of androgyny is extraordinarily acute. Hercules with a distaff is of course an inversion of the terms in which androgyny is usually represented—the androgyne is customarily seen as a *Venus armata* or a female knight—but the figure also exposes what both the armed Venus and the female knight imply. Contemporary voices, whether male or female, were generally male-identified; the rules of conventional marriage required the woman to assume the voice of her husband and be his echo, to be masculine to the extent that she identified herself with the interests of men, a condition that is emblematized by a Venus or a woman bearing arms. Sidney understands that a female-identified voice will have to signal its nature with the attributes of woman; a male feminist bears a distaff and, in the symbolism of gender that appears later in the romance, his female counterparts, the princesses, renounce or do not take up arms. (The two women who are forced by circumstances to assume male disguise and fight, the first Zelmane and Parthenia, do not survive.)

Pyrocles, disguised as Zelmane and accused by Musidorus of accepting the "peevish imperfections" of woman and utterly subverting "the course of nature," apologizes for his newly assumed double identity by arguments that might well have been lifted from contemporary defenses of women. Pointing out that he was "born of a woman and nursed of a woman," he insists that women "(if we will argue by reason) are framed of nature with the same parts of the mind for the exercise of virtue as we are." As proof, he adduces "this estate of Amazons (which I now for my greatest honour seek to counterfeit) that doth well witness that if generally the sweetness of their disposition did not make them see the vainness of these things which we account glorious, they neither want valour of mind, nor yet doth their fairness take away their force" (134–35). Pyrocles maintains that woman is capable of behaving in a virile fashion naturally, but that as the maiden Zelmane he declines to use such valour and force to achieve glory. For him as a biological male to assume a distaff is not to deny attributes traditionally valorized as masculine, but rather to renounce the signs—the "glorious things"—men have devised to recognize them. For him as a male *suitor* to assume a distaff is, moreover, to include in a program of courtship the manners and values of woman. In short, the distaff in male hands means, according to Sidney's gender symbolism, a renunciation of the *primacy* of the man over woman and male over female interests. (Later, Zelmane's rival for the hand of Philoclea is Amphialus, the suitor who, by relying on force, symbolically rejects the distaff and ends by killing himself.) Sidney hints at further distinctions. When Musidorus charges Pyrocles with being "woman-ish," by which he means vain and frivolous, the term is clearly deroga-tory and could be translated as effeminate. But Zelmane responds by accusing Musidorus of an "unmanlike cruelty of mankind," a kind of brutality expressed by men and usually visited on women (134).[84]

Revealed here is a complexity within gender. Zelmane represents what might be called the positive valence of gender; Musidorus, by contrast, sees and reveals both genders in a negative light. Zelmane represents herself virtuously, as both virile and feminine; she terms Musidorus cruel in an unmanly way in response to his denigratory vision of her as effeminate. The androgyny Zelmane incarnates is of course positively exemplary for both man and woman. As an Amazon she is a double androgyne: both a man who behaves like a woman and a woman who behaves like a man. In sum, Sidney posits androgyny as the rule of gender in contrast to sex; masculine and feminine behaviors that are not specifically procreative are not restricted by biological sex.[85]

[84]There is no negative term to denote a masculinity that corresponds to the negative "effeminacy"; Sidney is forced to use this circumlocution. A number of his characters seem to me to suffer from the negative aspects of masculinity—Musidorus here, Philanax and Euarchus later. Rebecca Bushnell has pointed out to me that the negative aspects of both genders—cruelty and effeminacy—are united in the figure of the tyrant as he is repre-sented in contemporary drama.

[85]Sidney's view contrasts with that of many modern feminists who see that in twen-tieth-century industrial cultures sexuality necessarily defines behavior in a way that does not admit much of the psychological latitude provided by the dominant feminist view of gender in the Renaissance. Catherine MacKinnon, for example, speaks of sex as the basis for gender in contemporary culture, although an understanding of the process of con-structing gender reveals that it is not synonymous with sex:

> The discovery that the female archetype is the feminine stereotype exposed "woman" as a social construction. Contemporary industrial society's version of her is docile, soft, passive, nurturant, vulnerable, weak, narcissistic, childlike, incompetent, masochistic, and domestic, made for child care, home care, and husband care. Conditioning to these values permeates the upbringing of girls and the images for emulation thrust upon women. Women who resist or fail, including those who never did fit . . . are considered less female, lesser women. . . . If the literature on sex roles and the investigations of particular issues are read in light of each other, each element of the female *gender* stereotype is revealed as, in fact, *sexual.* Vulnerability means the appearance/reality of easy sexual access; passivity means receptivity and disabled resistance, enforced by trained physical weakness; softness means pregnability by something hard. ["Femi-nism, Marxism, Method, and the State," in *The Signs Reader,* ed. Elizabeth Abel and Emily K. Abel (Chicago: University of Chicago Press, 1983), 242]

Renaissance feminists tried, among other things, to theorize about gender so that the "meanings" MacKinnon says our culture assigns to women's physical beings (including many more that are less negative than the ones she describes) are not restricted to females, but inclusive of males whenever possible (e.g., "softness" will never be a general charac-teristic of males; mercy, its virtuous correlative, however, can or could be). Renaissance feminists make this judgment of gender because they regard it as a cultural rather than a physiological phenomenon. Without such a concept of gender, the purely human dimen-

The episodes describing the various kinds of love the persons in Ba-silius's household feel for Zelmane clarify Sidney's conception of the psychological significance of androgyny. For Philoclea, representing the interests of the young and inexperienced woman, sexual difference is both fearful and obscure. She cannot detect Zelmane's sex under the feminine guise as her mother, Gynecia, can, and she falls in love with her as with a narcissistic self-image rather than as a different other. The process begins with a "friendly affection" and moves by imitation to "a commonalty of passion" to which "reason" agrees: she "[conformed] herself to that which she did like, and not only wishing to be herself such another in all things, but to ground an imitation upon so much an esteemed authority," she marked "all Zelmane's doings, speeches, and fashions" and took them "into herself as a pattern of worthy proceeding." By degrees her passion to imitate Zelmane as a model of woman is transformed by intimacy and companionship to a love of Zelmane as a man; she moves from wishing the two could live together, "like two of Diana's nymphs," then in the "natural band" of sisterhood, and finally she wishes "either herself or Zelmane a man, that there might succeed a blessed marriage betwixt them." Then "indeed love pulled off his mask and showed his face unto her, and told her plainly that she was his prisoner." Love has had to wear that mask because the "captivity" her father has forced her into has created a "suspicion" of marriage and she has vowed to devote herself to "Chastity . . . which mak'st us most immortal shape to wear" (238–41).

The entire sequence of events has both a psychological and a moral reference. Zelmane's feminine behavior draws Philoclea into an intimacy that finally seeks sexual expression with Zelmane as a male. By growing to love the androgynous Zelmane as an image first of self and then of other, Philoclea comes to recognize herself in that double, and conversely that double in herself. The basis is therefore established for the mystical union of two persons in one flesh extolled by defenders of marriage. In his version of this union, however, Sidney makes the process of mirror-ing reciprocal rather than uniquely a woman's experience: Pyrocles as Zelmane mirrors an earlier female androgyne, Zelmane the lady knight. Sidney rejects the notion that chastity in itself constitutes moral purity and leads to immortality, a notion endorsed first by the fearful Philoclea. In fact, he calls into question the very idea of "purity" by his image of the

---

sion of male or female existence (imagined as an attribute of the human being as *homo*) is difficult if not impossible to project. Of course a projection of this kind does not mean that relations of authority and power between male and female do not require negotiation.

androgynous self who experiences both sexes, at least at some level of consciousness.

Sidney's representation of androgyny illustrates what might be termed gender's functional flexibility; for him, a literal gender identity does not exist as more than an abstraction, its nature conveyed by what Zelmane says about "virtue"—the ability to do what we do well and decently: "we love it *in a creature*, not as a word" (135; my emphasis). This flexibility explains the virile woman and the uxorious man, the armed Venus and the spinning Hercules. (It presupposes a degree of *choice* in matters of behavior which would probably have struck a responsive chord in the queen, although she might have been less pleased to find a similar latitude generally available.) Beside this flexibility, however, Sidney posits the biological given of sex. This is apparent in behavior and works as a constraint upon the exploitation of the resources of androgyny, which thus are clearly not limitless. Philoclea's mother, the experienced Gynecia, sees through Zelmane's disguise and knows she is a man, despite her behavior. And when Philoclea is ready to see Zelmane as a man, Pyrocles' physical sex becomes evident to her, too: "love straight stood up and deposed that a lie [that she is not Pyrocles] could not come from the mouth of Zelmane" (329). The image suggests that sexual difference is principally if not exclusively registered in sexual behavior.

Sidney is also quite precise on the question of sexual behavior and the conventions that cause gender identity to be regarded as natural rather than flexible, as distinctive rather than oxymoronic, and thus as the reason for giving the sexes different social and political statuses. His representation of Zelmane's supposed seduction functions as the second stage of his defense of women. Having established in Zelmane's words that woman is as virtuous as man in all her activities, he then condemns male behavior that denies her virtue. Basilius has determined to keep his nubile daughters from marriage and, whatever significance the oracle may have to him or to Sidney's readers, the plot certainly suggests that the king is partly driven by incestuous desires. He falls in love and seeks to have intercourse with Zelmane, who is of his children's generation. He is joined in this error by Gynecia, who makes its incestuous character clearer by deliberately wishing her daughter dead so that she could take her place. An experienced woman, she detects Pyrocles in Zelmane's bearing and manners, and responds by jealously forbidding Philoclea to see him. Her passion (if not her thoughts) is in some measure excusable, as Sidney is careful to characterize Basilius as old (a full generation older than she) and foolish. His infatuation, by contrast, is complicated and implicates patriarchal practice. Apparently he cannot detect Pyrocles in Zelmane and persists in seeing her entirely as a woman; his seems to be the superficial reading of gender that Pyrocles inveighed against earlier. More important, Basilius's oversight can and, I think, ought to be interpreted as a defense against a repressed love of the Pyrocles in Zelmane; Basilius's love for Zelmane may actually be homoerotic and narcissistic, whether or not he is aware of it.

How directly (if at all) Sidney intended to engage the question of lesbianism in the case of Philoclea and Zelmane is unclear. The inexperienced Philoclea interprets Zelmane as female, associating the signs of femininity with the female sex; as she matures, she learns to separate the two. Sidney may have wished his readers to see her growing understanding as a process in which she also approaches lesbianism, only to reject it. If so, he is cautious about the evidence he conveys to the reader. In seeking to explain Philoclea's sexual development, we may refer to Sidney's representation of the pressures of patriarchal culture to ensure that women do not make love to each other, but the extent to which he intended such a reading can be determined only by inference. Basilius's love for Zelmane can be understood differently, although it too is not clearly represented as homosexual. Apparently Basilius, like Philoclea, mistakenly reads the signs of femininity as indicating a sexual female. But he is an experienced lover and ought, presumably, to be as sophisticated in such matters as his wife, and Gynecia reads Zelmane perfectly. It is therefore possible that Basilius does in fact read Zelmane accurately, if only at an unconscious level. On the other hand, when he encounters Gynecia and thinks she is Zelmane, he gets what he has been expecting. His case is also inconclusive, at least as far as his sexuality is concerned.

In depicting both love affairs, Sidney seems to be interested chiefly in describing relations that either promote or endanger the welfare of the persons involved. Nothing in the text suggests that Sidney condemns outright passionate male friendship, or what Eve Sedgwick has aptly termed homosociability, even as it moves toward eroticism—the intense relations of the *Arcadia*'s cousins make that clear.[86] But there is evidence that he saw the expression of male bonding as debilitating to women, less in sexual than in social situations—Basilius appears more likely to prefer the company of men to women not because he is attracted to Zelmane but because he is so dismissive of his wife, his daughters, and finally of Zelmane herself. What seems to be at issue here is the moral and political

---

[86]Eve Kosofsky Sedgwick, *Between Men: English Literature and Male Homosocial Desire* (New York: Columbia University Press, 1985). Homosexuality was a subject much discussed in Renaissance moral literature; lesbianism was not. See Judith Brown, *Immodest Acts: The Life of a Lesbian Nun in Renaissance Italy* (New York: Oxford University Press, 1986), esp. 6–20.

well-being (and, at last, the justice) of a society in which male affection is really focused on men and their interests, despite the fact that its biologically experienced expression is directed for the most part to women. Such a society will tend to valorize masculinity and seek to control its feminine elements in order to maintain its sources of authority and power. This much becomes clear in Sidney's description of Basilius's wooing of Zelmane and the bed trick that concludes it.

In his attempts to seduce Zelmane, Basilius resembles parodic versions of the prospective husband of treatises on the conventional marriage. Like Panurge, he regards women as objects to be manipulated for his own pleasure. "Alas," he exclaims, proposing to Zelmane that they meet for "mutual delight," "let not certain imaginative rules, whose truth stands but upon opinion, keep so wise a mind from gratefulness and mercy, whose never-failing laws nature hath planted in us" (671). And he insists that his wife's interests do not need to be considered: "Shall my wife become my mistress? Think you not that thus much time hath taught me to rule her?" he asks (673). His appeal to "nature" over "opinion" is typically that of the impatient young lover asking to pick his lady's rose, but the context renders it comically ironic: Basilius is too old to pick a rose of this kind, and as the plot unfolds, Basilius's wife *will* be his mistress.

Nature and natural law were of course important authorities for establishing the inferiority of woman and her subordination as a wife; they are here given a dramatic articulation in Basilius's indifference to the "opinion" that Zelmane claims to respect, as well as to his duty to his wife. Zelmane, however, corrects Basilius's use of these terms: his "nature" is appetite, not a model of order; his "opinion" is actually "a true observance of nature" and not merely (as he charges) "imaginative." She finally and most convincingly defends her position by her witty bed trick, in which the "imaginative rules" she sets up for the tryst actually turn a wife into a mistress, as Gynecia not only takes the part of Zelmane but in her own person also that of a moral authority, who can lecture Basilius on the virtue of fidelity. In effect, Zelmane's trick exposes possible abuses of patriarchy. A father can control his daughter's sexuality to the point of denying it altogether, an act that is a form of incest, a usurpation of place in generational terms. A patriarchal husband can exercise a similar control over his wife, although it is differently expressed; she exists for his pleasure, he is indifferent to the point of denying hers. The fact that Zelmane's feminist morality prevails by virtue of her wit rather than her male strength illustrates the effectiveness of the resources of mind over matter or mere force. Zelmane's Herculean distaff thus becomes emblematic of the *intellectual* faculty of the governor which permits her to rule by telling tales, by weaving benign fictions to trap and contain within the law those who would break it.

The idea that a woman's rank assigned her no political role was probably expressed more often in treatises on marriage (where it was nevertheless contested) than in social life. Sidney considers the problem with a logic familiar from his treatment of sex and gender. While he insists that rank or "blood" is a final determinant of a person's social and political character, he also demonstrates that a virtuous person can imaginatively and dramatically create public personae of diverse ranks and occupations. These personae provide a means to contend with social distinctions and the divisiveness they can create, whether these are evidenced as the distance between a prince and a peasant or as factionalism between persons of the same rank. If Pyrocles playing Zelmane signifies a mediation of sexual difference, Musidorus playing Dorus transcends social distinctions. He exhibits behavior proper to his social opposite in order to further his own interests, which, given the nature of the body politic, cannot in fact be divorced from those of his opposite.[87]

By contrast to social behavior, Sidney represents rank as innate and, like a person's sex, beyond compromise. Just as Philoclea must recognize Zelmane as a man in order to be a wife, so Pamela must see Musidorus as a prince in order that she may be a queen. Musidorus has to court Pamela as Dorus, but it is important that she convey to him that it is not as a shepherd—however virtuous—that she will accept him as her lover. Complaining that to Pamela "a shepherd's service was but considered of as from a shepherd, and the acceptation limited to no further proportion than of a good servant" (221), Dorus tells Zelmane that he has been forced to court Pamela indirectly, by feigning love to Dametas's shep-

---

[87]The image of a king as the shepherd of his people is of course scriptural; see Ezek. 34; Jer. 23:1–8. Cf. Sir Thomas More, whose character Hythlodaeus, rejecting the notion that the king is the rightful owner of his subjects' property, argues that this condition does not abridge the king's responsibility for his subjects. "It belongs to the king to take more care for the welfare of his people than for his own, just as it is the duty of a shepherd, insofar as he is a shepherd, to feed his sheep rather than himself": *Utopia*, in *The Complete Works of St. Thomas More*, ed. Edward Surtz, S.J., and J. H. Hexter (New Haven: Yale University Press, 1965), 4:95. See also n. 94/15, p. 364. To Henry VIII is attributed the classic statement of the king as head of the body politic: "The judges have informed us, that we at no time stand so high in our estate royal as in the time of parliament; when we as head, and you as members, are conjoined and knit together into one body politic": "Ferrer's Case," in *Parliamentary History*, ed. W. Cobbett, 1:555, quoted in Margaret Atwood Judson, *The Crisis of the Constitution: An Essay in Constitutional and Political Thought* (New Brunswick, N.J.: Rutgers University Press, 1949), 83. For a study of political ideas in *Arcadia*, see, i.a., William Dunsmore Briggs, "Political Ideas in Sidney's *Arcadia*," *Studies in Philology* 28 (1931): 137–61 and 29 (1932): 534–42.

herdess daughter, Mopsa. Pamela has urged him to attend to "framing himself to his fortune," and when he protests that fortune is "the only rebellious handmaid against virtue" (225) and should be discounted by those in love, she answers:

> Dorus . . . you must be so far master of your love as to consider that since the judgement of the world stands upon matter of fortune, and that the sex of womankind of all other is not bound to have regardful eye to men's judgements, it is not for us to play the philosophers in seeking out your hidden virtues, since that which in a wise prince would be counted wisdom, in us will be taken for a light grounded affection: so is not one thing one, done by divers persons.   [226]

She rejects an abstract, literal, or philosophical view of behavior, in which "one thing" is always "one" no matter who does it, and argues instead that an evaluation of a person should be based on who he is and his fortune as well as on what he does. Behavior, in other words, is to be understood in light of rank. Her opinion reflects Sidney's sense of social distinctions but also his sense of a social reality that women appear to have experienced to their detriment. Pamela maintains that one who is reputed to be a wise prince is credited with behaving wisely; a woman who exhibits the same behavior is criticized for her levity. She implies that the expression of virtue as social behavior is, like the expression of gender, finally under a certain constraint, in this case of a "fortune" that confers not only rank but the character proper to it. For woman, moreover, the constraints are double and to an extent work against each other. Whatever rank her fortune has given her is affected by fortune's other gift: the condition of being female. Whatever her rank, she is inferior to man doctrinally and, for the most part, socially. At the same time, Pamela's comments reflect her realization that her social fortune (unlike her sexual fortune) is privileged; she is committed to retaining her rank, secure in her belief that it determines, if not virtue itself, at least the possibility of cultivating it, despite her enforced contact with her shepherd guardian and his wife and daughter. Implicit in her statements is the notion that a woman's rank has political meaning, even though that meaning must survive contestation by doctrine and social practice. (This idea is made explicit dramatically later, by Zelmane's example.) Dorus's royal birthmark later serves to certify his rank and hence his suitability as Pamela's consort (232); as a mark in and of the body, it functions as Zelmane's erect penis does: to ground social behavior (which is flexible) in a biological being (which is fixed).

At various points throughout the text, the concept of a virtue that must be evaluated in light of the "fortune" or rank of the virtuous is reconsidered in relation to politics and a theory of government. Sidney links it to a defense of woman's rule when, in Zelmane's address to Basilius's rebellious subjects (disaffected by the remoteness of his government), he insists on what the courtship of Musidorus and Pamela has previously implied: the primacy of rank *over* sex, that is, of one given status over another. If, as he has maintained, virtue is common to both sexes but varies in its manifestations according to rank, then rank is a social constant. Virtue is not linked to sexual difference. Basilius's Arcadian "clowns" do not know precisely what they want in place of him; factions appear and "at length they [fall] to direct contrarieties" (383). Zelmane, excusing her womanhood and her temporary assumption of magistracy, accuses these "clowns" of instituting a tyranny, for proper government is by law and requires direction by a person born to govern, that is, of a certain rank. She insists:

> Neither can your wonted valour be turned to such a baseness, as instead of a prince, delivered unto you by so many royal ancestors, to take the tyrannous yoke of your fellow subject, in whom the *innate meanness* will bring forth ravenous covetousness, and the newness of his estate, suspectful cruelty. . . . Do you think them fools, that saw you should not enjoy your vines, your cattle, no not your wives and children without government? And that there could be no government without a magistrate, and no magistrate without obedience, and no obedience where everyone upon his own private passion may interpret the doings of the rulers?   [385; my emphasis]

And as the mob calms down, she adds: "What need I use these words, since I see in your countenances, now virtuously settled, nothing else but love and duty to him by whom for your only sakes the government is embraced" (386). Her speech implicitly refers to the concept of a monarch at one with his people, which has been represented earlier when Dorus described to Pamela the character of his uncle Euarchus, an obvious foil to the feckless Basilius. That ideal monarch regards his subjects not as alien to himself, however different their respective ranks, but as united with him in "one politic body whereof himself was the head and even so [he] cared for them as he would for his own limbs; never restraining their liberty without it stretched to licentiousness, nor pulling from them their goods which they found were not employed to the purchase of a greater good; but in all his actions showing a delight in their welfare" (256). The power of Zelmane's authority as (in effect) the king's subaltern magistrate to quell the temper of the mob illustrates both the genderless nature of virtue and its variability in relation to rank. Equally significant is the substance of her argument. By emphasizing that the rule of the just monarch defies the tyranny of private passion in his subjects and also, more important, in himself, Zelmane constructs an image of the body politic in which distinctions of rank are bridged by a common subjection to law: the monarch does not violate the rights (that is, the property) of private persons because they are, in a sense, also his rights.[88] At the same time, she enforces the principle of a hierarchy of rank—a hierarchy that (like those of Tasso, Bruni da Pistoia, and Aylmer) is oblivious of sexual difference.

Dorus fulfills this concept of a monarch who governs yet is contained within the body politic—in a symbolic anticipation of his own future rule—when he tricks Dametas in order to leave Arcadia with Pamela. Dametas and his family embody the "innate meanness" that Zelmane had earlier termed characteristic of clowns, and it is only through appealing to their greed that Dorus can extricate Pamela from their unsuitable guardianship. And following Zelmane's example, as it were, Dorus also contends with the vice he confronts in fictions: Dametas is lured away from Pamela by Dorus's asinine tale describing the location of a cache of gold; Miso, his wife, pursues Dametas because Dorus tells her that Dametas has betrayed her with a strumpet called Charity; and Mopsa is paralyzed by the prospect, sketched for her by Dorus, that the god Apollo will make Dorus her husband. The venal credulity of the shepherds permits Dorus and Pamela to escape. While Zelmane had insisted on observing the "natural rules" against adultery,[89] Dorus has honored those against abuse of property, especially important to a monarch. Both princes thus preserve the integrity of the symbolic bodies they represent. To gain their ends, they have used not force but policy, the obvious weapon of the weaker party and typically of woman. Their common strategy underscores both the identity of woman and subject which is

[88]Some political thinkers identified a tyrant as a governor who stole his subjects' property; since property was the source of political rights in much Renaissance law, such theft was in effect a denial of the subjects' rights to be represented in government. See, i.a., John Ponet: "Evil governours and rulers will have all that their subjectes have common to themselves, but they themselves will departe with nothing but wher they ought not: no, not so muche as paie for those thinges that in wordes they pretende to buie of their subjectes": *A Shorte Treatise of Politike Power* (London, 1556), in Winthrop S. Hudson, *John Ponet (1516–1556): Advocate of a Limited Monarchy* (Chicago: University of Chicago Press, 1942), 80. Ponet later defines such an evil king as a "tyranne" (87).

[89]It is important that in Sidney's 1590 revision of the 1580 *Arcadia*, the sexual passion of the two principal lovers, Pyrocles and Philoclea, is not consummated, nor does Musidorus attempt to rape Pamela, as in the earlier text. The change has the effect of concentrating the reader's attention on the passion of those characters who are parents and also monarchs, and hence on the whole question of the proper role of passion in the governor and his or her government. The effect of this change on the conduct of and charges against the princes at their trial is discussed below.

such a consistent feature of the literature of household government and the effective instrumentality of feminine modes of prevailing over their opposition.

But the princes' recourse to socially constructive trickery almost wholly in the interests of satisfying private passions raises another and perhaps more imposing question with regard to the conduct of persons who are united in both marriage and the body politic. The "headship" of the husband and the monarch was conventionally justified by the belief that it would be based on reason as opposed to passion; reason was gendered as masculine and attributed to persons of rank, passion was gendered as feminine and characteristic of common people. But if the fate of society depended on the welfare of its mystical *composite* bodies—as the plot and characters of the *Arcadia* suggest—was there some way in which passion was to be recuperated in the interests of the private and public governments of the family and the state? Sidney's answer to this question is to be inferred from his representation of the princes' trial.

Like many of Elizabeth's courtiers, Sidney perceived his relation to his monarch partly in erotic terms. His own character in the *Arcadia*, the shepherd Philisides, speaks of his monarch as the "mistress" to whom he has "subjected" his thoughts (704). Elizabeth herself insisted not only on her virile attributes but also on her feminine capacity to govern her people with love (if not passion) as well as with reason. In Sidney's representation of royal justice, the strictly paternal Euarchus is in some sense a foil to the image of a maternal Elizabeth, an image that inheres in and through his act of judging and at last causes the reader to question the nature and limits of this king's vision of law. It is perceived to be constrained by his preference for punitive over constructive decisions and for simple justice over equity and mercy.

How convinced Euarchus is that a magistrate must himself observe the law at the expense of personal interest is illustrated when he condemns to death his own son and nephew, Pyrocles and Musidorus, for complicity in the supposed death of Basilius. His concern there, as before, is for the whole body politic bound together by law. What the episode explores is, however, the difference between law that is partial to the personal interests of the powerful and law that is socially constructive because it leads to decisions based on the principle of equity. By his rigorously just decision, Euarchus actually suppresses the virtue of equity that he was credited with earlier (783, 793), a virtue important to the assessment of a judgment handed down by a king and father, since it is traditionally both a consideration in the interpretation of law and gendered symbolically as feminine.

As a concept, equity had both a juridical and a philosophical meaning.

Ranulf Glanvill, in his fourteenth-century treatise on the law of England, declares that it is restricted to cases involving property and intended to provide relief for poor or common persons who cannot defend their rights by judicial combat.[90] He designates it specifically as the king's law—in contrast to the common law—which "tempers" justice on behalf of the "humble and meek" (Prologue, 1); cases in equity are decided by a jury rather than by battle. Considering equity as constitutive of an attitude and an approach to legal decisions in general, Sir William Blackstone states that equitable judgments depend "upon the particular circumstances of each individual case"; as a principle, equity leaves decisions "entirely in the breast of the judge"—a dangerous situation if carried too far, since it would deny law and allow "almost as many different rules of action [to be] laid down in our courts as there are differences of capacity and sentiment in the human mind."[91]

Equity is certainly more broadly significant in this sense, as a concept addressing the problem of interpreting the law. In the *Ethics* Aristotle defines the "equitable" as "a correction of law where it is defective owing to its universality," a correction that may be necessary if the nature of a case is in some way unique or special.[92] In the *Rhetoric*, he justifies equity further by describing conditions under which a case can be considered equitably:

> Equity must be applied to forgivable actions; and it must make us distinguish between wrongdoings on the one hand, and mistakes, or misfortunes on the other. . . . Equity bids us be merciful to the weakness of human nature . . . not to consider the actions of the accused so much as his choice, nor this or that detail so much as the whole story; to ask not what a

[90][Ranulf Glanvill], *The Treatise on the Laws and Customs of the Realm of England Commonly called Glanvill*, ed. and trans. G. D. G. Hall (London: Nelson, 1965), 28–29.

[91]Sir William Blackstone, *Commentaries on the Laws of England* (London, 1811), 1:61. Arthur F. Kinney points out that in the development of sixteenth-century jurisprudence in England, common law, which relies entirely on precedent and tends to insist on rigid applications of rule to case, came to be identified with the monarchy and its interests. Equity, by contrast, allowing an interpretation of the rule to fit the circumstances in which the crime was committed, is associated with the rights of the subject, particularly of conscience, in contrast to the prerogatives of the monarch. Hence equity and its court, the Court of Chancery, came to be identified with Protestant causes: "Sir Philip Sidney and the Uses of History," in *The Historical Renaissance*, ed. Heather Dubrow and Richard Strier (Chicago: University of Chicago Press, 1988), 293–314. Cf. Blackstone on courts of equity, *Commentaries*, 1:91; later (3:49) he traces the origin of the concept of equity to the distinction in Roman law between the "*ius praetorium* or the discretion of the praetor" and the "*leges* or standing laws." For the courts of common law as they practiced equity, see Theodore F. T. Plucknett, *A Concise History of the Common Law* (Boston: Little, Brown, 1956), 681.

[92]*The Complete Works of Aristotle*, ed. Jonathan Barnes (Princeton: Princeton University Press, 1984), 2:1797.

man is now but what he has always or for the most part been. It bids us remember benefits rather than injuries, and benefits received rather than benefits conferred; to be patient when we are wronged; to settle a dispute by negotiation and not by force; to prefer arbitration to litigation.[93]

Strictly speaking, equity, which enters into the decision of a case, is to be distinguished from mercy, which is granted after a case is decided. But Aristotle sees that mercy is a feature of the equitable mind, and the sixteenth-century English lawyer Christopher St. Germain concurs. His Doctor claims that "Equytye is a [ryghtywysenes] that consideryth all the pertyculer cyrcumstaunces of the dede the whiche also is temperyd with the swetnes of mercye. . . . And the wyse man sayth: be not over moch ryghtwise for the extreme ryghtwysenes is extreme wronge. . . . And therfore to folowe the wordes of the lawe were in some case both agaynst Justyce and the common welth; wherfor in some cases it is *good and even* necessary to leve the wordis of the lawe." To render such departures permissible, St. Germain invokes divine and natural law, in effect equating equity with these higher forms of law and distinguishing it from positive law. Equity is, he asserts, "no other thynge but an excepcion of the lawe of god or of the lawe of reason from the generall rewles of the lawe of man: when they by reason of theyre generalytye wolde in any partyculer case Juge agaynste the lawe of god or the lawe or reason *the whiche excepcion is secretely understande in every generall rewle of every posytyve lawe.*"[94]

For readers not versed in the law, the most vivid and accessible representation of equity, gendered as feminine and attributed especially to female magistrates, was to be found in Spenser's "Book of Justice." Here Spenser sees that "true justice" emanates from "highest Jove" and is manifest in the god Osyris and his consort, Isis, who "in her person cunningly did shade/ That part of justice which is equity."[95] In the exercise of justice, "the cruel dooms" of Osyris are often superseded by the "clemence" of Isis (V. vii. 22)—an iconographic relation that is translated dramatically later, when Spenser depicts Queen Mercilla, the monarch in whom ideal justice is realized, surrounded by the Litae, the daughters of Jove, who "do . . . his cruel vengeance stay" (V. ix. 31). Hence, when Mercilla is called to decide the case of the treacherous Duessa, who is "guilty by right," she exhibits "piteous ruth," not "just vengeance." Her actions are the consequence of "passion," typically

[93]Ibid., 2188–89.

[94]Christopher St. Germain, *St. German's Doctor and Student*, ed. T. F. T. Plucknett and J. L. Barton (London: Seldon Society, 1974), 95, 97; my emphasis.

[95]Edmund Spenser, *The Faerie Queene*, ed. A. C. Hamilton (London: Longman, 1977), V. vii. 22.

feminine, which mitigates pure reason, typically masculine (V.ix.50). Spenser concludes his portrait of Mercilla by valorizing the feminine part of justice. Like St. Germain, he sees that equity is activated by mercy and improves on simple justice: justice, to "preserve inviolated right/ Oft spills the principal to save the part," whereas equity, without departing from "doom of right," seeks "to save the subject of her skill," to "reform" rather than "to cut off" (V.x.2).

Sidney repeatedly demonstrates his concern for equity as the feminine complement to justice throughout his description of the trial of the princes and Gynecia.[96] Philanax, the prosecutor, epitomizes the revenger who uses the law for a personal end. Suppressing pity for the accused, he promises to prosecute them with "dead pitiless laws" (751–52). He himself has a "perfect persuasion" of their guilt before examining the evidence, and is subsequently so moved by anger, the narrator tells us, that he would have overlooked "the form of justice" altogether and killed the accused for reasons of state as he saw them (772). And finally, during the trial, he refuses to read the princesses' letters declaring their wishes to marry their abductors, "doubting that his own heart might be mollified" (827)—a suppression all the more crucial because it eliminates from consideration the simplest legal remedy for the princes' crime: marriage.[97] His foil is the temperate Kalander, who, though not a spokesman for the defense, argues for clemency, because punishment would jeopar-

---

[96]Sidney's representation of equity in the *Arcadia* has, I believe, both a philosophical and a political reference. Because the truth of the past is elusive, judgments are subject to error; because judgments are subject to error, a monarch and judge must consider both equity (interpretation of rule in light of the extenuating circumstances surrounding the performance of a crime) and mercy (pardon in light of repentance and reform). In my reading, both princes ask for and should get equity, largely because the circumstances of their crimes justify it. This is especially true if the trial scene is read as the conclusion to the 1590 text, in which Pyrocles is wrongly charged. The rigidity of Euarchus then seems willful, the fanaticism of Philanax vicious. Arthur Kinney brilliantly suggests that Sidney saw the ending of the 1580 version as suited (and I would argue well suited) to the revisions he made in the 1590 version: "Sir Philip Sidney," 311. For a different view of equity and its part in Sidney's depiction of Euarchus's jurisprudential character, see Nancy Lindheim, *The Structures of Sidney's Arcadia* (Toronto: University of Toronto Press, 1982). She makes the useful distinction between equity, "dispensed by a regular court and [aiming] at ethical justice," and mercy, "a 'divine' prerogative of the rule [which has] no necessary connection with merit" (160). In her view, the princes, who are guilty of rape and abduction (although Pyrocles does not in fact rape Philoclea in the revised 1590 text) and who could not plead extenuating circumstances in the hope of eliciting an equitable decision, are eligible only for mercy. By contrast, Gynecia, who did not commit the crime with which she is charged, could expect a judgment in equity. The key question here is, I think, the meaning of guilt: equity enlarges the meaning of innocence to include the possibility of deciding that a particular criminal act is in some way excusable and therefore that its perpetrator is in fact innocent in the eyes of the law. This I take to be Blackstone's point when he insists that to set law and equity "in opposition to each other . . . [is] either totally erroneous or erroneous to a certain degree": *Commentaries*, 3:429.

[97]Cf. *Measure for Measure*, I.iv.45–50.

dize the future of the state. Advocating Pamela's marriage with Musidorus, Kalander "wills [the people] to consider that when all was done,
Basilius's children must enjoy the state: who since they had chosen, and
chosen so all the world could not mend their choice, why should they
resist God's doing and their princesses' pleasure? This was the only way
to purchase quietness without blood" (772). Kalander does not support
his position by an appeal to equity (although such an appeal is implicit in
the nature of his request), but the princes do later, when speaking in their
own defense.

Euarchus lacks the retributive vengefulness of Philanax but also the
political understanding of Kalander; although in no way unjust, he falls
short of justice in ruling out a consideration of equity from the very
beginning of the case. He challenges its pertinence initially when he
claims that his judgment must avoid "a free discourse of reason and skill
of philosophy," the loci of natural law, and rather "be tied to the laws of
Greece" or positive law. His position denies the kind of enlightened
interpretation of positive law that equity makes possible. Appearing to
take Musidorus's protest seriously, he alludes to the "services" the princes
have rendered the state (cf. Aristotle's idea of the importance of character,
"what a man . . . has . . . been"), but maintains that they are "not worthy
to countervail with a following wickedness." His reasons directly contradict the usual understanding of equity as soliciting respect for circumstantial differences among cases and persons accused or convicted: "It
hath been determined [he declares] in all wisdoms that no man, because
he hath done well before, should have his present evils spared, but rather
so much the more punished as (having showed he knew how to be good)
yet would against his knowledge be naught." Such reasoning overlooks
the possibility (mentioned by Aristotle) of a "mistake," the kind of
wrong that is done by a person who does not do wrong habitually. And
despite the fact that, by his own subsequent characterization, the case
involves the theft of property—the princes have "ravished [the prin-
cesses] from him that owned them which was their father"—and thus is
especially suited to a decision in equity according to English law, he
decides against the equitable and politically expedient solution advocated
by Kalander and supported by the victims, which is marriage (835–37).

He continues to rule out pity in the interest of maintaining not the law
but an image of the law that will prevent further crime:

> But herein we must consider that the laws look how to prevent by due
> examples that such things be not done, and not how to salve such things
> when they are done. For if the governors of justice shall take such a scope as
> to measure the foot of the law by a show of conveniency, and *measure that*
> *conveniency not by the public society but by that which is fittest for them which*

offend, young men, strong men, and rich men shall ever find private conveniences how to palliate such committed disorders as to the public shall not only be inconvenient but pestilent.   [838; my emphasis]

But it is precisely in the interest of what is "fittest" for the parties to a case that equity comes into play; that Euarchus associates this flexibility with abuse suggests that he denies equity in principle because he rejects what it may come to be in practice.[98]

True, by maintaining his decision after knowing who the criminals are, Euarchus demonstrates what he would have appeared to demonstrate earlier: that the monarch and the magistrate are indeed bound by the laws of the country they rule. To the princes he says, "I prefer justice . . . before you." But when he *disowns* them—in this case a personal rather than a legal decision—and so violates what would have been considered natural law ("never had I shepherd to my nephew, nor ever had a woman to my son" [842]), the princes remind him again of the place of equity in judgments. Pyrocles warns against "seeking too precise a course of justice, [lest] you [Euarchus] be . . . thought most unjust in weakening your neighbours' mighty estate by taking away their only pillar" (844). And Musidorus—who has earlier characterized the function of law in society as preservative, not destructive: "laws are not like lime-twigs or nets to catch everything that toucheth them, but rather like sea-marks to avoid the shipwreck of ignorant passengers" (833)—terms "insupportable" his uncle's pitiless "dominion" (845). Euarchus's act of disowning his near relations, gratuitous to his representation as a magistrate, underscores the paternal and masculine nature of his justice and implies its limitations. If a people are the monarch's children, and the monarch is, whether male or female, behavioristically androgynous, a monarch's responsibility as judge must include respect for the feminine aspects of justice: equity and mercy.

Finally, the images describing the conclusion to the trial point to equity and mercy as a feature of providential intervention in history.[99] They

---

[98]The danger that equity might be abused had already been addressed in legal and political commentary—a fact that makes Euarchus's position more rather than less questionable. Edward Hake, for example, objects that *mutatio legis* is not *correctio legis*; in other words, to interpret the "sowle and spyrit" of the law is not be "licentiously caryed awaye both from the letter and the sense of the lawe to the private interpretations of . . . fancy." In fact, it is to observe the law in a more accurate way: *Epieikeia: A Dialogue on Equity in Three Parts*, ed. D. E. C. Yale, Yale Law Publications no. 13 (London: Oxford University Press, 1953), 28–29.

[99]Several critics have written on the fictional resurrection of Basilius and the consequent pardon of the princes and Gynecia as Sidney's illustration of the workings of Providence in history. See, i.a., Kenneth Thorpe Rowe, *Romantic Love and Parental Authority in Sidney's "Arcadia"* (Ann Arbor: University of Michigan Press, 1947); Margaret E. Dana, "The

have already been validated implicitly by references to the natural debility of "human reason," which must generally give way to "divine
providence" (715). Philanax welcomes Euarchus as one brought by
"heavenly powers" (785); but Euarchus characterizes himself as "a creature whose reason is often darkened with error" (797), and hence (the
reader concludes) in need of forgiveness. The two characters who have
committed crimes for which there is no constructive remedy, Basilius
and Gynecia, deserve punishment and receive it, but only in what might
be termed a fictional mode: Basilius's "death" is only a pretense and
actually a sleep, a prelude to his rebirth; Gynecia pays for her crime (in
fact a lesser one than that with which she is charged) by her own torments
and public humiliation; and both monarchs are reformed through the art
of love, whose active agent is Zelmane (striving to gain Philoclea) and
whose passive agent is the supposed love potion of the mysterious
"Queen of Cyprus" (Venus) which exposes *and* restores them. Basilius
returns Gynecia to her former status, and in the course of her subsequent
life she earns a reputation that she does not initially deserve: that she is a
"perfect mirror of all wifely love." "So uncertain are mortal judgements,
the same person most infamous, and most famous, and neither justly"
(847), Sidney concludes, offering yet another reason to praise a discriminating and exculpatory feminine justice.

Nicholas Breton's brief essay "The Praise of Vertuous Ladies" (1599)
could serve as a witty postscript to Sidney's generously developed conceptions of sex and gender. Breton begins his critique of the woman-
hater by assuming that a human being is androgynous; a man is male but
he contains the female insofar as he can behave as woman does. Hence
any attack on her is actually an attack on himself: "For let a man not quite
forget himselfe, and but a little look into himselfe, hee shall see so great a
part of a woman in himselfe, as that except hee will runne from himselfe,
hee cannot but with as great honour account of them as of himselfe." And
because the other and the self are one, to flatter her is also a self-reflexive
act, and as damaging as to criticize her: "the hyre of flatterie is but hate"
and thus the flatterer of woman really "floutes" himself, expressing his
sense of his own inadequacy. Breton condemns both kinds of discourse as
"fantasticall," and notes that woman is not such a "fool" as to believe
them. She will "finde a falshood [even] in a faire tale."[100]

Providential Plot of the *Old Arcadia,*" *Studies in English Literature* 17 (1977): 39–57; see also
Lindheim, *Structures of Sidney's "Arcadia,"* 160–62. Yet it is important that Sidney's Providence be understood to derive the manner of its interventions from human wit: the proper
government is restored to Arcadia because decisive political events are made possible
through the creation and persuasive power of fictions.

[100]Nicholas Breton, "The Praise of Vertuous Ladies," in *A Mad World, My Masters, and
Other Prose Works,* ed. Ursula Kentish-Wright (London: Cresset, 1929), 2:173–74.

For Breton, to deny androgyny is necessarily to link behavior to biology, and to see gender as constituted by sex and not as a matter for improvisational choice. Men and women then inevitably perceive each other as different and antagonistic. Answering a fictional critic who claims it a "pittie" that Breton is not "made" a woman (since he goes to the trouble of defending women), he exclaims: "I woonder why? My beautie is not such to allure a wanton eye nor mine eye so wanton to allure a wicked mind, my qualities are not onely fit for a chamber, nor in my chamber alwayes in bed" (176). In other words, were he a woman, he would not be the kind his critic has in mind. Assuming, for the sake of his defense of women, the unsympathetic point of view of his critic, who can see nothing in woman to defend, Breton facetiously defines woman as his critic sees her: in purely sexual terms. Thus he insinuates that his critic is the one whose "wanton eye" and "wicked mind" constructs woman as fit only for sexual intercourse.

Breton analyzes what he has just shown to be the illusion of gender difference as primarily a matter of language by using and comparing terms that privilege a given behavior in a man and disparage the same behavior in a woman: "if shee . . . bragge of her beautie, hee is as proude of his proper personage. . . . [S]ome will say women are covetous, are not men as handfast?" (178).[101] Linguistic usage can also acquire the additional weight of the proverbial: "Some will say women are foolish: hee never heard [from a misogynist, presumably] that the wisedome of a woman should bee no more than to goe out of the raine, when shee is in it, and know her husband's bed from another man's" (179). Here he reveals the folly of the statement "women are foolish" by referring to a proverbial rendering of it and allowing the reader to evaluate the intelligence of the person who resorts to such statements. The statement "women are foolish" is refuted by the quality of mind of the person (again, one assumes, Breton's critic) who assents to it. More generally, Breton's concern with attacks on women which have achieved the currency of the proverbial suggests that he sees in linguistic conventions the reinforcement of ideology. He concludes his "Praise" by identifying the activity responsible for creating and sustaining ideology in language as that of the poet, whose "conceits" express not nature or some subject that

[101]Like Bruni da Pistoia and others, Breton makes an economic argument—essentially of comparable worth—praising woman's worth in relation to man's. His strategy here is to show that the vocabulary describing various kinds of activities is not gender- or sex-specific except when it refers to sexual activity (here perhaps alluded to equivocally). Hence work is simply work, to be evaluated according to the skill with which it is performed: "For qualities worthie commendation, see who is to bee preferred, the man or the woman? Without the house for husbandrie: if he mowe, she can tedde; if he tedde, she can turne; if he cocke[?], she can rake" (183).

exists outside his mind and as it were objectively, but *the reflections* such subjects cast in his mind. As reflections, they are colored by the nature of the medium in which they are represented. To the question whether woman is a necessary evil, Breton answers:

> That shee is necessarie I graunt, but evill I denie, except it be meant onely in respect of man, that desireth not anything that is good, and by his desire makes her ill in estimation of minde, for that shee is the content of an ill conceite: but (indeed, well considered) he should finde, that the ill were in his conceite onely and not in the woman, who is no other substance then another himselfe. Therefore let man first mend his minde, before he so discommend a substance of his owne naturall kinde.   [189]

Insofar as generic woman is thought to be evil, she is no more than a man's fiction, the "content of an ill conceit" that has its origins in negative desire, that is, in a kind of self-hatred, a desire "for nothing that is good."[102] Returning to the image of an androgynous human being, Breton insists that man and woman are one "substance"; neither can be "discommended" except as an act of self-repudiation.

Woman's Rule: Mary Stuart

Doubts about the succession continued to inflame debate on woman's rule in England and on the continent even after the accession of Elizabeth. The queen's place as monarch was of course assured; challenges to her rule came from Catholics and were generally made on specifically religious grounds. She continued to have Protestant defenders. Henry Bullinger, in his *Confutation of the Pope's Bull* (1572), argues against the propriety of her excommunication on grounds of his reformist understanding of ecclesiastical law. Terming the pope no more than the bishop of Rome, Bullinger asserts that Scripture declares that "kings of Gentiles shall rule over pastors," who are not themselves to rule but to serve rulers. In any case, he adds, Scripture cannot be used as evidence against woman's rule: "For we know that the thinges which the

---

[102]In her *Protection for Women* (London, 1589), the writer known as Jane Anger complains of a transformatory process comparable to that which Breton describes: "We woo them with our vertues and they wed us with vanities, and men being of wit sufficient to consider of the vertues which are in us women, are ravished with the delight of those dainties whiche allure and draw the senses of them to serve us, whereby they become ravenous hawks, who do not only seize upon us, but devour us. Our good toward them is the destruction of ourselves, we being wel formed, are by them fouly deformed" (B2v–3). In both cases, it is male desire that "deforms" the woman it seeks to possess. For an edited version of Anger's treatise, see Katherine Usher Henderson and Barbara F. McManus, eds., *Half Humankind* (Urbana: University of Illinois Press, 1985), 172–88.

Apostle speaketh concernyng the obedience of wives and the silence of women in the congregation of God are not to be wrested into reigning. For it is certain that the Lord's Apostles impeached not the successions in kyngdomes. . . ."[103] Mary Stuart's place in the succession was, on the other hand, a cause for comment. Dedicated to refuting what Bishop John Leslie calls Knox's "pestiferous pamphlet," his *Defence of the Honour of Marie, Quene of Scotlande* (1569) goes much further than Aylmer's *Harborowe* in defining woman's place in divine and natural law, and in the *ius gentium*, largely because he grounds his argument in a *linguistic* critique of scriptural interpretation. Like most defenders of women (and in contrast to Knox), Leslie sees in woman's first creation the basis of all her virtue and autonomy, including her right to magistracy: "Was not she created to the image of God as well as man? And dothe she not represente the maestie of God?" For if God's majesty signifies "rightuousnes and trewe holynes," "memorie," "will," and "understandinge . . . what thing ys there that reason, wytt and understandinge maye reatche to that woman hathe not or may not atchieve and attayne?"[104] Rather than contend directly with the meaning of woman's second creation, Leslie moves on to consider a second passage that Knox had adduced as evidence against woman's rule, in which the children of Israel are instructed to choose a monarch "from brethren," or, as Leslie says, *ex fratribus*. This choice is not, however, to be understood as restricted to men, because in classical languages the feminine gender is always comprehended in the masculine. To prove his point, Leslie illustrates how absurd Scripture would become were all masculine pronouns understood as referring only to males:

> Frater is the masculine gender (ye saye) and therefor women are to be removed. Then by this rule women also muste be excluded from theire salvation, bycause Scripture sayeth: He that shall beleave and be baptized shalbe saved. . . . And by this rule women are excluded from the eight beatitudes. . . . He that hatethe his brother ys in darkenes. . . . Shall we inferre ther uppon that we may hate our sister? . . . Wherefore neither this worde brother excludethe a sister, nor this worde kinge in Scripture excludethe a quene.   [r6–7]

[103]Henry Bullinger, *A Confutation of the Pope's Bull* . . . (London, 1572), sig. Mr–v. Bullinger's text, originally in Latin, is translated by Arthur Golding, who dedicates his work to Edmund Grindall, archibishop of York; Richard Coxe, bishop of Ely; and John Jewell, bishop of Salisbury.

[104]John Leslie, *A Defence of the Honour of Marie, Quene of Scotlande* (London, 1569), reprinted in facsimile in *English Recusant Literature, 1558–1640*, vol. 12 (New York: Scolar Press, 1970), sigs. r8v–s.

Leslie extends his linguistic argument to include the use and understanding of gender in the language of positive law: there, too, "the masculine gender comprehendethe the feminine" (r6v). Therefore "the auncient statutes of the realme" which constitute the royal prerogative refer to queens regnant as well as kings.

Leslie's analysis of the use of gender in language has revolutionary implications in what it suggests about the interpretation of all kinds of law. Unless a woman is specifically designated as an exception (as she is, for example, in laws that govern the property of spouses), provisions pertaining to men must also be thought to apply to her. Would Leslie have agreed to permit all women to enjoy the liberty of the *feme sole*—a liberty analogous to that enjoyed by the queen regnant in affairs not strictly marital? That this might have been his position is at least possible, if his linguistic argument is taken seriously. What can be asserted with some certainty is that, for Leslie, contemporary linguistic usage, if uncritically accepted, prejudices the interests of women as a class. Since this usage is clearly a matter of convention, he implies that verbal expressions of differences of *gender* are socially constructed and not responses to nature. In fact, he goes so far as to examine what is understood by the very concepts of nature and natural law. Aylmer had attacked Knox's idea that nature could be made the basis of law, since nature is constantly violating its own norms and patterns of behavior by admitting exceptions that are nevertheless also natural. Like Montaigne in his *Apologie de Raimond Sebond*, Leslie dismisses as fiction the notion of any kind of law that antedates human society and therefore human systems of communication. In other words, the only true law of nature is the law of nations, the *ius gentium*, that is, written law, law that is conveyed in and through language: "I saye then that this ys a false and an unnaturall assertion, to make this surmised lawe everlastinge as nature it self is. The lawe of nature or *ius gentium* ys and ever was *after* the time that there were any nations or people and ever shalbe" (q7; my emphasis). To say this is to claim that the only law available to human beings is historical, the product of accumulated human reason operating on a succession of real situations and expressed in language. If the only law available to human beings is historically contingent rather than timeless and absolute, as Leslie asserts it is, a case can be made for the legality of woman's rule on the basis of past experience. Leslie maintains that the numerous instances in history in which women have assumed authority over men conform to rather than violate the law of nations.

Defenders of Mary Stuart's right to succession who were associated with the French court had specifically to contend with the theoretical implications of the Salic law, even though it had no bearing on Mary's standing in England. The Salic law was derived from what were asserted to be ancient prohibitions against women's inheriting certain kinds of property, principally allodial lands or fiefdoms, and hence also public offices. In his *Discours de la légitime succession des femmes* (1579), David Chambers, a Scots courtier of Catherine de Médicis, attacked the validity of the law (without ever openly condemning it) by showing that the property rights of women are guaranteed in natural law and the *ius gentium*. Natural law, he says, obtained in the "age of gold," when "all things were in common," and its protection of the rights of women was further reflected in the law of nations, by which women's property (as dowry) was defended for the sake of future generations: "it is the task of a republic to provide for the conservation of women's dowries, in order to foster the generation of human beings and fill cities with children." And while natural law has left no testimonies, it is evident that the *ius gentium* protected woman's property in the cases of the daughters of Zalphaad (Num. 27) and Rachel and Leah (Gen. 31). Positive law everywhere recognizes these rights: Chambers cites Roman laws of inheritance and their codification by Justinian. France is alone in denying them, he observes, and on feeble grounds doctrinally, since the Salic law is not implicit in the Deuteronomic command that a monarch be chosen from among brothers, which has reference only to elected monarchies; nor do Pauline dicta against women preaching refer to other than married women.[105]

Chambers also considers the general question of fitness. Here he does not resort to the legal fiction of the monarch's second body (as Aylmer did) but says simply that nothing in the nature of the act of governing would make government impossible for a woman. The issue most critical to his case—the relative physical weakness of women—had been discussed earlier; Christine de Pisan had argued against woman's rule on the grounds that women were too feeble to administer punishment to wrongdoers. Chambers (here like Aylmer) assumes an entirely different political world, one in which social order is maintained not by the personal rule of the magistrate but by the law. A woman can administer, in the sense of interpret, this law as well as a man; the sex of those who carry out the actual punishment is therefore a bureaucratic detail: "sexual difference [*la différence du sexe*] is not required for . . . executing [the laws] but rather prudence and reason" (B7v). And, he notes, while a woman has never been elected to a monarchy, there is no reason she should not be

[105]David Chambers [Lord Ormond], *Discours de la légitime succession des femmes aux possessions de leur parens et du gouvernment des princesses aux empires et royaumes* (Paris, 1577), sigs. A5, C8v, D3v, D7.

(B5v). Chambers's emphasis on the fitness of a woman to rule *under law* and his interest in representing women in elective as well as inherited offices suggest that he is prepared to extend the terms of his argument beyond the monarchy to include all magistrates. His is therefore the most liberal position on the question of woman's rule adopted during the course of the century.

Feminist appeals to the common experiences of men and women drew upon androgyny as a concept that elucidated human behavior. Implicit in these appeals was the ancient scriptural distinction between *homo*, a human being, in contrast to *vir* and *femina*. Every man and woman was also and *primarily* a human being. Feminists recognized that patriarchy undervalued feminine traits, especially in men who risked being described as effeminate, and they considered again and in a new light the virtues typically associated with femininity. The origins of their thinking were doubtless in the spiritual allegories of the high Middle Ages, celebrating *sophia, prudentia, constantia*, and so forth, but they made over this iconography so that it could readily apply to an analysis of human actions and activities. The jurisprudential figurations of equity and mercy furthered the valorization of the feminine by descriptions of an ideal kind of justice. And the contrast between the advantages of "policy" as a peaceful means of gaining and retaining the allegiance of a subject people or territory—in contrast to the disadvantages of "force"—encouraged a positive evaluation of feminine strategies of statecraft. Weight was accordingly taken from negative assessments of femininity; masculinity in turn acquired its negative dimension. Sidney speaks of an "unmanlike cruelty," and feminist descriptions of the domestic tyrant picture him as both violent and vain, cruel and effeminate.

Feminist argument on the question of sex and gender also had a vital link to the idea of a hierarchy of rank, and it was within such a familiar conception of social order that feminists could investigate the real nature of the work performed by men and women. Their intention was to explode accepted notions of the value of a woman's labor and of her economic or political function. As Bruni da Pistoia first noted in print, although the evidence was presumably ubiquitous and perennial, men and women of peasant and artisanal rank regularly not only did the same work but produced it up to identical standards. This practice was at once an affirmation of shared gender behavior and a way of equalizing men and women within a single office or rank. Arguments for woman's rule as well—whether direct, as in the case of Aylmer, or implied, as for Tasso—made use of the idea that within a single social category, a man and a woman had the same prerogatives. Feminists could point out, as

Labé did, that women, particularly in higher ranks, often declined to use these prerogatives in a constructive way, preferring to retain the marks of rank—jewelry, clothing—without entering into its responsibilities. (Not that such ladies were encouraged by social or economic realities to do what Labé so energetically recommended.) Directives such as hers move toward contesting the whole notion of inherited office and rank, inasmuch as her idea of virtue reflects not "blood"—as Sidney's does, for example—but rather talent, industry, and discipline. In the first decades of the next century, feminist discussions of the nature of equality enlarge upon these kinds of issues. The idea of rank had proved useful as a way of establishing equality; on the other hand, the *fact* of rank—with the privileges that it conferred or witheld—was subsequently represented as a means of discouraging feminist thought and protest.

4   *Equality*

Cᴇɴᴛʀᴀʟ to almost every defense of women in the sixteenth century had been the claim of equality. But how, exactly, that
claim could be pressed found little consensus. A woman was supposed to
be both man's spiritual equal and his political subordinate, but the precise
way in which her two conditions or personae were to be related in the
exercise of her conscience varied from treatise to treatise. Literary evidence frequently suggests that feminist positions theoretically endorsed
were practically dismissed, especially by conservative writers. Historical
evidence that might explain contradictions between theory and practice
is even more problematic. I cite a single case in point, which I trust is
representative of a general trend.

The historian D. E. Underdown has characterized the sixty years
before England's civil war as manifesting a "crisis in order" in which the
status of the patriarchal society was especially jeopardized. Seeking to
determine whether the antifeminist literature of the period had a real
social correlative, he notes that court records indicate that from 1560 to
1640 English justice was particularly concerned with prosecuting brawl-
ing, scolding women. A survey of cases in which such punitive devices as
the cucking stool and the scold's bridle were put to use reveals that
socially disruptive women were most common in areas where communities were not closely knit, where the local squirearchy was not usually in
residence, and where the land comprised woods and pastures rather than
enclosed, arable fields.[1] It seems reasonable to conclude that when fewer

[1]D. E. Underdown, "The Taming of the Scold: The Enforcement of Patriarchal Authority in Early Modern England," in *Order and Disorder in Early Modern England*, ed.
Anthony Fletcher and John Stevenson (Cambridge: Cambridge University Press, 1985),
116, 122–26.

constraints controlled occasions and opportunities for protest, incidents evincing protest increased, as did their legal prosecution in the communities in which they occurred. In this instance, the punishment of unruly women by means of cucking stools and other such instruments signifies not simply the power of patriarchy but also, in a more complicated fashion, its relative fragility. Here, too, the fact of control is itself evidence of a threat to order.

In defenses of women published in the early years of the seventeenth century, the issue of equality in principle and also in social, political, and economic practice is raised in a number of contexts. In general, the demand for equality is answered by discussions of the related concepts of complementarity and equity. Complementarity is implicit in the Aristotelian notion of the man as acquisitive, the woman as conservative, and arguments for the worth of woman sometimes find their strongest proof in examples illustrating how important a wife is as "lieutenant" to her husband, the "general." A woman's subordinate status is not perceived as a humiliation, inasmuch as her "command" confers upon her a degree of independence and autonomy. Perhaps paradoxically, whatever value and virtue she exhibits as her husband's "complement" make her the more liable to charges of insubordination. Writers debate whether or not beating is licit in cases of a wife's insubordination. For writers for whom it is not licit, the concept of complementarity obviously has real meaning. A wife can require that she be treated in a manner commensurate with her importance *to the couple*. Writers who regard wife-beating as routinely acceptable reduce the concept of complementarity to little more than a feature of the rhetoric of coercive compliment. Equity enters discussion of equality as the means by which the rule requiring a woman's subordination may be relaxed in certain cases. Unlike the concept of complementarity, which more often than not enhances the wife's position, equity tends to limit the extent of the husband's direction of the couple. It is often present by implication; writers ask that men overlook the mistakes of their women, or give them extra latitude in choosing a course of action that involves the couple jointly. For widows and women who had been granted the status of *feme sole* the rule of subordination is modified. In a sense, of course, equity (like complementarity) is important because equality itself is, or was thought to be, socially unworkable. Both function within the rules governing patriarchy, not outside or in contradiction to them.

Equality in principle is constantly celebrated in feminist literature of this period, however qualified it may be in particular cases. Equality in practice, by contrast, is mourned as a concept whose time has not yet come. This is in part a matter of custom, mores, language—in short, of culture. Some writers see that the impracticability of equality is most cogently analyzed in economic terms. A woman's worth, comparable to a man's, is best (because most realistically) assessed as her ability to acquire and administer property. And what is clear to them and to their readers is that women in possession of property in their own right are perceived to be socially anomalous. Prostitutes and women cross-dressers (who buy clothes that their husbands and fathers ought not to approve of, much less pay for) provide extreme cases in point. At the same time, it is also clear that what passes for law—that is, what establishes social rules—is a function of wealth. It was asserted that women were not allowed to go to law out of respect for the so-called *pudor sexus*. Feminists now argue that to go to law at all requires money: women are merely a class of persons disempowered through poverty.

ITALY

A Feminized Society

In the early years of the seventeenth century, as in the previous half century, a new society in which women could demonstrate the value of qualities considered to be feminine—compassion, temperance, charity—continued to be imagined in the context of ideas promoting the kinds of social change that would enhance the status of women. Giuseppe Passi's *Dello stato maritale* (1602), for example, shows the effects of contemporary feminist protest on its representation of wifely subordination. Passi himself was not disposed to support such protest per se. His earlier *Donneschi difetti* (1601) is a conventional misogynist diatribe categorizing woman as "inquisitive," "quarrelsome," and so forth, and citing the usual authorities—Plato, Aristotle, Vergil, Boccaccio.[2] Its only point of interest is Passi's comparison of a woman who intrudes herself into the affairs of men with a tyrant who usurps power not rightfully his. A woman, says Passi, is typically afflicted with a *"vana curiosità"*: "Seneca called it useless. . . . [W]omen are persons who rush into things immediately, always wanting to know another's business and taking little care of their own faults, even though they are covered from head to foot with vices and faults" (O8). A tyrant, too, "obtains power in a republic illegally"; like the curious wife, he appropriates the business of others (Q3). These remarks discredit the wife's ability to contribute to the welfare of her family while testifying to her wish to do so.

Passi's adherence to the misogynist stereotype represented in this text

[2]Giuseppe Passi, *I donneschi diffetti* (Venice, 1601), sig. br-v.

is later reflected in his *Dello stato maritale*. There, although he states that "the wife is equal to the husband in love, in charity, in rule, and in governance," and that this equality is the "mother of concord" in marriage, he also believes that a wife must be "principally . . . in all things subject to [her husband], as he is her head . . . for all laws whether divine, natural or civic give man, as the more fit for government, sovereignty [*maggioranza*] over woman."[3] It is assumed, moreover, that a husband will shape his wife's character: "If you take a beautiful woman, your good sense will make her well behaved; if you take an ugly woman, your affection will make her pleasant" (O2r–v). In any case, a man's authority ought to supersede considerations of social status, but to avoid disappointment on this score, Passi tells his male readers not to take a wife who is of a higher rank than he is. To call a wife "signore" is to make a husband her inferior, "a thing much too vile for a manly person even to contemplate" (P2). Writers on marriage had warned against such matches for at least a century, especially if the wife was also rich. To support the connection between shrewishness and wealth, Passi quotes Aristotle in the *Nicomachean Ethics*: "Wives dominate because they have great patrimony" (O3).[4] Underlying these statements is a conception of equality qualified by the need to protect male interests. Husband and wife may be theoretically equal in the "governance" of marriage, yet any superiority the wife can claim by virtue of rank or wealth is nullified by the law privileging the "governance" of the husband. A typical feminist would reason differently. Law privileging the male might be allowed to stand, but in practice it should be made equitable or fair by giving a certain latitude to the female. This is the sense in which equity is most often used in contemporary treatises. Flexibility in this regard may also be prudent. Passi later condemns wife-beating as an abuse of male governance which might well result in a loss of male control: a mistreated wife, he claims, "will build herself a palace of anger and hatred" (T2). He is clearly mindful of the possibility that these "palaces" might someday threaten the structures of patriarchy.

Concern to preserve the status quo could produce defenses of women which describe the deleterious consequences of marital abuse in more general terms. Pietro Canonhiero, in his *Della eccellenza delle donne* (1606), argues against misogynist slander because it violates laws of decency that must be observed if a state is to remain strong. The point of his conventionally laudatory description of woman is to establish, first,

---

[3]Giuseppe Passi, *Dello stato maritale* (Venice, 1602), sigs. D2, O3, V3r–v. Passi's text is dedicated to Giulio Spreti, who, Passi says, has himself praised marriage (a2v).

[4]Passi quotes a Latin version of this text: "dominantur uxores propter amplitudinem patrimonii."

that slander against woman is irrational; and second, that in a civil society it must be punished. No woman is required to return her suitor's affection, Canonhiero claims; but it is nevertheless frequently the case that men blame women for rejecting proposals of love. "It is evident that all those who have written against women have spoken because they have been moved by these powerful matters of affection and not because they have really thought that the situation was as they portrayed it." Such license is unacceptable, however; Canonhiero insists that a certain *severità* is necessary to control it. For, citing Cassiodorus, he observes that to show "pity" for infractions of the rules of social decency is to weaken the law itself. By contrast, "by severity the prince is honored, the law is not flouted, and the common people are saved."[5] Here feminism is supported by rules of decent conduct; no longer merely providing a rationale for an attack on practices underprivileging women, it has become the basis for a modified form of patriarchy that is shown to be threatened—paradoxically—by misogyny.

A similar warning of the perils misogyny presents to the welfare of the state is inscribed in Giulio Cesare Capaccio's *Principe . . . e più avvertimenti politici e morali* (1620). Like Canonhiero, Capaccio makes a feminist attack on abusive men an aspect of his program to institute civic order. His analysis of the psychology of the victim is not especially new, but his entertainment of it in the context of a treatise of government is. Stating that animals are more "reasonable" than men, Capaccio reports that

> the serpent leaves its poison when it mates with the female [but] the husband does not know enough to forget his pride when he deals with his wife. She, on the other hand, stubbornly refuses to endure the brutal habits of her husband. . . . Instead of love there is hate, instead of making his wife his subject, he makes her recalcitrant, instead of a lover, she is so full of dislike that she cannot stand him. Then he decides to be high-handed with his wife, as if he were dealing with an armed enemy. And she, because she is naturally given to impetuousness, pretends to be his superior, whether because of nobility or beauty or wealth, . . . she makes herself grand, loses respect for him, chases him from the marriage bed, harms the children, uses up the inheritance, and makes marriage hell.[6]

[5]Pietro Andrea Canonhiero, *Della eccellenza delle donne* (Florence, 1606), sig. C4v. Canonhiero follows Tasso in distinguishing between *donne* and *femine*; the former, he declares, are celebrated in lyric and chivalric poetry (A2v). Canonhiero is not, however, a feminist; his *Dell' introduzione alla politica, alla ragion di stato, et alla pratica del buon governo* (Anversa, 1627) is highly critical of women in government, because (he says) they have "for the most part those qualities that governors try to rid themselves of, and they are unskillful and incapable of business" (Eee3). Gynecocracy is against divine and natural law; "government by women is almost always disastrous and the ruin of republics. Examples from every age and all history make this abundantly clear" (Eee4).

[6]Giulio Cesare Capaccio, *Il principe . . . tratto da gli emblemi dell' Alciato, con ducento e più avvertimenti politici e morali* (Venice, 1620), sig. Dd3v–4.

The result is "the downfall of the state."

Capaccio's sense of the duty of a wife hardly admits the possibility that she might have a justifiable cause for complaint. But the fact is that his critical analysis of marital behavior makes her rebellion understandable and therefore also an aspect of the general state of the commonwealth. For the most part, sixteenth-century literature on marriage and the state tended to blame men for unruly households: they were weak or lacked the ability to command and control. Here they are blamed for being too much the superior, much as if Capaccio had heard and sympathized with the feminist plea for equal status whenever possible, and equitable treatment in any case.

Writers whose main concern was the future of the state probably entertained feminist notions of reform in order to contain them within the scope of a traditional politics. Others more visionary and perhaps in reaction to Counter-Reformation attitudes—namely, the Venetians Moderata Fonte and Lucrezia Marinelli—sketched the outlines of a wholly feminized society. There, qualities traditionally assigned to women—charity, temperance, compassion—take precedence over those traditionally assigned to men—rationality, courage, and justice. Fonte's dialogue *Il merito delle donne* (1600) illustrates a social order based on what she represents as a typically feminine experience of "friendship."[7] Nonhierarchical in structure, her feminized society is designed as an organic whole whose elements are interdependent. Rather than deriving proper behavior from rank and office, Fonte exploits a notion that feminists usually reject as unfair—that a woman has effectively no rank—to create an image of egalitarian relations among all persons, determined and maintained by "liberty," the relative freedom of the individual person. The dialogue as a whole makes explicit what other treatises valorizing feminine virtue have implied: a society of women can provide a model for the feminization of society at large; a feminine society (here exemplified by females) is the basis of a revolutionary feminized society.

Fonte begins by stating—almost as if to ratify—differences of gender according to conventional stereotypes: "Men are notable for their courage, common sense, and courtliness; women are remarkable for their beauty, courtesy, and chastity" (Bv). Beyond these differences, Fonte is concerned with others attendant on the particular station in life of each of the characters in her dialogue: Helena, newly married; Cornelia, a young wife; Leonora, a young widow; Virginia, just betrothed; Adriana, an old

---

[7]Moderata Fonte, *Il merito delle donne* (Venice, 1600), sig. Bv. Fonte dedicates her treatise to Livia Feltria della Rovere, Duchess of Urbino. This edition contains a brief life of the author by Giovanni Nicolo Doglione. For an account of Fonte, see Ginevra Conti Odorisio, *Donna e società nel seicento* (Rome: Bulzoni, 1979), 57–63, 69–73, which reprints portions of *Il merito*.

widow and Virginia's guardian; Corinna, a young woman spurned by the man she loves; and Lucretia, a middle-aged wife. With the exception of Corinna, who, as Lucretia says, is incomparably fortunate in that she alone has not been subject to a man, each woman, complaining of some aspect of her subordinate condition, justifies her presence in an exclusively woman's world. Helena, who has traveled from her new abode in the country to see her friends in Leonora's garden—the setting in which the dialogue takes place—has already encountered marital disapproval: "he [her husband] does not wish me to leave the house and I long for nothing else." Leonora rejoices that she is not married, "considering how beautiful liberty is." Virginia does not want a husband, but she "must obey [her] elders" and get married. Adriana is sympathethic to her ward but she too is controlled by men: "your uncle has decided that I must marry you off because you have so much property [*gran facultà*] that otherwise someone might take. I don't know what else I can do with you." Corinna, by contrast, rejoices in her solitude: "I would rather die than put myself under any man. The life I lead with you ladies without fearing the abuse of a man who can order me about is too blessed." Predictably, Lucretia concludes that the spinster's situation is uniquely favored—evidently an oblique way of commenting on her own situation. She calls Corinna and those who follow her example "most blessed," "especially because God has given you a wonderful wit that you express in virtuous actions, and in using your loftiest intellect in the wonderful study of letters, humane as well as sacred, you can begin heavenly existence while still in the difficulties and dangers of the world" (B2v–3v).

The structural features of Fonte's garden setting for this conversation are emblematic of the feminine society her characters are in the process of illustrating. The statues of women from whose breasts flows the water of the fountain at the garden's center represent a comprehensive allegory of womankind. The first three embody aspects of the happy condition of the single woman and are all, paradoxically, generative; "chastity," an ermine, destroys what attacks it; "solitude," a phoenix, dies to be reborn; and "liberty," a sun, gives light to itself and to the planets. The last three represent the self-destructive states that a woman's association with a man induces in her: "naiveté," a window, burned by that through which it has seen beauty; "falsehood," a peach and its leaf, experiencing the difference between tongue and heart; and "cruelty," a crocodile, which grieves for the creature whom it has killed (B4r–v). The iconic rigidity of the statues contrasts with their function within the garden: to supply it with fresh water. As a whole, the statues and what they do is an analogue for what is demonstrated by the dialogue of Fonte's women, "freely" conducted (C2): the constructive effects of an uncensored communication among individual persons. Fonte has situated her fictional garden in her own city of Venice (Venus?), a city both "free" and pluralistic: it is so favorably situated "that persons from all the other countries [in Europe] come to it. . . . [I]t is a city as free as the sea and, without laws itself, it gives laws to others" (Br–v).[8] Here, as in Fonte's garden, differences do not promote divisiveness but rather result in an exemplary order. The paradox that characterizes the life of her city—freedom provides the basis for law—is coupled with a myth of origins: Venice, like the sea, creates new laws and hence forms of life. A society modeled on that of the women's garden will, she implies, be similarly generative.

The old law of patriarchy must be dismissed, Fonte's Virginia begins by arguing, for women are no more subject to men than men are subject to women. The subjection to which women are ordered, she says, "one ought to understand . . . [as a subjection to] the misfortunes, weaknesses, and other accidents of this life to which everyone is liable. [This is] a subjection that elicits not obedience but patience; not a fearful service but a Christian support. These [forms of subjection] are given us for our spiritual well-being [*essercitio spirituale*]. But they [men] take this [our spiritual well-being] in a contrary sense and want to tyrannize over us" (C2v). She overlooks the usual interpretation of the second creation, so crucial in curtailing the scope of a woman's autonomy, by arguing that the true nature of the only subjection a human being must undergo is ethical and common to both sexes. In fact none of Fonte's characters discusses the traditional view of man as woman's head; on the contrary, all insist that woman has the moral capacity, and ought to have the material means, to be her own head. Corinna, for example, protests the practice of fathers who leave their property to their male heirs, "and prevent woman from their rightful inheritance." Penniless women therefore live with their male relatives as "slaves, deprived of their reason and joy, against every kind of justice" (C4). Leonora interprets an arranged marriage as a "selling" of a daughter for the "utility"—presumably through enhanced family connections—it brings her father. A dowry is no guarantee of a woman's status vis-à-vis her husband. When Helena maintains that without one a woman cannot keep herself in clothes and furnishings, Corinna complains that the use of dowries is frequently perverted: "for as soon as a woman has taken a husband, she has the expense of raising children and of maintaining a house." If she remains a

---

[8]For Venice as particularly conducive to feminist discourse, see chap. 1, n. 49; Odorisio remarks that the *libertà* to which Fonte alludes depends on the fact that in Venice "there existed a hope of balancing political forces": *Donna e società*, 48.

spinster, she can live "on her portion according to her station like a queen." But once married, "she loses the control of her belongings and puts her entire wealth in the hands of the man she has bought" with her dowry (H2). The irony is of course that she has bought the person who then owns her. Moreover, if economic deprivation is wrong, so Corinna's argument goes, personal humiliation is also. Both usurp a woman's legitimate control over her life. Corinna observes that wives do not enjoy even the limited autonomy they are traditionally owed as housekeepers: husbands "scream" and "strike" them "even for the least little thing," despite the fact that, as Cornelia will note, were no wife to care for him, a man would "be governed by servants who would rob him of his goods and his life, as is common enough" (D3, G2v). Corinna insists that men should acquire "a little discretion, so that at the very least they would desire that things be organized equally [for men and women] and that there be a parity between them" (C3v). Of course, women are undervalued from the start. At the birth of a daughter a man typically "gets angry at his own wife, . . . almost as if she alone had generated the child and not he also." Instead, according to Corinna, he should organize the most magnificent feast (Hv).

But finally what legitimates a woman's "free" society is her resources of reason and a free will. If, as Leonora maintains (echoing Fonte's opening remarks), woman has a different "nature" than man, "colder, more fearful, credulous, and easy to deceive," she also has, as Cornelia claims, an "intellect and the torch of reason to expose the deceptions" to which her sex is liable (E4). And when Helena worries that a woman's "nature" is inherently inclined to goodness and not the product of "will" (E4v), Cornelia disagrees: women "are moved by as much will as is suitable and necessary for them as human beings and in their situation of life." True, she continues, a woman's will is severely tested by her natural "softness," her tendency both to show compassion and to believe in the goodness of others. In this case her will to secure the good is in conflict with her will to please.

> You see [in woman] a double strength, as things are more difficult [for her than for a man]. For her natural mercy and kindness incline her to rejoice and take pleasure in [the welfare of] others rather than herself; [this is true] in all things and in that one which is contrary to virtue [i.e., chastity] to which she knows she is more bound than to her life or that of another. Choosing to suffer by not following her will, and denying herself any satisfaction . . . she does great violence to her heart and the merit of her victory [in this act of self-denial] is infinite and cannot be expressed.[9]   [F]

---

[9]This is a complicated passage: "Mirate doppia fortezza, che quasi l'è più dificile [sic], per la natural sua clemenza e benignità, che la inclina a giovar e compiacer ad altrui più, che a se

The idea of will here is complex. Clearly it is the psychic agency that controls feeling, for others as well as for the self, but it is also feeling (principally erotic, it is implied) that needs to be controlled. It is best expressed in oxymoron, as the controlled (or disciplined) emotion or the emotional (or compassionate) control that determines moral choice. Thus a woman can and indeed must, Corinna argues, always turn to reason: "Given, as I have said, the prudence and goodness of rationality, one can escape many evils and pursue much goodness despite one's disposition" (Iv).

Fonte's closing image of feminine friendship reveals that it is the fruit of her new law. Renouncing a hierarchical society energized by competition, Cornelia imagines a feminized society created by "higher forces" (*cagioni superiori*) making for cooperation (Iv). It will be free of the need for self-promotion: "this stupidity of wanting to make oneself esteemed" (*questa sciochezza di voler farsi stimar*) does not honor friends and in fact dishonors the ideal of friendship (I2). In the language and practice of patriarchy, a woman's "nature" has proved a kind of weakness. But in her society, as Corinna points out, it is a source of goodness and strength: "true friendship is the reason for every good; by friendship the world is maintained and marriages are made, by which the species is preserved; by friendship the concordance of our bodily elements is maintained." By friendship, even cities and kingdoms prosper (I3).[10] The paradoxically free law of Venice and the garden constitutes a society neither tyrannical nor anarchic, loosely yet firmly bound by the generative yet orderly principle of *amicitia* typically realized in relations between women.

Lucrezia Marinelli's *Nobiltà e l'eccellenza delle donne* (1601) also concludes with a model for a new society built on a feminine cooperation. Its ostensible object is to repudiate what Marinelli refers to as Aristotle's opinions on the position of women in the *Politics* and the nature of the female in his *Generation of Animals*. Her interpretation of these texts is overtly polemical; she selects particular passages for comment without addressing the work as a whole body of philosophical opinion. Her

---

stessa, in tutte le cose, e in questa per esser contraria alla virtù al che ella si conosce più obligata che alla vita propria ne d'altrui; volendo patire di non esseguire la sua volontà e negando a se stesso ogni suo contento . . . riceve pero gran violenza nel cuore e il merito della sua vittoria è infinito e non potrebbesi esprimere" (F). The signatures throughout this edition are out of sequence.

[10]Fonte appropriates the concept of friendship, so important to humanist male discourse, especially in relation to women, and sees that its finest expression is in female society, where it is not complicated by greed and ambition. She later dismisses as stupid the courtly excuse for rivalry among males, the *farsi stimar* of the lovesick knight; in other words, she sees that when men depart from their usual exploitive treatment of women as objects of exchange and claim love for their ladies in a courtly manner, they are in fact only disguising self-love.

conclusion is, however, of a philosophical kind: by demonstrating the changing nature of all truth over time, a development epitomized in the continuing revisions of Aristotelian science and morals, she is able to claim the correctness of a historicist view of the institutions establishing social and political orthodoxy. In itself, such a position is not new. Like Valla and Colet, Aylmer had adopted a historicist view of Scripture half a century earlier, and the work of historians such as Francesco Guicciardini continued to represent for his sixteenth-century readers the real weakness in the position of the anti-Machiavellians, who argued that history was constructed on a divine plan guaranteeing that the same values would prevail in and over time. What is unusual about Marinelli's historicism is that it undermines an important and representative authority for *patriarchy*, and consequently links historicism to feminism.[11] She denies the whole category of the authoritative with its implied opposition, the category of the specious, and substitutes her own concept of the author— one whose claim to the truth is no more than contingent.

She begins by considering the question of intention. Authors, she says, write either to demonstrate the truth or to hide it. In both cases, they employ any rhetorical means at their disposal to *persuade* their readers of the truth of what they say. The truthteller uses "every device" (*ogni diligenza*) not only in "constructing his argument" but also in "rendering it in the most elegant way clear and obvious." The liar uses "every possible tool [*ogni studio*] to make the world believe that the false is true, evil is good, ugliness is beauty, and with apparent reason they very often attain their desired end" (A). In other words, all texts claim to represent the truth, to be its authority—all, in fact, use the same language in that effort. How is the reader to distinguish what is correct? Self-contradiction indicates authorial uncertainty at the very least; a disjunction between authority and the evidence of experience suggests authorial bias. Attacking Aristotle on both these counts, Marinelli points out those of his statements on women which are in conflict with themselves and with common knowledge. Woman, he has asserted, is instable and lacks

[11]Marinelli, like Fonte, is nevertheless very explicitly critical of contemporary abuse of the custom of dowries: "I don't see discreet and kind women meddling with their husbands' patrimony; however, they bring with them enough dowry toward the enhancement of their husbands so that they pay not only their own way but even their husbands'. And how many men, because of this dowry, regain family status and rank, and puffed up with pride march around with their associates, men who would otherwise rot dishonorably in debtors' prison? Moreover, you never find a woman who ruins her husband's property as a husband does a wife's. There are many women who never possess a penny their entire lives . . . and if the truth be known are always beggars": *La nobiltà et l'eccellenza delle donne co'diffetti et mancamenti de gli huomini* (Venice, 1601), sig. I2v–3. For Marinelli, see Odorisio, *Donna e società*, 57–63, 69–73.

firmness; but she is also diligent and careful, perspicacious and wise. Elsewhere he claims that women are shameless; but in yet another place they are modest (B6r–v). Marinelli turns next to the examples provided by experience, and rehearses points by now commonly known to readers of this literature: women have governed fiefdoms and nations, they have waged war, built cities, written books. In effect, she argues the simplest case for shared gender: the existence of the virile woman. If women have failed fully to explore the possibility of masculine behavior, it is because "men, driven by their own stubborn ignorance, persuading themselves that women cannot learn what men learn, have forbidden it to them" (C). If those women who have succeeded in functioning in a masculine way do not appear numerous in the pages of history, it is because (male) historians are rhetoricians, concerned only to convince others of what they maintain, however doubtful its relation to available evidence or verifiable fact. Driven by "excessive self-love, they judge themselves to be better in intellect and inventiveness than women are" (G6v).

Marinelli's most astute move, as she argues from experience, is to give Aristotle a motive for being misogynist. This move brings her case against him into line with her opening comments on rhetoric. There may be no way to establish the truth of a literary subject on the basis of the language used to represent it, but at least some light is shed on it if its author's interests are known. In this case, Marinelli cites Aristotle's envy and dislike of his wife, reported by Diogenes Laertes, as the real basis for his condemnation of women (G7). The nature of her claim (quite possibly fictitious) suggests that she could very well be using "every tool" herself to present a lie as the truth. On the other hand, her use of this kind of evidence is appropriate from a theoretical point of view; she is supplying a text with an experiential context in order to reveal its actual meaning.

Marinelli sees that what persons accept as true is historically contingent in any case. Enlarging on the interpretive problems posed by Aristotle's texts, she notes that it is easy to see how he might have been mistaken, "just as we often see that many have thought that the earth and sky may be stable; others that there may be many worlds, and yet others that there may be only one . . . thus everyone defends his opinion with many reasons and very obstinately. Such are the answers one gives to those who slander the female sex" (G7v). Given the date of publication of *La nobiltà*, 1601, this is a remarkable statement. Copernicus had published his treatise on the changing shape of the heavens, *De revolutionibus*, in 1543. But for readers not versed in the mathematics of astronomy, the views it contained (as well as speculations derived from them) were known popularly through the lectures of Giordano Bruno, who was

burned in 1601 for having asserted that there were many worlds. Here
Marinelli places Bruno's heretical opinion beside the view she must have
known to be orthodox—there is only one world—and includes them
both in a historicist view of science that represents all knowledge of
nature as "opinion," changing with time and, presumably, the interests
of philosophers. She concludes her attack on authority by pointing out
that the Aristotelian science of sex and gender is another instance of such
opinion. By seeing it as symptomatic not of a particular circumstance
(the writer's uxoriousness) but of a general condition (no truth of science
is timeless or absolute), she not only broadens the basis of her attack on
misogyny but implies the existence of an alternative concept of woman.

To state what this concept might be requires Marinelli, like Fonte, to
postulate a feminine nature. Fonte had urged the value of the feminine
dramatically, by representing in the dialogue of her women characters the
generous principle of *amicitia*. Marinelli proceeds analytically, establishing, first, that categorical comparisons cannot be used to determine
absolute value; and second, that if they are made to seem to do so, it is
because an a priori decision has been made to see a category in one way or
another. This procedure permits her to question the validity of the whole
set of categories sustaining patriarchal distinctions of sex and gender and,
as a result, propose others. What use is it, she asks, to claim that woman
is colder than man, man is hotter than woman? "Indeed one sees many
countries, not to say towns and castles, in which women are hotter than
the men of other countries, as those of Spain and Africa are hotter than
men in the north and in Germany. And how many of us believe from
Aristotle and Plato that men were and are hotter and therefore nobler in
spirit?" Nor is physical strength an index of nobility—otherwise laborers
would be nobler than kings. The correct assessment of the value of
a characteristic depends entirely on the circumstances in which it is
brought into play. Again, Marinelli's argument becomes historicist. Denying that it was the strength of Roman soldiers that guaranteed the
viability of the Roman senate and its republican government, she declares: "This is what actually happened when strength [i.e., the strength
of the state] was merely in arms and not in reason or justice: a murderous
brother took over the government of the nation and assumed its leadership from the other brother who was frail and retiring." This usurpation
is precisely parallel to man's over woman: "in the same way the female
sex, frailer . . . than the male sex, by not being used to physical exercise
[*per non essere assuefatto alle fatiche*], have come to be tyrannized over and
downtrodden by insolent and unjust men" (H4r–v).

Marinelli closes with a statement that reflects the fruits of her own
literary experience of authorities (principally Aristotle) as abusive. Dis-

carding their comparative categories and aprioristic evaluations, she suggests the desirability of a feminization of men. For the supposedly positive and masculine characteristics of heat, suggesting the quality of
magnificence (and possibly pride), and strength, suggesting fortitude,
Marinelli urges the substitution of others generically feminine: "if
women, as I hope, would wake from the long somnolence into which
they have been plunged, men who have been scornful and proud would
become gentle and humble." Like Fonte, Marinelli imagines a feminized
society as one that sustains relations determined less by the authority and
power of individual persons than by a common and pluralistic good.

A Feminist Politics

Feminists realized that the androgynous models of conduct
they endorsed had to be free of traits that conduced to effeminate in
contrast to feminine behavior. Vices associated with women were open
to reevaluation; both vices and virtues were to be shown to be in men as
well. Equality in principle—that is, equality of men and women, not of
men and virile women—assumed that differences of sex (between male
and female) and of gender (between the masculine and the feminine) were
real, but that they did not derogate from the worth of either sex or
gender. And finally, feminists paid attention to the situations in which the
femininity of persons of both sexes was routinely undervalued.

Lucretio Bursati's dialogue *La vittoria delle donne* (1621) moves from
revealing the ambiguities inherent in the concept of the moral superiority
of woman to pointing out the advantages of granting women a role in the
activities of the state. In the process, he argues for the value of a feminine
perspective. Discussing the figure of the woman as *domina*, Bursati asks
whether or not she can provide men with what courtly conventions
mandate: a social ethic. His defender of women, Gaudentio Moreschi of
Verona, states that "the habits of women . . . give man the true and just
rule, the right norm [*la regola, la dritta norma*] of a life lived in this world in
a decent and praiseworthy manner"[12]—a claim that within the spectrum
of behavior shared by men and women implicitly gives a high value to
femininity. The problem, according to Bursati's skeptic, Alessandro
Saluti of Venice, is to be discerned in actual cases: "don't [men] often
completely lose their wits [over women], so they can't learn or study or
get any use from their knowledge?" (B5v). Gaudentio's reply is disarm-

---

[12]Lucretio Bursati, *La vittoria delle donne* (Venice, 1621), sig. B4v. Bursati dedicates his
six dialogues to Signor Luigi Giustiniano, and states that their setting is "the ceremony of
the marriage of the sea" (A8).

ing. He admits that men in love behave in bizarre ways but he insists that
it is despite the example set them by women: "many young men [in love]
devote all their skill to dressing in a feminine way [*in parer femini*]" (C3).
Moreover, a man in love is a squanderer: "He spends, he spends in jousts,
in tournaments, in games, in masked balls, for livery, for clothes, for
guests, for servants, for bodyguards, for secretaries, for spies, and for
presents; he behaves in bizarre ways . . . he rushes into fights . . . he never
rests . . . you always see him moping . . . in churches and in squares . . . at
the port or hanging around under windows . . . to his own guests, he
knows only how to complain. . . . But when was the beauty of a young
man ever enough to drive a woman mad with love?" (Dr–v). Gaudentio's
purpose in rehearsing the effects of a man's lovesickness is to distinguish
the effeminate man from the comparatively dispassionate and hence
virile woman. Continuing to insist that "the beauties and graces of
women have too much force and too great value" (D5), Alessando replies
by warning against the participation of women in the law:

> Men of consequence, knowing that unsophisticated males [*i poco accorti
> maschi*]—because of their own bad tendencies—are easily caught in the
> snares of women's amorous graces, have forbidden women to appear
> before tribunals to perform the functions of solicitor or lawyer; thus
> women, driven by men to promote unjust causes by their sweet ap-
> pearance and words and graceful gestures, will not corrupt the integrity
> and severity of justice; thus men will not be inclined to hand down er-
> roneous decisions following the wishes of the most beautiful and graceful
> ladies rather than *the sacred laws of evidence* that every honorable judge ought
> to protect, since on these depend both the public and private good of the
> republic. [D5v]

Here Alessandro assumes what Gaudentio will later question: that
women are excluded from the processes of justice for the sake of justice.
Gaudentio will show that the judicial system functions in response to
wealth and rank. The exclusion of women from courtrooms testifies
only to the fact that they cannot hold or administer property in their own
names.

Social in contrast to legal practice places the question of the value of
femininity in still another light. From the beginning of the previous
century treatises on the education of noblewomen had illustrated that
men and women might be of the same rank and yet have quite different
degrees of authority and power. As Alessandro observes, a woman's rank
is particularly important in Venice, where the republic has decreed that
"if any nobleman take a wife from the common people, their children
will not be admitted to governing councils nor will they be taken for

noble" (I2v). All the more reason, then, to ask why, given the dynastic importance of a woman's rank, she should not be accorded the same public responsibilities as a man (I5). Gaudentio asserts that the fact that she is not so honored has nothing to do with the value of woman or the feminine: "It is not always the worthiest who has the office or rank. The queen of France has no office and she is of greater worth and nobler than all the officeholders of the kingdom that are her subjects and vassals" (I5v). But the question remains: Why and how is the nobler person denied the authority and power of her status? What about femininity, finally, is held to be so detrimental to social order?

As if to answer these questions, Gaudentio examines the vices supposedly typical of woman—inconsistency, lasciviousness, stupidity, and garrulousness—and in each case demonstrates either that these vices are not vices or that men have them too. In other words, there is no experiential basis for denigrating the kind of behavior characteristic of women. Lust is obviously a shared vice; so is the greed that exploits lust. If women demanded as many male gigolos as men female prostitutes, Gaudentio claims, cities would have to be enlarged to accommodate the trade (Lv). All the more reason to condemn the unfairness of the double standard.

> If a woman gives herself imprudently to a man, she is pointed at by everyone . . . and considered . . . to be deserving of poison or the stiletto. The adulterous man, who commits a thousand other worse acts of dishonesty, does not lose honor, his dissolute life does not matter, no one rejects his company or refuses to speak with him; he is like the other men of the city: honored, appreciated, valued. And why ought a woman to be in a worse condition than a man? If the crime is the same, why does not a man suffer the same infamy . . . as a woman?   [L3v–4]

Alessandro's response to this question, his attempt to see a woman's infidelity as a matter of insubordination, is met with Gaudentio's flat rejection of the idea "that a man is better than a woman" (L4v)

Gaudentio also rationalizes charges that woman is ignorant and garrulous by commenting on her circumstances. Women "do not go to the city where there are public schools, not because they are inept at learning difficult subjects but because there are such crowds of students there at the present time," and because fathers want their daughters to occupy "their wits in spinning and weaving exclusively" (M6r–v). Men, he goes on to observe, are often also ignorant, even after schooling: "they come home as witless as ever despite their doctorates" (N2v). As far as chattering is concerned, men are as guilty as women. They talk of war, hostility, politics, the exchange, trade; similarly, women talk of what concerns them: children, husbands, household affairs. But the latter are "low matters," Alessandro objects; "they have too much of the peasant about them, they reveal a great inferiority of spirit." Women speak of the things they have been charged with overseeing, Gaudentio replies, demonstrating the circularity of his opponent's reasoning (N8). Men restrict women to domesticity, women's conversation is of domestic matters, hence women are good only for domesticity and men are right to prevent them from doing anything else.

The devaluation of the feminine was often linked to conventional notions of social status (as Gaudentio's earlier observations on noblewomen indicates) and it was clearly important to the promotion of femininity that the patriarchal practice of tying privilege to rank in the case of men but not women be regarded as culturally rather than naturally derived. The effects of culture on gendered behaviors and their evaluation could be (and had been) answered by reference to evidence of a proto-anthropological kind. This evidence—the quite different roles other peoples assigned to the sexes—usually indicated the conventionality of the roles of men and women in Europe. Gaudentio cites an especially telling instance. Among the Tartars, "as soon as a woman has given birth she rises from her bed, and after she has bathed and clothed the infant, her husband gets into bed in her place and holds the infant, and she feeds her husband fresh eggs and all kinds of delicate food, and she nurses the baby while her husband lolls around for forty days, visited by friends and relations" (L6v). Even if Bursati's readers could not believe in the literal truth of this report, they would scarcely miss its representation of feminine behavior as determined by convention and without a basis in nature. On the basis of the biological facts of reproductivity, Bursati suggests, not many of the roles assigned to men and women can be attributed to sexual difference. A (Tartar) woman gave birth and suckled, but the posture of weakness that was supposed to characterize these actions was easily assumed by a (Tartar) man, presumably with social sanction and credibility. In effect, Bursati distinguishes behavior that is natural to the female from that which can be adopted by either sex, whether it be valued positively, as feminine, or negatively, as effeminate.

The idea that masculine and feminine behaviors were culturally determined also led to questions concerning the ideological uses of convention in patriarchal societies. What, specifically, sustains ideas of gender? Bursati implies that it is the economic power of men, and that this power elicits a response on the part of disempowered women which identifies them as a *class*. The terms of Bursati's analysis are, I think, novel. The advantages to be gained by thinking of women as constituting a separate class in a political and economic rather than an ontological sense do not seem to have been evident to feminists of the previous century, perhaps because they were so concerned to establish their common nature with men. But Bursati sees merit not only in making the point but in stressing the justice of class actions by women. Noting that the Roman laws of the republic were increasingly severe in punishing women who ventured into public, Gaudentio justifies their rebellion. Neither "indiscretion" nor "frivolity" but rather "a desire for honor, for reputation, and for domestic peace" led them to complain to the senators "that they had shown themselves to be unprincipled [empi] persecutors of the female sex" (P3v). Theirs were clearly "unjust laws" deserving of protest (P4). Moreover, the moral power motivating feminine protest, a love of honor, was of a conventionally masculine character.

Bursati's treatise opens with a discussion of why women are excluded from the operations of justice and concludes by returning to the question, this time with a more searching answer. Gaudentio has earlier claimed that women are excluded from courtrooms because men have insufficient control over their senses to avoid being swayed by beauty and charm. Gaudentio now declares that women are excluded from justice because they are poor and lack economic power. Women, he declares, may spend (some) money on clothing and furnishings, but it is nothing to what men spend on their own self-advancement. "Do not those courtiers, bankers, magistrates, public administrators, accountants, and merchants—who, not content with what is honestly earned [de gli onesti guadagni], have no regard for anything except the money for which they sell justice by ounces or pounds, more to one who gives more, less to less—behave in a worse way than do these women?" The law actually permits, not to say encourages, the abuse of riches, so that men, who have property, are more, not less, likely to err. Nor are their errors often punished. For, Gaudentio concludes, justice is like a spider's web, "where only the little ones [animaletti picioli] get caught and not the big ones; for it often happens that with an execrable partiality, the rich escape punishment and the poor, who have nothing to give, are sent off to be whipped" (R2v–3). Not generally liable at law, Gaudentio's women contemporaries escaped the fate of the poor in one way. They were similar, however, in being a class of persons who, having "nothing to give," are unable to defend themselves against those with means. Bursati's entire argument comes to rest on a constellation of points familiar to feminist discourse of the period. Beyond the cultural construction of gender, he insists on the fundamental bias of the system of values by which society lives; in fact, there is nothing lofty about men or masculinity, at least in contrast to women or femininity. What is spoken of as morality, however confused its terms, is actually only the power to coerce. By being disempowered and hence incapable of coercion, women as a class acquire a paradoxical moral authority. If disempowerment does not automatically conduce to disinterestedness, it is at least in a better position from which to value it.

Christoforo Bronzini's dialogue *Della dignità e nobiltà delle donne* (1622) has a bipartite argument: he valorizes the feminine over the masculine, despite the apparently contradictory choice of women who assume, from time to time, a masculine gender; and he asserts the absolute value of equality of men and women to the welfare of the state—reasons, perhaps, that his treatise was placed on the index of prohibited books the year of its publication. His case unfolds in an extended argument between Onorio, who defends women, and Tolomei, who is their "adversary"; it begins by establishing what is actually implicit in the notion of shared gender, that is (as Breton had also noticed) that men who despise women are socially maladroit. For, Onorio asserts, the idea of "man does not exclude woman"; women "have the same vigor, the same ability to commit themselves freely and willingly . . . to honorable enterprises." Women are despised only by "low persons": "nothing conduces more to the dispraise of women than ignorance and bad upbringing." By contrast, the status of women is enhanced by "the prudence, the courage, and the discretion of men."[13] It is because only "low persons" condemn women and by extension femininity that Onorio can make his most outstanding claim, that woman is actually superior to man. She is "the absolute governor of every prince," "school of every virtue," "a tower of high courage" (A5v, A6). Abstracted like the ancient figures of Sophia and Philosophia, Bronzini's ideal seems remote.

The point of his idealization is, however, to valorize qualities that are exhibited by both men and women but are traditionally identified as feminine. He depicts what appears to be a new political hierarchy—"We [men] command all the other men in the world but women command us"—but is actually a traditional kind of (essentially Christian) moral order: "Nor do courageous women achieve such government by violence, by tyranny, or by wealth, but with the most gentle of customs, with piety. And with a thousand other excellent qualities, which were and are the arms by which they triumphed, victorious in a tranquil and loving peace. And now more than ever, they continue to triumph."[14]

[13]Christoforo Bronzini, *Della dignità e nobiltà delle donne* (Florence, 1622), sigs. A3, A4. This passage appears in the first signature, which runs through the "First Day" of the dialogue. (A new signature begins with the "Second Day.") Bronzini dedicates his dialogue to Maria Maddalena, Grand Duchess of Tuscany.

[14]By now a virtual cliché of feminist discourse, the irenic nature of gynecocracies could be rendered ironic by reference to the most famous (albeit legendary) of them: Amazonia. For a curious example of such an argument, see Francesco Agostino della Chiesa's *Theatro*

The status of women, as an index of the worth of the feminine, guarantees the stability and continuance of society by representing the cause of peace, not war. Hence what is feminine is naturally perfect—as naturally perfect as the masculine has always been held to be, and on stronger grounds. "Nature (and nothing is more opposed to war) has naturally fashioned women entirely for peace and concord" (B5v). Bronzini supports his view of the feminine by citing Scripture and philosophy; finally, reverting to allegory, he posits the feminization of the processes of history by citing the role of "that benign nymph, Immortality" (i.e., fame), "a woman" who is the record of all great human actions (G8r–v).[15]

Why, then, Tolomei eventually asks, do women take it upon themselves to behave from time to time in a masculine way? If human nature is androgynous, as Onorio will claim it is, they cannot really do otherwise: "sexual difference does not exist except in the difference of bodily parts that generation requires" (H6v). Androgyny, on the other hand, as it is described in Plato's *Symposium* and "the greatest of mysteries," explains human behavior: "it means that we are the same thing [*una cosa medesima*], of the same perfection as women; and that women seek us out and love us; and we seek them out and love them" (H6). Onorio advances the usual arguments from experience to demonstrate the virility of women. If evidence of their virility is sparse, it is because men restrict women's experience and because men write history. All the more reason, Onorio can claim, for women who are denied the opportunity to bring their masculinity into play to wish actively to be men. This wish reflects not their imperfection but their abuse, and the fact that the power to reform society belongs to men: "A woman wishes to be a man not to make herself more perfect but only to free herself from the most insolent tyranny of men, usurped unjustly in every sphere of life" (H8v). In marriage, the state in which most adult women live, she is stripped of her

---

delle donne letterate con un breve discorso della preminenza perfettione del sesso donnesco (Mantua, 1620), in which the author describes the bloody conquest of the Amazons (complete with cruelty to male children) and then alludes to the "bell'ordine" of their government. He concludes: "There is no kingdom, province, or city in the world that women have governed in which the people have not felt a great desire for their form of government [*suo modo di dominare*]" (Bv). In this case, the type of the virile woman is shown to suffer from a perverted masculinity, from which she unaccountably recovers when she gets political control of male society.

[15]Cf. his earlier celebration of the ideality of woman as a moral force in society. On the medieval origins of the argument from genders in language, see Joan Ferrante, *Woman as Image in Medieval Literature* (New York: Columbia University Press, 1979), 4–6; at this stage in the development of feminist protest, it seems so abstract as actually to function as a counterpoint to the main line of reasoning.

human qualities to become merely an economic resource: "when a woman [marries], she has to be given a huge dowry, today the most important thing in that institution" (I3v).

To conclude his defense Onorio represents a society in which men and women are socially and politically equal. Stabilized by the power of femininity, this society exemplifies peace and concord: "Equality, in the household as in ancient republics, was always the keystone and the base on which rested public and private happiness, because [equality] fostered peace, discouraged sedition, gave birth to love and concord, conserved unity and the relations of all the members of the body politic and of the family" (A3v–4).[16] To return to this equality (as Onorio describes it) is in part to recover a prelapsarian paradise, the concord of the first couple in their garden, in part to prepare for eternity. In the dialogues of the second day, he justifies his position by referring to Scripture: woman was created "free" (according to her first creation); her punishment as subject to man ceased with the birth of Jesus (who allows believers to enter Paradise again): "Woman herself [as Mary] has this advantage, regaining that legitimate lordship of the human race which she lost through diabolical wit" (A6v).

A feminist society such as this one of Bronzini's, based on what may be termed an equality in principle between men and women, clearly risks being criticized as visionary and unworkable in practical terms, even if its value as morally prescriptive is conceded. If it had been considered to be a blueprint for actual reform, it could have been charged with fostering the kind of anarchy associated with such marginal societies as the Anabaptist, based in theory solely on Christian love. In fact, like Bruni da Pistoia, Tasso, and Sidney, Bronzini does translate his idea of equality into what might be termed an equality *within* a particular rank, and in a more generalizable manner. This strategy has the effect of preserving the hierarchical order of society while at the same time purging it of structures based on sex and gender difference. His picture of society depends on maintaining rank but without the deceptive dimension it has for women, the largely ceremonial aspect of their honor. So Onorio can answer Tolomei's accusation that women are frivolous by comparing their behavior with that of men of the same rank: "Realize that each woman in her status may be as competent as a man [of a similar status] in performing her tasks, however grand or insignificant, [and they will be done] according to the status of the particular woman." The tasks "appropriate and peculiar to poor women are not for brave and magnanimous

[16]This and the following passages appear in the second signature, which runs through the second and third days of the dialogue.

women." Of a higher rank and capacity, these women, "compared to the most masculine and virtuous of men [*a paragone d'ogni altro virile e virtuoso huomo*], have made themselves worthy examples for the future." Onorio concludes by promising that "women . . . can be the equal" of a man in "all the actions [*operationi*] one expects from a worthy knight" (N2v–3). In other words, men and women of a given rank function at similar levels of performance, using qualities and demonstrating behavior characteristic of both genders.

FRANCE

Reform

In seventeenth-century France, such feminists as Jacqueline de Miremont and Charlotte de Brachart echoed the opinions of radical writers such as Bursati and Bronzini; and like their Italian counterparts, they had to contend with conservative exponents of patriarchy. French moralists could be no less traditional on the subject of domestic life, and perhaps for the same reasons. While Pierre Charron and François de Sales (for example) included elements of the feminist rhetoric of equality in their discussions of marriage, they failed to support the changes that feminists proposed to make in that institution. Both writers portrayed marriage as inferior to celibacy.

For Charron its justification is progeny; otherwise woman is a distraction to the main business of life. In *De la sagesse* (1601), he declares that "marriage is a corruption and a debasement of excellent and rare spirits, inasmuch as the flatteries and cajoling of the person one loves, the affection for children, the case of the household, and the advancement of the family slow, dampen, and diminish the vigor and strength of the strongest and most energetic of persons."[17] To excuse those who nevertheless wish to marry, he advances a weak defense: "I can only say that human nature is incapable of perfection . . . its best remedies are always a bit sick, shot through with inconveniences; these are all necessary evils; [marriage] is the best one can recommend for its preservation and multiplication" (351). The status of the wife is therefore problematic; though the couple are equals, they must relate to each other as superior and inferior. Their equality "consists in an entire and perfect communication and community of all things, souls, wills, bodies, goods . . ."; it is offset by the husband's "power [over] his wife," even if "she is much nobler and richer than he is . . . ; this superiority and inferiority is *natural*, and is

[17]Pierre Charron, *De la sagesse* (Paris, 1824; rpt. Geneva: Slatkine, 1968), 348.

based on the force and competence of one and the weakness and incom-
petence of the other" (354–56). As justification Charron returns to the
Aristotelian notion of woman as a *vir occasionatus*—a notion that had been
so frequently disputed by feminists that Charron's endorsement of it is
tantamount to an admission of misogyny. It is only in contrast to what
Charron terms the "paternalism" of marriages in antiquity, condoning
polygamy and divorce in the interests of enhancing the procreative end of
marriage, that his depiction of the contemporary state of the institution,
as a *Christian* institution, concedes any virtue to the wife. For, as he says,
Christianity sees in marriage a "lofty and noble rationale," and experience of it as such "demonstrates that indissolubility serves to enhance
friendship" (359). In other words, if a man has to restrict himself to one
wife for a lifetime, he is less likely to regard her as a commodity (i.e., not
a friend) than he would be were she one among many and their relationship of limited duration.

Like Charron, François de Sales affirms the natural inferiority of
woman. In his "Avis pour les gens mariés," included in his *Introduction à
la vie dévote* (1609), he defines marital love as mutual but between unequals. He asks husbands to be tolerant of their wives' limitations: "The
stupidity and weakness of your wives, whether of body or mind, should
not provoke you to feel any sort of disdain, but rather to a sweet and
loving compassion, for so God created them in order that they, being
dependent on you, would give you more honor and respect, and that
they as your companions would nonetheless have you as their head and
superior." Wives are urged to accept their status, "for really God created
men as stronger and more powerful."[18] François's subsequent discussion
of sexual relations in marriage points up the logical connection between
the idea that man and woman are naturally unequal in all respects, and the
preference for a life restricted largely to the company of men.

True, he concedes the importance of sexual intimacy when he observes
that even the saints "used to caress each other in marriage," and that "the
marriage debt" ought to be paid faithfully "as if there were a hope of
children even though there is sometimes not that hope" (241). But finally
such a sexuality seems designed to foster the welfare of man, to make
marriage the canonical a remedy for lust and no more. François concludes
by recommending the prudent elephant as a suitable model for a husband. (Nothing is said of the wife's sexuality.) The elephant "never

---

[18]St. François de Sales, *Introduction à la vie dévote*, in *Oeuvres de St. François de Sales*, ed.
André Ravier (Paris: Gallimard, 1969), 235. For studies of François de Sales, see, i.a.,
Fortunat Strowski, *St. François de Sales: Introduction à l'histoire du sentiment religieux en
France au dix-septième siècle* (Paris: Plon, 1928); and Ruth Kleinman, *St. François de Sales and
the Protestants* (Geneva: Droz, 1962).

changes his mate and loves her tenderly although he only mates with her every three years and so secretly that he is never seen in the act. He is, however, seen on the sixth day [of the mating season] when before he does anything else he goes to some river in which he washes his body completely, not wanting to return to the herd without purifying himself first" (243). Pollution is often considered to result from contact with creatures of a lower order; if the female is inferior to the male, it is logical that she should be regarded as a (if not the) source of his debility. The anonymous author of a *Brief Discours pour la réformation des mariages* (1614) expresses what François implies—marriage may be "necessary" but it is also regrettable. The first man should have been content to live alone, "in that state of innocence without any mad desire for a companion," and consequently would not have lost "that perfection and prerogative which God gave him at his creation"—that is, his immortality.[19]

Nor did an emphasis on androgyny always lead to endorsement of equality of the sexes. Louis Bermen, in his *Bouclier des dames* (1621), centers his apology for woman on the figure of the androgyne and relates that Plato regarded it as an index of the "indissoluble bond of friendship that ought to exist between man and woman," a bond that is reflected in their physical identity. Initially, Bermen appears to be speaking of the *species* or what is conveyed by the scriptural idea of the human being as *homo*: men and women are "animated by the same heart, breathe through the same lungs, and are governed by the same soul and will."[20] Contradicting Aristotle's view of woman as inherently defective—woman is different from man in an "accidental and inessential" way—Bermen postulates a Platonic grammar of character in which gender is shared: persons of both sexes are born with an intelligence of either gold or silver, and so forth (F2v–3). These are distinctions that could serve to justify a social and political order in which status is linked only to performance. But for Bermen, as he later makes clear, the gender and finally also the sex that constitute the androgynous norm are masculine and male.

Following Galenic theory, Bermen maintains that man and woman are reflections of each other sexually:

> Why are the organs of woman less susceptible to the influence of a beautiful spirit [soon to be identified as proper to man] than are those of a man, since they are the same? She has a body composed of homogeneous organs, such as bone, nerves [and so forth]. . . . And the seven heterogeneous organs [that is, brain, spleen, and so forth]. . . . As far as accidental [i.e., sexual]

[19]*Brief Discours pour la réformation des mariages* (Paris, 1614), vol. 4 of *Variétés historiques et littéraires*, ed. E. Fournier (Paris, 1856), 6.
[20]Louis [Le] Bermen, *Le Bouclier des dames* (Rouen, 1621), sig. A8v.

organs are concerned, man and woman go together. . . . Doesn't she have
all the members of nutrition and generation that man has?   [F5r–v]

The perfection of the body and its intellectual and moral capacities,
however, are to be seen in the man. To make this point, Bermen cites a
case similar to that mentioned in Montaigne's "De la force de l'imagination" and described in contemporary clinical terms by Jacques Ferrand: a
woman at her best can become a man—indeed, she *is* a man—"as we see
from the example of a girl from one of the notable merchant families in
Cassine. Much loved and coddled by her relatives, but at the same time to
discourage that fatuous indulgence and cuteness that make daughters
incapable of fear, without which they cannot be instructed, she was sent
to friends, who, going to punish her for some insolence suited to her sex,
found that she had changed sex and had all the parts that distinguish a
man from a woman" (F7). The force of this sensational report of hermaphroditism derives from its context in feminist apology. For here, as
in the literature of patriarchy in general, it is masculinity and maleness
that is valorized. Femininity and femaleness are identified with infantile
behavior; a girl must be educated not only in the masculine virtues but to
be male.

Feminists who seriously supported ideas of reform on the basis of an
equality of sex and gender were almost bound to consider natural law:
reform that was not based on a correct evaluation of the principles of
social and political order could not hope for success. But what were these
principles? Rejecting the literature of patriarchal authority, some feminists characterized patriarchal attitudes as *perversions* of a legitimate vision
of sex and gender relations as egalitarian rather than hierarchical. At the
conclusion of many of their inquiries was the prospect—represented
with ever more alarm—of a patriarchal society fundamentally aberrant
and perhaps beyond reconstruction on better and feminist principles.
Masculine behavior was associated with violence, envy, and, even more
important, greed. Feminists complain specifically of poverty, that they
cannot own or manage property; and of a lack of education, a consequence and a cause of their powerlessness.

Nicole Estienne, for example, in her *Misères de la femme mariée* (1619),
writes that there is nothing "more miserable . . . than a woman subjected
to wicked men who, incapable of affection, as is clear from their tyrannical laws, make themselves masters of [her] body and will." A marriage
based on such laws was not instituted by God, but is rather a corruption
of an original "happy accord."[21] Estienne's purpose in alluding to the first

---

[21]Nicole Estienne, *Les Misères de la femme mariée, Variétés historiques et littéraires*, ed.
Fournier (Paris, 1855), 3:323.

marriage is to find a basis to condemn male greed. The first couple lived without property and enjoyed a compatible harmony of interests; her male contemporaries are so hardened by their desire for wealth that love is irrelevant. "To arrange for a marriage, they think only of goods and lineage and do not consider conduct and character" (327). They care about property because it guarantees their authority. "A husband glorifies himself in the thought that it is only by his labor that his wife is sustained, and that he alone brings bread to the house." Her contribution is ignored, evidently because it is unremunerated; her opinion is not sought: "she has to expect to obey instantly whatever he commands without asking the reason for it" (330). Estienne describes this abuse in political language: it is a form of "injustice" because it usurps a "God-given right to self-government"; it is a theft of "cherished liberty" (331). Grounding her claim to equality in all respects in the first creation, Estienne's criticism implies a norm, a counterimage of marriage as a partnership of social and political and, more important, economic equals. She rejects the idea that a woman's worth is something like capital, to be used wholly at the discretion of its owner, rather than human, capable of initiating its own forms of wealth with its own kind of capital: wit, energy, resourcefulness. What Estienne sees that patriarchy needs to deny—woman not as a bearer but as a producer of wealth—indicates the instability of ideas of traditional domestic order. Writers even as late as Charron asserted that woman is categorically subject to man; Estienne, a feminist, assuming a natural equality, now links a man's authority over a woman to his possession and control of the couple's wealth.

Other feminists focus on the education available to women; some, such as Jacqueline de Miremont, return to questions of gender and consider "feminine" as opposed to "masculine" ways of thinking. In her *Apologie pour les dames* (1602), Miremont represents the fallen Eve, a figure of both respectful curiosity and enlightened humility, as a model of human intellectuality. She is contrasted to a typical man who has yet fully to discard the pride she had to relinquish when, after she succumbed to the temptation to know everything, God punished her for exceeding prescribed limits. Miremont bases her defense of Eve on a rejection of thought based only on logic and reason, which she identifies as masculine, in favor of thought that entertains logic and reason and also transcends them in the mystery of spiritual awareness, which she identifies as feminine.

Miremont quite pointedly rejects any connection between feminine thinking and the passivity characteristic of women who decline to be educated. She asks her women readers to acquire learning and repudiate the "false friends" who "teach them in their youth only ignorance, who exhaust their spiritual faculties in games of indolence, who want them to be capable only of spinning, who praise them as born for serving men and the exercise of their tyranny." Impatient with apologies that are designed to make women content with inferiority, she adds: "Would that these dwarfs who to raise themselves debase you, who cannot see your suns from their caverns [of ignorance], could love your shining glory."[22] High-minded ventures tend to be arduous, however, and before celebrating the advantages of a life beyond the distaff, Miremont distinguishes between a woman reader who is a feminist and will approve her program of education and her opposite, a woman reader who is an antifeminist and will not. In a sense, the distinction has been implicit in the literature of protest from the beginning of the previous century. Just as there were men who espoused feminism, there were women who rejected it.

The latter pose a logical problem. For if there are women who reject the notion that they have cause to protest *as a group*, the practices that have been judged to discriminate against woman risk being reclassified as correct. The protesters are regarded as exceptional and the acquiescent as confirming natural differences between the sexes. At the very least, Miremont will have to differentiate between kinds of weakness: the docile woman who declines the rigors of intellectual life is not to be confused with the feminist woman who nevertheless embraces the virtues of modesty, humility, compassion. "Blast with [your] lightning the pride of those who would deny you a place," she urges her female readers, only then to reflect on their reluctance: "No, you refuse; your quiet spirit wants to keep its repose, and let my frail spirit . . . show how more competence could result in greater power [*combien plus grand effect seroit plus grand pouvoir*]" (A5v).

Crucial to her enterprise is a reinterpretation of the figure of Eve. The nature of her original sin—to long for knowledge—testifies to her strength of intellect (in contrast to Adam, who merely follows her lead); but the nature of her punishment—to lose paradise and be subject to man—is a sign of the greater mystery of the divine will. Logic and reason are thus comprehended and superseded by paradox and faith, and the image of the temptation and Fall becomes a moral paradigm: reason is exercised to its limits, but pride in reason is chastened by a recognition of these limits. By Miremont's account, Eve's sin is almost heroic: "How much homage do we pay Satan," she asks, "not to know everything, as Eve did, but to have everything"; that is, we honor Satan by loving possessions, not knowledge. Miremont then withdraws from the implications of this statement with a disclaimer that puts her promotion of

---

[22]Jacqueline de Miremont, *Apologie pour les dames ou est monstré la précellence de la femme en toutes actions vertueuses* (Paris, 1602), sig. A4. This treatise is dedicated to the Countess of Mont-gommery (*sic*).

intellectuality in a Christian perspective. "What," she exclaims, "do you wish to approve Eve's action?" (A10v). Rationally, of course, she might well do so, since her argument is based on the conviction that women ought not to be content with their ignorance. But finally she makes a distinction between simple ignorance and an enlightened awareness of the true scope of human reason. It is true that "an ignorant person is rarely a heretic," and that "in the sacred labyrinth [of the problem of original sin] our reason is no guide; our ancestors fell," she argues. Therefore, "let us reverence the secret [of their fall] . . . we cannot explain it; he who does not want to learn about that knows more [*plus en sçait celuy là qui moins en veut apprendre*]" (A10v–11). A form of *docta ignorantia*, Miremont's feminized intellect avoids heresy not by endorsing ignorance and dismissing rational thought but by embracing knowledge through testing and at last accepting the limits of reason.

The full impact of the paradox—weakness as strength—is apparent when Miremont transforms the figure of Jesus into a complex androgyne whose masculinity demonstrates the weakness inherent in manifestations of pride, whose femininity reveals the strength expressed in merciful behavior. Jesus was a man, she claims, just as "he was poorly dressed . . . in order to conquer our enemies by the weakest part." As a man, he shows the futility of pride in a way no woman, made of the stronger stuff of humility, could do. Addressing her male readers, she adds, "He was a man in order to tell you that if you left your self-centered ways you could hope to share in his mercy. . . . Be therefore reluctant audaciously to raise your knowledge beyond the pure letter of Scripture, to astonish nature with your enormities. . . . I have neither the skill nor the power to show you the suffering you bring us" (B4v). Here femininity is valorized in the context of deprecatory references to a concept of knowledge that by going beyond Scripture loses its own moral relevance. Miremont condemns as masculine the kind of mental activity that takes a classical imperium over nature as its sole object and justification, a conquest that, understood as man's relation to woman, is simply tyrannical.

Charlotte de Brachart's *Harengue* (1604), which also apologizes for women's education, begins by defining knowledge as itself morally neutral; it is simply *science*, which can be used in the interests of furthering good or bad causes. Railing against those who think women should remain ignorant, she exclaims that "if knowledge [*science*] is not in itself erroneous [that is, if it is sound] . . . its effects can be good only in a wellborn spirit." But even if knowledge comes to one who is "of a malicious spirit," and therefore risks being put to bad uses, it is in fact "more likely to diminish vicious habits than to augment misdeeds."[23]

[23]Charlotte de Brachart, *Harengue faicte par damoiselle Charlotte de Brachart surnommé*

For, she adds, "the knowledge of letters" is always moralistic: "we never find in histories and stories, whether sacred or prophane, ancient or modern, that an evil act is left unpunished, and I would say in an exemplary manner" (A2). Brachart is not quite clear here about the difference between the amoral *science* to which she first refers and the moral *letters* that will probably contribute to the reformation of an immoral reader. But in a subsequent discussion of the experience of intellectual life, she brings the two together as components of a single endeavor of the mind which has as its purpose the trial and testing of the thinker in relation to his or her social and political circumstances.

"Ignorance" is "vice"—she claims—because it conduces to behavior that is unexamined; it allows persons to let themselves drift without judgment in "what is held to be custom." "Ignorance" will not, in any case, preserve a "simplicity" of soul, as is alleged by men who want to bar women from education, for "simplicity is a function of the heart and the will and not of the mind, and God asks it of men and women alike" (A2v). The operations of conscience are common to both sexes and a feature of their spiritual life, in which they are equally responsible. Knowledge is rather a matter of expertise, the means by which a defective or deficient society can be reformed. Nor should it be eschewed on the grounds that such reformation is socially disruptive; or if it is, then the act of disruption, admitting that it must move beyond anarchy, is itself constructive. The impulse to criticize rather than to accept the status quo is an affirmation of life: avoiding such effort, "you hide your life, which is really to hate life itself. For the person who envelops himself in ignorance . . . makes his life a death and seems to have left being . . . there is nothing in the world a great soul hates more than ignorance" (A4). Knowledge of and for woman is particularly critical in that custom and the status quo, the very things that always require examination, have systematically excluded her from authority and power. Like Bursati, Brachart implies that of the two sexes, woman is in a better position to perceive the need for social reform, because she has less to lose if it is realized.

Is woman also better suited to enact this reform? Brachart does not claim, and perhaps does not even believe, that woman is inherently more moral than man or that femininity, in its traditional association with the unshowy virtues, is more Christian than masculinity. She does, however, conclude that woman is inherently more adept than man at *using* knowledge for getting and retaining certain kinds of power, both politi-

---

Arétuse qui s'adrese [sic] *aux hommes qui veuillent deffendre la science aux femmes* (Chalon-sur-Saône, 1604), sig. Av.

cal and economic. Citing male envy as the reason for the disempowerment of women, "who are a little more clear-sighted in the affairs of the world," she indicates their real competence: "for with [even] the little attention they give to worldly matters, they make themselves more capable of reason, more prudent in every area, better tempered in their emotions, and . . . they conduct themselves according to a sounder judgment in the affairs of which they take charge." This superiority is so decisive that were women to escape "miserable subjection, . . . [men] would be constrained to renounce the management of important business in order to leave us in charge, recognizing that we are much more capable than they are in enterprises both great and small" (A3).[24] Feminists of the previous century had frequently commented on the marginality of woman, usually to offer reasons why it was unjust. Here Brachart suggests a further point: it is the very marginality of woman that gives her "clear-sightedness" its valuable perspective on society as a whole.

It seems likely, however, that the concept of equality stood a better chance of being approved when feminists focused mainly on questions of gender. The *Défense des femmes* (1617) of Le Sieur de Vigoureux depicts human beings as capable of both masculine and feminine behaviors but praises the latter as more conducive to social harmony. Vigoureux represents patriarchy as actually authorized by no more than a pervasive fantasy of male superiority in which women are the blameless accomplices. No reason is openly given for their acquiescence in a system that denies them so much. But, Vigoureux slyly hints, by protesting women will have to assume masculine traits and hence lose the high morality of femininity.

> Reason prevails with them, and the knowledge they have of their nature and their duty constrains them; they confess that having been extracted from the side of man they owe him obedience and service according to God and reason. If by being too obedient to their husbands they are called wells of stupidity, they should be praised rather than blamed, for they would rather be thought simpleminded than impudent and proud.[25]

The statement recalls the traditional view of the model wife as her husband's "mirror" and the ironic consequences of her unfailing obedience when her husband is in error, that is, her own misdoing. By reflecting on this "mirrored" vice of hers, Vigoureux makes apparent the

[24]Several of Brachart's contemporaries claimed the superiority of women over men. See, i.a., *L'Excellence des femmes* (1618) and Le Sieur de Gaillar, *Le Bouclier des femmes* (1621).

[25]Le Sieur de Vigoureux, *La Défense des femmes contre l'Alphabet de l'imperfection et malice des femmes* (Paris, 1617), sig. B5v. Vigoureux prefaces his defense by saying that "it's not reason that makes the author [of *L'Alphabet*] speak in this way, but madness [*une rage*]" (B).

perils in the rule of obedience: women are in a double bind; either they obey and are thought stupid or they rebel and are condemned as proud. Vigoureux later asserts that woman's belief in her nature as inferior to man is erroneous, actually imposed by men. Her humility is not to entail subservience; neither Plato's gratitude at not being created female nor all the laws that control women "can dismiss them from the rank they have by virtue of being creatures of God, vitalized by a soul, and of the same reason as man" (B5v).

It is man's behavior rather than woman's that is given to error; it is massively presumptuous, desiring constantly to exceed due place and decorum, and to profess moral rectitude when in fact to acknowledge a failing would be the more honest response. Objecting to criticisms of women's vanity, Vigoureux points out that theirs is merely "an excess in dress."

> As for men, [vanity] is manifest not only in dress but in everything you can think of. Men, not women, exhibit the vanity of wanting to make themselves gods; men by their ambition and vanity lose the rank and status they have; men by their vanity are imbued with fury, with maniacal desires that cause them to forget themselves; the vanity of man causes a failure to know God. . . . And because the vanity of woman is restricted to dress, it does not cause either the ruin of kingdoms, or murder and manslaughter, or cruelty and infidelity, or treachery and impiety, or treasons as that of man does. [I9r–v]

Suggestive, perhaps, of a counterreformist devaluation of the humanists' *vita activa*, Vigoureux's condemnation of men's vanity and ambition distinguishes between the kinds of virility women should cultivate and the kinds of femininity men should imitate. In both cases, perversions that lead to cruelty and vanity are condemned.

What, then, makes for normative relations? Paradise, Vigoureux claims, was the locus of a unitary sex and gender. And, he implies, wherever androgyny is currently experienced (even if imperfectly), some aspect of paradise is recreated; wherever it is suspect, paradise is lost anew. "Is not man unhappy," he asks, "who, being a creature of God to whom complete dominion was given, . . . lost it by [the original] sin? . . . [He also lost] the woman who had been created only for him, [the two together] being one flesh, one soul, though divided in kind and in behavior" (H4v). Vigoureux resituates the Fall in a timeless present in which man is always in the process of alienating himself from woman by rejecting their fundamental identity—an identity that, according to this retelling of the scriptural myth of origins, is the only evidence of man's own generativity. To see the woman as other and wholly different is therefore a repetition of an original mistake.

But just as the paradisal bliss of true union is lost through a repudiation of androgyny, so it is recoverable through a reformation of the relations of identity between man and woman. Vigoureux concludes by suggesting that generation symbolizes that recovery. The couple's child is a palpable manifestation not only of their union but of their unity. It is specifically not what it was for such writers as Barbaro and Alberti, who insisted that paternity alone had meaning. According to Vigoureux, "the blessedness that ought to have been present in human beings before the Fall is rediscovered in the joy of the father in his children, in the joy of the new mother in her baby. It must be admitted that only this sign of the works of God remains to man and woman" (H4–5). In a sense, Vigoureux bases his entire idea of a just and beneficent society on the fact of generation as a process into which man and woman enter together.

To attack deeply held beliefs in the superiority of maleness and masculinity was never easy, however, and some feminists abandoned the demand for equality in favor of an examination of the social and political contexts in which inequality was sanctioned. This investigation revealed what feminists had always asserted, that women served as the scapegoats of patriarchy, and demonstrated (or tried to demonstrate) what feminists had come to claim, that social ills were created by men, particularly by their desires to possess and to control not only women but each other. The so-called Chevalier de L'Escale, in his *Champion des femmes* (1618), takes as the object of his attack a certain "Anonymous Misogynist," the author of an unidentified treatise blaming women for the world's vice. To complement his protest against such generalities, L'Escale looks at discrete issues.

Exemplarity, he insists, has nothing necessarily to contribute to a notion of type; the example can be unique or representative: "if in so many centuries and among so many millions of women, you can find one Messalina . . . whom our lying pedant describes at such length, you can find every day among us thousands of Sardanapaluses and Heliogabaluses."[26] What an example signifies is, in other words, a function of the argument in which it appears: L'Escale's strategy is to supply instances of misogynist blame with an appropriate context. If, as the Misogynist has claimed, women stock the bordellos, it must be remembered that "it is [men] who build them, who situate them, who furnish them, who maintain, preserve, and defend them" (C8). Nor is sexual morality ever a simple matter, he goes on to say. Phryne was a notorious prostitute, but "the way of life of her century made it in some way excusable for her to sell her body. She was praiseworthy in that everything she got from her

[26]Le Chevalier de L'Escale [Joseph-Juste Scaliger?], *Le Champion des femmes* (Paris, 1618), sig. C9v.

dirty pleasures she spent on respectable buildings and public works, to the honor of her country and to the confusion of men" (C12). L'Escale follows a similar procedure when he contends with such standard misogynist complaints as that a woman's work is trivial (the education of children is the basis for future security); women are treacherous (how can they be when they lack positions of responsibility?); women speak too much (they have no other weapon); witches are women (but they are also men); and so forth. In one instance, his perception of the contexts in which women are blamed for what society suffers includes an attempt to analyze the relations of authority and power informing context. Women, he observes, are said to be notoriously given to causing jealousy in men as well as to experiencing it themselves:

> What man who, wanting to see the way the world works with a sane and honest eye, is not constrained to admit that men live today in a way that makes jealousy an utterly useless burden for women. And not only in France . . . but whoever travels through Italy, Spain, Muscovy, Tartary, Turkey, in short all Asia, Africa, and America, will find that poor women in all regions are so tyrannized by the jealousy and control of men [*trop exacte garde des hommes*] that they are miserable.   [P2v]

Thus he establishes that the proposition "women are responsible for jealousy, whether in themselves or in men" is refuted by "the way men treat women." The value of his argument from contexts lies less in its claims than in its method: it brings to the understanding of misogyny a knowledge of the real circumstances in which, as he would have us believe, it is supposed to but does not in fact have meaning. In effect, L'Escale maintains that women cannot be jealous because they do not find themselves in situations in which jealousy is possible.

Fairness Dismissed

Yet the foundation on which Renaissance feminism came to be constructed was inherently fragile, largely because the theories used to advance arguments for women's rights were philosophical and literary. More precisely, these theories lacked a clear and demonstrable reference to the increasingly complex economic developments that were taking place in the large urban centers of Europe. Changes in property law, modes of production, and control of trade affected the status of women directly and critically, but they were rarely the subjects of feminist protest. Literature attacking the abuses of patriarchy did not consider the chief impediment to women's welfare—their poverty—in the kind of detail that would have made reform likely. Whatever the jurisdiction, married women in particular suffered. They owned little in their own right and of these limited portions controlled almost nothing. The notion of shared gender, the valorization of the feminine, the presumption of an equality of some sort within marriage and throughout society were ideas that helped to focus upon and to undermine, to a degree, certain of the assumptions of patriarchy. But they did little to encourage an analysis of the factors that contributed to the actual conditions in which women lived. A return to a consideration of the ideology of patriarchy—the pervasive, uncritical, and apparently often unconscious acceptance of the inferiority of women—provided at least one feminist with a chance to take note that her project had practically failed. Moving from hope to despair, the essays of Marie de Gournay illustrate *in nuce* the main features of a development that took over a century to unfold.

Gournay's principal feminist work, *L'Egalité des hommes et des femmes* (1622), presents her case with the evident expectation that its points on issues of fairness will be accepted in good faith. Her analysis of the abuse of patriarchal authority and power begins with the analogy that has featured so frequently in earlier discussions: the household as the state. But rather than attempt to determine how superior and subordinate should relate to each other within the hierarchy of these governments, she submits as her ideal the humanist (and Montaignesque) concept of *mediocritas*. Like most contemporary political theorists, she sees that the notion of the prerogative is conflicted: the actual power to enforce behavior (however it is expressed) is not always in line with the nature of the office or the right to use that power (however it is circumscribed by law). The higher the rank of the officer and the more extensive the forces at his disposal, the greater the risk that the prerogative will be abused. Like François Billon, she insists that monarchs must seek the virtue of humility above all others, "inasmuch as they have the power but not the right to violate the laws and equity, and encounter as much danger and more shame than ordinary persons in so doing."[27] In effect, she suggests that political power should be self-regulating; the most powerful are to be most wary of exercising their power. She assumes the value of an

[27]Marie [Jars] de Gournay, *L'Egalité des hommes et des femmes, 1622*, in Mario Schiff, *Marie de Gournay, fille d'alliance de Montaigne* (Paris, 1910), 58. Gournay dedicates her treatise to Anne of Austria, daughter of Philip II of Spain. On Marie de Gournay, see, i.a., Tilde A. Sankovitch, *French Women Writers and the Book* (Syracuse, N.Y.: Syracuse University Press, 1987), 73–99; Marjorie Henry Ilsley, *A Daughter of the Renaissance: Marie le Jars de Gournay, Her Life and Works* (The Hague: Mouton, 1963); and Domna Stanton, "Autogynography: The Case of Marie de Gournay's 'Apologie pour celle qui escrit,'" *Autobiography in French Literature*, French Literature ser. 12 (1985): 18–31.

equality of persons, conceived in the moral and spiritual terms common
to Christian and especially reformist political thought.

The significance of Gournay's discussion of *mediocritas* to her subject,
the equality of men and women, becomes clear when she addresses Anne
of Austria (to whom she dedicates her treatise) as a model of both royal
and feminine propriety. In the queen as monarch *and* woman is to be
realized the ideal of an equality of man and woman: "you will serve as a
mirror to women and the object of emulation to men throughout the
universe if you raise yourself to the rank and standing I shall represent to
you" (60). The figure is a paradox: if the queen as woman is raised as a
monarch, as monarch she is also lowered as a woman, that is, as a human
being. And a female monarch stands a better chance of governing with
mediocritas, since from birth she has experienced the effects of being
judged inferior by virtue of her sex. Gournay then makes her political
paradox the pretext for the philosophical principle underpinning her
thesis. Dismissing writers who prefer women to men, she says: "I, who
flee from all extremes, content myself with equaling women with men;
in this matter, nature is as opposed to superiority as to inferiority."
Appearances may seem to give the lie to the idea that men and women are
equally virtuous. But, Gournay maintains, an analysis of patriarchal
practice can remedy this impression. One would be justified in thinking
women inferior *only* if it were not clear that men confined them "to an
unquestioned and necessary preoccupation with the spindle and only the
spindle." Hence they seem to lack "dignity" and the "means," the "temperament," and the "faculties" to develop it (61).

The analysis of ideology such as Gournay undertakes inevitably presents methodological difficulties. As she realizes, a critique of an ideological position needs to use a language comprehensible to ideologues.
Because the misapprehension she has just outlined—that women are inferior to men—is not generally subject to any kind of critique, she
observes, male "eloquence" is able to develop (proverbial) expressions of
prejudice against women which then come to be associated with an
enhanced social status for men and a view that male wit is *au courant*: "But
what of the fact that they think they have the right to be considered
accomplished gallants and declare themselves such as if by edict; why
should they not also judge women to be idiotic by a corollary edict?"
(63). By this account, the mentality of the ideologue is despotic; it has the
same disregard for reality as does that of the tyrant. Hence, she concludes, she will not attempt to prove her thesis by "reasons, for the
opinionated will contradict them, or by examples" (that is, by experience, the traditional resource of defenders of women), but will rely on the
"authority of God, of the Fathers of the Church [*des Arcsboutans de son
Eglise*] and the great men who have served as the light of the world" (63).

Gournay's reliance on these authorities defies the example of much feminist protest—beginning with Christine de Pisan, who realized that hers must be a counterauthority of a purely feminine voice—but it is in keeping with her belief in the wisdom of an egalitarian politics, and perhaps also with her humanist training. Considering philosophy, she speaks of the role of women in Plato's *Republic*, of the divine insight of Diotima in his *Symposium*, of Plutarch's assertion that the virtue of men and women are the same, of the similar beliefs of Seneca and Aristotle(!), and of Erasmus, Poliziano, Agrippa, and Castiglione. In history she sees a record of circumstantial and cultural rather than natural and sexual differences: "do we find more difference between men and women than between women themselves, according to their education, and whether they have been brought up in a town or a village, or in a cosmopolitan environment?" (65). She indicates the irrational features of customary and positive law. The Salic law proves nothing about the competence of women but instead is the product of political circumstance; it is in any case invalidated by the equality of authority among the male and female peers of the realm and by the practice of appointing regents (68). Sexual difference has to do only with reproduction, despite the fact that gender is registered regularly in language: "there is nothing that resembles a cat [*chat*] on a windowsill more than a cat [*chatte*]. A man and a woman are so much the same that if the man is more than the woman, the woman is more than the man" (70).

Gournay scrutinizes divine law in a similar manner, selecting texts that substantiate her case for equality, overlooking the many others that do not. She especially insists that women have prophetic gifts just as men do. This argument bears on the ability of women to enter public life: "God [established] them also for judges, teachers, and priests of his people in peace and war" (71). Paul's dictum to the contrary is, like the Salic law, circumstantial, and refers only to a particular congregation. Even the sex of Jesus is historical accident. Had he been a woman, he could not have preached to crowds (75). Gournay even reinterprets the status of a married woman: "if Scripture has declared the husband head of the wife, it would be the height of stupidity for him to suppose that this automatically gives him dignity." His headship is rather a reflection of the greater physical strength of the "male, who cannot permit himself to accept submission" (76). The tendentiousness of these interpretations can have escaped few readers, nor would any acquainted with Scripture have found it difficult to challenge them or to refute Gournay's argument from divine law as a whole had she not concluded with an oblique but extended reference to woman's spiritual equality: "woman was found worthy of having been made in the image of God." To find Genesis 1 invoked to justify an assertion of equality may appear rhetorically weak, since this text had always had to stand against its contradiction in Genesis 3. Gournay chooses to comment on it because she sees it as the basis for the sacraments, the acts and privileges commonly available to all Christians, which are, in turn, the basis for all social and political privileges. Because woman has a divine image, she states, she can participate in the "holy Eucharist, the mysteries of Redemption, in Paradise, and in the vision and even possession of God." Is it then logical to deny her the "advantages and privileges of man"? Or is this not to elevate man above "such [sacred] things and thus commit the most grievous of blasphemies"? (77). Gournay's argument for the equality of men and women rests on the same foundation as the arguments for constitutional monarchy made by the more radical political thinkers of the previous century. For the author of *Vindiciae contra tyrannos* and others—such as John Ponet in England and George Buchanan in Scotland—the monarch is finally beholden not to his subjects but to their conscientious assessment of his devotion and obedience to divine law. Luther had claimed that the right of resistance to political authority was derived from the spiritual equality of Christians. Later writers included in that right an obligation to depose a godless ruler. For Gournay, the political importance of spiritual equality is discovered not in the common obligation of monarch and people to observe divine law but in the shared privileges of men and women before customary and positive law.

Gournay must have hoped that her treatise would meet with approval and conceivably even begin to alter the status quo. But her subsequent essays, *Le Grief des dames* and *L'Ombre* (1626), show her studied disappointment at her reception by contemporary writers. The substance of *Le Grief* may derive from her preface to the 1595 edition of Montaigne's *Essais*. If so, it indicates something of her intellectual development as she moves from editing Montaigne's *Essais* to participating in and finally renouncing the defense of women. The content of the preface is determined largely by its author's use of the topos of modesty, which nonetheless also reveals a measure of true self-deprecation. Imitating but also distinguishing herself from her mentor, she declares that she is

> a confused woman, inferior in everything, of extremely slow understanding and wit, with a memory so feeble that three points of an opponent in debate are sufficient to overwhelm it with its own simplemindedness, and above all possessing the most ridiculously nondescript appearance in the world. I wish to punish this imperfection that wounds me so much that I have to draw attention to it in public.[28]

[28]Marie [Jars] de Gournay, *Le Grief des dames* (Paris, 1626), 91.

But whatever Gournay's hope that the readers of the *Essais* would take her self-portrait rhetorically (as Montaigne's readers certainly took his), she had realized by the time she wrote *Grief* that she could no longer afford to be apologetic, even in a conventional way. There she represents herself as the victim of mistreatment that causes the kind of self-deprecation she expressed earlier. The irony of the figure of the writer as *folle* which appears in her preface mutates to the pathos inherent in her isolation from her peers in her later work:

> Be happy, reader, if you are not of that sex to which is forbidden all good things inasmuch as it is forbidden liberty. Yes, it [being female] denies them just about all the virtues, which are formed for the most part by the discipline of power, with the result that the sex believes that its only happiness, its sovereign and sole virtues are to live in ignorance, play the fool, and serve. Especially happy is the person who can be wise without being criminal: maleness gives you that just as it denies women all action, judgment, eloquent expression, and the credit of being believed or at least listened to.   [89]

For, she concludes, even if a woman has the eloquence of a Carneades, she is dismissed with a smile or shake of the head: "a woman speaks." Implied in this accusation is, once again, the assumption of an equality between the sexes. Men refuse to read women authors "without wanting first to know whether they themselves can write something that all kinds of women ought to read." In order to justify their decision, "they ought to demonstrate that their skill is everywhere better than ours; or at the very least that it is equal to their neighbor's, if they are below the highest rank" (94). Rejecting a concept of merit that rules out achievement by women, she argues that both sexes should be evaluated by a single standard.

L'Ombre, as its title suggests, establishes that Gournay knew her position on equality was untenable, given the intellectual mores of her society. In her "Advis au lecteur," she paradoxically rejects her reader, who she imagines is male and therefore hostile: "I realize that we will get along best if we separate. Is it not an act of charity to put distance between two irritable characters [*deux esprits scabreux*] before they actually quarrel?"[29] But the rejection is also a warning, for, revising further the use to which she put the topos of modesty in her preface (there using it as a disclaimer) and in *Grief* (there as an indictment of prejudice), she imagines that her book has become a weapon to attack and reform her reader should he ignore her words and persist in reading. It is "an openly simple book, its

[29]Marie [Jars] de Gournay, *L'Ombre: Oeuvre composé de méslanges* (Paris, 1626), sig. ii.

designs woven after its own fashion, its lack of method and doctrine displeasing to my well-wishers, its feebleness to me." Nevertheless, even in its weakness it is "a thing of contentiousness . . . a perpetual refiner of manners and morals [*perpetuel raffineur de moeurs et de jugemens*]; it hunts you down from corner to corner to put you in doubt, sometimes of your prudence, sometimes of your learning" (iiv). Here the fragmented and disorganized quality of her *Ombre*—its deliberate openness, presumably to criticism by men—is reconceived as a means of entrapment, much as if Gournay had come to believe that her reader could be moved only by expressions of distress and anger. Reason and eloquence had not worked.

Yet the success of such self-representation remains at last uncertain. Describing herself once again in her "Advis," Gournay now terms herself "the shadow of a dream." Her writing is therefore the shadow of a shadow of a dream, reflecting its author obliquely in symbolic references. In a humanist context this image might be interpreted as supporting the Pyrrhonism exemplified in Montaigne's *Apologie de Raimond Sebond*. As an image of a woman writer in a patriarchal society, however, it conveys an experience of nothingness of a different and nonphilosophical kind. Explaining the impresa on the title page of *L'Ombre*, a pine tree, with its subscript, "Man is the shadow of a dream and his work is his shadow," she states that "this device serves to declare that I feel the opprobrium of my time and I accuse my century, which holds me back in it as much as I strive to move out of it." Her book will find no contemporary reader; it will only testify that her beliefs "ought to be reborn in a season friendlier to the Muses and in a spirit more resolute than mine" (iii).

In short, she recognizes that her writing has been without a present effect, not because it lacks merit but because—being unseasonable—it has not been given a hearing. She is despairing, yes, despite the possibility that her "grief" may be a device to catch her reader's sympathy and turn him (or her) into an ally. She trusts in a future audience, perhaps. But finally she is unique among Renaissance feminists, as far as I know, in giving her readers a sense of the history of her protest, and of feminist protest as her generation knew it. The past, present, and future of her text suggest that she sees it as part of a movement in history.

ENGLAND

Depoliticizing Marriage

To write conventionally of marriage and insist on a hierarchy of sex and gender in the early years of the seventeenth century was implicitly to invoke the main tenets of feminist protest, if only in order to argue against them. By contrast, treatises conceding legitimacy to a wife's demands for more autonomy were often committed to what might be termed the depoliticization of marriage. They qualified, first, the extent to which the family constitutes a little government or state; and second, the kinds of power and authority husbands and fathers can exercise within it. This effort produced a picture of marriage as personal in nature, excellent to the extent that it reflected the goodwill of its parties rather than their willingness to perform specific duties. In most cases, however, attention to the affective side of marriage did not alter its essential character: husbands were to control wives, their minds, bodies, and property. Love and devotion were important but they were still elicited in relations between a superior and his subordinate.

In contemporary Protestant literature on marriage, the repressiveness of the institution is sometimes mitigated by an emphasis on the dignity of the wife and her nurturing functions as well as on the husband's duty to love. Such apologists stress the Pauline concept of marriage and its analogy in the relation of Christ and his church. Yet in their view a husband's love also mandates a wife's obedience—to the point of legitimating severe corporal punishment. Thus William Whateley's *A Bride Bush or A Direction for Married Persons* (1623), on the whole sympathetic to the humanity of woman, permits a husband to beat his wife to the point of "knocking her brains out"—a degree of brutality not envisaged by the most conservative moralists. A close analysis of the duties of a married couple as they are described in many of these Protestant treatises often reveals that writers who insist on an emotional intimacy and even a kind of moral equality between husband and wife see no need to alter the customary relations between them.

In fact, what I have called the depoliticization of marriage was in some ways an illusion—important because it testified to a certain embarrassment on the part of apologists for that institution, apparently moved by feminist protest, but of little effect in practice. Most marriage treatises of this period condone behavior that ratifies patriarchal discipline: cases of conscience aside, a wife must never repudiate her husband's authority. If she does, she is liable to punishment. The more impressive the concessions to some sort of equality, the more dextrous the manipulation of evidence in support of the male-headed household. Latent in all such accounts is the fear of anarchy. Robert Pricke's *Doctrine of Superioritie and of Subjection* (1609), a treatise on the need for obedience within the family and the state, exemplifies this ambivalence. It strongly qualifies the assertion that "husband and wife are yoke fellowes in one estate," "joynt companions in many workes and duties which serve to the glorie of God": as the husband has greater "authoritie," "courage," "strength," "sharpenesse and quickenesse of witte," "insight and forecast," than his wife, he "is to governe and to order her in all things."[30] And even if he has none of these qualities in reality, he nevertheless has them in theory, a condition that continues to justify his rule. What if

> sometimes the wife is wiser, more discreete and provident then the husband? It is true: but yet this doeth not overthrowe the superioritie of the man: and therefore if occasion be offered to admonish and advise her husband, she is to performe this dutie with humilitie and reverence; shewing herselfe more willing to heare, then to speake: to be ruled, then to rule and governe her husband. [L1v–2]

A similar message is preached in the various homilies of the period. In "An Homilie of the State of Matrimonie" in *The Second Tome of Homilies* (1623), the writer promises that a couple will live in "concord" if "hee will use moderation and not tyranny and if he yeelde something to the woman." Yet this "something" could not have been much; "the woman is a weake creature, not indued with like strength and constancie of minde, . . . the sooner disquieted and . . . the more prone to all weake affections and dispositions of mind, . . . and more vaine in their fantasies and opinions."[31]

The "forbearance" enjoined of men was the kind required of a parent. It was predicated on the powerlessness of its object; in a wife's case, it served to perpetuate that powerlessness. And it was easily translated into forms of control. Alexander Niccholes, in his *Discourse of Marriage and Wiving* (1620), for example, sees in love—where "there is no envy; no jealousie, no discontent, no wearinesse, for it digesteth and maketh sweet the hardest labour"—a preventive for the "mismatches" that produce "these lamentable jarres of housholds, worse then the open warres of kingdomes."[32] But such compatibility is possible only if a wife is restricted to certain activities: "bring her to the city, enter her into that schoole of vanity, set but example before her eies, she shall in time become a new creature . . . she shall not blush to do that unlawfully which before shee was bashfull to thinke on lawfully" (E2v). Once again, the quality of the affective life of a married couple depends upon the extent to which a husband can control his wife. She, in any case, is the

---

[30]Robert Pricke, *Doctrine of Superioritie and of Subjection, Contained in the Fifthe Commandement* (London, 1609), sigs. I6v, K2r–v. This edition contains a prefatory letter signed by Samuel Egerton.

[31]"An Homilie of the State of Matrimonie," in *The Second Tome of Homilies, of such matters as were promised and entituled in the former part of Homilies* (London, 1623), sig. Xx.

[32]Alexander Niccholes, *A Discourse of Marriage and Wiving* (London, 1620), sigs. F4v, D4v. The text is dedicated to Thomas Edgeworth.

spouse who is thought most likely to be out of line and hence responsible for the couple's "jarres."

Claims for an equality of husband and wife were sometimes occasioned by discussions of divorce. This was especially the case for those Protestants who considered that marriage was not a sacrament but a "thing indifferent" and to be adjudicated by a civil magistrate.[33] The Protestant clergy, debating the legality of both divorce that permits remarriage and divorce as separation, or *a mensa et thoro,* asked whether women had the same right to leave husbands as husbands did wives. Did they also have the same right to remarry? M. W. Perkins, in his *Christian Oeconomie* (1609), declares that adultery is grounds for divorce and that either party may request it:

> In requiring of a divorce, there is an equall right and power in both parties, so as the woman may require it as well as the man; and he as well as she. The reason is, because they are equally bound to each other, and have also the same interest in one anothers bodie; provided alwaies, that the man is to maintaine his superioritie and the woman to observe that modestie which beseemeth her towards the man.   [I4v]

He also insists that they both may remarry. His reference to 1 Corinthians 7:4—the wife shall have power over the husband's body—may be the reason he later denies the husband much of his customary headship: "Though the husband be the wife's head, yet it seemeth he hath no power or libertie granted him in this regard [i.e., over her whole being, as if that were no more than his body]. For we read not in Scripture any precept or example to warrant such practice of his authoritie. He may reprove or admonish her in word only [but not] with stripes and stroks" (I7v–I8). In other words, Perkins asserts that a husband cannot forcefully compel his wife to do his command, however much she ought to obey him. Here Scripture is used against custom and law to establish limits to the hus-

---

[33]M. W. Perkins, for example, argues that marriage is a sacrament to Roman Catholics in order that "they might by this means raise a commoditie to the sea of Rome, by the sale of their dispensations" (i.e., annulments). He terms marriage a "thing indifferent . . . [because] the kingdom of God stands not in it" (i.e., it is irrelevant to salvation), yet also a state "farre more excellent then the condition of single life": *Christian Oeconomie* (London, 1609), sig. A2. The text is dedicated to Lord Rich. Paul's dictum requiring a couple's mutual sharing of power over the body was evidently sometimes interpreted to license wife-beating; Perkins clearly rejects this interpretation. Against divorce, see R. Snawsel, *A Looking Glasse for Maried Folkes* (London, 1610). For a brief history of divorce in England, see Keith Thomas, "The Double Standard," *Journal of the History of Ideas* 20 (1959): 195–216. For a study of the correspondences and differences during this period between ideas of the marriage and social contracts, including the right to abridge those contracts, see Mary Lyndon Shanley, "Marriage Contract and Social Contract in Seventeenth-Century English Political Thought," *Western Political Quarterly* 32 (1979): 79–91.

band's government. John Raynolds's *Defence of the Judgment of the Reformed Churches that a man may lawfullie not onelie put awaie his wife for her adulterie but also marrie another* (1609) refers to the same passage in 1 Corinthians to make the same point on the question of divorce: "eche having interest in the others bodie, shee may as lawfully depart from an adulterer as he from an adulteresse."[34]

In general, however, discussions of marriage produced subtle reaffirmations of the divine origin of the hierarchy of sex and gender, irrespective of whether the contractual arrangements leading to marriage were represented as based on affective rather than economic or political relations. Thomas Gataker's *Marriage Duties Briefly Couched Togither* (1620) stresses mutual love and its expression in common desires. He tells his reader that if he "accountest her [his wife] one flesh with thee the same with thyselfe . . . there will be no true contentment to thee while thou perceivest discontentment in her."[35] Yet no topic concerns him more than the wife's subjection, established in divine and natural law. An authoritative or "mankinde" woman, he claims, is a political liability; she is a "monster in nature" and threatens "utter ruine oft of the family and of their whole estate" (Cv). Recalling the language of political absolutism, he represents the husband as God's representative on earth, the incarnation of divine will, at least as far as his wife is concerned. A wife's "feare" of him should be "a liberall, free and ingenuous feare (like that feare that the godly beare unto God)" (C2v); if she condemns her husband, "she contemneth God and God's ordinance in him" (C3v). In case of differences, she (like the typically Protestant subject) has the right only to the dictates of her conscience—her submission must be "in obedience of God." Even if she makes decisions for her husband, she must disavow them: "so every action in the family shall gaine itself more weight and procure more them both credit and carry more authoritie with it when it passeth through the husband's hands and is ratified and sealed as it were with his seale" (C4v).

How far such marriage doctrine conformed to actual practice or even

[34]John Raynolds, *Defence of the Judgment of the Reformed Churches that a man may lawfullie not onelie put awaie his wife for her adulterie but also marrie another* (London, 1609), sig. G. Raynolds is principally concerned to prove that Scripture, specifically Matt. 5:32, makes adultery an exception to the rule against remarriage, at least as it is stated in Mark 10:11 and Luke 16:1. These appear to be the texts cited on both sides of the question. He then adduces other situations in which remarriage is also a possibility: the desertion of a Christian woman by an "unbeleeving man" or the taking of monastic vows by either spouse (sigs. D4, E4, F3).

[35]Thomas Gataker, *Marriage Duties Briefly Couched Togither* (1620), sig. Gv. Gataker describes his work as the "raw notes of a sermon," and dedicates it to Robert and Dorothie Cooke, members of the family of his patron, Sir William Cooke.

to general opinion is another question. Gataker's treatise and others like it, notably William Gouge's *Domesticall Duties* (1622), seem primarily defensive when placed in the context of the growing body of writing arguing for the rights of wives. Gataker actually testifies to the existence of his opposition when he declares: "For howsoever women may thinke it an honour to them [to have authority over husbands] yet it is indeede rather a dishonour. A masterly wife is as much despised and derided for taking rule over her husband as he for yeelding it to her" (Cv). Gouge's rather more subtle disclosures on the related questions of equality and rank reveal that the concept of a household government had been at the very least called into question, apparently by persons who took the privileges owed to rank seriously. A woman of high social status had always represented a political anomaly. From the publication of Anne de France's *Instruction* to Bursati's *Defese* the noblewoman's lack of preroga- tive seemed to elicit either justification or protest. The literature on marriage frequently comments on aspects of her dilemma. "Equality" can refer merely to the fact that husband and wife are of the same rank. But because she cannot exercise the same prerogatives within that rank, their equality can be, and sometimes was, perceived as no more than nominal.

Gouge admits that an "equalitie" between spouse in age, estate, and piety are desirable; he also concurs with Perkins and others that husband and wife are equally bound to married chastity.[36] A wife's superiority in any of these respects—especially in rank—does not, however, impinge upon a husband's superiority, given him as a "civill honour" by God (T). True, of all degrees of "inequality" owing to "civill" distinctions there is least between husband and wife (S8). But no wife should judge that instances of near or actual equality with her husband (as in rank or wealth) should provide a reason for seeing a full parity of interests between them. These interests, Gouge argues, are governed by another principle: that of their "common equitie," which functions because of degree, not despite it. Just as magistrates and the clergy acquire their jurisdiction "equitably"—that is, by virtue of their accession to office and without regard to their personal competence to rule—so does a husband; if there are differences, the husband "must have stroak" of his wife's acknowledgment of her inferiority (S8–v). Thus equity determines the

[36]William Gouge, *Of Domesticall Duties* (London, 1622), sigs. T, Ppr–v. Nor is a husband's authority diminished by bad behavior: even if he is a "drunkard, a glutton, a profane swaggerer" and his wife is "sober, religious," her obedience is required. A husband may bear an "image of the devill," yet for "place and office," he bears the "image of God . . . so doe magistrates in the commonwealth, ministers in the church, parents and masters in the familie" (T).

actual *irrelevance* of rank: "in giving herselfe to be his wife, and in taking him to be her husband, she [a woman of higher rank than her husband] advanceth him above herself." And equity permits degree to obtain even when there is mutuality and "fellowship": "for fellowship hath respect to the thing itselfe, inferiority to the measure and manner . . . in giving light the sunne and the moone have a fellowship, but in measure and manner the moone is inferiour" (Aa3r–v).[37] For a wife to judge otherwise is, according to Gouge, an instance of "monstrous selfe-conceit . . . [and] intolerable arrogancy, as if she herselfe were above her owne sex and more then a woman" (T). That wives did so judge is clear subsequently from Gouge's accounts of their disobedience, which also reveal, paradoxically, that the order he champions in theory may work badly in practice: "If an husband be a man of courage and seek to stand upon his right, and maintaine his authoritie by requiring obedience of his wife, strange it is to behold what a hurly burly she will make in the house; but if he be a milke-sop and basely yeeld unto his wife, and suffer her to rule, then, it may be, here shall be some outward quiet" (T7v). Gouge's proposition—that "equitie," not "equality," characterizes relations between husband and wife—is challenged by his own description of domestic "hurly burly"—a social reality that defies the model of marriage he has constructed.

William Whateley's *A Bride Bush or A Direction for Married Persons* (1623) registers a similar wish to liberalize marriage doctrine without any loss of the husband's power and authority. He sees that marriage is founded on intimacy: "let one house and one bed hold them constantly; let them be as much in each others presence as business of their callings will permit; let them often talke together and be sorry together, and be merry together and communicate their joyes and griefes each with other and this will surely knit them if anything will."[38] Legally they are also a unit; they enjoy a "community in their estates" (which are actually at the disposition of the husband), but a wife's material requirements must be respected: "without all question she that hath a part in himselfe cannot

[37]Gouge's application of the principle of equity to relations within marriage takes as the relevant "rule" the equality of man and woman in both social and spiritual senses. He derives their different political statuses from an equitable interpretation of their respective functions, that is, from the "measure and manner" in which they behave toward each other. This is, of course, a circular argument; their behavior is mandated by the very political relations it seeks to justify. As it was conceived in law, equity in the sphere of domestic affairs ought to address the conditions under which the political relations of the spouses are actually realized; that is, the circumstances in which the rule of the wife's subordination is mitigated or abrogated.

[38]William Whateley, *A Bride Bush or A Direction for Married Persons* (London, 1623), sig. G2v. Whateley dedicates his text to his father-in-law.

want right unto that which is for his honest purposes; how can any man with good conscience forget that part of his publike and solemne covenant wherein he endowed her with al his worldly goods?" (M1r–v). And the husband ought not to limit in any way the exercise of his wife's conscience; "not alone in things that are unlawfull but also in things that to the wive's erring conscience seem unlawful must the husband forbeare the urging of his authoritie. What she upon some reason (to her thinking though not indeed and truth) grounded upon the Word of God doth account a sinne that the husband ought not to force her unto" (Q2v). He cannot, in other words, interfere with the exercise of her free will, even if it leads her to error. And when he does use his authority, it must conform to certain rules of decorum. He must not command his wife "foolishly," lest she think "that he doth nothing now but even upbraide her with her inferioritie" (V4v), or unreasonably, for "even a gentle natured woman is apt to prove refractary and hardly can she hold her heart so much under but it will mutinie at the least if not breake forth into open acts of rebellion" (Xv). In supervising her generally, he should never be "overly harsh":

> If the wife but forget a little businesse; if she but tarry a little longer in company of her neighbours than he thinks fit; if she but answere him a little angerly or so forth, the fist is up, or cudgell snatched, and she must little lesse then smart and bleed. Thou mad and mankind bedlam, who taught thee to bee so cowardly tyrannous towards so neere a person though an underling? [Z2]

When a wife's disobedience can be clearly established, however, her subordinate status and its political consequences are emphasized. What is remarkable in Whateley's account is not that he finds it necessary to preserve traditional domestic order but that he is at such pains to justify the brutality that it entails. A wife's overt insubordination automatically cancels her husband's obligation to treat her gently and with consideration. He must not use violence routinely,

> but if she will raile upon him with most reprochfull terms, if shee will affront him with bold and impudent resistances, if she will tell him to his teeth, that she cares not for him, and that she will doe as she lusts for all him; if she will flie in his face with violence and begin to strike him, or breake into any such unwomanly words or behaviour, then let him beare awhile and admonish and exhort and pray; but if still she persist against reproofes and perswasion, if her father be living, let him be intreated to fight; if she have none, or he cannot or will not, I think that husband shall not offend in using a fool according to her folly [i.e., with a rod on her back; Prov. 26:3]. [P2r–v]

And because a husband beats a wife not "to ease his stomacke" but rather "to heale his owne flesh with a corosive," his recourse to corporal punishment "may well stand with the dearest kindnesses of matrimony" (P2v). Certainly a husband is entitled to resort to whatever form of punishment he judges correct because his power, like that of a magistrate, is from God (P3).

It is in fact for Whateley's endorsement of the essentially *political* concept of marriage that his *Bride Bush* is memorable. Far from endorsing the concept of woman as equal to man, Whateley repeatedly stresses the *inferiority* inherent in the office of wife; "she must acknowledge her inferioritie," "she must carry herselfe as an inferior" (Bb3); "after the tying of this knot [marriage]," he warns the wife, "God will have thee subject." Assuming for the sake of debate her actual moral and intellectual superiority, he terms it inconsequential, and even a detriment: "better were it for a woman to be of meane capacitie and slow wit and every way simply qualified (so that she can put upon her the spirit of subjection) than to be adorned with all the good qualities of nature . . . and thereby be made selfe-conceited against her husband" (Bb4v). Unlike Vigoureux, who saw in the obedience enjoined of a wife the pretext for a universally salutary humility and proposed it as a model for her husband and society in general, Whateley regards the subordination of the wife simply as the condition of *her* subjection. In his view, an abused wife, like the subject of a tyrant in an absolute monarchy, has no right to dissent, to resist, or to rebel against an unreasonable rule. A husband's command is always legitimate, even when it is unwise, unkind, unjust, or irreligious; a wife's refusal to obey it does not include her right to resist being punished for disobedience (Ee2v): "Most times women are ready to thinke in such cases that they may lawfully take leave to depart from their husbands but Paul saith plainly no" (Ee3). What if, Whateley asks in conclusion, she is "in danger to have her braines knocked out"? She must go to a magistrate "and seeke safetie with a purpose of returning upon such securitie" (Ee3v). The guarantor of such "securitie" is unspecified.

Whateley's picture of the dark side of marriage testifies to the profound social unrest that the traditional form of the institution, on a collision course with feminist protest, was in the process of creating during the period in which he wrote. He represents wives who resent and resist the "inferiority" he insists they must accept; conversely, he portrays husbands who are desperate to hold on to what he regards as their rights. At the same time, certain of his remarks suggest that the kind of marriage he proposes has more life in theory than chance of serving as an actual model for contemporary practice. He disapproves of a wife's giving her husband a nickname, such as "Tom, Dick, Ned, Will, Jacke, or the like," for it indicates that she is "overbold of her husband's kindnesse." But acknowledging that he has heard "many *good* wives" do so (Cc4), he admits that this is a practice not only common but accepted by persons of whom he cannot disapprove on other grounds.

The effort to depoliticize marriage by insisting on the importance of marital love did little to alter the status of the wife as subordinate. Attempts to reformulate the laws and customs that controlled the activities of women represented a more concerted attack on the hierarchy of sex and gender. The more assumptions sustaining the superiority of the husband were questioned, the stronger and more insistent were arguments for equality between the spouses—and not merely spiritual and intellectual but political as well. Two important concepts emerged in the course of this debate. First, that performance is distinct from position and posture: a competent, courageous woman is not a virago and her autonomy need not invariably entail rebelliousness. And second, that positive law protecting persons from some kinds of abuse, especially assault and battery, applies to activities in the private as well as the public sphere: the husband cannot function as an absolute lawgiver within his family, nor can the exercise of his prerogative be unlimited.

An Apologie for Women (1609) by W. H. (William Heale), focusing directly on legal questions, resumes the discussion of the relation of natural law to the law of nations and positive law which had earlier preoccupied critics and defenders of woman's rule. Unlike John Leslie and David Chambers, who had to discredit what was advanced as the natural law of sex and gender insofar as it could be made to bear on the conduct of political life, Heale invokes the natural law of kinship or "kindness" as the basis for establishing licit marital conduct. Nature mandates that the "sovereign union of male and female" is fundamentally kind: "in all kindes between them there is found no unkindnesse."[39] If positive law is, as Heale then maintains, "an artificial collection of naturall precepts" (B2v), it ought not to legitimate unkindness between men and women. That it does in certain circumstances is wrong. Divine law had always mandated that husbands love their wives, but it could also be understood to mean that such love is to be expressed as harsh discipline. Heale's notion of kindness forbids such actions and in so doing effectively reinterprets divine law. The particular example of unkindness he chooses to examine is wife-beating, a subject actually being debated at Oxford: "how can it [positive law] dispense with [i.e., approve] so unnatural an

---

[39]W. H. [William Heale], *An Apologie for Women, or An Opposition to Mr. Doctor G[ager] his assertion, who held in the Act at Oxforde Anno 1608 that it was lawfull for husbands to beat their wives* (Oxford, 1609), sig. Bv.

action as for a husband to beate his wife, the one part of himselfe, nay his other selfe, or his better halfe?" (B2v). That this behavior, a form of "tyrannie," was sanctioned he attributes to "ancient ages of barbarisme" (B3)—custom is, in this respect, erroneous.

Heale is sensitive to the possibility that the positive law he is discussing risks being more or less ideological, that it was enacted to foster the interests of the most powerful and so is especially resistant to analysis. To justify his interpretation of positive law as naturally promoting marital kindness, he has to deny that man, however powerful in matters of government, has any authority over woman *in nature*. That is, if creation is organized as a hierarchy, which he does not dispute, the fact of place is irrelevant politically: men have no "priviledge" over women. Heale claims that the "supposed infirmities" of the latter derive "either from a prejudicate opinion, which ever miscarieth, or from particular example, which never concludeth" (D2). Excellence and depravity are not gender-specific qualities, instituted in nature, but rather are common to both men and women. With respect to women, "prejudicate opinion" can and often does become explicit and prescriptive as positive law, justifying behavior that ought to be strictly illegal according to "true" judgments. "For where trueth seemeth to have taken up her seate, there authority disguiseth her; and where she cannot be found, there fancie would needs discrie her. Everie man making an idol of his owne conceite, and partially impairing an other man's judgment" (E2v–3). By so acutely discerning the role of male "conceite" in establishing the "authority" that validates customs and, presumably, makes laws that enforce the inferiority of women, Heale points to the ideological character of the concept of a hierarchy of sex and gender. He repudiates it by advancing a radically different countermodel in which woman is the political equal of man.

First, he declares, the law gives a woman the right to leave a husband who beats her. He is obliged to maintain her while she is absent from him for this reason; she is required to return only if he gives her assurance that the beating will stop (G2v). Second, by extension, any "absolute *indecorum* in manners (as they confesse the beating of a wife to be) is an absolute breach of the law"—wife-beating is only one instance of such indecorum (G4). Whether it is also grounds for separation, *a mensa et thoro,* is unclear, but presumably a case might be made on these grounds. And third, women, and specifically wives, are protected legally against beating and other such kinds of indecorum by the fact that they are "in the law free burgesses of the same citie whereof their husbands are free, and free denisons in the same land wherein their husbandes are free: both participating [in] the same rightes, both injoying the same liberties" (G4). This is an extraordinary claim, given the scarcity of rights that wives appear to have been able to claim by law. The rights to which Heale refers are obviously those established in positive law and associated with social and economic status. Although they may, as he suggests, derive from divine law (Hv), such as the right to active resistance in the political thought of radical reformers, they are owed to women by virtue of their membership in the political bodies of the city and nation (or land). In conclusion, Heale blames the "serpent" for instituting marital discord and an unjust allocation of rights between husband and wife (I3v), an important theoretical point because it implies not only that inequality in marriage postdates Eve's creation from Adam's side (a point other apologists have also made) but also that it is simply divisive rather than constructively complementary or necessary, as conservative thinkers had often maintained. No other critic of marriage envisaged such profound changes in the legal status of the wife as did Heale.

Popular Polemics and Their Contradiction

The most popular vehicles for feminist debate in the previous century had been such ostensibly misogynist satires as Gosynhill's *Scholehouse.* By the turn of the century, however, there was a considerable London market for frank polemic on the woman question. Ester Sowernam, the author of one such work, states that the subject of the virtue of woman is widely discussed in both print and ordinary conversation.[40] Conspicuous for its role in stimulating controversy was Joseph Swetnam's *Arraignment of Lewde, Idle, Forward and Inconstant Women* (1615), which drew passionate responses from feminists, including Sowernam.[41] Many of the points rehearsed on both sides are commonplace.

---

[40]Ester Sowernam, *Ester Hath Hang'd Haman; or, An answere to a lewd pamphlet entituled The Arraignment of Women* (London, 1617), in *Half Humankind,* ed. Katherine Usher Henderson and Barbara F. McManus (Urbana: University of Illinois Press, 1985), 219. For an overview of feminist polemic of the period, see, i.a., Betty Travitsky, "The Lady Doth Protest: Protest in the Popular Writings of Renaissance Englishwomen," *ELR* 14, 3 (1984): 255–83; Linda Woodbridge, *Women and the English Renaissance* (Urbana: University of Illinois Press, 1984), 74–113; and Elaine V. Beilin, *Redeeming Eve* (Princeton: Princeton University Press, 1987), 247–66. The treatises of Swetnam, Sowernam, and Munda, in addition to the *Hic Mulier/Haec Vir* pamphlets, are reprinted in part in Henderson and McManus, *Half Humankind.*

[41]Joseph Swetnam, *The Arraignment of Lewde, Idle, Forward and Inconstant Women* (1615), sig. B. Swetnam addresses the "common sort of woman" and he allies himself with the narrator of the *Corbaccio:* "wronged men will not be tongue-tyed," he declares (A2). A good deal of the information about Swetnam derives from the play that satirizes his misogyny: *Swetnam the Woman Hater, Arraigned by Women.* For a discussion of Swetnam and the controversy surrounding his pamphlet and the play, see Coryl Crandall's introduction to *Swetnam the Woman Hater: The Controversy and the Play,* ed. Coryl Crandall (West Lafayette, Ind.: Purdue University Press, 1969).

But new to the literature defending women is the demonstration of links between the social value placed upon chastity, the practice of prostitution, and the legalized poverty of women. This element is theoretically important, since it is the discussion of economic issues, generally scarce throughout this period, that explains in some measure the failure of feminist protest to inaugurate political change. Women had economic value—that is, received material compensation for their services—typically as wives and as prostitutes. Neither form of compensation provided them with significant authority or power. Wives held a rank but not the command that usually went with it; correlatively, they possessed wealth but could not spend or manage it. Prostitutes actually earned money—if we assume it was not appropriated by their pimps—but were regarded as social outcasts. Wives were protected by patriarchy and hence had some stake in the system. Prostitutes had implicitly rejected the system but were not capable of overturning it; as a result, they were its unwilling victims. Of the two possibilities, marriage was clearly much better. Equality under law, as feminists were beginning to envisage it, was simply impracticable, given economic facts.

One of the first responses to Swetnam's *Arraignment,* Rachel Speght's *Mousel for Melastomus* (1617), questions the extent to which the husband's status as "head" confers on him the right to control the activities of his wife: "no authoritie hath hee [God] given him to domineere, or basely command and imploy his wife as a servant." It rather enjoins "an extraordinary affection."[42] Constantia Munda's *Worming of a Mad Dogge* (1617) continues the attack but focuses on misogyny as ideology. Since printed invective against women is now very common, she notes, some might think that "community in offense could make an immunitie," and fail to condemn the wrong.[43] Astute women are nevertheless obliged to speak out against misogynists: "Know therefore that wee will cancell your accusations, travers your bils, and come upon you for a false inditement" (B4). She then proceeds to discount Swetnam's charges by terming them false and derivative: his is merely the "refuse of idle-headed authors . . . a mingle-mangle gallimauphry" (D4). She implies that when "community" takes "gallimauphry" seriously, "some" are persuaded that "gallimauphry" loses its nonsensical character and becomes acceptable opinion or establishes a moral consensus. What passes for the truth about woman ought therefore never to be immune to criticism simply because it is uncontested. Her own analysis of the rationale for preferring the male and masculinity over the female and femininity reveals that bias

[42]Rachel Speght, *A Mousel for Melastomus* (London, 1617), sigs. D4v, E.
[43]Constantia Munda, *The Worming of a Mad Dogge* (London, 1617), sig. B2v.

against women actually results in the moral and political degeneracy of men.

Challenging Swetnam's apparent celebration of war and its hardships, she asks: "[Is it] more agreeable to humane nature to march amongst murthered carkasses, which you say man rejoyceth in, than to enjoy the fruition of peace and plenty, even to dance on silken carpets, as you say is our pleasure? What man soever maketh warre, is it not to this ende, that he might enjoy peace?" (Fv). To deny gender stereotypes, she has implicitly appealed to the concept of androgyny. For if to make war is masculine and to love peace is feminine, then clearly men are both masculine and feminine. Nor is their masculinity necessarily preferable—her critique of war refers to the arts of peace. She does not, however, then pursue her investigation further to ask what an understanding of misogyny can reveal about the relations of power that are at stake in the society that both sponsors and is shaped by it. Sowernam's *Ester Hath Hang'd Haman; or, An answere to a lewd pamphlet entituled The Arraignment of Women* (1617) provides a partial answer to this question.

Sowernam's defense of women, conducted through the fiction of a "trial" of Swetnam and his *Arraignment,* examines the nature of scapegoating and the economics of prostitution. Her analysis of scapegoating is familiar to feminist protest; she argues the general point (established at least as early as Champier's *Defense*) that if woman is deemed inherently weak, she cannot be held responsible for the ills of the world. If considered realistically, the misogynist argument from provocation common to scapegoating—men sin because women provoke them—indicates the responsibility of the "provoked" and the innocence of the "provoker." "What," demands Sowernam, "do women forcibly draw? Why, men are more strong. Are they so eloquent to persuade? Why, men are too wise. Are they mischievous to entice? Men are more holy. How then are women causes to bring men to ruin?" (237). The passage places the misogynist in a double bind. Women cannot be accused of violent crime (including rape) because they cannot "draw"; men must therefore bear responsibility for all social activities that depend on sheer physical force. But because men deny women the wit necessary to overcome male intellectual force, they must also bear responsibility for the general state of society. Men can blame women for sin only if they admit to losing control over women—that is, their own fallibility. Such an admission would undermine the rationale for that control. Sowernam compounds the logical impasse in which she has placed her opponent by entertaining further the myth of male superiority. How is it, she asks, that men so often reject the consequences of their own influence? Her case in point is the widow: although men value a young woman for her impressionability, they scorn widows for their stubbornness. "How cometh it then that this gentle and mild disposition [of the maid] is afterwards altered?" If (weak) women can only reflect the treatment of men, men must have "framed" them to the "froward conditions" they exhibit in maturity. The only other explanation contradicts another assumption of patriarchy, that women are not strong enough to be their own teachers and have no reason to develop their independence. Sowernam understands that to preserve what she regards as the fiction of their superiority over women, men choose the immature woman to represent the norm and consider the mature woman aberrant, not only unattractive but unmarriageable: "you [Swetnam] give a great charge not to marry a widow," she observes (239).

Sowernam finally addresses the crucial issue of wealth. This discussion, too, follows from her earlier one. For if woman is inherently strong and capable of cultivating "frowardness," at least with respect to the demands of men, why has she so little real power? Why, indeed, is she the object of systematic slander? Sowernam suggests that the ideology of patriarchy sustains and is sustained by the related institutions of marriage and prostitution, that it is manifest in the comparable lives women lead in the family and in the brothel. Answering the charge that women are "lascivious, wanton and lustful," she begins her analysis by referring to the scapegoat theory: woman is blamed for the sexual indiscretions of man. She goes on to show that *this* type of scapegoating, an essential feature of patriarchy, sets up the basic parameters of women's lives as her contemporaries know them. Denying that woman is innately lustful, Sowernam claims that more often than not she is deceived by man. A woman who prostitutes herself does not prefer that life, she is forced to accept it: in order to seduce her, some man "will pretend marriage; another offer continual maintenance. But when they have obtained their purpose, what shall a woman find: just that which is her everlasting shame and grief: she hath made herself the unhappy subject to a lustful body and the shameful stall of a lascivious tongue." Once fallen, a woman becomes notorious. Her sexual indiscretion does not go unnoticed because it is in the interests of men to publicize it; thus they can know that a woman, having lost her value as a bride, can continue to be bought and (probably) at an even lower price. Men, Sowernam argues, must not think that they can have it both ways; they cannot extoll the honest woman who is in her own right always destitute and reward the whore who is never morally acceptable: "if a woman or maid will yield unto lewdness, what shall they want? But if they would live in honesty, what help shall they have? . . . How many pounds will they [men] spend in bawdy houses, but when will they bestow a penny upon an honest maid or woman, except it be to corrupt them?" (241).

The inference Sowernam asks her reader to draw from her analysis of prostitution indicates something about her view of marriage. The acts of respecting and impoverishing on the one hand and seducing and remunerating on the other bear directly on the economics of that institution and, more particularly, on the real poverty of wives. Such practices guarantee that the chaste and marriageable woman will be poor in terms of the wealth she can acquire on her own; that the promiscuous and rich woman will be unmarriageable because of the way she has acquired whatever wealth she has obtained. These distinctions are, admittedly, rather abstract. Married women could and did possess property, although they could use it only at the discretion of their husbands; women could and did earn money in trades other than prostitution, although they were prohibited from pursuing certain kinds of business and, more generally, from acting as free economic agents. Given the economic structure of patriarchy, however, Sowernam's point is theoretically valid: a woman gets rich because she sells the only property over which she has any control, and this action puts her outside the bounds of civilized (patriarchal) society. Within that society and (presumably) enjoying the benefits of civility, she is and must remain without economic power.

The failure of sixteenth-century feminist debate to produce any social change was due to a variety of factors, one of which may have been the ambivalence that women could be made to feel toward the prospect of securing rights as representatives of their sex irrespective of rank. Any interest that women might have in securing equality of the sexes could be depicted as if it threatened privileged social status. The pamphlets titled *Hic Mulier* and *Haec Vir* (1620) show feminism in relation to this conflict. Feminism is here perceived less as a protest against patriarchy than as advocacy of a *social change* that by effacing differences between sex and gender—allowing women to behave or sign themselves as men—would also efface those between social ranks. Cross-dressing, a mode of behavior in which a person's sexual identity is not declared openly and his or her gendered character is deliberately registered as fluid or androgynous, is represented as an invitation to anarchy. Social order, it is implied, is maintained by an identification of sex with gender, an identification that, as Renaissance feminists had recognized in the terms available to them, denied women the possibility of assuming masculine virtues and the scope for public life which they make possible. These pamphlets criticize a feminism that they represent as furthering the possibility of a social leveling implied by such earlier protests as Bruni da Pistoia's. No longer a question of a lack of distinction between man and woman within a rank, feminism is now associated with a lack of distinction between ranks.

Distinctions of rank were of course observed in many ways, dress being the most common and visible. Their preservation had been the object of sumptuary laws throughout the previous century, and especially during the reign of Elizabeth. [44] Differences of sex and gender were also marked by dress (a long gown signified that a person was either clerical or female and would behave in feminine ways), and were similarly controlled by law and custom. Vives and others had insisted that women should not wear men's clothes, a view echoed later and parodically by Ben Jonson's Puritan, Zeal of the Land Busy. Dress had social importance partly because it determined behavior, at least to some extent; women's clothing inhibited the kind of physical activity characterized as masculine. These differences were not, however, understood as absolute. The celebration of virility in women, particularly by literary or historical example, had rendered restrictions on dress open to question; and the notion of shared gender had revealed the behavior of men and women—including their choice of dress—as a matter of convention rather than of divine or natural law. As these pamphlets indicate, sumptuary laws were not strictly enforced in Jacobean London, the locus of new "City" wealth. The signs of gender (masculine or feminine) and rank (gentle or base) were, in other words, subject to qualification. Their increasingly uncertain meaning in the early years of the seventeenth century was the pretext for attacks on what the writers of these pamphlets saw as a principal agent of social destabilization: the concept of shared gender, epitomized in the figures of the mannish woman, *hic mulier,* and the womanish man, *haec vir.* Both figures had real counterparts, women and men who appeared cross-dressed in public. The charges against their literary representations are directed at what these figures could be made to signify—that is, the effacement of rank and hence an inevitable decline into anarchy. It is through seeing feminist issues in relation to the well-being of civil society that the writers of *Hic Mulier* and *Haec Vir* cast doubt on the goals of feminist protest. True, these pamphlets are in some ways endorsements of opposing points of view, *Hic Mulier* more obviously against the cross-dressed woman, *Haec Vir* apparently a defense of her, at least in part. But *Haec Vir*'s is such a poor defense and its conclusion—that men must resume control of women—is so orthodox that its function as polemic is like *Hic Mulier*'s. Like the earlier work, it gives feminism a context that renders it practically indefensible. [45]

---

[44]See the account of Elizabethan sumptuary laws in Frank Whigham, *Ambition and Privilege: The Social Tropes of Elizabethan Courtesy Theory* (Berkeley: University of California Press, 1984), 155–69.

[45]On the relation of these pamphlets to contemporary drama and the representation of

The authors of these pamphlets are strategically astute in associating the signs of gender with social status. The numerous defenders of women who had claimed equality for men and women within ranks had not explored what its economic consequences might be. Equality of virtue, or comparable worth, was rarely imagined as conferring legal or economic rights on the women whose work was now to be as valued as a man's. In reality, the only authority and power to which a woman could lay claim was in almost every case inextricably bound up with her status as daughter, wife, or mistress; with certain exceptions it was entirely dependent on the goodwill of the man who exercised patriarchal rights over her. The writers of the *Hic Mulier/Haec Vir* pamphlets exploit the fact that women were dependent on men in this way. They attack feminism by using as weapons the very conditions feminism endeavored to change. They assume that they can make a case against feminism by reminding their readers (and they are implicitly readers of the gentry rather than of the "middling sort") that it is more advantageous for women to hold on to the privileges of rank that they enjoy as dutiful dependents than to renounce them in favor of taking a stand for equality with men. The linkage of such a position with the destruction of existing society further strengthens their case. Money was crucial to their antifeminist argument: as long as most women of every rank were financially dependent on men, whether or not they had property, there was a chance that all their activities, and especially those that took place in public, could be controlled merely by threats of material deprivation. To present feminism in this light makes it appear prospectively counterproductive of the welfare of the ordinary woman. Still more pernicious is the fact that the movement, now seen as misguided, is reduced to an event that can take place only if men, whose money sustains these protesting women, allow it to go on. These points illustrate the nature of a reaction that may have guaranteed that feminism would remain a subject of literary and philosophical debate rather than be realized in new privileges and responsibilities.

Hic Mulier ties privileges of rank to sex and gender. The critic of the mannish woman and her companions, virtual caricatures of the great

---

women, especially in *The Roaring Girl*, see Mary Beth Rose, *The Expense of Spirit: Love and Sexuality in English Renaissance Drama* (Ithaca: Cornell University Press, 1988), 64–92. Rose describes the recent interpretations of the *Hic Mulier/Haec Vir* pamphlets; I concur with her reading of the first, but see the second as thoroughly antifeminist as well, although rhetorically different. See also Valerie R. Lucas, "*Hic Mulier*: The Female Transvestite in Early Modern England," *Renaissance and Reformation/Renaissance et Réforme* 24, 1 (1988): 65–84; and for a view of cross-dressing in nondramatic literature, Winfried Schleiner, "Male Cross-Dressing and Transvestism in Renaissance Romances," *Sixteenth Century Journal* 19, 4 (1988): 559–75.

female knights of legend, begins by charging them with monstrousness and, more important, licentiousness. By making "your bodies like an-ticke boscadge or crotesco worke, not halfe man, halfe woman; halfe fish, halfe flesh; halfe beast, halfe monster: but all odyous, all divell," he declares, "[you] have cast off the ornaments of your sexes to put on the garments of shame."[46] What concerns the critic is not the meaning of the female androgyne as a sign of protest against patriarchy but her indif-ference to modesty, which he regards as a form of attack on society as a whole. He sees that the androgyny of *hic mulier* indicates that she is not socially enlightened (as the tradition of feminist representation suggests) but rather degenerate. To the critic, female androgynes are either "ragges of gentry, torne from better pieces for their foule stains . . . or . . . the stinking vapours drawne from dunghils, which nourisht in the higher regions of the ayre become meteors and false fires . . . till the substance of their pride being spent, they drop down againe to the place from whence they came and there rot" (B). Whether "ragges" or "vapours," they defy their inherited and customary status in society, and their proper place is consequently at its lowest levels. Neither money, which has enabled them to effect such horrible changes—"such as are able to buy all at their one charges . . . will bee man-like not only from the head to the waste but to the very foot and in very condition"—nor rank can mitigate their shame: "no more shall their greatnesse or wealth save them from one particle of disgrace which these monstrous disguises have cast upon them" (B2). In effect, the critic of the mannish woman has testified to the fact that he perceives feminism as an action undertaken by women *as a class,* however it had been perceived in the previous century. And because the critic also sees that women *as a class* have no social status apart from what they can claim individually, as a wife or a daughter, he can go on to maintain that insofar as women are feminists, they are without social status, both declassed and antisocial.

The mannish woman's reply discredits feminism further and along lines similar to those already sketched by the critic, although in apparent contradiction to him. Herself a gentlewoman, she excuses her androgyny by confessing that it is not a protest in support of women's rights and hence is not destructive of rank, as he has claimed; rather it champions the rights of persons of particular ranks who happen to be women. She suggests that were not the status and privileges of aristocratic and gen-tlewomen threatened by women in the City, the wives of burgesses, who ape the clothing and manners of their betters, she would renounce her

---

[46]*Hic Mulier; or The Man-Woman* (London, 1620; facs. rpt. Exeter: Scolar Press, 1973), sig. A4.

masculine attire. As it is, she insists that there must be a "difference amongst women."

> Must but a bare payre of sheeres passe between noble and ignoble, betweene the generous spirit and the base mechannick; shall we be all co-heires of one honor, one estate and one habit? . . . What is it that eyther the lawes have allowed to the greatest ladies, custome found convenient, or their bloods or places challenged, which hath not been ingrost into the Citie with as great greedinesse and pretence of true tytle. [B4v–C]

Now City women, she complains, are even copying their betters' feminist cross-dressing, which is "as frequent in the demy-palaces of burgars and citizens, as it is either at maske, tryumph, tilt yeard or play house" (C).[47] Removed from discussion altogether are the vital issues of feminist protest; it is represented as no more than a quarrel concerning the propriety of a stratified society.

Hic Mulier's conclusion indicates the importance of economic issues in the containment of feminist protest. The critic of the mannish woman, taking seriously her objections to the pretensions of upstart City women, which at least in theory have no place in feminist argument, proposes that the solution to the problem of anarchy is not to efface gender differences by cross-dressing, as *hic mulier* has misguidedly done, but to insist more vigorously on the sexual determination of gendered behavior by forcing women into positions of greater economic dependency. The relevant power here is the power not of symbolic action by women but of the purses held by men. To fathers and husbands belongs the cure of social degeneracy: "doe you [men] but hold close your liberall hands," he states, "and these excesses will either cease or else dye smothered in prison in the taylors' trunkes" (C2v). Women who contest differences of gender or distinctions of rank are the disruptive elements of society. What the critic is concerned to crush is, arguably, not only or perhaps principally feminism as it supports the rights of women as opposed to men, or even the rights of rank over wealth, but rather what feminism represents in practice: women of whatever rank, or claiming no rank and hence "of the dunghill," who manage to take action as a class in their own interest.

To press the case against feminism in *Hic Mulier*, the writer of *Haec Vir* represents the chief points of protest in a context that both restates and further discredits them. The mannish woman of the earlier work reappears, this time to determine whether her "deformities" are more or less

---

[47]The text is here difficult to read in its first edition; the speech is the mannish woman's. See the punctuation in Henderson and McManus, *Half Humankind*, 272–73.

"injurious to nature" than those of her counterpart in androgyny, the womanish man.[48] *Hic mulier* argues first that she merely exercises "free-dome of election" and follows her "owne will and pleasure" (A4v)—a habit that is neither "base" nor "slavish" but rather the special gift of nature. Cross-dressing makes her not therefore unnatural but only "an enemie of custome," and "for custome, nothing is more absurd, nothing more foolish" (Bv). The fact that she flouts the manners that conventionally characterize young women is to her credit: "[I] that am not dumbe when wantons court mee, as if asse-like I were ready for all burthens, or because I weep not when injury gripes me, like a worried deere in the fangs of many curres; am I therefore barbarous or shame-lesse?" (B3). Her statements might have been lifted from the literature of protest but with this crucial difference: they all raise questions that cast doubt on the integrity of the speaker. "Freedom of election" is given to every Christian but not to follow a personal "will and pleasure." The status of custom is mixed (especially in England); it can grow stale and inhibit necessary change but it is also the basis for much common law. There the concept of custom was regularly referred to when rights were asserted for the people as against their limitation by statute. *Hic mulier's* sturdy rejection of helplessness is clearly virtuous but it is also expressed in unfortunate circumstances, among "wantons" and "curres." Her conclusion, a declaration of woman's equality to man, is weak in comparison with contemporary feminist discourse:

> We are as free-borne as men, have as free election, and as free spirits, we are compounded of like parts, and may with like liberty make benefit of our creations: my countenance shal smile on the worthy, and frowne on the ignoble, I will heare the wise and bee deafe to ideots, give counsell to my friends, but bee dumbe to flatterers, I have hands that shall be liberall to reward desert, feete that shal move swiftly to do good offices, and thoughts that shall ever accompany freedome and severity.   [B3]

This declaration stops short of endorsing the kind of equality that offers a direct challenge to the superiority of man politically—the kind actually envisaged by Heale and others. As a protest, it might well have found a place in one of the more moderate treatises on domestic government. By avoiding any mention of the most contentious points of feminist protest, the writer of *Haec Vir* is able to render the mannish woman's position identifiably feminist but at the same time no substantive challenge to patriarchy, and so to prepare his reader for his final point.

---

[48] *Haec Vir; or The Womanish-Man: Being an answere to a late booke intituled Hic Mulier* (London, 1620; facs. rpt. Exeter: Scolar Press, 1973), sig. A4.

Man must resume his hegemony. Throughout the previous century, literature on household government condemned the uxorious husband, he who rejected his vocation as head of his family and so confused the divine order of things. The writer of *Haec Vir* invokes the concept of a hierarchy of creation as the basis for reforming a society now corrupted by persons who share gender and obscure rank. His is a reaction to feminist protest, a counter–reformation of what appears to have been the elements of a popular movement. Revealing her new docility, the mannish woman confesses what her reader has long since intuited, that for her the distinction of rank that she so desires is dependent upon identifying sex with gender and that such an identification is what she really desires. Because men have abandoned their masculinity (and ceased to control women), she asserts, the authority and power belonging to men have been (reluctantly) adopted by women lest distinctions of rank disappear: "no other meanes was left us *to continue our names* and to support a difference" (C2v; my emphasis). She echoes her critic's association of anarchy with androgyny and thereby draws attention to the source of the greatest weakness in the program of Renaissance feminism: that women had no control of wealth and therefore could not determine their place in the social order independently of men. Antifeminism here represents its opposition as caricature, the mannish woman who is desperately unhappy, anxious only to resume her former dependence, her only guarantee of economic security and social acceptance.

Afterword

RENAISSANCE literature in defense of women was pan-European and transgeneric. It appeared in virtually all kinds of narrative, in epic poetry and prose fiction as well as in political and philosophical writing. Written by hacks in hope of patronage, by great writers (perhaps for the same reason), printed in the centers of the book trade—Venice, Paris, Lyon, and London—as well as by a few regional presses, it must have reached vast numbers of persons, some of whom may not have been literate. Ostensibly concerned with the fate of women in patriarchal societies, it actually addressed issues beyond those of sex and gender.

Its larger reference is always to the nature of authority and the status of the subject in relation to authority. The reason is obvious. If the primordial couple—figured in the androgynous and yet to be divided Adam, the only true *homo* that human history can claim—can be said to represent the first subject, then the woman who breaks out of this couple is the second subject and one more representative of historical experience. While Adam as *homo* is directed to obey the eternally true Word in his (or their) felicitous state of paradise, Eve as *femina* must obey the reduced and de-ribbed Adam as *vir*, her fallible yet absolute governor. Hers is therefore the position of the quintessential political subject, forever bound conscientiously to honor divine law and also assiduously to obey her human superior. Her predicament is exemplary: the various claims made for the autonomy of woman in Renaissance literature reflect more general and imposing social conflicts. What, for example, is the proper role of the governor in a society in which the law must protect everyone? What are the protections owed the weakest and most subordinate subject? What is the calculus by which to determine the human virtue or value of persons of different ranks? On what basis is virtue discriminated among persons of the same rank? And because virtue has no certain relation to rank or social office, what is the language—the forms and modes of communication—that ought to obtain between the subject who is powerful, cunning, and competent yet without authority and (typically) her male superior, who has the right but not the skills to command? As Jean Bodin saw, the question here is one of accountability: the actions of a subject who is powerful yet without authority are not necessarily bound by the laws that ordinarily limit that authority. Hers is therefore the power of the usurper and potentially it is limitless, as in a tyranny. Conversely, the failure of a person in authority to exercise his rightful power invites anarchy. Bodin's solution to these irregularities is framed in terms of sexual difference and as if in view of the original Fall: he concedes the power of the female subject but denounces its deployment.

Successful in providing the substance of political debate, Renaissance defenses of women had no standing at all as the pretext for a social revolution. Their proposals for reform—in education, marriage law, and public life—never came to constitute an actionable program; there was no single party to press for change and no locale from which to lodge particular complaints. The loyalties of these writers were, moreover, always divided. I believe they took more seriously than twentieth-century sociologists can imagine the real meaning of androgyny, in part because they were so used to thinking figuratively. To win concessions for woman meant also to benefit man; to feminize society was to open possibilities for the human male. Through the early decades of the seventeenth century, feminists never stopped invoking the principles of fairness which they believed could be derived from the common origin of man and woman in the image of God, even after, like Marie de Gournay, they had given up hope of seeing such principles acted on. Their efforts expose what today we call the cultural construction of gender. More boldly, they envisage gender not only as distinct from sex but also as flexible. Gender is androgynous.

Of course, feminist theory came into inevitable conflict with patriarchal practice. Feminists learned, among other things, that power is rarely if ever renounced because of appeals to principles. And in fact their protests became progressively more focused on the consequences of poverty and, in particular, of the economic deprivation of women. The privileges that law and custom allow are to a large degree purchased by wealth: this they knew and stated with increasing vehemence. It was commonly accepted that formal rights and duties were to be derived from the possession of property; feminists drew attention to the more insidious ways the rich could control the creation and interpretation of the law, as well as access to it. In any case, the poor or propertyless subject, a member of a category comprised of some men and virtually all women, enjoyed the religious, intellectual, or artistic fruits of his or her autonomy only on sufferance. In the spectrum of sexual difference and social distinction, the rich woman of rank, one who had perhaps secured the status of *feme sole*, was obviously in quite a good position. Was it better than that of a poorer man of lesser rank? Like all women, her poor sister enjoyed the dubious advantage of not being liable at law, since her wrongdoing was the responsibility of her next male kin. But again like all women and more than her brother, she was the object of deals and exchanges over which she had little control. In the late Middle Ages and early Renaissance slavery was primarily a female institution. Feminists recognized and denounced this most thorough denial of autonomy for women. Women who were actually enslaved became points of reference for those who condemned the prejudicial treatment of women in general; women who were recognized as greatly virtuous brought others to consider that the institution of slavery, *de iure* or *de facto*, might contravene divine or natural law.

Defenders of women had more than misogynists as critics, however: some (commonly male) critics saw change as a threat to their rights of command and control, others (commonly female) as a threat to their rights to protection and nurturance. The writers of the *Haec Vir/Hic Mulier* pamphlets expressed a powerful argument against the feminists' push for equality for women: the economic power of men was comprehensive and could be comfortable. It was, moreover, virtually unassailable. It probably guaranteed the material well-being of most dependent women; it could, and perhaps would, destroy the woman who attempted to be independent. Centuries earlier, Christine de Pisan had implied that in her society, feminist victories were for women pyrrhic victories; that this position could still be maintained in the seventeenth century was a function of the poverty of women, continuous throughout these centuries. It is to their poverty, too, that we can look to explain the relative infrequency of feminist appeals to resist faintheartedness; the woman who declined to protest, whether from fear or laziness, may well have been the most prudent. There is generally no feminized version of the Hercules paradigm, depicting the heroine at the crossroads, tempted by pleasure but led on by virtue. The game that defenders of women were playing was dangerous; when arguments moved beyond topics in natural law and the nature of sex and gender and on to demands for the social and economic equality of men and women, the stakes grew impossibly high. I have suggested that the logic and rhetoric of feminist protest were instrumental in opening issues of political and philosophical moment to examination, and I think arguments on these topics from a feminist perspective were as subtle as those offered from other points of view. But when protest criticized, however indirectly, patriarchal notions of property as the basis for misogyny or the devaluation of women, it became a cause too risky for most persons to endorse. In our own century, women got the franchise, the formal acknowledgment of their political maturity, only *after* they were permitted to own and manage their own property.

Index

Library of Congress Cataloging-in-Publication Data

Jordan, Constance.
    Renaissance feminism : literary texts and political models /
Constance Jordan.
        p.   cm.
    ISBN 0-8014-2163-2 (alk. paper). — ISBN 0-8014-9732-9 (pbk. :
alk. paper)
    1. European literature—Renaissance, 1450–1600—History and
criticism.   2. Feminism in literature.   3. Feminism and literature.
4. Women in literature.   5. Sex role in literature.   6. Women—
History—Renaissance, 1450–1600.   I. Title.
PN721.J67   1990   89-46172
809'.031—dc20